EXILE

AND THE

NATION

EXILE
AND THE
NATION

*The Parsi Community of India
and the Making of Modern Iran*

AFSHIN MARASHI

University of Texas Press Austin

Requests for permission to reproduce material from this work should be sent to:
Permissions
University of Texas Press
P.O. Box 7819
Austin, TX 78713–7819
utpress.utexas.edu/rp-form

♾ The paper used in this book meets the minimum requirements of ANSI/NISO
Z39.48–1992 (R1997) (Permanence of Paper).

Library of Congress Cataloging-in-Publication Data

Names: Marashi, Afshin, author.
Title: Exile and the nation : the Parsi community of India and the making of modern
    Iran / Afshin Marashi.
Identifiers: LCCN 2019040609
ISBN 978-1-4773-2079-2 (cloth)
ISBN 978-1-4773-2080-8 (paperback)
ISBN 978-1-4773-2081-5 (ebook)
ISBN 978-1-4773-2082-2 (ebook other)
Subjects: LCSH: Parsees—History. | Zoroastrians—History. | Iran—History. |
    Zoroastrianism.
Classification: LCC DS432.P3 M37 2020 | DDC 305.6/950955—dc23
LC record available at https://lccn.loc.gov/2019040609

doi:10.7560/320792

For Kathleen

CONTENTS

NOTE ON TRANSLITERATION AND DATES

This book uses a transliteration system based on the *Iranian Studies* and *International Journal of Middle East Studies* guidelines, with some simplifications and modifications to accommodate Persian language pronunciation. Short vowels are rendered as a, e, and o. The long *vav* is rendered as u. Diacritics and macrons have been omitted in most cases. *Ayn* and *hamzeh* have generally been rendered as (') and (') respectively. For the Persian *ezafeh* I have used –e (following a consonant) and –ye (following a vowel). Names and proper nouns that have common English-language renderings have generally been preserved in these more familiar English forms. In most bibliographic entries, dates have been converted to the common Gregorian calendar.

ACKNOWLEDGMENTS

I have incurred an embarrassing number of personal, professional, and intellectual debts during the writing of this book. Acknowledging these debts can serve as only a small gesture toward what I hope will be the ultimate repayment of these obligations. Foremost is the debt I owe to Jim Burr and everyone at the University of Texas Press. Jim was an advocate for this project from the outset. After working with him on the 2014 volume *Rethinking Iranian Nationalism and Modernity*, coedited with Kamran Aghaie, I knew that Jim would be the ideal editor for this book as well. The University of Texas Press was the first publisher that I approached to consider this manuscript, and I am grateful to Jim, Sarah McGavick, Lynne Ferguson, John Brenner, and everyone else at UT Press for the professionalism and personal care with which they saw this project to completion.

Many others were generous in helping to locate source material, share ideas, read drafts, correct errors of both fact and judgment, and provide general encouragement and insight. I especially want to record my gratitude to Kaikhosrov D. Irani (1922–2017), for sharing with me memories of his father, Dinshah J. Irani. These recollections helped me to write chapter 2 of this book. I am also grateful to Ehsan Yarshater (1920–2018), for sharing with me memories of his teacher, Ebrahim Purdavud. His recollections helped in the writing of chapter 4. I wish I could have presented the published version of this book to both of these men, who were generous with their encouragement and who embody the best of the history connecting Parsis and Iranians.

Others were generous in innumerable other ways. Touraj Atabaki was very kind in helping me to gain access to material at the International Institute for Social History in Amsterdam. Much of chapter 5 could not have been written without his assistance. Houchang Chehabi was equally generous in sending unsolicited primary source fragments that seemed to add the essential detail that arrived uncannily at just the right moment. Important revisions to chapter 3 owe themselves to Houchang's help. I am also grateful to Nawaz B. Mody for drawing my attention to the remarkable figure of Madame Bhikaiji Cama, and the important and still underacknowledged role that she played in this history. The story of Madame Cama surely deserves a full-length biography. I am also grateful to Nawaz for the invitation to present some early material relating to this research at Mumbai's Cama Oriental Institute. Presenting at the Cama Institute was a dream come true. Dinyar Patel and Daniel Sheffield were also generous to include me in the 2013 Dastoor Meherjirana Library anniversary conference. It was a wonderful introduction to India and to the Parsi community. Dinyar was especially generous in reading and providing important suggestions for revisions to several of the chapters in this book. Dan was kind to share with me source material from his vast personal library of all things Zoroastrian. I am fortunate to count both Dinyar and Dan as peers, colleagues, and friends.

Touraj Daryaee, Alka Patel, Talinn Grigor, Monica Ringer, Mohamad Tavakoli-Targhi, Ali Gheissari, Nile Green, Farzin Vejdani, Mana Kia, Samuel Hodgkin, Reza Zia-Ebrahimi, Sarah Kayali, Kevin Schwartz, and Mitchell Numark were also generous with their ideas, criticism, comments, suggestions, corrections, and encouragement. At the University of Oklahoma, I am grateful to my colleagues Manata Hashemi, Alexander Jabbari, Samer Shehata, Gershon Lewental, Carsten Shapkow, Paul Goode, and Alan Levenson for their intellectual camaraderie and comradeship. Thanks are also due to Kamran Aghaie, Mikiya Koyagi, and Lior Sternfeld for helping to make UT-Austin a second scholarly home during my years in Norman, Oklahoma. I am glad that my former OU students, including Andrew Akhlaghi and Elizabeth "Libby" Ennenga, have also found UT-Austin a welcoming place to continue their own work in the field of Iranian studies.

All of those listed above, as well as students in my "Modern Iran" courses, have heard earlier versions of the material in this book. I have also presented portions of this research at numerous conferences and invited lectures, including at: UCLA, UC-Berkeley, UC-Davis, UC-Irvine, UC-San Diego, UT-Austin, the University of Washington, NYU, Princeton, Simon Fraser University, Pomona College, the Cama Oriental Institute, the Dastoor Meherjirana Library, Phillips-Universität in Marburg, Germany, and to audiences at the University of Oklahoma's Farzaneh Center for Iranian Studies. Portions were also presented at various Middle East Studies Association (MESA) conferences, and at the Association of Iranian Studies (AIS) biennial conferences in London (2006), Istanbul (2012), and Vienna (2016). I thank all of my hosts, as well as my copanelists, discussants, and audience members, for their constructive comments and criticisms.

An earlier version of chapter 2 was published in *Iranian Studies* (vol. 46, no. 2), and an earlier version of chapter 3 was published in the *Journal of Persianate Studies* (vol. 3, no. 1). I am grateful to Taylor and Francis, Brill Publishers, and the editors of both journals for permission to reproduce the material here. Some of the ideas in this book also grew out of the "After the Persianate: Cultural Heritage and National Transformation in Modern Iran and India" conference that I organized in 2014 at the University of Oklahoma's Farzaneh Center. I am grateful to the Farzaneh Family Foundation, the PARSA Foundation, the Iran Heritage Foundation-America, the OU College of International Studies, the OU Department of History, the OU Center for the Study of Nationalism, and the other cosponsors for the financial support that made the conference possible. In addition to helping to shape the content of this book, some of the ideas generated at that conference also found their way into the special section I coedited with Mana Kia for the journal *Comparative Studies of South Asia, Africa, and the Middle East* (vol. 36, no. 3 [2016]).

Other funding that supported the research and writing of this book came from the Farzaneh Family Chair in Modern Iranian History, OU's Department of International and Area Studies Faculty Development Grant (2012), the OU President's International Travel Fellowship (2012, 2014, and 2016), the "Big 12" Faculty Exchange Fellowship (2013), the OU College of International Studies' Senior Faculty Research Award (2014), and an OU Sabbatical Leave Fellowship (2017–2018). These funds provided me with time devoted to writing, and also enabled travel to the following research libraries and archives: the Young Research Library at UCLA, the Getty Research Institute in Los Angeles, Doe Library at UC-Berkeley, the Perry-Castañeda Library at UT-Austin, the New York Public Library, the British Library, the British National Archives in Kew (UK), the International Institute for Social History (Amsterdam, Netherlands), the K. R. Cama Oriental Institute Library in Mumbai (Maharashtra, India), and the Meherjirana Library in Navsari (Gujarat, India). The interlibrary loan staff at OU's Bizzell Memorial Library, and the many lending libraries from throughout North America, were also enormously patient and generous in helping me to gain access to source material necessary to complete this book.

Last, but certainly not least, I would like to thank my family for their support during the writing of this book. My parents remain a source of inspiration, and I am happy that they are both able to see my second monograph in published form. My sister, Nooshin, remains a great source of support, and my biggest booster. I have also been privileged to see my niece and nephew, Desi and Darius, grow into maturity since I completed *Nationalizing Iran* more than a decade ago. It brings me great joy to see them now poised to make their own indelible marks on the world. As with my first book, I hope they will see something of themselves in the pages that follow. Finally, I owe the greatest debt to my wife, Kathleen A. Kelly. She has read and commented on every word that I have written here, and knows the twists and turns of this saga better than I do. I owe her everything that is in this book, and so much more.

EXILE

AND THE

NATION

INTRODUCTION

AN OCEANIC ECUMENE

When Ebrahim Purdavud's steamship sailed past the Gate of India and into the harbor of colonial Bombay in late October of 1925, the first-time visitor to the bustling and cosmopolitan imperial city could not help but reflect on the relative ease with which he had made the four-day journey from Iran.[1] The thirty-nine-year-old Purdavud (1886–1968) had traveled to India with his wife and daughter from the Persian Gulf port at Basra via an ocean liner owned and operated by the British India Steam and Navigation Company. The company, known colloquially as "B.I.," was a private firm, established in 1862, for the purpose of facilitating the transport of passengers, mail, and commodities between the network of commercial entrepôts dotting the British Empire's political and economic presence in the western Indian Ocean.[2] By the time of Purdavud's journey to India in 1925, however, the relative comforts of steam-powered sea travel had not only fostered economic links—and all the so-called "virtues of free trade"—but also facilitated an acceleration of contact and communication among the peoples, cultures, and societies of the Indian Ocean world.

Purdavud's 1925 journey to India was one of the cultural exchanges enabled by the increased ease of long-distance travel linking the shores of this oceanic ecumene. His trip to India, and what ultimately became a two-and-a-half-year intellectual sojourn in Bombay and the surrounding cities in the Indian states of Maharashtra and Gujarat, had been conceived and sponsored by civic leaders associated with the two main Zoroastrian communities of South Asia. Both the long-established Zoroastrian "Parsi" community of India, whose members had emigrated from Iran and settled in the subcontinent following the seventh-century Arab-Muslim conquest of the Iranian plateau, and the more recently arrived Iranian Zoroastrians—known as the "Iranis"—who had settled in western India

1

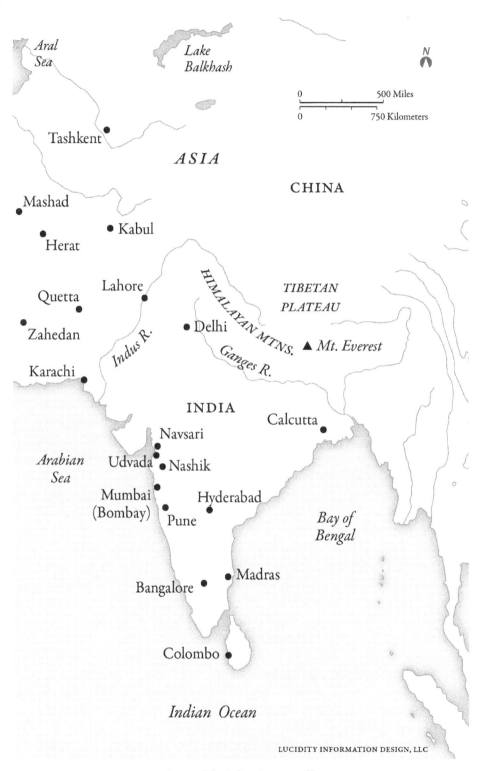

Iran and the Indian Ocean world.

in increasing numbers during the eighteenth and nineteenth centuries, had learned of Purdavud's talents as a budding scholar of Zoroastrianism. The Bombay-based civic organizations representing these two Zoroastrian communities—the Iranian Zoroastrian Anjoman (established in 1918) and its closely allied organization, the Iran League (established in 1922)—both recognized the utility of inviting Purdavud to India to encourage his intellectual collaboration with the local community of reformist Zoroastrian priests, scholars, and lay intellectuals. Born into a prosperous Shi'ite family from the Gilan region of northern Iran, Purdavud had demonstrated a precocious talent for poetry and the study of languages early in his life. Family resources enabled him to pursue his education, first in Tehran and Beirut, before traveling to Paris and Berlin, where he continued his studies with some of the most senior scholars in the early twentieth-century German orientalist tradition of Iranian Studies, including Josef Markwart (1864–1930), Fritz Wolff (1880–1944), and Hans Heinrich Schraeder (1896–1957). Purdavud's reputation as an emerging scholar, poet, translator, and activist eager to revive the culture of Iran's pre-Islamic Zoroastrian heritage spread quickly through networks of intellectuals in Iran and Europe, as well as among Indian Zoroastrians. This reputation was built on the distinction he had gained as the first modern Iranian to master the "Old" and "Middle" Persian languages of Avestan and Pahlavi. His knowledge of these languages, along with his recognized talent as a poet of the Persian language and his command of Arabic, as well as the major European scholarly languages of German, French, and English, made it clear to Bombay's Zoroastrian civic leaders that Ebrahim Purdavud was uniquely qualified to translate the corpus of Zoroastrian religious texts into the "New" Persian vernacular of modern Iran. The goal of translating these texts—chief among them the *Gathas*, the *Yashts*, and the *Yasna*—into the poetic idiom of the New Persian language had become an important objective for the Zoroastrian civic organizations of India, as well as the community of modern nationalist intellectuals inside Iran. Both Indian Zoroastrians and Iranian nationalists had come to see the importance of making these texts available to modern Iranian readers as part of a campaign to encourage a broader revaluation of Iran's classical heritage.

For the Zoroastrians in India, the intellectual renaissance that they had experienced since the mid-nineteenth century had sharpened their self-perception as a diaspora community displaced from their ancient and ancestral homeland of Iran. As Monica Ringer has noted, Iran came to increasingly play "a central part in the Parsi imagination," and histories of the Parsi community produced by reformist Zoroastrian priests and scholars during this period were conspicuous in their emphasis on "the myth of exile and return."[3] Equally important for explaining this Parsi fascination with Iran was the shifting political terrain in British India during the early decades of the twentieth century. Despite their long association with the culture and society of the Indian subcontinent, the Parsi community's position as one of the most favored communities of the British Raj became increasingly precarious as the Indian independence movement gained momentum. While many Parsis were active in the cause of India's independence, others were not averse to considering other possibilities, including the prospect of negating their increasingly felt diasporic and exilic condition and taking steps to prepare for a possible return to Iran. These fantasies of a Parsi repatriation to Iran paralleled both Zionist arguments of "return" and "negation of exile" as well as the cultural logic of eighteenth- and nineteenth-century settler colonialism. As the chapters in this book will detail, this romanticized dream of a Parsi return to Iran animated much of the Parsi-Iranian cultural and intellectual exchange in the early decades of the twentieth century. From the Parsi point of view, the translation of the corpus of Zoroastrian texts into modern Persian, and the broader charity and cultural philanthropy that the Parsis sponsored inside Iran, were therefore partially intended to promote Iran's renewed appreciation of its own classical civilization. Just as important, however, was the Parsi intention to make the Zoroastrians of India known to modern Iranians as their distant—and kindred—compatriots.

This shared sense of transnational belonging connecting Parsis and Iranians is precisely what began to take shape as a result of increased travel, cultural exchange, and Parsi-sponsored philanthropy. As Purdavud himself wrote some years later, his initial impression of the Parsis confirmed their deep ties to Iran. "Anyone who arrives by boat at the port of Bombay," he wrote in describing the welcome that he received from Zoroastrian civic leaders upon his arrival in October of 1925, "will understand that the Parsi people in that land were born and nourished from another spring."[4] For Iranian nationalists like Purdavud, the discovery of this shared history connecting Parsis and Iranians was, however, more than a simple acknowledgment of a forgotten cultural heritage. The recognition of this common history also came to have important implications in the context of Iran's political history.

As with the Parsis, the shifting political terrain of the first few decades of the twentieth century came to shape—with some urgency—the way that Iranians came to perceive their rediscovered cousins from the distant shore. As Iran's nation-building project began to unfold, first in the years following the 1905 Constitutional Revolution and subsequently with the rise of Reza Shah and the Pahlavi state of the 1920s and 1930s, debates surrounding Iran's cultural, religious, and literary heritage were at the forefront of efforts to reconsider, redefine, and, in the words of Mohamad Tavakoli-Targhi, "refashion" the cultural definition of the Iranian nation.[5] The Iranian encounter with the Parsis was an important element of the debates during this period, and for many Iranian nationalist intellectuals, the Parsis came to represent a direct link to a living tradition of Iran's pre-Islamic classical past. As Iranians increasingly came to imagine a culture of neoclassicism during the late nineteenth and early twentieth century, the seventh-century displacement and resettlement of the Parsi community in the subcontinent was understood as insulating these émigré Iranians from the cultural effects of Arabization and Islamization that had transformed Iran following the Arab-Muslim conquest. Purdavud's journey to India and the broader possibility of renewed contact and connection with the Parsi community was therefore perceived by many Iranian nationalists as something more than an exercise of cultural tourism made possible by the newfound comforts of steam-powered sea travel. The new Iranian engagement with the Parsis was instead perceived as a rediscovery of Iran's classical past, and as inspiration for a renaissance of a putatively lost—and now found—authenticity that had been preserved by the Parsis in India, and which could now serve as a blueprint for the political project of Iran's twentieth-century history of nation-building and cultural nationalization. This Iranian encounter with the Parsis was therefore inspiring, but at the same time unsettling. To paraphrase Raymond Schwab, while it is possible to document the intellectual consequences of Iran's own *oriental renaissance*, "what we cannot reproduce is the great shock with which a whole buried world arose to unsettle the foremost minds of an age."[6] The creative inspiration accompanying the initial Iranian rediscovery of the Parsis was coupled with an equally powerful mood of anxiety that grew from the stark realization of contemporary Iran's own relative decay in comparison to the progress and prosperity that their now-perceived Parsi cousins had achieved during their long sojourn in India. Both of these emotions were engendered by the renewed contact between Parsis and Iranians. Ultimately, it was precisely this dialectic between mimesis and alterity, between recognition and difference, that both captured and troubled the imagination of Iranian intellectuals like Ebrahim Purdavud and the others discussed in this book.

For Iranian nationalist intellectuals and activists who were seeking strategies to reform Iranian culture in order to overcome what they perceived as a long period of cultural degeneration, economic impoverishment, and political weakness, this discovery of the Parsi community in western India can be read as one of those examples of "the intervention of enchanted agency" that was conjured from the increased circulation of peoples and printed materials in what Nile Green has described as the "religious economy" of the Indian Ocean world.[7] From the point of view of Iranian nationalist intellectuals, their aspirations for bold transformations inside Iran were shaped not only by purely theoretical, fictive, and phantasmagorical *utopias* of modernity, but also by the very real, more immediate, and directly tangible *heterotopias* that Mohamad Tavakoli-Targhi has defined, following Michel Foucault, as "alternative real spaces" through and against which the Iranian present came to compare, conceive, and ultimately construct versions of its possible future.[8] While the term "heterotopia" has most often been used to analyze the epistemic genealogy of the European encounter with the colonial world,[9] the concept can also be useful in understanding the nature of the Parsi-Iranian encounter. The Iranian discovery of the Parsis was one of these heterotopic encounters engendered by the circulation of peoples and ideas within the Indian Ocean world of the late nineteenth and early twentieth century. As Green has argued, an intellectual history of the Indian Ocean world can be built most fruitfully within a framework that recognizes the cultural-philosophical effects engendered by these "waves of heterotopia" produced by the manifold encounters set in motion by industrialized travel and the proliferation of vernacular print technology.[10]

The simultaneously inspired, yet troubled, enchantments that were engendered by these stark transoceanic encounters—like the ones produced by the Parsi-Iranian exchange—would not, however, stay contained within the imagination of adventurous and impressionable travelers, but came to have very real implications as the source for twentieth-century political projects in the societies that bordered this oceanic zone. In the Iranian case, the encounter with the Parsi community produced profound implications for how intellectuals and nationalists came to imagine an Iranian modernity rooted in a rediscovered, reconceived, and reconstructed culture of Indo-Iranian neoclassicism. This imagination was neither spectral nor illusory, but was instead vividly apparent through the now-animated example of western India's Parsi community. The impressive prosperity that the great Parsi merchant families and industrial barons had achieved in India, as well as the general respect afforded by dominant British imperial standards to the Bombay community's modern educated and professionalized middle classes, made this Parsi model of Iranian regeneration an especially attractive one for early twentieth-century Iranians debating the best strategy for their own path to modernity.

For both Parsis and Iranians, therefore, the acceleration of their mutual engagement within this culturally fertile oceanic ecumene of the late nineteenth and early twentieth century produced simultaneous heterotopic visions that, while bearing some correspondence with one another, were by no means mutually equivalent. For Parsis, their newly romanticized longing for an ancestral Iran was imagined as a *territorial displacement* from an original homeland; for Iranians, their enchantment with the Parsis was conceived in terms of recovering faint cultural remnants resulting from a *temporal displacement* from a lost antiquity. Both of these interconnected—and ultimately unrealized—Parsi and Iranian imaginings unfolded across the cultural landscape of the Indo-Iranian world during the long nineteenth century; both ultimately came to realize their most potent consequences in the respective political histories of Iran and India during the twentieth century.

MYTH AND HISTORY

The modern Parsi-Iranian encounter did not materialize abruptly with Ebrahim Purdavud's journey to Bombay in 1925. The mutually enchanted engagement of Parsis and Iranians was instead the outcome of a much longer history that had unfolded gradually over a number of centuries, and had only accelerated since the mid-nineteenth century. Conventional accounts of Parsi history suggest that the Zoroastrian-Parsi community of western India originally migrated to South Asia in the aftermath of the seventh-century Arab-Muslim conquest of Iran.[11] In the pre-Islamic era of Iranian history, Zoroastrianism had been the official religion of the Sasanian Empire, and the Zoroastrian faith was practiced by the vast majority of the empire's population. In the aftermath of the seventh-century Arab-Muslim conquest, a gradual process of conversion to Islam took place. While a small but significant minority of Zoroastrians remained inside Iran—gradually concentrating in the central plateau towns of Yazd and Kerman—and were recognized as a protected religious minority within the conventions of Islamic law, others from among the Iranian Zoroastrian population chose to seek a new home in South Asia. According to Parsi lore, these émigrés first migrated from the central plateau to the island of Hormuz, before setting sail from the Persian Gulf and landing on the western Indian coast near the town of Sanjan.

Scholars disagree as to the historicity of this conventional Parsi migration story. The narrative's echo of the biblical exodus story suggests a reworking of the Parsi past within frameworks of religio-historical knowledge derived from other sources. Recent scholarship has found evidence for a history of cultural and commercial contact between Sasanian Iran and India in the centuries before the Arab-Muslim conquest, with colonies of Zoroastrians probably already inhabiting the western coast of India prior to the "exodus" of Iranian Zoroastrians in the aftermath of the conquest.[12] Similarly, this scholarship challenges the notion of a singular migration of Iranian Zoroastrians to India in the immediate post-conquest period, suggesting instead a continuous process of emigration that unfolded over a number of centuries both before and after the Arab-Muslim conquest.[13] The more conventional exodus narrative of Parsi migration to India is ultimately derived from a single source written between eight and nine centuries after the purported events that it claims to describe. This text, the *Qesseh-ye Sanjan* (Story of Sanjan), is a Persian-language poetic rendering of a Parsi exodus from Iran composed by the Zoroastrian priest Bahman Kay-Qobad Sanjana in Navsari, Gujarat, at the end of the sixteenth century. This poetic account of the Zoroastrian exodus from Iran has come to shape both the mytho-historical imagination of the Parsi community's perception of their own origins and a modern Iranian nationalist conception of the Parsis as a diaspora community that has preserved a culture of Iranian classicism under the conditions of exile and displacement. As Alan Williams has convincingly argued, this Zoroastrian "myth of migration" as poetically composed in the *Qesseh* should not be interpreted as a historical account derived from oral testimony of an original Parsi exodus, but instead as a literary text produced and conditioned by the context of its sixteenth-century composition.[14] While acknowledging the salience of this narrative, and the powerful effect that it has produced in shaping Parsi and Iranian understandings of a common past, Williams argues that this salience should not be conflated with the *Qesseh*'s historicity. Despite the challenges of untangling the interconnectedness of history and myth in the Zoroastrian migration and settlement in India, scholars agree that over time this immigrant community of Iranian Zoroastrians in India became known by the ethnonym *Parsi*, in reference to their original place of origin in the Pars, or Fars, region of the Iranian plateau. Scholars also agree that contact between the Parsis of India and their coreligionists inside Iran was intermittent in the centuries that followed.[15]

Within Iran, the remaining Zoroastrian community decreased in population over the course of subsequent centuries, and the community's religious institutions began a process of erosion. Historians also agree that the decline of the community inside Iran was likely due to social and economic conditions—including the imposition of the *jizya* tax on non-Muslims—which had the effect of inducing a steady process of conversion to Islam. The vagaries and inconsistencies associated with the Zoroastrian population's status as a protected *dhimmi* community placed additional pressure on the community and also precipitated conversion.[16] The thirteenth-century Mongol conquest of Iran also had devastating social consequences for the entirety of the plateau's inhabitants, including the Zoroastrian community. The community's already declining fortunes on the eve of the Mongol conquest made its social consequences even more acute for the remaining Zoroastrians in Iran.[17] Furthermore, the sixteenth-century reconstitution of central authority by the ascendant Safavid dynasty, and their vigorous campaign of promulgating Twelver Shi'ism as the official religion of their empire, further eroded the fortunes of Iran's Zoroastrians. Due to their formal *dhimmi* legal designation, the Zoroastrians—like Iran's Jewish and Christian communities—were technically exempt from the Shi'ification campaigns that the Safavids principally deployed against Iran's Sunni communities. Nevertheless, the Zoroastrian community's protected minority status was considered controversial among some interpreters of the *sharia*, and instances of harassment, forced conversion, and large-scale massacres of local Zoroastrian populations further eroded the demographic presence of the Iranian Zoroastrians.[18] By the second half of the nineteenth century, the community's presence was almost entirely limited to the remote and semi-isolated towns of Yazd and Kerman, with only a sprinkling of Zoroastrians found in other parts of the plateau. When A. V. Williams Jackson (1862–1937), the Columbia University professor of Indo-Iranian languages, traveled throughout Iran in 1903 to document the textual and archaeological record of its classical past, as well as to visit the remaining Zoroastrian communities, he estimated that the total population had dwindled to little more than ten thousand adherents.[19]

By contrast, in India the Parsi community's fortunes generally improved over the centuries. While source material other than the *Qesseh* is sparse for the early period, it is clear that the Zoroastrian communities in western India grew over time. The initial settlements, believed to have been in and around Sanjan, expanded to include other concentrations in other towns and villages of the Gujarat region. The community also adopted Gujarati as its vernacular language, while Avestan and Pahlavi continued to be used for scholarly and liturgical purposes. Until the early modern period these Parsi communities of the Gujarat region were principally engaged in the locally focused agrarian economy.[20] Over time, however, the community shifted its economic focus to the growing commercial economy of western India's port cities and achieved great success in the trade of numerous commodities, chief among them textiles and opium. The commercial history of the Parsi community began with Portuguese, Dutch, and French merchants, but greatly prospered following the British East India Company's arrival in India beginning in the seventeenth century.[21] The fortunes of the Parsi community steadily improved in the following centuries, and reached their apex in the decades following the consolidation of the British Raj in 1858. By the second half of the nineteenth century, the bulk of the Parsi community's prosperous industrial and merchant class had settled in Bombay, and the city came to serve as the nodal point for a Parsi global trading network connecting commercial ports in the Indian Ocean and the Persian Gulf to East Africa, the South China Sea, and the Mediterranean.[22]

It was in this period of Parsi political ascendency and economic prosperity that the community began a concerted effort to reach out to their Zoroastrian coreligionists inside Iran. While epistolary exchanges on matters of scripture, dogma, and ritual—in what is known as the *revayat* literature—had intermittently connected Parsis and Iranian Zoroastrians in Yazd and Kerman since the late fifteenth century, a formal Parsi representative was not sent to reestablish permanent links between Zoroastrians in India and Iran until 1854. The first of these representatives, Manekji Limji Hataria (1813–1890) was sent to Iran by the newly established Society for the Amelioration of Conditions of Zoroastrians in Iran, a charity foundation established by Sir Dinshaw Petit (1823–1901).[23] The Petit family had prospered during the eighteenth and nineteenth century along with the growth of the industrial and commercial economy of the era. Sir Dinshaw Petit's immediate family was related by marriage to recently arrived Zoroastrian Iranis who had migrated to India at the end of the eighteenth century and brought with them accounts of the deteriorating social conditions of the Zoroastrian communities in Yazd and Kerman. These personal and philanthropic motives inspired Sir Dinshaw to help in the establishment of the Amelioration Society, sending Manekji Limji as the Society's first official representative to Iran in 1854.[24] Manekji has been rightly described by Reza Zia-Ebrahimi as a Parsi "emissary from the Golden Age," in large part because of his efforts to revive and restore the culture of Zoroastrianism and neoclassicism inside Iran.[25] Manekji spent the next thirty-six years in Iran working to encourage this renewed interest in ancient history among Zoroastrian and non-Zoroastrian Iranians. He also distributed exhaustive resources in rebuilding *atash bahrams* (fire temples) and *dakhmehs* (ossuaries), as well as building new schools, orphanages, and medical facilities among the economically impoverished Iranian Zoroastrian communities. Through Manekji's lobbying, the *jizya* tax was also repealed by decree of Naser al-Din Shah in 1882. When Manekji died in Tehran in 1890, he was succeeded first by Kaykhosrow Khah Saheb Tirandaz between 1890 and 1894, and then by Ardeshir Edulji Reporter (1865–1933) from 1894 to 1933. Like Manekji Limji's long and productive residency in Iran, Ardeshir Reporter's thirty-nine years as the official Parsi representative in Tehran was profoundly consequential in building bonds of connection between Parsis and Iranians. Also like Manekji Limji, Ardeshir Reporter played an important role in encouraging the revival of interest in Zoroastrianism and Iranian antiquity among Iran's nationalist intellectuals.

AFTER THE PERSIANATE

The twentieth-century evolution of Iranian nationalism grew from this modern culture of neoclassicism, as encouraged, enabled, and facilitated by Iran's encounter with the Parsi community of India. Historians of Iranian modernity, however, have long placed primary emphasis on the cultural and intellectual encounter with European thought in shaping debates within Persian-language modernist texts of the nineteenth and twentieth centuries. These accounts are grounded in diffusionist models of modernity shaped by assumptions of "modernization" and "westernization" that trace the dissemination of ideas from a purported

European place of origin outward to the various colonial and semicolonial regions of Asia and Africa. From the work of Max Weber to Arnold Toynbee and Eli Kedourie, this sociology of knowledge—defined in terms of a unidirectional process of diffusion and reception—has underestimated the complexities involved in the encounter between multiple systems of knowledge, and has likewise underestimated the agency of non-Western intellectuals in the appropriation of Western thought. Just as consequentially, scholars working within critical Saidian and postcolonial paradigms of knowledge often arrive at analogous conclusions by overemphasizing the discursive power of orientalism in shaping forms of thought outside of Europe. According to the logic of some postcolonial-inflected historiographies, the intellectual history of modern Iranian neoclassicism is therefore inevitably written as a modular or derivative history.[26] Historiographies grounded in both Weberian and Saidian paradigms of knowledge therefore run the risk of defining modern Iranian intellectual history in passive rather than dialogical terms.

While the ideas of European positivism writ large, and the allied field of orientalist science, played a central role in shaping modern Iranian intellectual history—often in terms that were refracted indirectly through Parsi sources in what Talinn Grigor has called "reviving the invented"[27]—the local cultural and political landscape that defined the Indo-Iranian world, and out of which novel forms of thought invariably emerged during the modern period, was equally consequential. The role played by this Indo-Iranian cultural and intellectual landscape is still largely unmapped and unaccounted for in histories that attempt to explain modern Iranian and Indian encounters with ascendant European forms of knowledge. Chief among the elements that defined this Indo-Iranian terrain was the complex and multilayered cultural fabric that Marshall Hodgson first described as the "Persianate zone" characterizing the eastern frontiers of the Islamic world during medieval and early modern periods.[28] The cultural elements that defined this Persianate zone—or what Richard Eaton and Phillip Wagoner, following Sheldon Pollock, have called a "Persianate cosmopolis"[29]—served as the intellectual setting out of which the various modernities of the Indo-Iranian world ultimately sought to emerge during the nineteenth and twentieth centuries.

The traditional reticence of scholars of the modern period to acknowledge this early modern Persianate context is rooted in a number of interrelated factors. We can look, for example, to the modernist penchant to overemphasize the discursive power of "modernity" in rendering irrelevant all systems of culture and thought that preceded it. The assumptions of historicism that are built into the language of modern thought make it easy to assign such a discursive power to modernity that in turn produces such casual elisions. Equally important is the more recent historiographic tendency to emphasize the novel and constructed nature of nationalism in Iran and India as a way of compensating for equally stubborn and still-entrenched ahistoric, perennialist, and primordialist arguments for the histories of the nation across the Indo-Iranian world. For these and other reasons, a broader historiographic boundary separating the "early modern" and "modern" eras has until recently institutionalized our inability to read the past across arbitrarily erected historiographic periodizations. Beyond these conventions of periodization, however, are equally formidable and ingrained spatial divides. Mid-twentieth-century area-studies paradigms of knowledge—determined and defined by the exigencies of geopolitics and security concerns—have further partitioned our knowledge of the Persianate past into spatial divisions that have conceptualized "Iran" and "India" into discrete and divergent domains of *area* knowledge.

This book aims in part to challenge these conceptual conventions, and seeks to extend a mode of transtemporal and transspatial *connected history* that traverses the arbitrary divides of "early modern" and "modern" history, and "Middle East" and "South Asian" area studies.[30] From within the field of seventeenth- and eighteenth-century scholarship, the work of Kathryn Babayan,[31] Mana Kia,[32] and Daniel Sheffield,[33] among others, has already eroded these temporal and spatial boundaries. In the historiography of nineteenth-century Iran and India, the work of Mohamad Tavakoli-Targhi,[34] Nile Green,[35] and Monica Ringer[36] has also situated the onset of the modern period against the backdrop of what came before. Both of these traditions of scholarship have already helped to illuminate important connections between Iran and India that would otherwise remain concealed behind the barriers of conventional historiography.

As this book argues, the cultural and intellectual history of Iran and India during the seventeenth, eighteenth, and nineteenth centuries also has implications for the history of Iranian nationalism in the twentieth century. When considered in this transtemporal and transspatial context, the Parsi-Iranian cultural and intellectual engagement can be identified as one of the newly empowered strands of thought that had long existed within a much more complex Persianate cultural system. As the early modern Persianate system of thought began to fray during the nineteenth century, its component elements did not disappear or melt away, but were in many cases reconfigured, empowered, and enabled to operate as the basis of modernist projects of culture and politics. Parsi-Iranian neoclassicism was only one of these newly empowered strands of culture to emerge after the Persianate cultural system's gradual eclipse. Also to emerge from the peripheries of the Persianate system were territorial vernaculars associated with the many regionalisms within the Indo-Iranian world. Linguistic reconfigurations of local vernaculars into Urdu, Dari, Baluchi, and other languages are perhaps among the most noted new cultural-political forms to emerge during the era of the Persianate's slow and uneven decline. The Iranian *bāzgasht-e adabī* (literary return) movement, which reified not a pre-Islamic past, but a literary classicism associated with a reconfigured canonic tradition of tenth- to thirteenth-century New Persian literature, was another of these reconfigured and newly empowered strands of culture and thought to emerge from the margins of the Persianate. In sharp contrast to Parsi-Iranian neoclassicism, the belle-lettres proponents of this movement did not seek new connections with India, but to the contrary designated the Indian style of Persian poetry—the so-called *sabk-e hendī*—as inferior in comparison to the putatively "original" and "authentic" style associated with the plateau.[37] Similarly, the multiple strands of religious modernism—whether Muslim, Hindu, or otherwise—that emerged in the nineteenth and twentieth centuries also had their origins in fertile cultural terrains rooted in Persianate culture and thought of the early modern period.

As even this cursory survey indicates, the strands of culture that emerged from this polyvocal early modern Persianate system were themselves infinitely varied, frequently coextensive, and often mutually contradictory. What we observe as the subsequent "politics" of the twentieth century is in large measure a history of the cultural-political contestation of these newly empowered—and now competing—strands of the former Persianate system as they vie for dominance within the communicative arenas of newly formed polities. When understood in this way, the slow decline and transformation of the early modern Persianate world becomes crucial to any understanding of the politics of nationalism in the twentieth-century Indo-Iranian region. While the emerging historiography of the connected histories of the Middle East and

South Asia has been suggestive in identifying the early modern origins of much that we consider as the "modern" culture in this transregional zone, this historiography has also stopped short of analyzing the twentieth-century trajectories of these various and varied cultural strands.

POLITICAL TERRAINS

The twentieth-century political trajectories that evolved out of the Parsi-Iranian exchange are an ideal illustration of how the complexities of contrasting contexts produced very different historical outcomes for strands of culture emerging from the Persianate cultural landscape. As the chapters in this book will argue, the Parsi reformists in India and the community of Iranian nationalists inside Iran grew to develop very different understandings of Zoroastrianism and their shared classical heritage. For the Parsis, the intellectual renaissance of reformist Zoroastrianism was produced within the social milieu of a favored minority community living within the multiconfessional and polyglot colonial rule of the British Raj. The terms of this context produced what was ultimately a liberal, cosmopolitan, and ecumenical reading of Zoroastrianism as a progressive faith that conformed with post-Reformation and post-Enlightenment understandings of religion, culture, and society. Parsi concerns about India's political future did not ultimately negate their commitment to these understandings. The only political question requiring consideration for the Parsis was whether those values would be realized in the context of a continued history for the British Raj, or whether those understandings would be realized after a Parsi "return" to Iran. The Iranian context, by contrast, was very different, and in turn produced what became an alternative appropriation of Iran's classical heritage that was shaped by the context of Iran's twentieth-century nation-building project. Iran's position as a semicolonial polity, conscious of its relative underdevelopment, produced a political logic that engendered a search for a cultural blueprint to serve as the basis for a radical project of compensatory transformation characteristic of defensive modernization nation-building projects. By the Reza Shah period, the culture of neoclassicism that had grown out of the exchange with the Parsi community came to play an important part in this Pahlavi project. Far from promoting liberal, and culturally and religiously ecumenical, readings of the past, the Pahlavi appropriation of Zoroastrianism contained an insurgent quality vis-à-vis what were now perceived as hegemonic Arab-Islamicate cultural forms. By the logic of Pahlavi nationalism's construction of neoclassicism, Iran's Islamic history was seen as an unnatural imposition and—as Reza Zia-Ebrahimi has argued—a civilizational "dislocation" from a more authentic and pristine culture of Iranianness.[38] This pristinely imagined version of Iran's heritage, shaped by a romanticized understanding of Zoroastrianism and pre-Islamic Iranian history, as well as a mythic attachment to an idealized Aryanism, was adopted as part of the Pahlavi project of nationalization and normalized through the authority and techniques of twentieth-century state power. The political form that this Pahlavi appropriation of Parsi-Iranian neoclassicism assumed during the 1920s and 1930s ultimately took the form of a Bonapartism that only oscillated within the limited range of authoritarian modernization and quasi-fascism. Like other political projects of the interwar era, Pahlavi nationalism's political form was very much a product of its times, and grew naturally from what Ali Ansari has described—following Eric Hobsbawm—as Iran's "age of extremes" during its short twentieth century.[39]

As this book asserts, despite their rediscovered roots in a shared past, the cultural and intellectual exchange between Parsis and Iranians was principally defined by a tension between these liberal and cosmopolitan intentions of the Parsi community, and the more culturally assertive and nationalist intentions of Iranian intellectuals and activists. As the chapters that follow will illustrate, this growing tension came to have increasing political consequences by the 1930s and the eve of World War II. As chapter 1 will document, the contradiction between the liberal and nationalist readings of Iran's Zoroastrian heritage will play out as a family drama between Kaykhosrow Shahrokh—Iran's most well-known liberal-minded Zoroastrian reformer and longtime Majles deputy—and his son Shah-Bahram Shahrokh, who by the late 1930s will appropriate the language of neoclassicism to become Iran's most infamous promoter of Nazi ideology. Chapter 2 will shift the focus to the life and work of Dinshah Irani, the most active civic leader among the Zoroastrians of Bombay, and cofounder of both the Iran League and the Iranian Zoroastrian Anjoman. Dinshah Irani was also a prolific author of popular books on Zoroastrianism that were intended for export to the growing print marketplace inside Iran. As an analysis of his life and work will illustrate, while he promoted a reformed and liberal interpretation of Zoroastrianism, there was also an inherent tension within much of his writing that invited more nationalist readings of his books. In chapter 3 this same tension is analyzed through the official visit to Iran in 1932 by the Indian poet, artist, and Nobel Prize laureate Rabindranath Tagore. Tagore's visit to Iran was organized in large part by the Bombay-based Zoroastrian civic organizations as another attempt to build bonds of cultural exchange between India and Iran. As this chapter will highlight, however, Tagore and his Iranian hosts projected very different meanings onto the trip. For Tagore, his visit represented a gesture of liberal ecumenism highlighting the cultural bonds of a multiconfessional and cosmopolitan Pan-Asianism. For his Iranian hosts, by contrast, Tagore represented an archetype of a lost Iranian authenticity associated with deep Indo-Aryan roots, and his presence in Iran was defined as a symbolic *return* and cultural assertion of this national authenticity. Ebrahim Purdavud's life and work—detailed in chapter 4—represents the most formidable intellectual contribution to emerge from the Parsi-Iranian exchange. His engagement with the Parsi scholarly community during his time in Bombay, along with his equally important collaboration with German orientalists, ultimately rendered the Zoroastrian Avestan texts into the living language of twentieth-century Iranians. As a reading of his work will also suggest, Purdavud's work reflected not only the liberal ideals of his Parsi colleagues, but also the political logic of twentieth-century Pahlavi nationalism. While the tensions within Purdavud's writings were inconspicuously woven into his scholarly work, the journalistic appropriation of neoclassicism in the work of Abdulrahman Saif Azad—as discussed in chapter 5—brings the radical nationalist and quasi-fascist implications of these ideas squarely into focus. Saif Azad's long history as an anticolonial and proto–Third Worldist activist preceded what became his tactical association with Parsi benefactors to publish the *Iran-e Bastan* (Ancient Iran) newspaper in Tehran between 1933 and 1935. As this chapter will detail, *Iran-e Bastan*'s editorial content had its origins in promoting the liberal Parsi cause inside Iran, but quickly adopted the tone and content of Nazi propaganda once Saif Azad found new supporters in the Nazi government's propaganda bureau. This abrupt shift in editorial policy reflected the inherent tensions contained within the Parsi-Iranian cultural and intellectual exchange.

The contrasting political trajectories emerging from the Parsi-Iranian exchange also highlight the larger question of how to conceptualize the networks of contact and connection that were enabled in the Indian Ocean world during "the age of steam and print."[40] The assumptions that underlie much of the existing portrayals of this cultural zone often anticipate idealized cultures of cosmopolitanism as the natural result of newly enabled transoceanic encounters. Amitav Ghosh's literary-historical writings have perhaps most evocatively depicted this world as one characterized by an ethos of cosmopolitan optimism.[41] As both literary and historical critics have suggested, however, Ghosh's eloquent renderings of the past may be rooted in a nostalgia for a history that erases the complexities that were also inscribed throughout the Indian Ocean cultural-spatial zone.[42]

In the case of the Parsi-Iranian history of neoclassicism, for example, while the acceleration of Indian Ocean exchange from the mid-nineteenth century onward enabled Parsis and Iranians to build stronger bonds of social, cultural, and intellectual exchange, rather than engendering a simple telos of liberal ecumenism, the newly enabled engagement produced very different cultural and political imaginings for Parsis and Iranians. While Parsi liberal-cosmopolitanism was one of these outcomes, for Iranians the consequence of their discovery of the Parsis also engendered very different emotional-cultural responses, and very different political-historical outcomes. For both Parsis and Iranians, the introspection engendered by the stark encounter with the other produced not only imaginings that conformed with Ghosh's cosmopolitan optimism, but also existential anxieties that were perhaps more reminiscent of Albert Camus's literary meditations on the relationship between France and Algeria. Like the Indian Ocean, the oceanic ecumene of the Mediterranean produced its own history of manifold encounters and array of responses, including imaginings that encompassed both a transcultural "Mediterranean humanism" that Camus invoked in some of his journalistic writings, and—just as consequentially—the murderous impulses of Meursault on the beach in *The Stranger*, or the allegory of fascist petulance sweeping over the shores of Oran in *The Plague*.[43] Like its analogous Mediterranean cultural-political contact zone, the Indian Ocean similarly produced myriads of conflicted, ambivalent, and often contradictory responses stemming from the same experience of newfound transoceanic contact. A close reading of the Parsi-Iranian exchange will therefore detail a fuller range of cultural, emotional, and philosophical complexities emerging from one such encounter in the Indian Ocean ecumene, as well as the concomitant cultural and political outcomes that those encounters produced.

CHAPTER 1

TO BOMBAY AND BACK

Arbab Kaykhosrow Shahrokh
and the Reinvention of Iranian Zoroastrianism

The Iranian public scarcely noticed the sudden and mysterious death of Arbab Kaykhosrow Shahrokh (1874–1940) on July 3, 1940. The semi-official Tehran daily, *Ettela'at*, made only scant reference to Shahrokh's passing in a brief 250-word column on page 2 of the July 5 issue.[1] The strangely truncated obituary made only brief mention of Shahrokh's civic contributions to Iran's nation-building project—as part of a thir-ty-one-year career as an elected member of the Iranian Majles, and as the universally acknowledged leader of the Iranian Zoroastrian commu-nity—before tersely stating that "on the night of July 3rd [12th of Tir], as he was walking home, he suffered a heart attack and died."[2] The funeral services for Shahrokh, the newspaper's death announcement continued, were already completed, and a memorial service had likewise already taken place at the Firuz Bahram High School in central Tehran.[3]

It was an ignominious end to a life that had begun in the remote and impoverished Iranian Zoroastrian heartland of Kerman, on Iran's central plateau, before he managed to find the means to travel across the waters of the Indian Ocean to the distant metropolis of colonial Bombay.[4] The sixteen-year-old Shahrokh made the journey to India in 1891 to pursue his education at the Parsi community's well-respected Sir Jamsetjee Jejee-bhoy Zartoshti Madressa. After completing his education and returning to Iran, Shahrokh went on to play a key role in nearly every important aspect of Iran's modernization and nation-building efforts during the first four decades of the twentieth century.

The impressive litany of Shahrokh's civic contributions would have—under normal circumstances—received fuller notice than what

Kaykhosrow Shahrokh (1874– 1940). Forugh-e Mazdayasna, *1919 Bombay edition.*

appeared in the *Ettelaʿat* obituary. A more complete accounting would have also acknowledged Shahrokh's efforts, during his long public career, of working to improve the social conditions in which Iran's Zoroastrian minority community lived.[5] These efforts included working closely with charity and philanthropy-minded Parsi benefactors to transfer funds and other resources from India for the building of schools and hospitals in Yazd and Kerman, the two Iranian towns with the highest concentration of Zoroastrians. Kaykhosrow Shahrokh's efforts also included reestablishing, after a protracted hiatus, the Iranian Zoroastrian Anjoman of Tehran, an institution that became the community's principal civic organization, and which raised funds and advocated for the rights of the growing Zoroastrian community in Iran's capital city. Shahrokh served as the president of the Anjoman from its reconstitution in 1906 until his own death in 1940.[6] Under his leadership, the Tehran Anjoman built numerous schools in the Iranian capital for the education of both boys and girls. While the schools were sponsored and constructed through the efforts of the Zoroastrian community, enrollment was open to students of all religious backgrounds. Shahrokh's work as president of the Iranian Zoroastrian Anjoman also led to the establishment of the first *ātashkadeh*, or fire temple, in the Iranian capital, to serve the religious needs of Tehran's Zoroastrian community.[7] His efforts to build religious institutions also led to the establishment of the first Zoroastrian cemetery, or *ārāmgāh*, in the capital region. The cemetery, which came to be known as the Qasr-e Firuzeh Aramgah, was established in the eastern outskirts of Tehran in 1936 and ultimately became Shahrokh's own final resting place.[8]

In addition to his work within Iran's Zoroastrian community, a more complete obituary for Shahrokh would have also detailed his efforts as part of the broader nation-building projects of both Iran's constitutional revolution era and the reign of Reza Shah. During the debates surrounding the drafting of Iran's 1905 constitution, it was Kaykhosrow Shahrokh who emerged as the strongest advocate for formalizing the representation of Iran's religious minority communities.[9] His work on this issue with Jamshid Jamshidian, the prominent Iranian Zoroastrian merchant, banker, and Majles deputy, ensured that Zoroastrians and other recognized religious minority communities would receive designated representatives in Iran's newly established legislative body. Shahrokh's leadership in drafting this constitutional provision helped to secure his own election in 1909 as the Zoroastrian deputy to the Majles, following Jamshidian's political retirement. Shahrokh went on to hold his seat on the Majles for twelve successive elected terms over the course of the next three decades.[10]

As a Majles deputy, Shahrokh became an outspoken fixture of the body and was entrusted with numerous important assignments, including the administration of the critically important office of the Majles' auditor general. His work during this period also extended to his efforts to establish the Majles Library and the Majles Press, two key national institutions that he initiated and oversaw during his tenure as deputy.[11] He was also the founder and initial editor of the *Salnameh-ye Pars*, the long-running official government chronicle during the Reza Shah years.[12] During this time, Shahrokh was also periodically tasked with contributing to a number of other high-priority nation-building projects, such as the creation of Iran's nationwide telephone system, rural and provincial electrification initiatives, and the management of the trans-Iranian railway.[13] As a member of the National Heritage Association (Anjoman-e Asar-e Melli), Shahrokh also played a key role in the cultural history of nationalization during the Reza Shah period, including his important role in building the Ferdowsi memorial in Tus and convening the Ferdowsi millennium conference in 1934.[14]

Aside from his civic and political work, a fuller accounting of Kaykhosrow Shahrokh's record of accomplishment would have also included his contributions to the intellectual history of modern Iranian nationalism. In this regard, he wrote two books that became important texts in redefining the Zoroastrian faith in the context of Iran's pre-Islamic national heritage. The first book, *A'ineh-ye A'in-e Mazdayasna* (Mirror of the Faith of the Mazda Religion), was published initially in a 1907 Tehran lithographed edition.[15] Monica Ringer has rightly described this work as a modern "Zoroastrian catechism," written to present a new Parsi-inspired reformist understanding of the faith to an audience of Iranian Zoroastrians and other interested early twentieth-century readers of the Persian language.[16] Shahrokh's second book, *Forugh-e Mazdayasna* (The Illumination of the Mazda Religion), was first published two years later in a 1909 Tehran lithographed edition.[17] This book consists of an extended essay written by Shahrokh promoting his modernist, universalist, and ecumenical understanding of Zoroastrianism. Significantly, the book also contains Shahrokh's translations of excerpts from selected English-language sources originally written by Parsi and British orientalists, theosophists, and Victorian and Edwardian-era occultists, all of whom had come to praise Zoroastrianism as one of humanity's earliest expressions of a perennial doctrine. The importance of these two books—both of which will be analyzed more closely later in this chapter—has been overshadowed, if not ignored, when considered against the backdrop of Shahrokh's larger body of work as a Zoroastrian civic leader and Iranian politician. In the context of Iran's cultural and intellectual history, however, these books deserve more careful consideration as two of the foundational sources for what became the ideology of twentieth-century Iranian nationalism.

Given Shahrokh's record of accomplishment in all of the areas outlined above, the brevity of his obituary in the pages of *Ettela'at* is surprising. The most obvious explanation for the truncated death announcement is that almost immediately following his death, rumors began to circulate within his family, within the Iranian-Zoroastrian community, and within the salons of Tehran's political class that Kaykhosrow

Shahrokh's death was the result of foul play. In a report sent back to the US State Department in Washington, DC, just days following Shahrokh's death, the American ambassador to Iran, Cornelius Van Engert (1888–1985), who had a close and cordial relationship with Shahrokh during his tenure as the US representative to the Pahlavi court, reported that there was "suspicion that he [Shahrokh] did not die a natural death."[18] Engert, like others at the time—and many others ever since—went on to speculate that Reza Shah had ordered the assassination of Kaykhosrow Shahrokh in retaliation for the political activities of Kaykhosrow's son, Shah-Bahram Shahrokh (1910–1976).[19]

The younger Shahrokh had quickly become a notorious public figure inside Iran during the waning years of Reza Shah's reign, gaining infamy as Iran's most prominent advocate for the Nazi ideology. After completing his education in Iran and Germany, and after a series of brief but failed business ventures in Tehran, the multilingual and by all accounts articulate and charismatic Bahram Shahrokh made the fateful decision in the spring of 1938 to travel to Germany to volunteer his services to the Nazi government's Propaganda Ministry.[20] Once in Berlin, Bahram Shahrokh was quickly assigned as the principal spokesperson and propagandist for what became known as the Nazi government's "Radio Berlin" Persian service.[21] His broadcasts over the new medium of radio quickly gained a widespread listenership inside Iran and earned him the designation of "the most dangerous of all Iranians"[22] by Allied military intelligence officials who documented his activities and became concerned by the extent of his popularity inside Iran. Reza Shah, who by 1940 was under great pressure by the Allies to maintain Iran's political distance from the Nazi government, saw Bahram Shahrokh's radio broadcasts from Berlin as both troublesome and dangerous. For a political class that had become accustomed to Reza Shah's growing authoritarianism—including the imprisonment, disappearance, and death of numerous politicians and intellectuals who were deemed by the Shah as disloyal, incompetent, or otherwise inconvenient[23]—it was easy to interpret the sudden death of Kaykhosrow Shahrokh as an example of his decision to punish the father for the political sins of the son.

When considered in the larger context of these circumstances, the truncated death notice in the pages of the semiofficial *Ettela'at* is therefore understandable. Given this context, presenting a complete obituary for Kaykhosrow Shahrokh would hardly have been appropriate in the pages of Pahlavi Iran's newspaper of record. Shahrokh's mysterious

Kaykhosrow Shahrokh and family. Bahram Shahrokh, still an adolescent, is standing at left. Courtesy of Mohamad Tavakoli-Targhi/Iran Nameh.

death, however, is more than just a graphic indication of the growing climate of authoritarianism in Reza Shah's Iran or the increasingly pervasive mood of fear and paranoia among Iran's political class that there were hidden hands lurking in the shadows of Iran's politics.[24] Rather, what the mysterious death of Kaykhosrow Shahrokh brings to the surface is the larger question of the tenuous fate that had befallen the civic project of liberal Iranian nationalism by the eve of the Second World War. How could a figure such as Kaykhosrow Shahrokh, whose life and work had coincided with the civic, liberal, and ecumenical project of Iran's 1905 constitutional revolution, fall victim to the encroaching politics of Iranian authoritarianism? Similarly, how could a figure whose religious and intellectual contributions had helped to revive a progressive and pluralistic reading of Iranian Zoroastrianism come to pay such a heavy personal price for the emergence of the Nazi ideology inside Iran? To answer these questions requires a consideration of the details of Kaykhosrow Shahrokh's life, as well as an examination of the inherent tensions and contradictions that were rooted within the culture, politics, and ideology of Iranian nationalism during the first four decades of the twentieth century.

BETWEEN KERMAN AND BOMBAY

Kaykhosrow Shahrokh was born in the south-central Iranian plateau town of Kerman, on June 28, 1874, into a Zoroastrian family with deep roots in Iran's history.[25] According to the family's own ancestral lore, they descended from the lineage of Bahram Gūr V (r. 420–438), one of the more fabled shahs of Iran's pre-Islamic Sasanian dynasty. As he describes in a memoir written just two years prior to his death, in addition to this illustrious lineage, Kaykhosrow Shahrokh's more immediate ancestors were also traditionally recognized as figures noted for their learning and government service. Shahrokh's great-great grandfather, Bahman, and his great-grandfather, Goshtasp, were both employed as treasurers and astronomers in the respective courts of Karim Khan Zand and Agha Muhammad Khan Qajar.[26] By the time of Shahrokh's birth, however, the family's fortunes had precipitously declined to the level of menial and semirural subsistence. This decline of the family's fortunes reflected both the more general social and economic decline of the Qajar era and the deteriorating conditions affecting the Iranian Zoroastrian community in particular.[27] To escape the growing poverty in Kerman and Yazd, members of Shahrokh's father's and grandfather's generations emigrated to India in search of opportunity. Most importantly, two of Kaykhosrow Shahrokhs' great-aunts had successfully made the journey to Bombay early in the century, married, and settled into new lives among the Parsi families of Gujarat.[28] This pattern of Zoroastrian contact, travel, and migration to western India would become increasingly commonplace during the Qajar era, and consequently worked to build networks of social, cultural, religious, and familial bonds connecting the Zoroastrians of Iran and India.[29] The importance of India, and the city of Bombay in particular, would come to play an especially important role in Kaykhosrow Shahrokh's life as well.

Kaykhosrow Shahrokh's father, Shahrokh Pur-Eskandar—from whom Kaykhosrow would later adopt what became his legal family name—had already made the journey to India.[30] After completing his education at one of the new Parsi-sponsored schools in Kerman established by Manekji Limji Hataria (1813–1890), the first of the Parsi emissaries to Iran, and embarking on a career in trade, the elder Shahrokh had gone to Bombay in 1873, only to return ill to Kerman prematurely and die of disease just after Kaykhosrow's birth.[31] As he states in his memoir, "I do not remember my father. I was still in my mother's womb when he went to Bombay, and on his return, he became ill and passed

away."[32] With the death of his father, the fortunes of the family continued to decline. His mother, Firuzeh, nineteen years old and now wid-
owed, was forced to support herself and her two young sons by working
as a textile weaver in the local craft economy.[33] Both Kaykhosrow and
his older brother Rustam were also put to work to support the family.
Kaykhosrow's education while still in Kerman was rudimentary, consisting of basic literacy through the traditional *maktab* method. When
his mother remarried as Kaykhosrow was entering into adolescence, he
and his brother chose to leave Kerman to live with their paternal uncle
Aflatun in Tehran.[34]

There is some discrepancy in the sources regarding the date of
Kaykhosrow's initial migration to Tehran, as well as the length of his
stay in the city, before traveling to Bombay for additional education. He
states very clearly in his memoir that he arrived in the capital city "one or
two months"[35] before the death of Manekji Limji Hataria, and as a consequence, "I never met him."[36] Most sources definitively date the death
of Manekji Limji to February 15, 1890.[37] By this account, Shahrokh
would have arrived in Tehran sometime between December of 1889 and
January of 1890. Shahrokh also states that he spent four years in Tehran and one additional year in Bombay[38] before returning to Iran on
the same ship that carried Ardeshir Edulji Reporter (1865–1933), the
most important successor to Manekji Limji as the Parsi community's
official emissary to Iran. As he recalls in his memoir, "I was on the ship
with him as he [Ardeshir Reporter] sailed from Bombay to take up his
assignment in Iran . . . we disembarked in Bandar Abbas; I proceeded
towards Kerman, and he travelled to Tehran."[39] Shahrokh does not give
an exact date for this return trip from India, but other sources definitively date Ardeshir Reporter's initial arrival in Iran as taking place in
1893.[40] If this is the case, then either Kaykhosrow spent much less time
in Tehran and Bombay than the five years in total that he claims, or he
made his initial trip to Tehran earlier than 1890 and is mistaken that
his arrival in the capital coincided with the death of Manekji. It is most
likely that Kaykhosrow and his brother made the journey from Kerman
to Tehran in 1887, as he states in his memoir, "when I reached twelve
years of age,"[41] and that his time in Tehran in fact overlapped with the
final years of Manekji's life, but that the young Shahrokh never crossed
paths with Manekji Limji Hataria. Writing from the vantage point of
1938, Shahrokh's occasionally inconsistent chronology of his early adolescence is understandable.

What is more clear, however, is that when he arrived in Tehran his uncle made arrangements for Kaykhosrow and his brother to enroll in the newly established American Presbyterian boarding school.[42] The American Presbyterian mission had begun their work among Iran's Armenian community much earlier in the nineteenth century, in the northwestern city of Urmieh.[43] By the 1870s, they had also established services in Tehran. The missionary boarding school for boys—under the direction of the Reverend Samuel Ward—was a new initiative that began its operations in 1887,[44] the year that Kaykhosrow most likely arrived in the capital city. Shahrokh remembers his four years at the boarding school vividly, describing Samuel Ward as "a very kind and noble man."[45]

It was during this period that Kaykhosrow Shahrokh began to excel in his studies, especially with respect to the English language. In addition to the establishment of the mission school, the American Presbyterian mission in Tehran had also established a hospital in the capital during this period. When a severe cholera epidemic broke out in 1891[46]—which claimed the life of Kaykhosrow's uncle—Shahrokh and other students began work at the hospital. With the money he earned from his hospital work, Shahrokh next began to consider embarking on his journey to Bombay.[47] With the death of his uncle, the resourceful Shahrokh used his connections via the American mission and the Zoroastrian Anjoman in Tehran to correspond with his still-living great-aunts in India. These elder relatives had migrated to colonial Bombay many years earlier and married into the prominent Petit and Panday families.[48] As he writes in his memoir, "because of the family connections, we were helped."[49] The result of Kaykhosrow's resourcefulness, as well as the intervention of his great-aunts, was that Sir Dinshaw Petit (1823–1901)—the great Parsi textile industrialist and prominent philanthropist—arranged for Kaykhosrow Shahrokh's admission to the Sir Jamsetjee Jejeebhoy Zoroastrian School in Bombay.[50]

The Jejeebhoy School that Shahrokh attended—also known as the Jamsetjee Jejeebhoy Benevolent Institution—was the first of numerous cultural and educational institutions endowed by its eponymous industrialist and social reformer.[51] The school was primarily built for the purpose of providing a new generation of Zoroastrian youth with the cultural and intellectual capital necessary to succeed in the middle-class prosperity engendered by the Parsi community's participation in the colonial economy of the British Raj. Just as importantly, however, the Benevolent Association, like its sister organization, the Sir Jamsetjee Jejeebhoy

Maddresseh (established for the training of a new generation of Zoroastrian priests), was designed to produce a new Parsi intelligentsia committed to fostering a liberal, reformed, and modernist understanding of the faith.[52] All of the principal nineteenth- and early twentieth-century proponents of what came to be called the Parsi renaissance, reformation, and enlightenment, including such key figures as Kharshedji Rustomji Cama and Jivanji Jamshedji Modi, were intimately associated with both of these institutions.

Kaykhosrow Shahrokh only spent one year at the Jamsetjee Jejeebhoy School, between 1892 and 1893, before returning to his native Kerman. The climate of Bombay did not suit Shahrokh any more than it had his father, and as he writes in his memoir, he was frequently ill during his time in the city.[53] Despite the brevity of his sojourn to Bombay, however, Shahrokh was clearly affected by his experience among the Parsis. He excelled at the school, and as he recalls, despite his frequent illnesses, "my teachers appeared very pleased with my progress and I received several awards."[54] Shahrokh also made a strong impression on the leaders of the Parsi community's Society for the Amelioration of the Conditions of the Zoroastrians in Persia. The Society had been established in 1854 by Sir Dinshaw Petit to promote philanthropic initiatives to improve the social and economic conditions of Iran's beleaguered Zoroastrian community.[55] Manekji Limji Hataria's nearly four-decade career as the Parsi community's emissary to Iran was the first initiative sponsored by the Amelioration Society. Kaykhosrow's resourcefulness and educational achievement impressed the Society's leadership, and when poor health required that he return to Iran, Shahrokh was recruited to serve as a new emissary to continue the Society's philanthropic work in Kerman.[56]

Kaykhosrow Shahrokh returned to Iran in 1893, and as he states, "I was paid my travelling expenses [by the Amelioration Society], and in Bandar Abbas, I bought a donkey for ten tomans, and riding on the beast, I somehow managed to reach Kerman."[57] For the next eleven years, from the age of eighteen to twenty-nine, Shahrokh received a modest salary from the Parsi Amelioration Society in Bombay, and served as a community organizer and social reformer among the Zoroastrians of Kerman. Expanding educational opportunities became his primary goal during this period. His own education at the American mission school in Tehran and the Jejeebhoy School in Bombay gave him the essential tools needed to build new schools and a modern curriculum. When he began his efforts, Shahrokh recalls, there was only one school in the

Zoroastrian quarter of Kerman.[58] Over the next decade, with the initiative of local Zoroastrians and Parsi assistance, Shahrokh established three new schools for boys and three schools for girls.[59] These schools were organized as primary schools, which provided only basic literacy and elementary civic education. Higher levels of education remained scarce in Kerman and Yazd, and would have to wait another generation before becoming locally available. In the interim, however, Shahrokh's new Zoroastrian primary schools represented an important expansion of the initial efforts of Manekji Limji Hataria.

Shahrokh's other major effort during the eleven years that he spent in Kerman was his work in challenging both the social and religious conservatism within elements of the local Zoroastrian community, and his efforts to overturn the Jim Crow–like social restrictions that had traditionally been imposed on Iran's Zoroastrians.[60] The social restrictions that were imposed on the Iranian Zoroastrian community—and other non-Muslim communities in Iran—were not institutionalized legal codes rooted in Islamic jurisprudential sources. They were likewise neither uniform nor ahistorical in their practical implementation. Rather, the restrictions that did in fact exist—such as physical separation of Zoroastrians from Muslims on rainy days in order for the majority population to avoid "pollution" from Zoroastrians, or the general prohibition on Zoroastrians from riding horses, donkeys, or mules in public spaces where Muslims were present, or clothing restrictions that had the effect of publicly identifying Zoroastrians as such—were all informal local accretions that had accumulated to become enforced social practices over the course of many generations.[61] In a place like Kerman, by the late Qajar period these customary social codes had become particularly egregious. As Shahrokh recalled in his memoir, when he returned to Kerman as the emissary of the Bombay community's Amelioration Society, "I vowed to myself that I would return home with the sole aim of changing all of this."[62]

Shahrokh had the good fortune of returning to Kerman during the governorship of Prince Abdolhossein Mirza Farman-Farma (1857–1939), one of the most formidable, farsighted, and progressive members of the extended Qajar family.[63] The eighteen-year-old Shahrokh cultivated a good relationship with Farman-Farma, impressing the governor with his travels to Bombay and his command of English. Shahrokh went on to serve as Farman-Farma's personal secretary during his governorship of Kerman and worked as a teacher of English to the members of the governor's household.[64] With the support of Farman-Farma, Shahrokh set out to challenge the informal restrictions that had been imposed on the Zoroastrians of Kerman. He writes, for example, that as he would regularly go to the governor's mansion to work, he consciously chose to make a public spectacle of defying the prohibition against Zoroastrians riding horses in public. He described this defiance as "a dangerous thing to do, for which I was threatened." He added, "I refused to be intimidated and continued with my practice of riding horse-back, and later, this came to be accepted by the Muslims."[65] Shahrokh's social reform efforts also extended to challenging the traditional sartorial regulations imposed on local Zoroastrians. As the headmaster of the newly established schools in Kerman, Shahrokh took the initiative to institute a new dress code that would apply to all pupils, irrespective of their religious affiliation. The initiative was met with resistance, including from conservative elders of the local Zoroastrian community, who Shahrokh claimed were fearful that challenging the sartorial codes would "endanger the community."[66] Despite the initial resistance, Shahrokh insisted that Zoroastrian students dress in the same manner as their "Muslim brothers."[67] As with his other efforts of social reform during his Kerman years, Shahrokh credits the Prince-Governor Farman-Farma with supporting his initiative and ensuring that the changes he had instituted would succeed.[68] However, the governorship of Abdolhossein Mirza Farman-Farma was in some respects the exception to the more general pattern of capricioius Qajar rule in the provinces. Other governors who followed, such as Mozaffar al-Saltaneh and Zill al-Soltan, were described by Shahrokh as "tyrannical and cruel," and were known to arbitrarily confiscate property and otherwise persecute Kerman and Yazd's Zoroastrian, Bahai, and Jewish communities.[69]

By 1904, after eleven years in Kerman and a productive but mixed record of success in improving the lives of the local Zoroastrians, Kaykhosrow Shahrokh chose to explore new opportunities. His time in Kerman had led to contacts with figures such as Sir Percy Sykes, the British general who spent some time as consul in the city.[70] Shahrokh describes Sykes's eager curiosity for exploring the region in and around Kerman, including his excavation of a frieze from the tomb of the fifteenth-century Shah Nematollah-e Vali in Mahan, just outside of Kerman. "Later," Shahrokh writes, "it was discovered that Major Sykes sold this to the Louvre Museum in Paris at a very high price."[71] Shahrokh also became associated with a Russian doctor who was likewise appointed to work in the local Russian consul. After exchanging English lessons for lessons in Russian, a language that Shahrokh came to have a passing proficiency in, he was encouraged by the Russian, Dr. Vinogradav, to travel to Odessa, the Russian commercial port city on the Black Sea, to explore the potential there for business opportunities.[72]

His journey to Odessa was ultimately cut short by the political unrest that unfolded throughout Tsarist Russia following the Russian defeat in the Russo-Japanese War of 1904–1905. Shahrokh spent only four months in the city, leaving just before the June 1905 workers' strike and mutiny on the battleship *Potemkin* led to the outbreak of what became the Russian Revolution of 1905.[73] As he recalled, "I left Odessa for Tehran the moment I felt the disturbances would spread to the Black Sea port. The day after I left, Odessa was shelled by the navy and disturbances erupted there as well."[74] By the early twentieth century, Russian Odessa, like British Bombay, was a largely modernized and cosmopolitan port city of several hundred thousand inhabitants. The city also had substantial commercial links that connected its people and its economy both regionally and internationally.

FOUNDING FATHER

Despite the brevity of Shahrokh's stay in the city, when he reached Tehran sometime in early 1905, his travel experience in both Bombay and Odessa, combined with his linguistic skills and personal qualities, led him to quickly find employment with the Jamshidian Trading Company.[75] The company, founded by the Iranian-Zoroastrian entrepreneur Jamshid Jamshidian (1850–1932), was Iran's largest trading company at the time, with interests and holdings throughout Iran as well as the Indian Ocean, Black Sea, and beyond.[76] Shahrokh quickly rose through the ranks of the Jamshidian organization from clerk to principal administrator of the company and also became one of Jamshid Jamshidian's closest associates. The position gradually made Shahrokh a wealthy man, with significant ownership in land and business investments of his own.

Shahrokh's return to Tehran also coincided with the beginning of Iran's Constitutional Revolution of 1905–1911. His initial involvement in the revolutionary movement appears to have been minimal. He does describe writing articles in support of the constitution in the Tehran newspaper *Neda-ye Vatan*, and using the pure-Persian form of the Persian language—devoid of Arabic loan words—claiming to introduce new "pure" words such as *kangāshestān* (assembly), *novīn* (new), *jāygāh* (place), and *vïjheh* (special) into Iran's political lexicon.[77] Like others of the era, Shahrokh quickly came to see Iran's constitutional revolution as not only a political movement, but also an occasion for a national rebirth. The role that Zoroastrianism and the Zoroastrian community—and Iran's classical heritage as a whole—would play in that political and national rebirth now became the major preoccupation for the rest of his life.

It was during this period that Shahrokh came to combine his social activism to improve the conditions of Iran's Zoroastrian community with his political activism in the cause of Iran's constitutional revolution. His close association with Jamshid Jamshidian—the wealthy Iranian-Zoroastrian merchant and elected Zoroastrian deputy to the first Majles—greatly facilitated Shahrokh's efforts in this regard. During the early debates of the constitutional assembly, one of the divisive issues that quickly emerged was the conservative proposal to limit the definition of Iranian citizenship to members of Iran's Muslim-majority population. As Shahrokh recalled, "the draft stated that, 'Muslims are equal under the law,' thereby excluding non-Muslims."[78] Shahrokh went on to write that he "protested in the strongest possible terms to Jamshidian, even though I was his employee."[79] Though Jamshidian was a member of the Majles, he acknowledged that he was not adept at the language of constitutional law. He therefore encouraged Shahrokh to lobby for a change to the draft provision. Shahrokh worked with other prominent Zoroastrians in Tehran, and likewise reached out to the leadership of Iran's Jewish and Armenian communities, before approaching the speaker of the Majles. After additional consultations with other Majles deputies—and after receiving a *fatwa* from the progressive Najaf-based Marja al-Taqlid, Mohammad Kazem Khorasani, endorsing the principle of legal equality of non-Muslims—a new draft bill extending equality to "all Iranian subjects" was approved.[80]

Following this incident, Shahrokh's social and political activism accelerated rapidly. When Jamshid Jamshidian chose to step down as Majles deputy following the royalist coup d'etat of 1908, Shahrokh became his natural successor. After the restoration of the Majles in 1909, Shahrokh was elected to the second Majles and went on to serve until his death during the twelfth Majles, in 1940.[81] During this period, Shahrokh reestablished the Zoroastrian Anjoman of Tehran, the main organization promoting the civic life of Zoroastrians in the capital city. Kaykhosrow Shahrokh was elected as president of the Anjoman, and under his leadership it built a series of other Zoroastrian institutions in Tehran, including schools, libraries, a fire temple, and the first Zoroastrian cemetery in Iran. The headquarters of the Anjoman was located on a city block off of Naderi Street in central Tehran, adjacent to the British and Russian embassy compounds. The site gradually grew to become the de facto civic home of Tehran's growing Zoroastrian community. Jamshid Jamshidian's personal estate and business headquarters, as well as Kaykhosrow Shahrokh's own home, were also located on this same city block. In later years, the community's fire temple and the Firuz Bahram Zoroastrian High School were also built there. The Parsi community's official emissary to Iran during this period, Ardeshir Reporter, also resided on the Jamshidian property, and kept an office in the Anjoman's building.[82]

A ZOROASTRIAN CATECHISM

In addition to his energetic work as a civic and political leader during this period, Shahrokh also made an important contribution to the cultural and intellectual history of Iranian nationalism. Between 1907 and 1909 he wrote his two principal works, *A'ineh-ye A'in-e Mazdayasna* (1907) and *Forugh-e Mazdayasna* (1909). The first of these books, the *A'ineh*, was published in at least two editions during Shahrokh's lifetime. The initial publication was in a lithographed Tehran edition of roughly three thousand copies. A second edition, which as he states was necessary to produce because the first edition had become unobtainable, was published in 1921—also in a lithographed edition—at Bombay's Mozafari Press.[83] Like the first edition, the 1921 Bombay edition was also produced in roughly three thousand copies. The second edition is also important because the Parsi charitable foundations collaborated with Iranian Zoroastrians to sponsor the book's publication and distribution costs. It contains an appendix that includes the names of the dozens of Parsi and Iranian Zoroastrian *moshtarekīn* (subscribers) who prepurchased copies of the 1921 lithographed edition.[84] Both editions were also produced with a primary audience of schoolchildren and interested lay Zoroastrian readers in mind. As the number of Zoroastrian schools in Yazd, Kerman, Tehran, and elsewhere began to increase, Shahrokh came to realize the necessity for a foundational text that would present the essential teachings of a modernist and reformed interpretation of Zoroastrianism.[85] In the context of the upheavals underway during the constitutional era, the *A'ineh*, like its sequel work, the *Forugh*, also found an audience among Iranian readers who were reevaluating Iran's cultural, religious, and political heritage.[86]

In the case of the *A'ineh*, the book was written in the simple and accessible format of a catechism. The thirty-five chapters of the text were each organized around an essential theme or doctrine relating to the faith. Within each chapter, the format of the text was presented in the form of a series of questions purportedly made from a student-initiate, followed by a careful and succinct presentation of what is presented as official doctrine. This format has roots in earlier textual traditions of "manuals," wisdom literature (*andarz*), and "books of instruction" that can be found in other religions, including Zoroastrianism.[87] The precise format of this text, however, seems to most clearly approximate the Christian catechisms that Shahrokh had encountered through contacts with missionaries in both India and Iran. As Monica Ringer has described, Shahrokh was in fact explicit in revealing how close he had come to converting to Christianity following his years as a student at the American Mission School in Tehran and his encounter with Christian missionaries during his time in Bombay. Rather than conversion, it seems that Shahrokh chose to embark on a project of reinterpreting and reforming Zoroastrianism.[88] The format of the *A'ineh*—as well as its content—can therefore be broadly interpreted as an exercise in *apologia*, designed to present doctrines derived from a normative Christianity within the template of a reformist Zoroastrianism.

This becomes very clear in the thirty-five chapters of *A'ineh-ye A'in-e Mazdayasna*. Among the chapters are ones relating to theological principles concerning the nature and attributes of God (*dar shenāsā'i-ye khodā*),[89] as well as chapters outlining ethical doctrines such as duty,[90] prayer,[91] neatness,[92] abstinence,[93] and the ethics of marriage.[94] The content of many chapters are also clearly organized to address and dispel common "misconceptions" traditionally held by detractors of Zoroastrianism, whether they be conservative Muslim jurists, proselytizing Christian missionaries, or by some Zoroastrians themselves. In discussing the nature of God, for example, there is an inordinate emphasis on the singular and indivisible nature of the creator-deity. To the question "Who is God?" as posed in chapter 1 of the catechism, Shahrokh replies, "God is the singular (*yektā*) creator of existence (*hastī*) who was not born and will not die, and exists and will always exist, and all of creation (*āfarīneshhā*) is from him."[95] This emphasis on the principle of monotheism was intended as a retort to the accusation of dualism and polytheism often leveled against Zoroastrianism by its traditional detractors. Shahrokh's modernist Zoroastrian catechism suggests that the source of the misconception is the use of the word "Ahuramazda" to describe the creator-diety. "What is the word for God in the *Avesta*?" asks Shahrokh's imaginary student-supplicant.[96] The reply the reader receives is that "in the *Avesta*, which is the book of the Zoroastrians, the word 'Ahuramazda' has come for God, which some have shortened to Ormozd, Hormoz, or Hormozd."[97] Shahrokh's explanation continues by resorting to a linguistic explanation of this name: "the meaning of 'Ahura' is lord and bestower of creation (*hastī-bakhsh*) and supreme radiance (*shaydān-shīd*) and 'Mazda' means great and peerless knower (*dānā-ye bīhamtā-ye bozorg*)."[98] The precision of Shahrokh's philological explication notwithstanding, his intention in describing the God of Zoroastrianism in this way is clear. Ahuramazda becomes not a proper name within an earthly or celestial pantheon of deities, but simply the Avestan term that equates the Zoroastrian creator-god with the same monotheistic conception as found in the Abrahamic tradition.

In addition to emphasizing a strict monotheism, Shahrokh's rendering of a modernist Zoroastrian catechism also underscored additional reformist readings that bore a remarkable resemblance to normative elements of the Abrahamic tradition. In describing the text of the *Avesta*, Shahrokh echoes what had become the reformist Parsi interpretation of placing emphasis on the *Gathas* as the scriptural core of the faith. The *Gathas*, he writes, "are portions of the utterances (*sokhanān*) of Ashu-Zartosht and are in five parts . . . each one of these *Gathas* are portions and selections of worship and devotion to the one God (*khodā-ye yektā*) in the form of songs."[99] He goes on to explain that the many supplementary texts in the later Zend, Pahlavi, and other Middle Persian linguistic traditions should not be afforded the same lofty status as the original *Gathas*. These later texts are merely commentaries (*gozāresh*) or, as he states, "commentaries on commentaries" (*gozāresh-e gozāresh*).[100] By limiting the textual foundation of the faith to the *Gathas*, Shahrokh's reinterpretation of the faith—like those of his Parsi reformist contemporaries and predecessors—came to elevate the scriptural authority of the *Gathas* in terms resembling the hermeneutical and exegetical understandings found in Christianity and Islam.

Other doctrinal and ritual elements of Zoroastrianism were similarly redefined. On the issue of "prayer" and "fire worship," for example, Shahrokh is determined to dispel the popular notion that fire is itself the object of veneration in Zoroastrian ritual life. "During the performance of worship to the one God," Shahrokh writes, believers are instructed to "turn their gaze towards light" (*rū be sū-ye forūgh*).[101] He continues: "In seeing this illumination (*shaydān*), which is a representation (*nemūneh*) of the light of truth, their hearts will be drawn towards understanding the bestower of illumination."[102] The fire itself, he suggests, is not the divinity, but is intended as a symbol, representation, or reminder of a more "profound illumination" (*rūshanā'ī-ye amīgh*).[103]

We see this reformist theology as well in his treatment of issues such as "proselytism," "burial practices," and "polygamy." On the contentious issue of proselytism, Shahrokh's position reflects the debates within the Parsi community of the time. While arguing against the practice, he suggests that it is proper to "offer" or "present" (*pazīrā'ī*) the teachings of the faith to all.[104] He then goes on to cite *Yasna* 30, verse 2, which is the verse emphasizing the principle of "choice" and "selection" in one's faith, and is likewise one of the Avestan verses often invoked by Parsi reformers who expressed openness to—if not proselytism—then to the possibility of conversion to Zoroastrianism.[105] With respect to death and burial practices, Shahrokh does not use the *A'ineh* as a platform to question the traditional *dakhmeh* practice of exposing the remains of the dead on platforms—the so-called "towers of silence"—to be consumed by vultures. Instead, following Parsi reformist ideas, he places emphasis on exercising modern hygienic precautions involving ritual cleaning of the deceased in order to prevent the Zoroastrian towers of silence from becoming breeding grounds for communicable disease.[106] In later years, Shahrokh took the much more radical step of advocating for the abandonment of *dakhmeh* practice, and instead initiated the practice in Tehran of burying the dead, in coffins lined with stone, cement, or metal, in the city's Zoroastrian cemetery, or *ārāmgāh*. This method, he argued, had innumerable advantages, including the principles of cleanliness, purity, and hygiene, while also conforming Zoroastrian death and burial practices with modern tastes. As he writes in 1937, the traditional *dakhmeh* practice was contrary to "progress, health, moral purity and goodness, as well as hygiene."[107] On the issue of the *dakhmeh* debate, Shahrokh's reforms in fact outpaced the ideas of his contemporary Zoroastrian reformers in Bombay.[108]

His ideas relating to marriage (*zanāshū'ī*) likewise showed little hesitation in breaking with customary practices and beliefs in the interest of conforming Zoroastrianism to contemporary standards. Though Zoroastrianism had a complex history with respect to customs of marriage and the status of women—including polygamy, incest, and female seclusion—Shahrokh's rendering of the issue in the pages of both the *A'ineh* and the *Forugh* clearly draws from a modernist tradition which sought to find "progressive" elements in an "original"—if now corrupted—Zoroastrian heritage. This practice of returning to a purported original form of the faith that was deemed to be in harmony with modern values had the effect of *authenticating modernity* as a cultural restoration of a putatively original Zoroastrianism. Corruptions and accretions over time had, according to this logic, concealed the original content of the faith that was, in fact, in conformity with the culture of modernity. In following the structure of this logic, Shahrokh followed the work of progressive Parsi priests and scholars of the era, including Darab Dastur Peshotan Sanjana and Maneckji Nusservani Dhalla,[109] to argue that "in the Zoroastrian religion it is permissible to have one wife, and if she should die, after some time it is permissible to take another."[110] He returns to this issue in the *Forugh* where he is likewise clear to argue that "a woman cannot take more than one husband . . . and a husband does not have permission to take more than one wife."[111] Shahrokh's modernist critique of matrimony also focuses on what he describes as the "outmoded" practice of child marriage.[112]

WEIRD SCIENCE

Shahrokh's willingness to pose sometimes bold reinterpretations of the Zoroastrian faith along these modernist lines was, however, a far more delicate and precarious procedure than what may at first appear as the simple logic of doctrinal "modernization." The reformist desire to synthesize Zoroastrian thought with the most *up-to-date* intellectual novelties of the late nineteenth and early twentieth centuries also exposed reformists like Shahrokh to the danger of grafting tenuous and fringe doctrines, which had nevertheless managed to acquire a novel if precarious currency, onto the Zoroastrian tradition. With respect to "progressive" doctrines, such as the emancipation of women, the modernization of burial practices, the codification of scriptural authority, or a refined, reinvented, and redoubled emphasis on a Zoroastrian monotheism, the desire to conform the Zoroastrian heritage to the demands of "contemporary standards" was largely unproblematic.

What was equally unproblematic was Shahrokh's willingness to draw inspiration from the many Western commentators on religion, philosophy, and science who praised Zoroastrianism as a faith that had uniquely foreshadowed the foundations of modern thought. The bulk

Title page of Forugh-e Mazdayasna. *1919 Bombay edition.*

of Shahrokh's second major work, *Forugh-e Mazdayasna* (1909), in fact consists of translated excerpts from the writings of these sympathetic critics and commentators of Zoroastrianism. Some of these flattering— if often eccentric—excerpted examples of what can be termed *philo-zoroastrianism* include the ideas of the popular Victorian-era science writer Samuel Laing (1810–1897). Laing argued in his 1887 work, *A Modern Zoroastrian*, that the doctrine of duality, for example, as personified by the anthropomorphic figures of Ahuramazda and Ahriman, that is at the core of Zoroastrian understandings of the cosmos is a mytho-religious expression of the same "law of polarity" that latter-day researchers have identified as the science of electromagnetism.[113] Laing illustrates this point by posing a correspondence between the principle of attraction and repulsion as seen in magnets and the notion of cosmic duality as expressed in Zoroastrian doctrines.[114] He goes on to trace other similarities between core doctrines of Zoroastrianism and findings in the fields of geology, chemistry, biology, zoology, and botany. These doctrinal affinities between Zoroastrianism and modern science suggest for Laing that "Zoroastrianism . . . in its foundational ideas . . . reconciles the conflict between faith and science."[115]

For Victorian- and Edwardian-era thinkers still burdened by the debates surrounding Darwin's theory of evolution, Zoroastrianism, rather than receiving the dismissive judgment of orientalist scholarship, was instead heralded as the paragon of a religion that could be at home in the culture of modernity and the Enlightenment. In this way, the Zoroastrian tradition escaped some of the more imperial pronouncements of orientalism and found a form of quasi-scientific redemption through one of orientalism's minor offshoots, which Edward Said has called "the Romantic Orientalist project."[116] This "scientific" endorsement of the faith—its patronizing and paternalistic subtext notwithstanding—was particularly appealing to Shahrokh, who was eager to translate excerpts of Laing's work for his audience of Iranian readers. "Men of science like Huxley, philosophers like Herbert Spencer, poets like Tennyson, might all subscribe to it [Zoroastrianism],"[117] according to Laing. Shahrokh was also eager to translate Laing's pronouncement that Zoroastrianism approximates "the best of modern thought" (*behtarīn khiālāt-e jadīd-e emrūzeh*).[118] Equally important for Shahrokh was his eagerness to render into Persian Laing's notion that the Zoroastrian conception of the divine was analogous to the modernist notion of a creator-god defined as a First Cause, which Shahrokh translates as both *elat-e aval* and *sabab-e nokhostīn*. Laing, like many other thinkers of his day, saw Zoroastrianism's cosmological and theological teachings as analogous to the religio-philosophical ideas of Deism that were in harmony with an understanding of a perfectly ordered universe governed by the laws of nature. As Laing writes, in a phrase Shahrokh eagerly rendered into Persian, "The Parsee has no reason to tremble for his faith if a Galileo invents the telescope or a Newton discovers the law of gravity."[119]

The affirmation that Zoroastrianism received from these Victorian-era commentators was particularly appealing to Shahrokh. Another measure of this affirmation, as Shahrokh explains in the *Forugh*, was the growing popularity of Zoroastrianism in Europe and North America— not only as an example of a historical artifact and doctrinal precursor of modernity, but as a living and growing tradition of faith that was attracting new adherents. He pays particular attention to the growth of a small but significant Neo-Zoroastrian cult led by the self-styled Reverend Doctor Prince Otoman Zar-Adosht Hanish (1856–1936). As Shahrokh explains, "these Neo-Zoroastrians [which he translates as *jadīd-ol-zartoshtīan*] total several thousand people in America and Europe."[120] Referring to Hanish, Shahrokh continues, "one person among these preachers and scholars of spirituality [*'olamā-ye rūhāni*] and the science of holiness [*'olūm-e 'ālī*] in America has established a society and named it Mazdaznan . . . and every single day there are those . . . who follow and spread the word about this faith."[121] The Mazdaznan movement that Shahrokh takes great pride in introducing to his Iranian readers was in fact a small but significant cult that combined vegetarianism, calisthenics, tantric disciplines, and sun worship with Zoroastrian-inspired doctrines and symbolism.[122] Its founder, whose given name was Otto Zachariah Hanisch, had purportedly lived in Iran as a child and was the son of Russian diplomats.[123] In the first half of the twentieth century, the Hanish cult also intermittently published a monthly periodical promoting his eccentric ideas.[124] The Mazdaznan Neo-Zoroastrian movement had established a network of affiliated religious centers throughout Europe, as well as in New York, Chicago, and Los Angeles. As detailed in chapter 2, the Parsi community of Bombay took a particular interest in the ideas of the Hanish cult, and it is quite likely that Shahrokh was introduced to the Mazdaznan movement through his network of Parsi intermediaries.[125] Like his Parsi colleagues, Shahrokh took particular pride in the fact that Westerners "from the highest ranks of scholars and people of learning" had recognized and converted to what Shahrokh describes as "the light of truth of this pure religion."[126] In the *Forugh* he is also quick to use the authority of Zoroastrianism's recognition by Western commentators and converts to encourage his Iranian readers to reconsider the value and importance of the faith as part of Iran's own heritage:

> and it is hoped that the light of truth (*nūr-e haqīqat*) of this pure faith (*ā'īn-e pāk*) will be appreciated as a luminous science (*'elm-e tābnāk*) and discovered, strived for, and inspired by, so that you Zoroastrians who are followers of this monotheistic faith will not fall behind those who have newly arrived (*noresīdegān*) to your own religion.[127]

Shahrokh's eagerness to acknowledge the authority of Otto Hanisch and the Mazdaznan cult as a legitimate arbiter of the value of the Zoroastrian faith—like his eagerness to accept the generous pronouncements of Samuel Laing and other Western commentators—brings to the surface one of the underlying tensions at work in his writing. While Shahrokh was eager to accept the endorsement of Western commentators with respect to the culture of Zoroastrianism and Iranian classicism, that eagerness also led him to uncritically absorb other far more dubious cultural, historical, and quasi-scientific pronouncements. In Shahrokh's case, orientalism as a form of scientific flattery was culturally enticing, but it also led to the adoption of assumptions that were intellectually contradictory and morally questionable. The pronouncements of the Mazdaznan sect, for example, may have been curious, eccentric, and ultimately harmless, but other eagerly accepted authoritative judgments from Western commentators regarding Zoroastrianism had far more complex and problematic implications.

We see this especially with respect to Shahrokh's casual invocation of doctrines associated with race science, philology, and the occultist ideas derived from the then-ascendant theosophical movement. His understandings of language and race, in particular, are especially rooted in assumptions of cultural purity connected to popular romantic understandings of the nation. We can identify these assumptions sprinkled throughout the text of both the *A'ineh* and the *Forugh*. In the *A'ineh*, for example, Shahrokh places great emphasis on his conscious use of a pure-Persian language that is conspicuous in its avoidance of Arabic loan words. As he states in the preface to the text, one of his main goals was to produce a work "written in the Persian language without Arabic"

Otoman Zar-Adosht
Hanish (1856–1936).
Mazdaznan, *Chicago,*
1908.

(*be zabān-e pārsī-ye bi-tāzī*).[128] Even here he is explicit—if not ostentatious—in his use of the Middle Persian term *pārsi* to refer to the Persian language, rather than the more familiar Perso-Arabic use of *fārsi*. His use of the term *tāzi* to refer to Arabic linguistic influence on Persian is likewise an archaic form that carries a derogatory connotation in his writing. The text of the *A'ineh* is replete with other pure-Persian neologisms and pseudo-archaisms, such as, for example, the use of the word *farjūd*[129] in his discussion of Zoroastrianism's understanding of "miracles," rather than the more commonly used *mo'jezeh*; or *varshīm*[130] for "section" in referring to the different segments of the *Avesta* instead of the more common Perso-Arabic terms *qesmat, fasl*, or *bāb*; or *farāzmān*[131] for "commandment" in the discussion of the juridical *Vendidad* text instead of the vernacular *farmān* or *qānūn*. To assist his readers in deciphering these awkward archaisms and neologisms, Shahrokh also included a glossary at the end of the *A'ineh* that lists over six hundred words along with their more familiar Perso-Arabic equivalents.[132]

THE SUN WORSHIPER

DEVOTED TO
Oriental and Occidental Philosophy,
Sociology. Religion. Science.
Cultivation of the Higher Senses,
and the Development of the Body.

One Dollar a Year   Ten Cents Single Copy

The Sun Worshiper *monthly magazine. Otoman Zar-Adosht Hanish, editor.* Sun Worshiper, *Chicago, 1902.*

Shahrokh's strident emphasis on the importance of linguistic purity contradicts his broader objectives of cultural and political pluralism as reflected in his civic work as a member of the Iranian Majles and as the President of Zoroastrian Anjoman of Tehran. While advocating for civil and religious rights for Iran's minority communities, and operating within the parameters of a liberal-constitutional political project of post-1905 Iran, he also seems to hold the view that the Arabic language, and Arab-Islamic civilization more broadly, represents an external intrusion into a now sullied Iranian purity. This tension is clearly reflected in how Shahrokh approaches the problem of language in the *A'ineh* and the *Forugh*.

A similar tension is at work in Shahrokh's discussions of history and race. In both the *A'ineh* and the *Forugh*, he places special emphasis on identifying the racial origins of the Iranian people as a whole, and in identifying the racial identity of Zoroaster (*nezhād-e aslī-ye Zartosht*) in particular.[133] In the 1909 text of the *Forugh*, Shahrokh gives a brief but lucid discussion of the essentials of the Aryan theory, as understood in his time, presenting the hypothesis of the ice-age origins of the Aryan tribes and their subsequent migrations and dispersions to various sub-regions of the Eurasian continent. He gives the etymology of the related terms *Iran, Arya,* and *Aryan* to their Sanskrit and Avestan forms. "The essential meaning of the word *āryā* is purity (*pāk*) and noble (*najīb*)," he states, "according to the Sanskrit and Avestan languages."[134] In the *A'ineh* he also echoes some of these ideas by tracing Zoroaster's lineage to leg-endary kings described in the mytho-historical *pīshdādīān* sections of Ferdowsi's *Shahnameh*. Zoroaster, according to Shahrokh's account, is therefore identified as not only a religious figure, but becomes part of a romanticized definition of, as Shahrokh writes for his audience of Ira-nian readers, "our race" (*nezhād-e mā*).[135]

Shahrokh's familiar—and perhaps tedious—nationalist predilection to point out the racial identity of Iranians via invocations of nineteenth-century anthropological, orientalist, and linguistic theories is coupled by his equally familiar echoing of nationalist readings of Iran's history. In the *A'ineh*, for example, he includes a chapter describing the "peak" (*bolandī*) and the "downfalls" (*oftadegīhā*) of Iranian-Zoroastrian his-tory. "How many times has Zoroastrianism been attacked since the beginning of this religion?"[136] he asks. His answer is that Zoroastrianism has suffered exactly five periods of great suffering in its history. As he details these five episodes, it becomes clear that in his understanding, the history of Zoroastrianism and Iran are equivalent and interchange-able. Iran's national history becomes congruent with the history of Zoro-astrianism, and therefore becomes worthy of inclusion in a text, like the *A'ineh*, which presents itself as a manual of essential tenants of the faith. The posing of the question itself, therefore, carries with it the assump-tions of a romanticism that connects religion and nation. What is also clear in the subsequent answer to this question is that the challenges that have befallen Zoroastrianism have been levied against it by its *external* ethno-religious rivals. The first of these rivals, he argues, in this case borrowing from the familiar demonology and myth-history of the *Shahnameh* as well as modern romantic nationalist sensibilities, came at the hands of Ferdowsi's fabled serpent-king and villain "Zahhāk-e Tazi." Emphasizing Zahhāk's tribal Arab origins, he writes, "it was in the time of Shah Jamshid that Zahhāk-e Tazi shed the blood of the Iranians."[137] As a consequence of this assault, he continues, "the nation of Iran was under oppression for one thousand years."[138] He also makes mention of the trials of Rustam against Turan, as well as Kiyanid battles against the Assyrians, before depicting the conquest of Iran by Alexander the Great in stark detail. "The Estakhr-e Pārs [Persepolis] was set on fire,"[139] he writes. This conquest of Iran by the Greeks was particularly egregious, because—as he suggests—it led to the destruction and loss of much of the corpus of Zoroastrian literature. As he describes, "the books of religion and knowledge (*dīn va dānesh*) of the Zoroastrians, which were stored in the library (*nāmeh-khāneh*) were burned."[140] Intriguingly, he then claims that some of these books survived and were carried off to Greece, where they subsequently spawned the Greek philosophical and scientific tradition.[141] The fate of Iran and of the Zoroastrians are again rendered here as equivalent. The two are defined by Shahrokh as not only suffering victims of external conquerors but also the forgotten seeds of what grew to become the Western philosophical tradition. Finally, in describing the fifth—and by his account final—conquest of Iran, he laments the fall of Yazdegird III, the last of the Iranian-Zoroastrian monarchs, to the "tāziān" (the Arabs), who "became the possessors of this worthy treasure (*ganj-e shāygān*) . . . that is Iran."[142] Shahrokh has little to say about the subsequent thirteenth-century Mongol conquest, which in his reading of Iran's history was more pertinent to the Islamicate historiographic imagination. By Shahrokh's logic, Iran's conquest had already become irreparable by the time of the seventh-century Arab-Muslim conquest of Zoroastrian-Iran. As he writes, "and until today it is in their hands."[143]

Despite Shahrokh's casual invocations of many of the racialized and exclusionary assumptions of romantic nationalism and scientific orientalism of his day, there remains a countervailing tension at the core of both the *A'ineh* and the *Forugh*. Shahrokh frequently tempers his racialized assumptions with a language that simultaneously reflects assumptions rooted in a liberal, democratic, and pluralistic political philosophy. In the *Forugh*, for example, he is blunt in suggesting that appeals to racial pride (*eftekhār-e nezhād*)[144] do not adequately measure the value or worth of individual believers. After a long discussion of Zoroaster's racial genealogy and the Aryan origins of the "Iranian nation," Shahrokh concludes by asking, "Now that our origins and race have been explained in this way, should we be contented with this pride?"[145] He then goes on to argue that the true achievements of the Iranian-Zoroastrian people should instead be measured by their creation of the moral-ethical system of good thoughts, good deeds, and good words that they introduced into the world. These are the values, he concludes, that should be the source of pride and accomplishment, and which should be measured as most worthy in the "highest realm" (*'ālam-e ā'li*).[146]

This tension between Shahrokh's racialized reading of Iran's history and his liberal-constitutionalist credentials is also on display in his description of the treatment of Iran's Zoroastrian community during the more recent epochs of Iran's history. In the *A'ineh* he turns to this issue by expressing praise for the inclusive governance of Shah Abbas as well as Muhammad Shah Qajar, Naser al-Din Shah Qajar, and Muzaffar al-Din Shah Qajar, all of whom, he argues, "allowed this community [Zoroastrians] to live in tranquility and freedom" (*āsāyesh va āzādi*).[147] These rulers, he continued, marked the beginning of a period of enlightened rule after a long period of repression following the Arab-Muslim conquest of the seventh century. He concludes that the signing of the 1905 constitutional decree represented the culmination of this long period of overcoming the legacy of post-conquest Zoroastrian decline. Writing in 1907, and from the vantage point of the debates surrounding the constitution of 1905, Shahrokh argues that the signing of the constitutional decree by Muzaffar al-Din Shah, along with its supplementary laws, "established the equality of all Iranians."[148] The resulting system of government and law, he continued, helped to nourish what he calls "the tree of unity and brotherhood and freedom and friendship."[149] He goes on to describe with great optimism his expectation that this metaphorical tree will "grow leaves and branches" and mature to provide "shade for love and justice"[150] (*mehr va dād*) for all Iranians regardless of faith or background. While Shahrokh's writing is replete with casual and critical comments that assume the detrimental effects of Arab-Islamic culture on Iranian-Zoroastrian history, he is simultaneously quick to invoke the broader principles of liberalism and pluralism in Iran's new constitutional government. This tension at the core of Shahrokh's reading of Iranian and Zoroastrian history remained unresolved in his writing. Throughout all of his writing, liberal, pluralist, and democratic notions are invoked alongside casual assumptions rooted in the racialized and exclusionary forms of historical, scientific, and orientalist thought of his era.

Kaykhosrow Shahrokh was of course not alone in grounding his religious and political reading of Iran's long history in what was ultimately a fundamental contradiction between liberalism and illiberalism. Critics of Western culture from Frantz Fanon to Dipesh Chakrabarty have long argued that hidden and unacknowledged contradictions—including the histories of empire, white supremacy, and eurocentrism—were at the core of the Enlightenment project of modernity from its inception. Shahrokh's intellectual and ideological shortcomings therefore echo larger tensions and contradictions that were rooted within not only his own reading of Iranian history but also the philosophical system that he was perhaps uncritically aligning himself to. In his case, however, these unacknowledged contradictions produced outcomes that must be described as more than simple intellectual or theoretical inadequacy. For Shahrokh, these tensions and contradictions also reflected a broader collection of symptoms that ultimately came to afflict both Iran's twentieth-century political history and Shahrokh's own personal fate.

WHO KILLED KAYKHOSROW SHAHROKH?

In a curious and unfortunate way that demands explanation, it is very likely that Kaykhosrow Shahrokh ultimately became a victim of the political and ideological contradictions that were inherent in his own work. Seven years after his mysterious death on July 3, 1940, his son, Bahram Shahrokh, published a six-part serialized memoir in the pages of the popular Tehran daily newspaper *Mard-e Emruz*.[151] This newspaper, published by the intrepid Iranian journalist Mohammad Masud (1901–1948), had gained a wide readership during its relatively short life for its sometimes courageous, and more often sensationalist, exposés on politically taboo topics.[152] The years of the Allied occupation of Iran had lifted the press restrictions that had been in place during the Reza Shah years, and *Mard-e Emruz*, like many other newspapers that were published during this politically fertile era, took full advantage of these new freedoms. Bahram Shahrokh's serialized memoir, published in six successive issues between December 27, 1947, and January 31, 1948, was presented as the first of a series of articles detailing the activities of Nazi collaborators inside Iran during the war. Masud's introduction to this series, which he called "Khakestar-e Garm" (The Warm Ash), promised readers that the story of Bahram Shahrokh was only one example of a larger "fifth column" (*sotūn-e panjom*) inside Iran who worked with the Germans. "When you are introduced to the spies," Masud wrote, "you will be amazed. . . . I will reveal officers, ministers, deputies, mullahs, merchants, nobles, and royalty, all received money and committed betrayal."[153] The first of these articles, Masud promised, was to be the story of Bahram Shahrokh, perhaps the most infamous and notorious of the Iranian Nazi collaborators. In addition to the scandalous details of his wartime activities, the serialized memoir by Bahram Shahrokh

Kaykhosrow Shahrokh's grave in Tehran's Qasr-e Firuzeh Zoroastrian cemetery.
Hukht, *Tehran, 1972.*

also included his detailed recollections of the circumstances surrounding the death of Kaykhosrow Shahrokh. Collectively, Bahram Shahrokh's *Mard-e Emruz* articles read as both a confession of his wartime collaboration with the Nazis and a sharply worded indictment of the forces that ultimately led to what he believed was the politically motivated murder of his father.

Bahram Shahrokh included in his *Mard-e Emruz* articles an account of his father's last moments. The uncontested details of this account are that on the night of July 3, 1940, Kaykhosrow Shahrokh had attended a wedding reception at the residence of a friend within walking distance of his family compound. As the reception drew to a close, he took leave of the gathering and, following his customary practice, began walking in the direction of his home, located adjacent to the Iranian Zoroastrian Anjoman's headquarters, the Adrian Fire Temple, and the Firuz Bahram Zoroastrian School just off of Naderi Street in central Tehran, on a street that is today known as "Kucheh-ye Shahrokh" (Shahrokh's Alley). Also uncontested is that Kaykhosrow Shahrokh's body was found the next day by the side of the road, near the intersection of Kakh and Naderi Streets, at the corner of what is today Palestine Street and Jomhuri

Boulevard.[154] Though the official cause of death, as reported in *Ettela'at*, was that the sixty-six-year-old had died of a heart attack while walking home, Bahram Shahrokh was quick to challenge this official conclusion. As he asserts in the pages of *Mard-e Emruz*, "Still today it is not clear to the Iranian public who was responsible for killing my father. . . . However, that he was caught in the politics of Berlin is not in doubt."[155] Bahman Shahrokh and his brother Manuchehr later reported that others at the reception recalled seeing their father escorted out from the reception by two men who appeared to be security officials.[156] There were also secondhand accounts of a confession by one of the security officials involved in the incident, who claimed that Shahrokh's heart attack was not from natural causes, but was instead caused by an embolism induced by the forced injection of air into his veins via hypodermic syringe after he had been involuntarily sedated.[157] What made this account so believable was that this method of execution had some precedent during the years of Reza Shah's reign, as an efficient means of eliminating opponents to the government as well as those who were deemed excessively troublesome.[158] In his *Mard-e Emruz* articles, Bahram Shahrokh made his own conclusions very clear: "I am of the opinion that this order came from the direction of the monarch of Iran."[159]

What led Bahram Shahrokh to draw this conclusion was his awareness of Reza Shah's displeasure with the younger Shahrokh's wartime activities. Between the fall of 1939 and the spring of 1940, Bahram Shahrokh's activities as the head of Nazi Germany's Persian-language programming on Radio Berlin had gained wide public notice inside Iran. The novelty of radio technology, the eagerness for information about the progress of the war, and the universally acknowledged charismatic radio presence of Bahram Shahrokh worked to attract a wide listenership for Radio Berlin in Iran's major cities. As Hedayat Matin-Daftari recalled many years later, "Everyone would listen to Radio Berlin every night . . . one of our neighbors had a radio and we used to take it on the roof and listen to Persian service of Berlin."[160] Others also recalled hearing Bahram Shahrokh's "booming" and "towering voice"[161] as he would begin the daily programs with his trademark introduction, "This is Berlin. This is Berlin. I am Bahram Shahrokh from Berlin."[162] The 230-foot shortwave radio tower broadcast Radio Berlin's Persian service from its transmitter station in the town of Zeesen, just south of Berlin.[163] The programming itself was aired three times per day—in the morning, afternoon, and evening—with each program lasting approximately thirty minutes.[164] The content of the programming was notorious not only for its markedly enthusiastic reporting of German territorial conquests across both western Europe and the Russian front, but also for the dissemination of its virulently anti-Semitic propaganda.[165] Iranian Jews were instilled with great fear by Bahram Shahrokh's radio propaganda, and oral history testimonies document "painful memories" that remain to this day.[166]

Given the degree of attention that Radio Berlin received inside Iran, it was not a surprise that Shahrokh's broadcasts quickly drew the attention of Reza Shah. As the Shah was under increasing pressure by the Allies to maintain Iran's self-declared, if precarious, neutrality, Bahram Shahrokh's pronouncements encouraging his listeners to support the German advance toward Iran, combined with rumors of an impending pro-Nazi coup,[167] led Reza Shah—according to Bahram Shahrokh's account—to take steps to silence Radio Berlin. Among these steps was the Iranian government's pressuring the German Foreign Ministry to curtail the tone and content of Berlin Radio's broadcasts.[168] Shahrokh himself, in his *Mard-e Emruz* articles, describes diplomatic turf battles between the Nazi Ministry of Propaganda and the German Foreign Ministry's Near East office over the best strategy for promoting German interests inside Iran.[169] These turf battles eventually led to Shahrokh's termination as the Iranian voice of Radio Berlin.[170] Shahrokh also describes an emissary sent by Reza Shah's government to meet with Bahram Shahrokh in Berlin. The emissary, according to Bahram Shahrokh, was Sarhang Soheil, a well-known military official who had a reputation as one of Reza Shah's principal political enforcers. As Shahrokh recalls, Soheil met with him in Berlin, and, as he describes, delivered a thinly veiled ultimatum to terminate his broadcasts.[171] All of these efforts to moderate or curtail Bahram Shahrokh's broadcasts took place in the weeks just prior to the death of Kaykhosrow Shahrokh. In his *Mard-e Emruz* articles, Bahram Shahrokh interprets this sequence of events as a prelude to his father's murder.

Bahram Shahrokh's *Mard-e Emruz* memoir also includes the voice of Kaykhosrow Shahrokh himself, speaking through a letter that he wrote to his son in Berlin. The letter—a facsimile of which is reproduced by Mohammad Masud in the pages of *Mard-e Emruz*—is dated July 1, 1940, on what would be the day before Shahrokh's sudden death.[172] The letter reads as a final, fitting, and tortured testament to the ideological tensions that Kaykhosrow Shahrokh found himself entangled in by the end of his life. It begins with him describing the growing notoriety of his son's radio programs inside Iran. He states that he has heard "from trustworthy sources" that the programming broadcasting from Berlin "is said to be from you." He continues, with increasing concern, "the pronouncements that have come from you are the cause of great difficulty here."[173] Shahrokh then goes on to chastise his son for his political activities. "It is not pleasing," he writes, arguing that these actions "are completely in conflict with neutrality and the wise policy of the Shah."[174] He continues in the letter to argue that his son's activities in Berlin will have a direct effect on his own personal safety inside Iran:

> Even though you are far from here, however, I am close at hand. I have an official position as a representative in the Majles . . . and you are my son. . . . They will not believe that your methods and mine are entirely separate from each other. If you can refrain from the work which brings you into the realm of politics, you will have shown me great mercy. . . . If you are unable, then at least refrain from speaking about Iran. Pay close attention and choose wisely the correct path amidst these difficulties.[175]

According to Bahram Shahrokh, this letter was mailed via the Majles post office just prior to his father's death, and he received it in Berlin thirteen days later. By then he had already received notice that his father had died. As he writes in the *Mard-e Emruz* article, this posthumously received letter from his father "is the most important document of his murder."[176]

CONCLUSION

The exact circumstances of Kaykhosrow Shahrokh's death remain uncertain, and it is ultimately impossible to definitively conclude that his death was the result of foul play. As he himself detailed in his memoir, he had a documented history of heart trouble in his final years, and the possibility of his death resulting from natural causes is at least as likely as any more sinister scenario. In the historiography of modern Iran, however, as well as in the oral history of twentieth-century Iranian politics, his murder has come to be regarded as a truism reflecting the increasing authoritarianism of the final years of Reza Shah's reign.

What Kaykhosrow Shahrokh's final fate—whether real or imagined—also reveals is the ultimate untenability of the tension inherent within the ideology of Iranian nationalism. Kaykhosrow Shahrokh's life and work had been premised on the ideal of empowering Iran's

Zoroastrian community as part of the political project of the 1905 Constitutional Revolution. His efforts at institution building in Kerman, Yazd, and Tehran to promote the well-being and prosperity of Iran's Zoroastrians were similarly premised on a pluralistic and ecumenical interpretation of Zoroastrianism and its place within a liberal and democratic understanding of Iran's nation-building project. His cooperation with the Parsi community of Bombay was central to all of his efforts. As he describes in his memoir, the time that he spent in Bombay was transformative in terms of shaping his understanding of a reformist and modernist understanding of Zoroastrianism. The two books that he wrote—the *A'ineh-ye A'in-e Mazdayasna* and the *Forugh-e Mazdayasna*—can be read as testaments to the nature and extent of the Parsi cultural and intellectual influence that he had absorbed during his formative period.

What is also clear, however, is that there was a tension rooted within these cultural and intellectual influences. The ideas that Shahrokh expressed about Iranian and Zoroastrian history contained the elements of both a liberal and ecumenical interpretation of Iran and Islam, and current notions of orientalist knowledge, scientific racism, and romantic nationalist ideology. Curiously, but predictably, the text of the *A'ineh* and the *Forugh* contain traces of both a liberal and pluralistic reading of Iran's history, and a reading that marginalizes and dismisses the place of Arab-Islamic history in the making of Iran's cultural heritage.

For most of Shahrokh's life this tension was latent, but remained submerged and subsumed beneath the veneer of Iran's nation-building achievements and the empowerment and liberation of Iran's Zoroastrian community. By the end of the Reza Shah years, however, the political context of the coming war finally brought these latent tensions to the surface.[177] As the circumstances of Kaykhosrow Shahrokh's death suggest, by the end of his life he was caught between his more moderate and liberal understandings of Iranian nationalism, and its more unrestrained and extreme incarnations that now reached the same political conclusions as Nazi ideology. Ultimately, in the case of Kaykhosrow Shahrokh, the tension between these two incarnations of Iranian nationalism took the form of a family tragedy. The tension that was exposed in Shahrokh's life and work was, however, suggestive of a far more general political and ideological contradiction that would continue to haunt the history of Iranian nationalism.

CHAPTER 2

PATRON AND PATRIOT

Dinshah J. Irani, Parsi Philanthropy,
and the Revival of Indo-Iranian Culture

When the prominent Parsi lawyer, intellectual, philanthropist, and civic leader Dinshah Jijibhoy Irani (1881–1938) died in early November of 1938, the outpouring of tributes acknowledging his lifetime of service to the Zoroastrian communities of India and Iran took place almost simultaneously in Bombay and Tehran.[1] In Bombay, the city where he had been born to parents of Iranian-Zoroastrian extraction, it was the Parsi Panchayat—the long-established governing body and charity foundation of Bombay's prosperous Zoroastrian community—that organized a memorial service in his honor.[2] Bombay periodicals also published front-page obituaries marking the passing of one of the founding members of the Iranian Zoroastrian Anjoman (established in 1918) and the Iran League (established in 1922), organizations created to improve the social condition of Zoroastrians in Iran through the building of schools, orphanages, pharmacies, and hospitals, while also working to expand broader cultural, commercial, and political ties between Iran and India.[3] Both were also organizations to which, as Irani's obituary in the *Iran League Quarterly* stated, "he spared goodly time for numerous acts of public benefaction."[4]

The small but growing Iranian expatriate community in Bombay also expressed their grief at the death of Dinshah Irani. Iran's long-serving former consul-general in the city, Jalal al-Din Kayhan, whose office had previously worked closely with Irani in facilitating travel and scholarly exchanges between Iran and India, sent a message of condolence to the Iran League, stating that the passing of this key figure represented "a great loss to the Iranian and Parsi communities" and adding, "his patriotic

*Dinshah J. Irani
(1881–1938). Jehangir
Coyajee, ed.,* Dinshah
Irani Memorial
Volume, *Bombay,
1943.*

services in the cause of Iran will never be forgotten."[5] Within Iran, news
of Dinshah Irani's passing also spread quickly through the local Zoroastrian community, as well as among Iran's modernist and nationalist
intellectuals who had come to know Irani through his widely circulating
Persian-language writings on Zoroastrianism and pre-Islamic Iranian
history, as well as his correspondence and collaborations with important Iranian intellectuals and literary figures such as Ebrahim Purdavud,
Aref-e Qazvini, Sadeq Hedayat, Sa'id Nafisi, Rashid Yasami, Mohammad
Qazvini, and numerous others.[6] The Zoroastrian deputy to the Iranian
Majles, Kaykhosrow Shahrokh, who also had a long-term personal col-
laboration with Irani, organized a memorial service at the Parsi-endowed
Firuz Bahram School in Tehran, where he and others paid tribute to
their friend, colleague, and patron.[7] Following the memorial service,
Shahrokh sent a telegram to the offices of the Iran League informing the
Parsi community in Bombay of the memorial held in Tehran:

> On receiving the sad news on the 7th of November, a cere-
> mony was performed in his honor in the Firooz-e Bahram
> High School Hall, and the whole community, eminent

persons of high positions and the President and a great number of members of the Parliament were present at it . . . newspapers also showed their feelings in announcing his death. Also telegrams were sent to Kerman and Yazd, and they too have done their duty towards the esteemed deceased.[8]

These expressions of sympathy in both India and Iran at the moment of Dinshah Irani's death demonstrate the recognition that he had achieved by 1938 as an important cultural interlocutor between the Bombay Parsi community and Iran's modernist and nationalist intellectual millieu.

And yet, despite this record of affection expressed for Dinshah Irani at the time of his passing, and despite an equally explicit record of the important role that he played in the revival of interest in Zoroastrianism and Iranian antiquity among Iranian intellectuals of the early twentieth century, it is surprising how minor a place he has come to occupy in the historiography of interwar Iranian and Indian cultural and intellectual history. Resituating Dinshah Irani within this history brings to the surface a number of overlooked themes that characterized India and Iran's cultural history during that time. Most importantly, acknowledging Dinshah Irani's contribution to the history of Iranian nationalism, and to the Zoroastrian and pre-Islamic revival inside Iran during the interwar period, helps to highlight the important role that the Bombay-based Parsi community played in encouraging a rediscovery of Iran's classical heritage to shape a new Iranian culture considered suitable for the demands of modernity.

This rediscovery of Iran's pre-Islamic heritage by Iranian intellectuals was to a large extent tied to currents of thought already circulating within the Zoroastrian community of South Asia. By the early twentieth century, Parsi priests and lay scholars had for several generations engaged in an intellectual enterprise of rethinking the religious history of Zoroastrianism, as well as of the Parsi community's own history within India.[9] One consequence of this intellectual renaissance of the nineteenth century was a Parsi cultural history of Persophilia,[10] or phil-Iranism, associated with a renewed understanding of Iran as the Parsi community's ancestral place of origin and an appreciation of the broader heritage of a classical past shared by Indian Parsis and modern Iranians. Significantly, this process of cultural rediscovery and rearticulation was carried out across a broadly conceived Indo-Iranian cultural and territorial zone during a critical moment in the transition to modernity. As the early modern Perso-Islamicate—or Persianate—cultural system became increasingly challenged by the encroaching logic of a globalized system of nation-states, some long-dominant forms of culture began to recede while other, older, neglected, and submerged strands of pre-Islamic Indo-Iranian classicism were gradually rediscovered, reconstructed, and newly empowered as the basis of alternative cultural-historical genealogies for both Iran and India.[11] The nature of these articulations, as well as their political implications, remained undetermined, contested, and decidedly fluid. Nevertheless, articulating this newly empowered Indo-Iranian neoclassicism, and devising methods by which to circulate texts and other cultural forms that conveyed its message, became one of the key elements defining the transition to a post-Persianate cultural-political system. Dinshah Irani's life and work as a civic leader and cultural entrepreneur serves as perhaps the best example of how this transnational enterprise of cultural and intellectual articulation of a new post-Persianate Indo-Iranian culture of neoclassicism took shape in the early decades of the twentieth century.

Dinshah Irani made two very important contributions to this Indo-Iranian revival. First, as the founding president of the Iranian Zoroastrian Anjoman of Bombay, and as the cofounder and vice president of the Bombay-based Iran League, he played a key role as a civic leader who solicited funds from charity-minded Parsi patrons in Bombay for philanthropy intended to improve the social and economic conditions of the Parsi community's Zoroastrian coreligionists inside Iran, located primarily in the central Iranian cities of Yazd, Kerman, and their surrounding towns and villages.[12] Irani's close collaboration with wealthy Parsi philanthropist Peshotanji Marker in particular led to the allocation and distribution of substantial resources for establishing educational and medical facilities in these regions.[13] Irani's second major contribution toward the cause of the Indo-Iranian revival was focused on cultural philanthropy and his work in publishing books and facilitating intellectual exchanges between Parsis and Iranians. His most direct contribution in this regard was the writing of his own important trifecta of widely read Persian-language monographs: the *Peyk-e Mazdayasnan* (1927),[14] the *Akhlaq-e Iran-e Bastan* (1930),[15] and the *Falsafeh-ye Iran-e Bastan* (1933).[16]

These books were intended as accessible introductory essays on the teachings of Zoroastrianism, written for and targeted to general audiences of both Zoroastrian and non-Zoroastrian Iranian readers. Along with numerous other works that he and his Parsi colleagues in Bombay helped to write, translate, publish, and distribute inside Iran, the books represented quasi-missionary efforts to remind Iranians of their pre-Islamic national heritage, as well as to present a reformed, modernist, and sympathetic understanding of Zoroastrianism to an increasingly literate public of readers inside Iran.

Significantly, Dinshah Irani's goals—in all of his social, economic, and cultural projects—were always defined within the parameters of liberal and democratic political objectives. His own education in law, and his successful career as a tax attorney within the social, political, and economic system of Parsi middle-class prosperity characterizing late nineteenth- and early twentieth-century India, worked to shape his political outlook along lines that emphasized the classical liberal virtues of pluralism, compromise, accommodation, and the rule of law.[17] The status of the Parsis as a minority community within the multiconfessional politics of colonial India also came to underscore the importance of these liberal political virtues as the basis of the Parsi community's— and Irani's—support for an idealized liberal understanding of the British Raj. His own work as an attorney included extensive efforts of legal mediation between commercial clients from Parsi, British, Muslim, and other business communities. These liberal ideals, born of the Parsi experience in colonial India, came to shape Irani's approach to Iran as well. His efforts toward improving the social and economic conditions of Iranian Zoroastrians, as well as his Indo-Iranian intellectual and literary projects of cultural philanthropy, were ultimately carried out with the intention of promoting an inclusive, pluralistic, and ecumenical understanding of Zoroastrianism and pre-Islamic Iranian history.[18] The goal of these philanthropic projects, Irani and his Parsi collaborators concluded, would be to enable Zoroastrians to share in Iran's anticipated future of economic prosperity and to help elevate the status of Iran's Zoroastrian community to that of equal members in a liberal-minded and multiconfessional Iranian constitutional monarchy.

And yet despite these liberal ideals, there was also a tension at the core of Dinshah Irani's project of social, economic, and cultural philanthropy. While the cultural logic of reviving Iran's Zoroastrian heritage had the social effect of empowering Iran's Zoroastrian minority community as part of a goal of democratic pluralism—a goal originally born of Iran's experience of the Constitutional Revolution of 1905—the ideological effects of the Zoroastrian and pre-Islamic revival also conveyed the implicit possibility of enabling conservative—and proto-fascist—political and ideological outcomes. As a careful reading of Irani's religious and historical writings will suggest, the reformist project of a modernist interpretation of Zoroastrianism was always able to identify and highlight liberal and pluralistic readings of Iran's pre-Islamic heritage. At the same time, however, there were others, both in India and Iran, who saw the Zoroastrian and pre-Islamic revival as part of a project of dismissing, diminishing, or imaginatively *dislocating* Iran from the historical edifice of Arab-Islamic civilization.[19] In a still little-noted and paradoxical way, the cultural and ideological logic of Iran's pre-Islamic revival simultaneously enabled both liberal and extreme nationalist readings of Iran's Zoroastrian heritage. As Farzin Vejdani has noted, "cosmopolitan understandings of language, religion, and politics...often emerged side by side with nationalism."[20] It was the contrasting cultural-political terrains defining Iran and India in the early twentieth century that in large part worked to determine the distinct historical outcomes of these seemingly conflicting and paradoxical ideological projects. While Dinshah Irani's interpretation of a revived Zoroastrianism may have been born from the context of the liberal empire of the British Raj, it remained unclear how such a project would set its roots in the context of Iran's early twentieth-century political terrain. The complexity of this cultural-political terrain made any assessment of the potential historical outcomes difficult to foresee. Dinshah Irani was himself likely unaware of these complexities, and of the inherent tensions in the project of Indo-Iranian neoclassicism. Nevertheless, despite his own liberal intentions, the work that Dinshah Irani and his Parsi collaborators engaged in during the 1920s and 1930s marked an important stage in defining what became the contested cultural-ideological landscape defining Iran's twentieth-century history.

IRANIS AND PARSIS IN BOMBAY

The larger context of the Iranian expatriate community in Bombay during the nineteenth century played an important role in setting the stage for Dinshah Irani's career as a commercial, cultural, and intellectual intermediary with Iran. Irani was born into a family of Bombay Zoroastrians with relatively shallow roots in India. The "Irani" designation of his name was one that he himself adopted in his early adulthood as he embarked on his formal schooling.[21] "Irani" as a family name had become an increasingly common designation in Bombay during the nineteenth century and came to distinguish a subcommunity within Bombay's larger Parsi-Zoroastrian community of those who had immigrated to India from Iran beginning in the late eighteenth century and increasingly in the nineteenth century.[22] As Bombay's economy flourished during this period—especially the textile industry and opium trade[23]—and as the visible prosperity of the much older Parsi community became known to Zoroastrians in Iran, Bombay became an attractive destination for Iranians seeking to leave their ancestral home in search of a better life. By the time of Dinshah Irani's birth, the "Irani" segment of the Bombay Zoroastrian population was beginning to find success as a distinct subcommunity within the social, cultural, and economic context of late nineteenth-century cosmopolitan Bombay.

The "Irani" community of Bombay also played an important role as advocates for the Zoroastrian communities still residing within Iran. By the mid-nineteenth century members of the Irani community had married into some of Bombay's most prosperous Parsi families, including the Petit family. It was Lady Sakarbai (1826–1890), the Irani wife of Sir Dinshaw Manekji Petit (1823–1901)—one of the most prominent scions of the Parsi textile industrialist families of nineteenth-century Bombay—who encouraged her husband's philanthropy for the cause of Iranian Zoroastrians.[24] In part because of these personal familial ties, Petit worked to establish the Iranian Zoroastrian Amelioration Fund in 1853 to sponsor social services for the Zoroastrian communities in Kerman and Yazd.[25] This fund also had sponsored the journeys to Iran of the famous nineteenth-century Parsi emissary Manekji Limji Hataria.[26] Despite their relatively recent immigration to Bombay, the "Irani" subcommunity had already come to play an important role as intermediaries between the Zoroastrian communities of Iran and India by the middle of the nineteenth century.

The liminal and marginal position that the Bombay Iranis occupied within the increasingly transnational networks of social, economic, and cultural exchange across the Indian Ocean made the Iranis ideally situated to serve as intermediaries between Parsis and Iranians. On one level, the status of the Irani-Zoroastrian subcommunity within the larger Parsi community of Bombay came to make the "Iranis" a minority within a minority. This minority or marginal status has perhaps worked to obscure the important role played by members of the "Irani" community—including Dinshah Irani—in the cultural and intellectual history of Iranian nationalism. At the same time, however, this marginal position worked to make a person like Dinshah Irani ideally positioned as a figure who could imagine new configurations of culture, religion, and national identity that came to reposition the Parsis—and the "Iranis" in particular—as a *diaspora community* that could mediate between currents of thought in India and Iran. It was precisely because of his position as a diasporic and "marginal Iranian" that Dinshah Irani was able to conceive the possibility of forging connections between currents of thought circulating among the Bombay Parsis and those emerging within a maturing Iranian search for national identity.

EDUCATION AND EARLY CAREER

Two important institutions in Bombay helped to shape the direction of Dinshah Irani's civic career. The first was Elphinstone College of the University of Bombay. When he graduated in 1901 with a bachelor's degree in English and Persian literature, Irani's linguistic skills had so distinguished him that he was offered a teaching fellowship at the University of Bombay's St. Xavier's College as instructor of Persian.[27] By the end of the nineteenth century the established Irani community had largely ceased using Persian as a vernacular language in favor of Gujarati and English. Dinshah Irani's interest in pursuing the study of Persian at Elphinstone College was very much grounded in mastering it as a "classical language."[28] The time that he spent at Elphinstone College and St. Xavier's College ultimately led to his collaboration with his colleague Khodabakhsh Irani on a number of translation projects of classical Persian texts.[29]

Unlike Dinshah Irani's later work, these early translations were not texts intended for Iranian audiences; rather, they were texts intended as pedagogical handbooks for students learning the Persian language at the colleges of colonial Bombay. His commitment to preserving and promoting the Persian language in India continued later in his life as well, when he led fund-raising efforts to encourage the establishment of Persian language courses in Bombay and western India.[30] Aside from these pedagogical efforts, however, his early translation projects were also important in establishing a pattern of scholarly collaboration, which in his later career led to his more important collaborative efforts in publishing introductory books on Zoroastrianism and pre-Islamic Iranian history, as well as translations of Zoroastrian religious texts intended for general audiences inside Iran.

The other key institution that came to inspire Dinshah Irani's later literary and scholarly collaborations, as well as his civic projects of promoting Zoroastrian culture, was the Jamsetjee Jejeebhoy Zartoshti Madressa. This institution was originally founded in 1863 through the philanthropy of the Jejeebhoy family to train a new generation of Zoroastrian priests.[31] By the 1880s the school took on a broader liberal arts mission to attract students from the growing constituency of modern middle-class Bombay Zoroastrians. In the process the mission became one of educating students—like Dinshah Irani—who would become part of a new Bombay-Parsi intelligentsia consisting of middle-class lay scholars of a reformed Zoroastrianism. By 1902, when Dinshah Irani began studying Avestan and Pahlavi at the J. J. Zartoshti Madressa, Kharshedji Rustomji Cama (1831–1909), the great Parsi social and religious reformer and pioneer in the modern Parsi study of Zoroastrianism, was in his final years as head of the school.[32] Under his directorship the J. J. Zartoshti Madressa became a major Parsi academic institution for teaching a modern Parsi reinterpretation of Zoroastrianism. It was also during his tenure that the teaching of the Avestan and Pahlavi languages became the major focus of the school's curriculum.[33] The logic of this emphasis was rooted in Cama's reformist interest in encouraging modern Zoroastrians to go back to the original sources and reinterpret the textual foundations of Zoroastrianism from a modernist perspective. It was to this intellectual, literary, and theological enterprise that Dinshah Irani came to devote himself under the direct influence of K. R. Cama.

In an autobiographical fragment written in 1922, Dinshah Irani described the encounter he had with Cama that came to radically change the direction of his intellectual curiosity:

> One Sunday evening, about twenty years ago [1902] I saw standing a venerable old sage, with a silver-grey beard, explaining to a band of University students some points in a passage of the Holy Gathas. . . . He was the late Mr. K. R. Kama. The great Parsi Orientalist was trying to bequeath to the younger generation the fire which burned in his old heart. . . . I will never forget the sight nor the zeal of that veteran scholar. My love for the study of the Gathas took its birth that day.[34]

This encounter with Cama came to shape much of the course of Irani's subsequent civic and scholarly endeavors. It was from this point that Irani began the serious study of the Avestan and Pahlavi languages. Irani also came to increasingly associate himself with reformist currents of Parsi thought in Bombay, such as the "Gatha Society," the "Zoroastrian Reform Society," and the Parsi calendar reform movement.[35] All of these Zoroastrian reform movements advocated for a simplified and modernized understanding of Zoroastrianism, emphasizing its universalist and ecumenical values, its essential monotheism, antinomian and spiritual qualities, a deemphasis on ritual, and a growing romantic association of Parsi religious and cultural life with the classical history of Iran.

BETWEEN PHILANTHROPY AND REMIGRATION

The reformist Zoroastrian community of Bombay also placed a great deal of emphasis on the virtue of charity and civic philanthropy. In addition to its role of defining codes of Zoroastrian ethics and practice, the long-established Parsi Panchayet of Bombay had since the eighteenth century made an enormous effort of gathering and distributing funds to promote the social and economic well-being of the Zoroastrian communities of Bombay and western India.[36] Some of these funds were also designated for the benefit of the Zoroastrian communities inside Iran. To further this effort, the Iranian Zoroastrian Amelioration Fund was established in 1853 by the Petit family and was closely associated with the Parsi Panchayet. Inspired by this earlier tradition of philanthropy, and hoping to expand its mission, Dinshah Irani set out to establish a new civic and philanthropic organization whose primary objective would be to improve the lives of the Zoroastrian communities inside Iran. This organization—the Iranian Zoroastrian Anjoman of Bombay—was established in 1918, with Dinshah Irani as its principal founder and first president.[37] The leadership of the Anjoman consisted primarily of members of the "Irani" subcommunity within the larger Parsi community of India, but its financial supporters were drawn from the Parsi community as a whole. The Anjoman's sister organization—the Iran League— was established four years later in 1922. While the two organizations shared many of the same aims and objectives, as well as benefactors, the Iranian Zoroastrian Anjoman's efforts were directed more narrowly toward charity work among the Zoroastrian rural and poor communities residing in Yazd, Kerman, and surrounding areas, as well as among recent "Irani" migrants to western India. The Iran League's mission was, by contrast, focused more broadly on building larger cultural, economic, and political ties between the Parsi community of India and the government of Iran.[38]

It was through the civic leadership of Dinshah Irani that the philanthropic efforts of wealthy Parsi benefactors came to serve the objectives of both organizations. The establishment of the Iranian Zoroastrian Anjoman and the Iran League marked a new phase in the history of Parsi philanthropy toward Iran. Initial charity efforts dating back to the mid-nineteenth century—especially in the area of education—had been directed toward promoting basic literacy, with the establishment of primary schools in and around Yazd and Kerman. Many of Manekji Limji Hataria's efforts during his four-plus decades of residence in Iran were directed toward these educational initiatives.[39] The emergence of a figure like Kaykhosrow Shahrokh, as discussed in chapter 1, was made possible largely as a result of these early educational efforts. Funding for these early primary schools came from both local Iranian sources and through the philanthropy of Parsi benefactors associated with the Parsi Panchayet in Bombay.[40]

By the early 1920s, however, it had become clear that new investments were needed to expand the educational opportunities available to Iranian Zoroastrians. As Iran's nation-building project gained momentum in the early 1920s, Dinshah Irani and other leaders among the Iranian Zoroastrian Anjoman of Bombay recognized the social benefit of helping a new generation of Iranian Zoroastrians acquire the educational skills and social capital needed to join the ranks of Iran's new professional, entrepreneurial, and technocratic middle classes. To facilitate these expanded opportunities, Dinshah Irani and other leaders associated with the Iranian Zoroastrian Anjoman of Bombay searched for patrons to help build a number of high schools, both in Yazd and Tehran, to serve as conduits for the most promising graduates of the primary schools.

These initiatives bore significant fruit during the 1920s and 1930s. Among the benefactors who contributed to these new educational facilities was Mrs. Ratanbanu Bamji Tata, the sister of the Parsi industrialist Jamsetji Tata.[41] The Tata endowment was used to transform the existing Zoroastrian middle school in Tehran into a much larger facility that would now include a high school for girls capable of accommodating five hundred students. The school eventually came to be known as the Anushirvan Dadgar High School.[42] The Tata family had previously donated funds to establish a medical mission among the Zoroastrian communities in Yazd.[43] Also contributing toward the cause of expanding educational opportunities for Zoroastrian youth in Iran was Bahram

Anushirvan Dadgar School for Girls in Tehran. Iran League Quarterly, *Bombay, 1940.*

Bicaji, who donated funds in memory of his deceased son, Firuz, to establish what became the Firuz Bahram School in Tehran.[44] Both the Anushirvan and Firuz Bahram schools, in addition to the previously established middle schools, were placed under the management of the Zoroastrian Anjoman of Tehran with funds that were administered via the Iranian Zoroastrian Anjoman of Bombay. As the president of the Bombay Anjoman, Dinshah Irani played a central role in soliciting funds for these facilities and in the management of the schools. Kaykhosrow Shahrokh, as the president of the Tehran Anjoman and the Zoroastrian representative to the Iranian Majles, also played a key role in the administration of these schools, as well as in maintaining lines of communication with Dinshah Irani and the Bombay Anjoman.[45]

The other key figure who mobilized the interest and resources of the Parsi community of Bombay for these efforts was Ardeshir Reporter, the longtime representative of Bombay's Parsi Panchayet in Tehran and the successor of Manekji Limji Hataria.[46] On one of his periodic visits to Bombay in the spring of 1930 to report on the progress and opportunities in Iran, Reporter convinced Ratanbanu Bamji Tata to make the significant contribution toward the expansion of the Tehran school.[47] While in Bombay, Reporter gave a number of pubic lectures describing the work of Parsi philanthropy in the area of education.[48] The schools that Hataria had established, Reporter argued, had produced students who were now working in the areas of business and commerce.[49] The

Ardeshir Edulji Reporter (1865–1933). Iran League Quarterly, *Bombay, 1933.*

prominent Iranian Zoroastrian businessman Arbab Jamshid Jamshidian had himself employed over two hundred Iranian Zoroastrian graduates of the existing schools.[50] The result of these investments, Reporter told his audience of Parsi benefactors, was that the Iranian Zoroastrians were no longer restricted to agrarian labor, but were now poised to enter the urban professions. It was for this reason, he argued, that educational investments should also be made in Tehran as well as Yazd and Kerman. Tehran, Reporter explained, was more cosmopolitan and tolerant, and it was also the nation's cultural, economic, and political capital. Growing the Iranian Zoroastrian presence in the capital city would facilitate the progress and prosperity of the community.[51]

At his public lecture in Bombay, Ardeshir Reporter also reflected on the progress that the Zoroastrian community of Iran had already achieved—with Parsi help—toward the goal of promoting pluralism and inclusion in Iran:

How differently were the Zoroastrians treated in 1854, when the first schools were started! They [Zoroastrians] were

Ratanbanu Bamji Tata (d. 1930). Iran League Quarterly, *Bombay, 1935.*

regarded as "impure" like the "untouchables" of India. The epithet implied deep contempt. A puddle that they crossed over in wet weather was regarded as impure and polluted. There were countless civil restrictions against them. All these are forgotten today. It is realized that Moslems and Zoroastrians are of one race and so the latter are called "baradaran-e Zartoshtian" (brother Zoroastrians) today. All are regarded as equal under the Pahlavi regime and that gives us great joy and fresh hopes.[52]

Reporter's comments in part reflect the liberal ideal of Parsi philanthropy, as an effort to overcome what was perceived as the traditional exclusion of Zoroastrians as equal members of Iranian society. Education, especially of Iran's Zorostrian community, seemed the most useful means by which to promote these liberal, pluralistic, and inclusive social objectives.

There were also those within the Parsi community, however, who had trepidations about excessive involvement in Iran's internal affairs. G. K. Nariman, the Parsi historian and original editor of the *Iran League*

Quarterly (when it was known as the *Iran League Bulletin*), was outspoken in raising concerns about the nature and direction of Parsi involvement with Iran. As Sohrab J. Bulsara wrote in the editorial note of the October 1931 issue of the journal, in announcing his own assumption of the editorship of the quarterly, Nariman's tenure as the journal's original editor had been tumultuous and ultimately cut short. Without going into explicit details, Bulsara describes disagreements with the executive council of the Iran League and Nariman's subsequent resignation.[53] Bulsara then went on to write:

> Often a cry is raised from certain and varied quarters that the Iran League is attempting to trifle with the established creed of Iran when it is showing active sympathy . . . and endeavoring to help her know her past.[54]

Bulsara may be referring to Nariman's criticisms of the Iran League's support for the pre-Islamic revival in Iran under Reza Shah and the potential of unknown cultural and political consequences that such a policy might set in motion.[55] There clearly seems to have been a tension within the Bombay Parsi community between those who saw charity work as part of a liberal mission of social and economic philanthropy and those who saw engagement with Iran as an opportunity to enable a broader neoclassical resurgence in Iran's culture and politics. As Bulsara continued in a somewhat strident and defiant tone,

> And if . . . Iran is keen to know her past, why should she not do so? Why should she not yearn to revive in herself that which made her once so glorious . . . and if the Parsis assist her in doing so, they serve their dear old motherland, and a cause approvable before God and Goodness . . . no amount of difficulty or opposition shall deter them from that cause and effort.[56]

Bulsara was not the only one to express these culturally assertive goals among the Parsis. Ardeshir Reporter, despite his efforts to raise funds for schools and hospitals inside Iran for the general improvement of Iranian-Zoroastrian living conditions, also encouraged Parsi assistance in promoting what he described as "Persia's re-Iranization."[57] This process, he argued in one of his letters written from Tehran to the Parsi

The
Iran League
Quarterly

نامه چهارم سالین ایران لیگ

Official Organ of the Iran League, Bombay

| Vol. V | APRIL, 1935 | No. 3 |

CONTENTS

Annual Subscription : Iran Rials 50 : Foreign sh. 9 : India Rs. 6

Cover, Iran League Quarterly. Iran League Quarterly, *Bombay, 1935.*

THE IRAN LEAGUE

EST. 1922.

ایران لیگ

Aims and Objects.

To renew and continue the connection between the old land of Iran and Hind ; to continue and encourage fraternal sentiment towards and interest and enthusiasm in the cause of Persia ; to confederate the Zoroastrian population in Persia with a view to increase, to ameliorate their condition and to strive for their uplift ; to make researches with reference to their religion and ancient Parsi history ; to stimulate commercial relations with Persia ; to encourage Parsis to visit the old land, as businessmen or as travellers, for change of climate and health ; to obtain and spread among Parsis and others, by means of literature, authentic information regarding the state of affairs in Persia ; to secure the sympathy of the Imperial Persian Government and the Persian subjects towards the cause of Parsis in relation to Persia.

President :

Sir Hormusji C. Adenvala, Kt., M.V.O., O.B.E.

Vice-Presidents :

J. J. Vimadalal, Esq., M.A., LL.B.
D. J. Irani, Esq., B.A., LL.B.
F. K. Dadachanji, Esq., B.A., LL.B.
The Hon. Mr. H. M. Mehta.
} Solicitors.

Patrons:

Sir Hormusji C. Adenvala, Kt., M.V.O., O.B.E.
Mrs. Dhunmai F. Arjani.
Peshotanji D. Marker, Esq.

S. R. Bomonji, Esq.
Pirojshaw R. Vakharia, Esq.
Ruttonji F. Ginvala, Esq.
The Hon. Mr. H. M. Mehta.

Hon. Patrons:

H. H. Sir S. M. S. Aga Khan, G.C.I.E., G.C.S.I., G.C.V.O., K.C.I.E., &c.
Malek-ut-Tujjar M. J. Shushtary.

Secretary:
Kaikhosro A. Fitter, Esq.

Hon. Auditor:
Capt. Sohrab R. Bamji.

Hon. Treasurer:
Phiroze S. Guzder, Esq.

Editor of the Quarterly:
Sohrab J. Bulsara, Esq., M.A.

Office : **Kamar Bldg, Cowasji Patel Street, Fort, Bombay.**

Telegrams: "**Iranleague**"

Aims and Objectives, the Iran League. Iran League Quarterly, *Bombay, 1935.*

community of Bombay, and published in the pages of the *Iran League Quarterly*, was "the great ambition of all the Persian nationalists."[58] He went on to observe:

> Now that the great founder of Pahlavi Persia has been exerting himself in this particular direction . . . and gaining marvelous success, Parsis of due vision and imagination could well conceive the moral and general transformation Iran is sure to undergo within a few decades hence to the immense advantage of herself and of ourselves as the true representatives of ancient Persia . . . in the next few decades, the results will find full expression to the amazement of the civilized world.[59]

Ardeshir Reporter's bold predictions for Iran's future—from the vantage point of 1932—inspired some Parsis to contemplate even more ambitious projects for engagement with Iran. Among these initiatives were those that included economic engagement with Iran, as well as projects of Parsi remigration and repatriation.

Throughout the 1930s there were, for example, various discussions among civic-minded Parsis of purchasing land in Iran for the establishment of a "Parsi colony."[60] Sir Hormusji C. Adenwala, the successful Parsi businessman and president of the Iranian League, proposed raising funds in Bombay "for the purchase of suitable land near Persepolis" to establish the nucleus for a Zoroastrian commune in Iran.[61] The Iranian government itself assisted the Iran League in acquiring agricultural lands and also actively encouraged the idea of remigration and establishment of a Parsi settler colony in Iran.[62] Reza Shah himself made overtures to Parsi industrial barons to visit Iran to assess the possibilities of investment and resettlement.[63] A few Parsi pilgrims had, in fact, already returned to Iran for permanent resettlement since the days of Manekji Limji Hataria in the nineteenth century.[64] Articles in the *Iran League Quarterly* also responded to the queries of some readers regarding the legal and economic procedures for purchasing land in Iran. According to one article, the purchase of land in the vicinity of the new Persian Gulf port of Bandar-e Shapur would be particularly ideal, as Iranian government plans to turn the port into the "gateway to Persia" would make any land purchased in that region very valuable. As the editor of the *Quarterly* noted, "This land will indeed be very valuable in the near future, in the same way as the land purchased in old Bombay by the forefathers

Dreams of remigration to Iran. Iran League Quarterly, *Bombay, 1930.*

of the Parsis some generations ago proved afterwards."[65] Similar plans were discussed for other Parsi settler-colonies inside Iran, where Iranian Zoroastrians from Yazd and Kerman might settle alongside Parsi pilgrims coming to resettle their ancestral homeland.[66] As one article envisioned, "Interspersing the colonisers with a sprinkling of agricultural families from Yazd in Persia, would hearten them to follow their example . . . the colony must form one compact mass of holdings to be owned by a thousand families at least."[67] Textile manufacturing, an industry that the Parsi communities of India had long excelled in, was also envisioned as one area of Parsi investment in Iran. This initiative made some progress with the establishment of the short-lived Khorsovi Textile Mill in Mashhad, based on a joint Iranian and Parsi ownership arrangement in which Iran would control 51 percent.[68] One idea posed in the *Iran League Quarterly* was to combine this industrial investment in the mill with the goal of establishing a Parsi agricultural colony. As Sohrab Bulsara noted, "If any agricultural colony is founded, a mill may be started in its midst for providing occupation to spare hands ordinarily or in the slack seasons."[69] Other projects for economic engagement were also discussed in Parsi periodicals that touted the "rich fields in Persia" awaiting Parsi investors.[70]

As the president of the Iranian Zoroastrian Anjoman of Bombay, Dinshah Irani was himself active in considering these plans for Parsi repatriation. His thoughts on the matter were shaped by not only the dream of a Parsi *negation of exile*, but also the context of a growing sense of Parsi unease for the future. Echoing the anxieties of the Parsi community in the age of the impending dissolution of the British Raj, Irani wrote in 1932:

> In the history of the Parsi community today we are face to face with a crisis . . . the ground on which the edifice of our prosperity rested is giving way. . . . In such a situation it is not wise to have all of our eggs in one basket. . . . I'm not a pessimist about Bombay, but at any rate the events of the last five years should make us pause and think. . . . To my mind a golden opportunity is coming. There is something providential in the fact that at this juncture the old and beloved country of our forefathers, Iran, makes such friendly gestures to us . . . let us think and act. Our future now rests in the hands of those who have some wisdom, some vision, some money, and the eternal spirit of enterprise.[71]

While large swaths of the Parsi community were active supporters of India's independence movement, others were also uncertain about what a post-independence India might mean for the Parsis. The long association that many of the Parsi community's industrial and commercial elite, as well as the prosperous Parsi middle class, had with the British government in India suggested to many civic-minded members of the community that Parsi fortunes might change in a post-independence India. Parsi loyalty to the Raj—a community whose association with the colonial system in South Asia earned them the moniker of "the good Parsis"[72]—had been largely unquestioned, and the growing momentum of the independence movement therefore posed a dilemma for how the community should plan for its future. As Dinshah Irani and other civic-minded Parsis observed, the prospect of remigration, resettlement, and repatriation in their *original homeland* of Iran might have arrived as a providential and fortuitous circumstance that could help to resolve the community's dilemma in the anticipated age of decolonization.

Despite these Parsi anxieties, and despite the imaginative notion of a Parsi return and negation of exile, the prospect of a large-scale exodus of Parsis out of India and back to Iran never became a serious possibility. Diaspora nationalist projects of "return to the homeland" face enormous challenges that are not only logistical, but also political, economic, and cultural as well. With the notable exception of the Zionist project of return, which was itself spurred to success in large part through the cataclysms of World War II and the Holocaust, few other diaspora nationalisms have been able to overcome the challenges inherent in these projects of return, remigration, and repatriation.[73] Parsi musings in this regard were ultimately only romantic illusions stemming from a newly formed nostalgia born of the culture of early twentieth-century Parsi *phil-Iranism* and a growing mood of anxiety in the waning years of the British Empire.

THE 1924 MARKER MISSION TO IRAN

Despite this unrealized dream of remigration, the Parsi community of India was able to achieve its long-held project of charity and philanthropy intended to elevate the social status of Iran's indigenous Zoroastrian community. The most successful project in this regard was the educational mission of the major Parsi benefactor P. D. Marker (1871–1965).[74] Peshotanji Dossabhai Marker was born in 1871 to the prominent Marker family, a Parsi family with deep ties to the Parsi communities of Bombay, Karachi, and Quetta. The family wealth had originated through business interests involving a military supply company in the mid-nineteenth century. The Markers' financial interests later expanded to include holdings in commercial, industrial, pharmaceutical, and banking enterprises.[75] After graduating from Elphinstone College in 1893, Marker worked briefly for his maternal uncle Seth Edulji Dinshaw (d. 1914)—the great industrialist, land owner, and primary developer of colonial Karachi—before embarking on his own business and commercial activities.[76] Seth Edulji Dinshaw was also a major philanthropist who made innumerable contributions to Parsi charities.[77] It was the example of his prominent uncle that led P. D. Marker to continue the family tradition of civic-minded philanthropy.

By the early 1920s, P. D. Marker had made the decision to focus his charity and philanthropy work on expanding the educational opportunities available to the Zoroastrian communities of Yazd and Kerman. This philanthropy ultimately earned Marker recognition as "the largest

*Peshotanji D. Marker
(1871–1965). Ebrahim
Purdavud, Iranshah,
Bombay, 1926.*

individual donor for amelioration work in Iran."[78] His personal friendship with Dinshah Irani was one of the primary reasons for his decision to engage in charity work in Yazd and Kerman.[79] Between 1918 and
1922, Irani, Marker, and the Iranian Zoroastrian Anjoman of Bombay
began an effort to expand already existing educational facilities in Yazd
and Kerman, as well as to allocate substantial funds for the construction
of new facilities. The first of these efforts led to the construction of the
Marker Zoroastrian Boy's Orphanage in Yazd, which opened its doors
in early 1923.[80] The orphanage soon expanded to include educational
facilities for a primary and secondary school. By the late 1920s, the
Marker Orphanage and Day School of Yazd included residential quar-
ters for orphans, as well as classroom space and teaching staff capable
of accommodating approximately 150 orphans and local students. The
school continued to grow in the following years with yet more support
from Marker, which allowed it to purchase a considerable amount of
land adjacent to the existing compound and build additional facilities
now capable of accommodating several hundred more pupils.[81] Due to
the impressive presence of the school in central Yazd, city officials chose

P. D. Marker presented with Neshan-e Elmi medal in Yazd by Iranian government,
1934. Iran League Quarterly, *Bombay, 1935.*

to rename the street where it was located "Khiaban-e Marker" (Marker Road), and to christen the neighborhood surrounding the Marker educational compound as "Markerabad."[82] P. D. Marker's philanthropy also extended to providing equal funds for the establishment of the Marker High School for Girls in Yazd, as well as funding primary and middle schools in the smaller towns and villages surrounding Yazd and Kerman.[83] While most of the students at both the boys and girls schools were from local Zoroastrian families, the enrollment policies of all of the Parsi-funded schools were self-consciously nondenominational.[84]

This policy of multiconfessional admission was in keeping with Marker, Irani, and the Parsi community's larger goal of promoting an ecumenical and pluralistic political culture in Iran. Years later, Marker commented on his hopes for the growth of this more inclusive Iranian political culture, but was clearly aware of the perennial challenges. "In India, a Parsi can become a magistrate, judge, or minister. It is not so in Iran," he commented.[85] Marker's tempered hopes and occasional frustrations were also reflected in comments he made during a private meeting with Princess Ashraf Pahlavi in 1949. At the meeting, she asked Marker why it was that the Parsis had not remigrated to Iran as Reza Shah had hoped. Marker replied that "your father, his late Majesty, had sent his first message to the Parsis to come to Iran through me. But even at that time, as the Zoroastrians of India had no assurance of getting political rights, they did not come."[86] Despite the progress made since the mid-nineteenth century and the Constitutional Revolution of 1905, a candid assessment of the limits of Iranian pluralism led Marker, Irani, and the Parsis to instead pursue a more realistic long-haul strategy of promoting gradual cultural change in Iran. Their hope was that by promoting a broader revaluation of Iran's classical heritage through educational philanthropy, Iranians would develop a newfound appreciation for the important role that Zoroastrianism had played in Iran's history and heritage. This appreciation, it was hoped, would help to enhance the social and political standing of the Zoroastrian community in contemporary Iran as well.

In addition to educational philanthropy, however, other strategies for promoting cultural change were also increasingly under consideration by Marker, Irani, and the Bombay-based Parsi organizations. In the spring of 1924, Marker made his first of three trips to Iran.[87] The ostensive goal of this trip was to visit the facilities of the newly built orphanage and school that he had funded in the previous year. Marker and his entourage of travel companions—who included his nephew Kekobad Ardeshir Marker, as well as Kaykhosrow A. Fitter, the energetic and capable secretary of the Iran League and Iranian Zoroastrian Anjoman—embarked on their mission to Iran in May of 1924.[88] The group first made their way by train from Bombay to Karachi and Quetta before arriving at what was the terminus of the Indian railway system in the Iranian border town of Zahedan. From there the group drove their specially outfitted Model T Ford van across the barely passable roads of southeastern Iran to their primary destinations of Yazd and Kerman.[89] Kekobad Marker's memoir of the trip provides a detailed account of this arduous journey. The memoir also provides valuable details of the Marker mission's observations of Iran during the four months that the group spent in Kerman, Yazd, Isfahan, Shiraz, Tehran, Hamadan, and Qazvin before returning via steamer through Baghdad and Basra to Bombay in August of 1924.

Among the recollections that Kekobad Marker records in his memoir is the welcome that the delegation received upon approaching their destination: "nearing Yazd at a distance of two or three miles from the town, we saw a large group of people awaiting to greet us. . . . As soon as we approached them, we were greeted with shouts of *zindibad* (long live) and other friendly slogans."[90] For the next two months the Marker delegation assessed the condition of the local Zoroastrian community, the orphanage and school established by the Marker endowment, as well as the medical facilities that had been funded by the Tata family. Jamshid Patel, a Parsi medical doctor sent from Bombay via the Tata charities, had been in residence in Yazd since 1919 when the Marker delegation arrived.[91] In addition to his medical duties, Patel also served as the official representative of the Bombay Anjoman in Yazd. The Tata-funded medical mission as well as the newly established Marker orphanage and school remained under the direct management of the Iranian Zoroastrian Anjoman of Bombay, with the Zoroastrian Anjoman in Tehran working as the local intermediary. This arrangement eventually evolved, and the management of the Marker charities ultimately passed from representatives sent directly from Bombay to local Iranians. Sorush Lohrasb (1906–1997), a member of the Iranian Zoroastrian community and a recent graduate of Alborz College in Tehran, assumed the management responsibilities for the Marker educational charities in 1927.[92] As the president of the Bombay Anjoman, Dinshah Irani maintained regular contact via post and telegraph with both Lohrasb and the head of the Tehran Anjoman, Kaykhosrow Shahrokh, in the management of these initiatives.[93]

Kekobad Marker's memoir also detailed conversations that the Marker delegation had with members of the local Zoroastrian communities in Yazd and Kerman. He recalled "how interested they were in the welfare of the Parsis in India, and asked us many questions about their status, habits, etc."[94] Although contact, travel, and communication between the Iranian Zoroastrians and the Parsis of India had increased since the mid-nineteenth century, the Marker mission of 1924 may have been the first substantial delegation of Parsis to travel to Kerman and Yazd. The resulting cultural encounter led to significant expressions of mutual curiosity. Kekobad recalled, "We informed them that some of our religious customs and habits changed as a result of our stay in India . . . our replies often delighted and surprised them."[95] The members of the Marker delegation were also greatly intrigued by what they learned about the Iranian Zoroastrians.

Among these discoveries was the degree to which local Zoroastrians had developed syncretic cultural and religious practices reflecting local Muslim customs. As Kekobad Marker described, "Our co-religionists having lived with Muslims for a long time, naturally adopted some of their customs."[96] Among these was either the total abandonment of wearing the traditional Zoroastrian *koshti* band around the waist or choosing to wear the band around the arm or neck in the manner of an amulet, talisman, or *ta'viz*, common in many vernacular forms of Islamic practice.[97] For the members of the Marker delegation, these examples of cultural syncretism were not only curiosities, but also were understood as cultural changes born of local ignorance of the Zoroastrian tradition. After two months of residence in Yazd and Kerman, the Marker delegation ultimately came to the conclusion that the local Zoroastrian community had an inadequate understanding of their own faith and needed help from the Parsis to *relearn* their heritage.

Having reached this conclusion, the Marker delegation began to consider strategies for promoting educational initiatives targeting not only children—as had been the primary objective of the Marker charities until this point—but also the broader public. As Kekobad Marker recalled in his memoir, "We discussed with uncle Peshotanji the necessity of imparting more information about our religion to the members of the community."[98] Following these discussions, P. D. Marker agreed to establish a permanent endowment for the publication of Persian-language translations of Zoroastrian-themed books intended for general audiences of Persian readers in Iran. By the mid-1930s, the "Marker Iranian Religious Literature Fund" had become a major publishing initiative for the "dissemination and printing in pamphlet form, the Persian translation of important lectures and discourses on the religion of Zoroaster."[99] As K. A. Fitter explained later, the Marker publishing initiative was intended to meet the "demand for religious literature from outside India."[100] The 1924 Marker mission to Iran, therefore, represented an important turning point in the history of Parsi philanthropy toward Iran. Not only did Marker, Irani, and the Iranian Zoroastrian Anjoman expand their efforts to build orphanages, schools, and hospitals, but the publication and distribution of books also became a major component of their ongoing charity work.

BOOKS FROM BOMBAY

Dinshah Irani took the lead in these publication efforts. Soon after Marker's visit to Yazd, Irani, the Iran League, and the Iranian Zoroastrian Anjoman identified and reached out to Ebrahim Purdavud to sponsor his translation of the Avestan-language Zoroastrian sacred texts into Persian. The full extent of this project will be discussed in chapter 4, but the critical year of 1924 and the collaboration between P. D. Marker and Dinshah Irani were decisive for putting this translation project into motion.[101] In addition to the Purdavud translations, however, Irani,

Marker, and the Parsi charitable foundations in Bombay set out on an equally ambitious project to produce, publish, and circulate a broader series of introductory texts on Zoroastrianism and Iranian history intended for general audiences inside Iran.[102]

The Indian subcontinent had long been important to the Persianate literary tradition, and had been a center of Persian-language book production for centuries,[103] largely in the older manuscript traditions, but also increasingly through the newer nineteenth-century technologies of lithography and even typeset printed works.[104] It was, however, only in the early twentieth century—when industrialized forms of typographic book production combined with new efficient technologies of long-distance commercial exchange—that a larger-scale network of book production and circulation connecting Bombay and Iran became feasible. The Marker initiative to produce Zoroastrian-themed books for Iranian readers took advantage of these new technological and commercial possibilities, enabling broader networks of textual circulation.

Technological and commercial innovations may have enabled the larger-scale production and export of Zoroastrian-themed books from Bombay to Iran; however, as the Marker expedition to Iran made clear, the more important set of interests that compelled Parsi book export to Iran was not principally determined by market-driven considerations. While an Iranian book market was clearly taking shape during these decades—and the Parsi books imported from Bombay certainly found a home in the marketplace of the modern bookstores now increasingly dotting the urban landscape of Iran's major cities[105]—it remained unclear if the still relatively high costs of typeset book production and long-distance distribution could commercially justify the enterprise of books bound for Iran.[106] By the logic of "print-capitalism," the Parsi book trade with Iran certainly remained a risky venture, and such an enterprise needed to be justified by an entirely different set of interests and considerations.[107]

Rather than commercial interest, the export of Zoroastrian-themed books from Bombay to Iran was instead tied to the broader goals of religious philanthropy—and to what might be termed a "quasi-missionary" motive—intended to help improve the social standing of the Zoroastrian community inside Iran as well as to encourage the nationalist revival of Iran's classical heritage. Like P. D. Marker's other philanthropic efforts, his collaboration with Dinshah Irani to produce Persian-language books for Iranian readers was certainly tied to these larger goals of cultural and religious charity. This practice of book production for purposes of religious philanthropy in fact had roots in Bombay's nineteenth-century colonial history. As others have argued, the evangelical Christian presses of the nineteenth century had long used mass production of inexpensive Christian-themed printed books in vernacular languages—what Leslie Howsam has called "cheap bibles"[108]—to proselytize to the indigenous communities of India as well as throughout Asia, Africa, and the Americas. Marker and Irani's 1924 project of producing mass-circulating Persian-language printed books on Zoroastrian themes for general audiences inside Iran—produced under Parsi auspices—was likely inspired by this practice of book production first pioneered by Christian missionaries in India. Instead of motives of "print-capitalism," therefore, the Parsi book trade with Iran can more appropriately be described as part of a tradition of "textual philanthropy" that saw the printing, export, and distribution of books to Iran as part of a larger history of cultural, religious, and educational philanthropy on the part of the Bombay Parsis toward their Zoroastrian coreligionists inside Iran, and toward the reading public in what they now considered to be their ancestral homeland. In contrast to their Christian missionary counterparts, however, narrow evangelism or proselytism to the non-Zoroastrian Iranian communities was never the goal of Parsi-sponsored textual philanthropy. The Zoroastrian-themed books produced in Bombay and bound for Iran were instead intended to promote new understandings of Zoroastrianism that would enable the local Zoroastrian community to gain a new modernist understanding of their faith, and to help promote a sympathetic understanding of the faith to audiences of non-Zoroastrians. Both of these goals were ultimately intended to elevate the social and cultural status of the faith in the eyes of non-Zoroastrian Iranians, to encourage an ecumenical and pluralistic dialogue between the Zoroastrian tradition and Iranian Shi'ism, and to bring Zoroastrianism more fully into the center of emerging debates surrounding Iran's national identity.

Dinshah Irani's own writings took the lead in producing books designed to convey this message to their intended audience. The first of Irani's three Persian-language introductory books on Zoroastrianism appeared in 1927 as *Peyk-e Mazdayasnan*.[109] The slim collection consisted of eight revised and expanded essays, complete with bullet points and concise statements of doctrine, all designed to be instructive and accessible. The essays had originally been delivered as lectures in English and Gujarati to audiences of Parsi youth in Bombay.[110] As part of his civic activities within the Parsi community, Dinshah Irani was also a frequent lecturer to community groups in Bombay and western India.[111] The introductory nature of the lectures made Irani conclude that a Persian-language edition would be suitable for Iranian audiences. To produce the Persian translation of the lectures, Irani turned—as he would on several later occasions—to Ebrahim Purdavud. As Irani states in the introduction to the work, "the beautiful Persian language in which these thoughts are clothed, is his and not mine."[112]

The *Peyk-e Mazdayasnan* is a remarkable work in a number of ways. Its purpose is to speak directly to Iranian reading audiences with a pedagogical tone, intending to inspire and provoke a renewed curiosity about Zoroastrianism. "Do you know anything about your religion?"[113] Irani writes pointedly as he introduces the book, addressing an Iranian audience of Zoroastrians, in a voice that is unmistakably that of an Indian Parsi-Irani speaking from a perspective of authority over his Iranian audience. He continues:

> In the olden days it was the custom that the Zoroastrians of India would go to Iran to consult with the wise sages of Zoroastrianism in order to learn of their faith. Today a different situation prevails in which the Iranian Zoroastrians have become ignorant of their religion and beliefs and it is the Parsis who have achieved knowledge of the faith and produced great scholars.[114]

The exchange of religious views between Iranian and Indian Zoroastrians had indeed taken place for several centuries in the form of epistolary exchanges (known as the *revayat* literature),[115] as well as occasional exchanges of priests to discuss matters of practice and scripture. During the premodern history of this religious exchange, the Iranian Zoroastrians had generally been seen as the caretakers of the religious tradition and the ultimate arbiters of orthodoxy.[116] By the early twentieth century, as Irani writes, this situation had changed, and "it is today proper that you [Iranian Zoroastrians] study with these scholars [Parsis] and send your future priests to India to study the most advanced knowledge."[117] India, and Bombay in particular, had now come to be regarded by Irani as the center of Zoroastrianism. And yet, Irani is also careful to present himself and the Parsis as part of a larger transnational community tied to a continuing loyalty to the Iranian nation:

Iran, our homeland, is in need of knowledge and national
feeling. It is because of a lack of national devotion that we
have succumbed to these dark days. You who still belong
to the ancient faith of Iran must not have any less devotion
to your homeland than others. It is true that prejudice is
a sin . . . but devotion in relation to a homeland like Iran
must be a duty to all the offspring of this land. So in relation to the homeland we should not withhold ourselves but
should work with our heart and soul to its improvement and
independence.[118]

The Parsis are presented here as a diaspora community, sharing a common identity with their coreligionists but residing outside of Iranian territory. Their mission, he suggests, is to make use of their more advanced
position in Bombay to help their perceived compatriots inside Iran.

In addition to emphasizing the diaspora status of the Parsis, Irani
also goes on in the *Peyk* to urge the Iranian Zoroastrians to join in common cause with their fellow Iranians of other religious backgrounds
as part of a pluralistic, inclusive, and civically defined understanding
of Iranian identity. In the eighth chapter of the *Peyk-e Mazdayasnan*—
titled "what we are and what we must be"—he writes, "Our sacred nation
has awakened and entered the road of progress . . . it has been twenty
years that it entered this new stage."[119] Writing in 1927, Irani is referring here not only to the nation-building project of the Reza Shah era
but more importantly to the legal and political changes put in place following the Constitutional Revolution of 1905. "The role of every Zoroastrian," he continues, "is to join the general population of Iranians in
one feeling and one purpose, for progress in Iran and the promotion of
happiness."[120] Irani's mention of the political and cultural changes taking
place in Iran underscores his understanding of a continuity between the
civic project of liberal nationalism ushered in by the 1905 revolution
and the cultural and institutional changes that were now being set in
motion by the government of Reza Shah. Irani suggests in the *Peyk-e
Mazdayasnan* that the new Pahlav state's *revival* of the Iranian nation,
and the Parsi community's promotion of a modernist understanding of
Zoroastrianism, were in harmony with each other, and with the goals of
the 1905 constitutional revolution. While many saw Reza Shah's authoritarian modernization as an abrogation of the principles of the 1905
revolution, many others—including liberal-minded Parsis like Dinshah

Irani—were optimistic that Reza Shah's methods would help to achieve some of the goals of 1905 and were an expression of what Ali Ansari has called "the Iranian Enlightenment."[121] For Irani, as for many others, chief among these goals was the creation of a secular-liberal political culture that would enable an inclusive and pluralistic polity to emerge in Iran, and which would guarantee the equality of all citizens of the nation, regardless of their religious or confessional backgrounds. The inherent tension between this liberal ideal and the authoritarian methods of the new Pahlavi state were either not understood by Irani and other interwar liberal intellectuals, or passed unacknowledged in the hopes of achieving broader social and political objectives.

What Irani clearly did understand, however, was that the success of any potential liberal-nationalist project of Iranian modernity would necessarily need to include an understanding of Zoroastrianism that stressed the ideas of "equality of all citizens" and "love of the homeland." By attempting to configure a new understanding of the Zoroastrian tradition that emphasized both of these liberal-nationalist principles, Irani hoped to promote a new normative understanding of Zoroastrianism that would reinforce both the values of the 1905 constitutional revolution and the cultural objectives of *national revival* associated with Reza Shah's nation-building project. Irani continued in the *Peyk-e Mazdayasnan* by encouraging his Iranian audience to read the newly available Persian translation of the *Gatha*: "Every Zoroastrian must read this important book in detail. We are hopeful that all of our compatriots, after studying this book will understand that what has been associated with Zoroastrianism has no basis, all the indecent suggestions have flowed from evil and prejudice."[122] Despite the traditional Islamic juridical designation of Zoroastrians as part of the *ahl-e ketab*, or an extension of the Abrahamic tradition of monotheism, Irani was acknowledging the existence of a parallel tradition of popular bias and mistreatment of Zoroastrians inside Iran.[123] A new understating of Zoroastrianism's place within the culture of Iranian nationalism, he argued, would help both Iranian Zoroastrians and non-Zoroastrians to overcome this tradition of bias and prejudice, and join together in a shared civic community. As he suggested, by reading the Zoroastrian scriptures, Iranians "will understand that one of our religious beliefs is that we love the land of Iran, and that we are loyal to the national language and literature. . . . Is this feeling not enough to make all of us understood as partners and participants in the land of Iran?"[124] Irani then goes on to discuss the nature of monotheism as understood in his interpretation of Zoroastrianism, arguing, "Zoroaster was the first man among the Aryan peoples to promote monotheism. This recognition, which is acknowledged by scholars of our homeland, is worthy of being a source of public pride for all Iranians."[125] His invocation of Aryanism in this context is seemingly unusual, and signals his liberal objective of bringing Zoroastrianism into harmony with the majority Shi'ite-Islamic heritage by using a language that emphasizes a shared *racial pride* of all Iranians in laying claim to Zoroaster as a pioneer of monotheism. While the language of Aryanism was increasingly invoked in conservative and divisively racialized forms during the interwar period, Irani seems here to be drawing on the racial language of the era for a very different political-cultural project, an ultimately contradictory project that might be described as *liberal Aryanism*. From within the framework of Dinshah Irani's reading of Iran's religio-cultural heritage, stressing an imagined racial bond that was common to all Iranians—regardless of faith—strengthened his ability to reach the conclusion that "we [Zoroastrians] are partners with our Muslim brothers in worshipping divine unity."[126]

The emphasis on finding common cultural threads that united Zoroastrianism and Islam was in fact a common theme in the popular texts produced in Bombay and exported to Iran during this period. In addition to Irani's *Peyk-e Mazdayasnan*, we see it again in his other popular books, the *Akhlaq-e Iran-e Bastan*[127] and the *Falsafeh-ye Iran-e Bastan*.[128] Of Irani's three published books that were designed to introduce the teachings of Zoroastrianism to audiences of Persian readers, it was his second book, the *Akhlaq-e Iran-e Bastan*, that became his most widely read work. Just over one hundred pages, the book was, like the *Peyk-e Mazdayasnan*, a slim volume intended to present a reformed and modernist understanding of Zoroastrianism to audiences of both Zoroastrian and non-Zoroastrian backgrounds inside Iran. Published initially in 1930 as part of the sponsored works funded by the P. D. Marker Iranian literature fund, it was republished in a second edition as early as 1933. A third edition was also produced in 1955.[129]

Like all of Irani's writings, the book included translated excerpts from other sources, including his own translations from the Avestan scriptures, translations from orientalist scholarship on Zoroastrianism, and translations of inscriptions from epigraphic source material. Also like his other works, especially the *Peyk-e Mazdayasnan* and his subsequent work, the *Falsafeh-ye Iran-e Bastan*, Irani included bullet-pointed

summaries, flowcharts, and concise encapsulated distillations of Zoroastrian teachings, all with the intention of making the material easily
understandable and accessible to his audience. Equally important was
his effort of making connections with other moral and philosophical
traditions, both within Iranian and Islamic thought, as well as with more
universal systems of ethics, morality, and philosophy. Irani's intention
of summarizing and generalizing basic Zoroastrian teachings is perhaps best represented by his use of a visual graphic in the first chapter of the *Akhlaq-e Iran-e Bastan*. He called this graphic, which took
the form of a diagram, the *dāyereh-ye kamāl* (the circle of perfection),
consisting of a visual representation of three concentric circles.[130] The
diagram was one element of the book's initial chapter, titled "Gatha va
ta'alimāt-e akhlāqi-ye ān" (the *Gathas* and their moral teachings), which
summarized the teachings of the *Gathas*. Of the three concentric circles,
the outermost was composed of six points, each of which was labeled
with the name of one of the Zoroastrian Amesha-Spentas, or "benef-
icent archangels" or "holy immortals," who according to the tradition
were begotten alongside Ahura-Mazda to "fashion the seven creations
which make up the world."[131] Each of these anthropomorphized principles is visually represented on the outer circle of the diagram in textual form, along with a succinct description of the core virtues that each
Amesha-Spenta represents: Asha-Vahishta (*rāsti*/truth),[132] Vohu-Manah
(*manesh-e pāk*/good mind),[133] Khshathra (*saltanat-e āsemāni*/holy sovereignty),[134] Spenta-Arma'iti ('*eshq va mohabat*/love and benevolence),[135]
Haurvatat (*sa'ādat*/happiness),[136] and Ameretat (*nejāt va jāvdāni*/salva-
tion and immortality).[137] Within this outermost circle, another smaller
circle consisting of three principles is represented. Here, Irani visually
represented the supreme principles of what he describes as Zoroastrianism's threefold system (*osūl-e se-gāneh*)[138]—or trinity—of ethics consisting of Humat (good thoughts), Hukht (good words), and Huvarasht
(good deeds).[139] At the center of the graphic is the innermost circle with
a single principle represented with the word Ahura-Mazda, described
as the singular and indivisible (*yektā*) creator-god of the universe.[140] In
the following pages of the chapter, the graphic is elucidated with further
elaboration and is accompanied by a more detailed flowchart that folds
out over six pages to include supplementary principles associated with
each moral-ethical concept visualized in the graphic.[141]

The purpose of visually representing the essential teachings of
Zoroastrianism in this way was twofold. First, as with all of Irani's

Dinshah Irani's "circle of perfection" in Persian. Falsafeh-ye Iran-e Bastan,
Bombay edition, 1933.

writings—and as with all of the sponsored works produced and distributed via the Zoroastrian charitable foundations in Bombay—the
primary objective of the text was to simplify the complexities of the
Zoroastrian faith into an easily accessible, tangible, and systematized
form. The graphic visualization of Zoroastrian teachings through the
use of the "circle of perfection" helped to serve this purpose. Second,
and perhaps more importantly, the succinct summaries of Zoroastrian
teachings accompanying the graphic helped to convey the universalist
foundations of Irani's understanding of reformed Zoroastrianism. The
distillation of the faith's essential moral and ethical foundations into a

THE CIRCLE OF PERFECTION

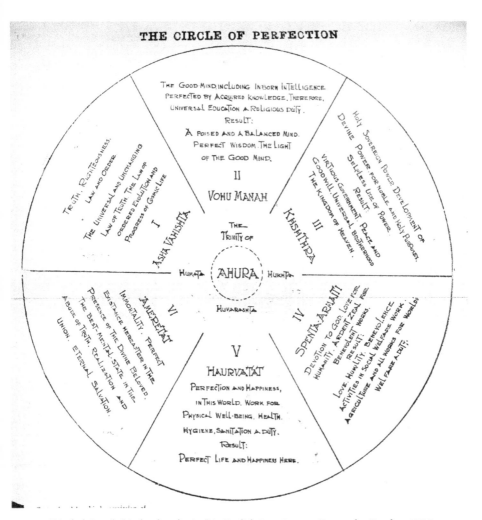

The outer ring contains, reading around the circle:

I — ASHA VAHISHTA: Truth, Righteousness. Law and Order. The Universal and Unchanging Law of Truth. The Law of Ordered Evolution and Progress of Cosmic Life.

II — VOHU MANAH: The Good Mind, including Inborn Intelligence Perfected by Acquired Knowledge, Therefore, Universal Education a Religious Duty. Result: A Poised and a Balanced Mind. Perfect Wisdom. The Light of the Good Mind.

III — KHSHATHRA: Holy Sovereign Power for Noble and Holy Purposes. Divine Power for Development of Virtuous Government. Selfless Use of Power. Good Will. Universal Brotherhood. The Kingdom of Heaven. Result: Peace and Brotherhood.

IV — SPENTA-ARMAITI: Devotion to God. Love for Humanity. Ardent Zeal for Benevolent Works. Result: Love, Humility, Benevolence. Activities in Social Welfare Work. Agriculture and all Works for World's Welfare a Duty.

V — HAURVATAT: Perfection and Happiness. In This World. Work for Physical Well-Being, Health. Hygiene, Sanitation a Duty. Result: Perfect Life and Happiness Here.

VI — AMERETAT: Immortality. Perfect Existence of the Divine Beloved. The Best Mental State in the Presence of the Divine Hereafter in the Abode of Truth. Realization and Union. Eternal Salvation.

Center — The Trinity of AHURA: HUMATA, HUKHTA, HUVARASHTA.

Dinshah Irani's "circle of perfection" in English. Iran League Quarterly, Bombay, 1930.

visualized rubric consisting of familiar ecumenical virtues was in large part intended to demystify Zoroastrianism and make it understandable to a population of readers acculturated into a moral-ethical heritage defined by normative Shi'ism and its related Perso-Islamicate religious systems. Perhaps most notably, the use of the "circle of perfection" echoed common Sufi representations of the doctrine of emanation as derived from neoplatonic traditions. The outer circle of Amesha-Spentas in this way came to represent generalized moral principles, with the inner circle representing practical-ethical techniques through which those moral principles were to be put into practice, and the ultimate goal being to achieve knowledge and *union* with the divine, as represented by the innermost circle of the diagram.

Dinshah Irani in fact made frequent use of the language of Sufism to convey understandings of Zoroastrianism that were intended to make the religion knowable and palatable to his audience of Iranian readers. This practice of utilizing Sufi ideas within a Zoroastrianism cultural-religious milieu had a complex cultural and religious genealogy. Since at least the sixteenth century a cultural history of syncretism between Islam and Zoroastrianism had taken shape, most notably through the heterodox teachings of Azar Kayvan (1533–1618) and his followers, both in Safa-vid Iran and at the court of the Mughal emperor Akbar.[142] This tradi-tion of religio-cultural syncretism—what Kathryn Babayan has called the overlapping "Mazdean and Alid domains of signification"[143]—drew from an eclectic mix of religious traditions, including Zoroastrianism and both gnostic (*'erfān*) and illuminationist (*'eshrāqi*) Sufism. The Kay-vani sect also produced understandings of Zoroastrianism that came to foreshadow later forms of religious heterodoxy, including the ideas of Madame Blavatsky (1831–1891) and Annie Besant's (1847–1933) Theo-sophical Society, ideas which found a wide resonance in nineteenth- and early twentieth-century India.[144] Dinshah Irani's efforts to render Zoroas-trianism knowable and accessible to an audience of Iranian readers drew from these earlier traditions of religious heterodoxy and ecumenism.

We see this theme expressed continuously throughout Irani's writings bound for Persian-reading audiences inside Iran. In the pref-ace to his 1933 book, *Falsafeh-ye Iran-e Bastan*, for example, he begins by emphasizing the connection between Zoroastrian and Iranian Sufi traditions:

> To my Islamic brethren in Iran, I hope this book may prove
> interesting and show how their forefathers, like themselves,
> had a fine philosophy which is so near and akin to the beauti-
> ful philosophy of Islamic 'erfān, thus bringing closer the bond
> of friendship now existing between the followers of the two
> great faiths of Iran, that is Zoroastrianism and Islam.[145]

Irani's deference to the *'erfān* tradition may seem unusual in the con-text of his simultaneous invocation of Iran's pre-Islamic Zoroastrian heritage. The cultural fault lines dividing Iran's pre-Islamic and Islamic epochs are perhaps more familiar to those with an understanding of

Iran's later twentieth-century ideological history.[146] This more familiar history makes Irani's invocation of a deep spiritual bond between Zoroastrianism and the Islamic *'erfān* tradition at first appear to be unusual. As with his equally unusual, if not unsettling, invocation of the notion of a *liberal Aryanism*, Irani's referencing of the *'erfān* tradition is, in fact, a concerted effort to identify a common ground—in this case a common spiritual ground—connecting Iran's Zoroastrian and Islamic heritage. As had also been the case in the time of the Emperor Akbar and the Kayvani sect, the terrain of Sufi mysticism serves Dinshah Irani well in his effort to find a place for Zoroastrianism as part of a liberal, pluralistic, and inclusive culture of Iranian nationalism.

There are in fact a number of doctrines from the Sufi mystical tradition that Irani returns to in the pages of the *Falsafeh-ye Iran-e Bastan*. The most substantial portion of this work—published as a sequel to his popular 1930 work, the *Akhlaq-e Iran-e Bastan*—consists of an extended discussion in which Irani describes what he identifies as the "seven spiritual stages" (*haft marahel-e ruhāni*) of the Zoroastrian tradition.[147] As with his discussion of the Zoroastrian "circle of perfection" (*dāʾereh-ye kamāl*) in the *Akhlaq-e Iran-e Bastan*, Irani once again summarizes the essential teachings of the Zoroastrian faith and places them within a systematized and easily accessible format. In the case of his excursus of these teachings in the *Falsafeh-ye Iran-e Bastan*, instead of using a visual rendering inspired by neoplatonic representational forms, Irani now makes use of an alternative and equally familiar pedagogical device of the *stages* of spiritual enlightenment. His use of this device to summarize the essential teachings of Zoroastrianism is a clear echo of common tropes found in multiple mystical traditions, including the Sufi traditions of Indo-Iranian Persianate poetry.[148] Irani describes the path of the spiritual seeker of Zoroastrianism as passing through the six stages of truth (*Asha-Vahishta/rāsti*),[149] good mind (*Vohu-Manah/manesh-e pāki*),[150] selflessness (*Khshathra/khedmat*),[151] love (*Armaiti/'eshq-e moqadas*),[152] happiness (*Haurvatat/saʿādat*),[153] salvation (*Ameretat/jāvdāni*),[154] and ultimately to the seventh and final stage of union (*vasāl*) with the divine truth (*haqiqat*).[155] Irani's language in articulating these stages is drawn from an eclectic mix of Zoroastrian terminology and Sufi heuristic devices drawn from the Persianate *'erfān* tradition. By placing the teachings of Zoroastrianism within a template of familiar ethical and spiritual forms, Irani underscores the theme of ecumenical universalism that served as the goal of all of his writings and which also served as the cultural message of all of the Parsi-sponsored books published in Bombay and bound for Iran.

We see this even more evocatively in Irani's references in the *Falsafeh-ye Iran-e Bastan* to the pantheon of classical Persian poets. As Irani goes on to argue, the great canonical poets of Iran's literary heritage all expressed a singular and transcendent universalism that was a reflection of a common tradition of Indo-Iranian metaphysics. Irani pays special care to place Zoroaster himself at the head of this chain of poets and sages that produced what became the later traditions of Persian mystical literature. As he writes, "We can see that the geniuses of the Iranian race were the cradle of philosophy (*falsafeh*) and *'erfān* from the beginning of history."[156] Zoroaster, therefore, represents "the first sage (*hakīm*) and poet (*shā'er*) of Iran . . . who came to us from these earliest times."[157] After proclaiming Zoroaster as the progenitor of this tradition, Irani goes on to make reference to the subsequent history of Persian mystical poetry as the heirs of Zoroaster's original vision of union with the divine. Zoroaster's use of the Avestan form of the Old Persian language—as in the *Gathas*—is identified by Irani as the original mode of spiritual-poetic expression that the later New Persian language also came to express. This continuity in the evolution of language, Irani argued, was congruent to the essential continuity of a singular vision of spiritual knowledge that transcended the Zoroastrian-Islamic temporal, religious, linguistic, and cultural divide. To further underscore this argument, Irani places special emphasis on Hafez, identifying him by the use of the literary-mystical appellation of *lesān al-ghayb* (tongue of the unseen).[158] "Hafez's only purpose and goal in life," Irani suggests, "was bearing witness to and achieving union with the unseen."[159] This unseen realm of spiritual perfection was the same state of knowledge that all of the other Persian mystical poets sought, from Ansari, Jami, and Rumi to Hafez. It was a mystical state that Irani describes as—again employing the language of Persianate mysticism—comparable to encountering the true beloved (*ma'shūq-e haqīqī*).[160]

And yet significantly, Irani is also careful to equate this supreme mystical state to language and forms of knowledge derived from Zoroastrian cosmology. Reaching the final state of mystical union, Irani argues, is the equivalent of entering into the heavenly realm of *garodemana* as described in both the Avestan and Pahlavi Zoroastrian literature.[161] This highest and most perfected heavenly realm is, according to the Zoroastrian tradition that Irani invokes, the final destination of the righteous

"Path of Truth." Falsafeh-ye Iran-e Bastan, *Bombay edition, 1933.*

seeker, a place in which the eternal soul reconciles itself into the presence of Ahuramazda. Irani describes this heavenly domain of *garodemana* as "the final dwelling of the spirit [*manzel-e rūhāni*] and the location of salvation and perfection [*nejāt va kamāl*],"[162] and as "a place of music and light" (*jāygāh-e sorūd va nūr*),[163] of "limitless illumination" (*forūgh-e bīpāyān*), and of "boundless radiance" (*anvār-e bīkarān*).[164] The implication of Irani's use of references to light, radiance, and illumination to describe the ultimate state of union with the divine is his effort to once again underscore the spiritual continuity that transcends the Zoroastrian-Islamic divide.[165] As Irani explains, these Zoroastrian descriptions of union in *garodemana* were the same as "the impressions [*tasavvorāt*] and understandings [*aqāyed*] of the various great mystics [*'orafā*] of Iran."[166] Irani concludes this final essay in the *Falsafeh-ye Iran-e Bastan* with one final description of the otherworldly place of perfect awareness of the divine:

> This place where, with unlimited happiness, we will come into awareness, is a place where all of the barriers and constraints which divide us from one another in this unholy earthly realm, are destroyed . . . and in that place, all of us, whether Zoroastrian, whether Jew, whether Christian, whether Muslim, will stand shoulder-to-shoulder as brothers and bear witness to the existence of the celestial father's (*pedar-e āsemāni*) eternal and divine grace (*tawfīq*).[167]

Irani's idealized invocation of this vision of spiritual unity ultimately reflects the broader goals of all of his writings. It also reflects the broader goals of the Parsi mission to Iran during the Reza Shah period. For both Irani and the community of reformist and civic-minded Parsi philanthropists, the ideal of political liberalism and civic pluralism had roots in religious traditions of ecumenism found in both the Zoroastrian and Islamic traditions. Reviving these traditions and producing books to remind Iranians of this shared heritage represented an important component of the Parsi community's larger mission to Iran.

CONCLUSION

This liberal ideal of modern Iranian nationhood nevertheless remained illusive. While the charity work of P. D. Marker and the Bombay-based Parsi philanthropic foundations was always advanced in the interest of achieving progressive ideals, the political implications of Marker and Irani's cultural project of promoting new understandings of Zoroastrianism inside Iran nevertheless remained undetermined. For the Parsis, the reformed Zoroastrianism articulated in the writings of Dinshah Irani—and promoted in Iran via Bombay-based publications—was uniformly envisioned as part of an ideal of utopian modernity in which the rediscovery of the core, essential, authentic, and unsullied values of Zoroastrianism would in turn enable the coming to fruition of a new and perfected Iranian culture characterized by equality, tolerance, and ecumenism. Despite the utopian ideals, for others this renewed interest in Zoroastrianism also carried the implication of a cultural resurgence of Iran's pre-Islamic heritage that threatened the long-hegemonic cultural and religious status of Iran's Shi'ite-Islamic culture. As is evident from his writings, for Dinshah Irani—as for many others—these two cultural systems were inherently reconcilable. In the later years of the interwar period, however, this ideal of cultural ecumenism would be challenged both by those Iranians who came to feel threatened by a loss of Islam's cultural dominance in Iranian society, and by growing cadres of political-cultural entrepreneurs who sought to mobilize the language of Zoroastrianism to promote more exclusivist configurations of culture, politics, and ideology.

CHAPTER 3

IMAGINING HAFEZ

Rabindranath Tagore in Iran, 1932

In the early morning of Wednesday, April 13, 1932, the plane carrying Rabindranath Tagore (1861–1941) and his entourage landed on a makeshift airstrip in the southern Iranian port city of Bushehr.[1] Tagore, who by 1932 had a well-earned international reputation as not only a patient activist for India's independence but also a Bengali poet, playwright, novelist, and 1913 Nobel Prize laureate, had come to Iran at the invitation of the Pahlavi state. Iranian diplomats at the Foreign Ministry and the Ministry of Education had originally conceived of a Tagore visit to Iran after learning of his 1926 visit to Egypt. Tagore's visit to Egypt as an Asian elder statesman bearing a message of "cultural revival" had impressed the Iranian diplomats. The ministry officials concluded that Iranians, like their Egyptian counterparts, would respond well to such a message.[2] Iran's consul-general in Bombay, Jalal al-Din Kayhan, had similarly conceived of a Tagore trip to Iran via associations he had developed with civic leaders from Bombay's Parsi-Zoroastrian community such as Dinshah Irani and Hormusji Adenwalla. Both Irani and Adenwalla had served as past presidents of the Bombay-based Iran League and Iranian Zoroastrian Anjoman, organizations that were keenly committed to promoting expanded cultural, commercial, and political ties between Iran and India. By 1931, Kayhan began to lobby the Iranian Foreign Ministry and the Ministry of Education to issue a formal invitation to Tagore.[3] The letter inviting the poet to Iran for a four-week official visit was issued on behalf of Reza Shah in September of 1931.[4] Tagore, for his part, wrote in his remarkable travel diary of the trip that he was eager to "know clearly how western Asia is responding to the call of the new age."[5] Accepting the invitation, he embarked on April 11, 1932, from his villa on the outskirts of Calcutta.

Tagore's journey to Iran by air was an unusual one for the seventy-year-old poet. The many years of international travel that he had undertaken since winning the 1913 Nobel Prize for literature—traveling to dozens of countries on virtually every continent in the world—had all been undertaken either by sea or rail.[6] The two-day journey aboard a twelve-passenger Dutch Air Mail Fokker Trimotor aircraft from Calcutta to Allahabad, Jodhpur, Karachi, and Jask before finally landing in Bushehr was thus a new experience for the poet, introducing him to the still new practice of international air travel.[7] Just as importantly, however, flying by plane—or by "sky-chariot" or "mechanical Pegasus" as he called it[8]—gave the poet an entirely new perspective on the geography linking the land of India and Iran.

Flying along the Makran Coast, where the frontier of British India approached the territory of Pahlavi Iran, Tagore wrote in his travel diary that "the field of view seen from the aeroplane is immensely larger [and] the apparent motion of objects below correspondingly slower."[9] In narrating his experience of air travel, Tagore seemed intrigued by the distortions of perception that he encountered while looking out across the landscape from the heights of air travel. In his travel diary of this experience, he took great pains to document these disjointed perceptions. The altered perceptions of space and time allowed him to imagine what he described as "a different creation." The world as "viewed from such heights is very different from our usual world," which, he explained, is ordinarily confined by "a limited range of sense perceptions." Seen from the vantage point of air travel, however, Tagore visualized an alternative geocultural imaginary where the distances of territory are minimized in favor of larger transterritorial cultural and geographic continuities. He writes that this alternative imaginary is ordinarily "beyond the scope of our imagination," but when seen from such heights, and with the aid of poetic intuition, the view below comes to reveal "another world altogether.... [reflecting] the play of a particular set of rhythms."[10]

Tagore's ruminations on air travel reflect many of the larger themes of culture and politics that preoccupied him throughout his years of travel to the societies bordering the Indian Ocean. As Ashis Nandy, Sugata Bose, Michael Adas, and others have written, Tagore's extensive and much-publicized travels throughout Asia and Africa were more than political trips designed to raise the diplomatic profile of gradually emerging anticolonial independence movements; his trips were also efforts to contest the geographic and territorial boundaries that had been imposed by Euro-imperial colonial regimes. The gestures and symbolism of Tagore's travels were efforts to assert the presence within the emerging international state-system of alternative geocultural notions such as "Indian Universalism," "Brahmanic Liberal-Humanism," "Pan-Asian Civilization," or the idea of an "Afro-Asian" cultural-political solidarity that stood in contrast to the monologic of "European civilization."[11]

In making these kinds of *civilizational* claims, Tagore did not shy away from strategically using the then-dominant romantic orientalist discourse to assert the notion of an "Eastern" solidarity defined by a *spiritual essence*, standing in contrast to a "Western" culture defined in terms of *materialism* and mechanization.[12] The substance and tone of his most famous book-length essay, *Nationalism*, for example, continuously contrasts the concept of "the Western nation," described as "steel unto steel, machine unto machine," with an understanding of "the East," which was understood to embody "all the sweet flowers of simple faith."[13] Much of Tagore's geographic, cultural, and political claims reflect this basic assumption common to the romantic orientalism of the early twentieth century. He derived these assumptions from both orientalism's disciplinary and scholarly tradition, with which he was familiar, as evidenced through numerous citations or passing references that he includes in his written works, and, just as consequentially, from the more diffused romantic orientalism of interwar European vernacular culture with which he was also familiar as a participant in the culture of "British India."[14] The tone of this vernacular orientalism affected not only Tagore's cultural-political assumptions, but notably also the style of his writing. In describing the style of Tagore's prose, more than one commentator—even one as generally sympathetic as Ashis Nandy—has described his choices of metaphors and literary style as "dated," "rococo," and "purple."[15] Nevertheless, throughout his European as well as his Asian and African travels, Tagore consistently used the available language to sometimes make crudely familiar essentialist statements describing an East-West dichotomy. However, despite the dated nature of his language, orientalism also gave Tagore room to make sometimes quite radical cultural-political claims. His numerous lecture tours to Europe during the 1920s, for example—as Europe was emerging from one catastrophic war and moving toward another—were all couched in terms of the language and symbolism of an "Oriental sage" coming to chastise "the West" for the devastation its civilization had wrought both on itself and the world.[16] In the aftermath of the crisis of European culture following World War I, there was enough cultural room within the discourse of orientalism for someone like Tagore to appropriate the mantle of a "morally superior" oriental critic of Western culture.[17] In Tagore's usage, therefore, the language of orientalism was not restricted to the notion of passive and powerless orientals standing mute before an ascendant Europe. Using assumptions, references, and even a tone which indicated that he was speaking from within the language of orientalism, Tagore simultaneously worked to invert and reorder the terms of that discourse to empower and give voice to parallel and coeval geocultural essences existing outside of Europe.

His April-May 1932 trip to Iran was intended precisely in this way. Throughout the four-week tour from Bushehr to Shiraz, Isfahan, and Tehran—where he met at every stop along the way with Iranian intellectuals, religious leaders, political figures, and ordinary Iranians—Tagore consistently emphasized the cultural and historic ties that linked India and Iran together. At archaeological sites then under excavation, while admiring the architectural style of early modern structures, or while discussing the legacy of Persian poetry, music, and food in South Asia, Tagore's public comments—as well as his private ones recorded in his travelogue—all reflect his interest in asserting the existence of a geocultural ecumene he called "Indo-Iranian Civilization."

IMAGINING INDO-IRANIAN CIVILIZATION

Tagore's thinking about the idea of an Indo-Iranian civilization was part of his larger understanding of a broadly unified Asian civilization. His long-standing interests in Japanese, Chinese, and Indonesian cultures were all similarly conceived. Despite the territorial and national distinctiveness of individual states, Tagore consistently argued for deeper cultural connections and a deterritorialized understanding of culture that moved beyond the borders of individual nations. In this way he was following a kind of thinking that, as Prasenjit Duara has argued, was common to the interwar period.[18] Under the influence of Oswald Spengler, Arnold Toynbee, and others, the concept of *civilization* was changing in significant ways during the early twentieth century; its older meaning of a singular concept associated with "civility" in contrast to "barbarism" was giving way to a new liberal internationalist notion of a world community consisting of multiple civilizational blocs existing alongside one another and each characterized by a distinctive moral-aesthetic essence. As Duara has argued, these civilizational essences became the cultural-historical genealogies in which newly independent and emerging nation-states sought to root themselves. The discourse of nationalism, as it was developing during the interwar period, required newly emerging nations to align themselves with larger civilizational genealogies. Membership in a particular civilizational bloc strengthened a would-be nation's political claim to independence by endowing those claims with the moral authority of a *civilization* and what Duara calls its "transcendent spiritual purpose."[19]

From the point of view of the Pahlavi state, Tagore's April-May 1932 trip to Iran posed an important opportunity to showcase Iranian nationalism's larger ideological project of promoting Iran's pre-Islamic culture as the basis of its modern civilizational affiliation. Like other emerging nation-states of the interwar period, Iranian nationalists of the 1920s and 1930s were eager to construct an appropriate cultural-historical genealogy for Iran. Central to their ideological project was the construction of an alternative civilizational genealogy that conspicuously dissociated—or as Reza Zia-Ebrahimi has termed it, "dislocated"—Iran from the long-dominant *Abrahamic-Islamicate* civilizational genealogy and instead repositioned Iran within an *Indo-Iranian* civilizational concept rooted in the classicism of the Avestan, Vedic, Hindu, and Zoroastrian heritage shared between Iran and India.[20]

This ideological project overlapped with Tagore's own transnational and "pan-Asianist" cultural notions, and as such Tagore showed great interest in the cultural and political developments taking place both within Iran and among the Parsis of India. In a letter written to a friend in the 1930s, he wrote:

> Culturally speaking Persia comes nearer to us than most
> Asiatic countries. In language, religion, literature, and arts we
> have very real affinity and all through the course of our past
> history communication of mind has been constant.[21]

Tagore's interest in an Indo-Iranian civilizational concept developed alongside his other pan-Asianist ideas. His already mentioned travels to East Asia, Southeast Asia, and the entire Indian Ocean world were an important indication of his interest in establishing intra-Asian cultural ties.[22] His close friendship and deep intellectual kinship with the Japanese writer and art collector Okakura Tenshin (Kakuzo) (1863–1913)—whose influential 1903 book, *The Ideals of the East*, began famously with the sentence, "Asia is one"—also indicates Tagore's search for finding the cultural strands of a common Asia.[23]

The Indo-Iranian portion of that broader Asianist project took shape through Tagore's readings of the latest historical and philological findings produced by European scholars in the fields of Indology and Indo-Iranian studies.[24] Tagore was also an important supporter of Indology as it was developing within Indian academic institutions. The Greater India Society—the early twentieth-century Calcutta-based network of Indian philologists and historians who, like Tagore, conceived of an Indian universalism stretching beyond the territoriality of India's borders—also greatly shaped his thinking about Indo-Iranian cultural and historical ties. Tagore was in fact such a key figure in the Greater India Society's view of itself that he was listed in its official publications as the Society's symbolic intellectual figurehead.[25]

Just as important for the development of Tagore's Indo-Iranian civilizational concept was his friendship with the prominent Parsi civic leader, Dinshah Irani. As discussed in chapter 2, Irani had been a longtime promoter of Zoroastrian culture and an advocate for greater Iranian-Indian political, economic, and cultural contact. In addition to his well-established career as a solicitor in colonial Bombay, Irani also worked for many years as a key figure in Bombay's Iranian Zoroastrian Anjoman (founded in 1918) and the Iran League (founded in 1922), organizations that sought to promote commercial and cultural ties between the two countries, as well as to enhance the position of Zoroastrians inside Iran. Irani's civic activities also extended to his work as a writer, translator, and promoter of Zoroastrianism. Under his direction, the Bombay Zoroastrian societies became instrumental in the publication of numerous Persian-language texts on topics relating to pre-Islamic Iranian culture, texts which in some cases, through Irani's sponsorship, became available to vernacular readers of Persian for the first time in many centuries.[26] Tagore came to know Irani through the Zoroastrian community's philanthropic work; Irani and the Zoroastrian philanthropic organizations eventually became important benefactors for Iranian and Zoroastrian studies at Tagore's Visva-Bharati Academy at Santiniketan.[27] Among Irani's personal scholarly efforts was the publication of his own collection of English-language translations from the *Gathas*, published as *The Divine Songs of Zarathustra* (1924), which helped to introduce Zoroastrianism to a wider audience in the English-speaking world.[28] As an indication of their friendship and collaboration, Tagore wrote an introductory essay, "The Indo-Iranians," for Irani's anthology.[29]

Tagore's essay on the Indo-Iranians, first published in the *Visva-Bharati Quarterly*, and then as the introductory essay of Irani's anthology, can be read as an important statement of the cultural premises animating both Tagore's own concept of Indo-Iranian civilization and the Neo-Zoroastrian ideological basis of interwar Iranian nationalism. The essay echoes much of the popular racial, linguistic, and anthropological writing of the time to argue for the deep racial and cultural connections between the peoples of Iran and India:

> Pods burst, and winged seeds are borne away by the winds to distant soils where, in combination with new environments, variations are produced, and nature, full of creative curiosity, is given opportunity for making new experiments. In the history of man, such experiments have been made with races, driven by some ethnic storm, who reached lands far away from their original habitation, different in climate and surroundings. . . . The Indo-Iranian people, like a giant river, started on their nomad career from their now-forgotten land of birth, in some obscure dawn of history. At last the current of emigration divided into two streams, one finding its destination in the west of the Hindukush, and the other pouring into the plains of India through some gap in its mountain barrier. . . . The two people, though racially one, were placed in environs which were greatly different.[30]

From this somewhat poetic rendering of the Aryan migration theory of Indian civilization, Tagore goes on to describe the deep similarities in the religious and cultural patterns in the subsequent histories of India and Iran, which he attributes to the "underlying strand of unity in their development of mind, owing to their common race."[31] He is prolific in his praise of Zoroaster—"the greatest of all the pioneer prophets"[32]—and emphasizes important similarities between the religious ethos of Zoroastrianism and Hinduism with respect to ritual, devotion, and sacrifice. He goes on to emphasize, however:

> It is interesting to note that the growth of the same ideal in the same race in different geographical situations has

produced results, that, in spite of their unity, have certain
aspects of difference. The Iranian monotheism is more ethical, while the Indian is more metaphysical, in character. Such
a difference in their respective spiritual developments was
owing, no doubt, to the active vigor of will in the old Persians
and the contemplative quietude of mind of the Indians. This
distinction in the latter arises out of the climactic conditions
of the country.[33]

Tagore accounts for the differences between Indian and Iranian culture
by pointing to cultural effects engendered by geography and climactic
variation. He suggests, however, that these variations are superficial, and
scarcely obscure the much more important continuities and connections
that link India and Iran to a common moral-aesthetic essence:

It nourishes my heart to know, that the peoples who had
nourished their seeds of civilization together, and blended
their voices in an original mother tongue which belonged to
them both, should, even after their long period of separation,
have kept some primal similarity of expression in the growth
of their respective histories.[34]

It was precisely the identification and promotion of this "primal similarity of expression" that became the central theme of Tagore's visit to
Iran in 1932. Throughout his four-week stay in Iran, Tagore—and his
Iranian hosts—made consistent reference to the symbolism of these civilizational bonds of "Indo-Iranian culture."

Significantly, despite the invocation of symbols linking Iran and
India, Tagore's visit to Iran was also characterized by a subtext of tension with respect to how Tagore and his Iranian hosts defined the political meaning of the symbolism associated with his visit. While Tagore's
vision of Indo-Iranian cultural contact and affinity was always articulated within the political logic of a liberal project of Pan-Asian solidarity, his Iranian hosts were more inclined to define the symbolism
of Tagore's idea of "Indo-Iranian Civilization" to a more narrowly conceived nationalist project of reviving Iran's Zoroastrian cultural history
at the expense of its Islamic heritage. This narrower conception of an
Indo-Iranian civilization also had clear echoes of emerging racialized
discourses of Aryanism among both Indian and Iranian intellectuals.

The tension between liberal and conservative nationalist articulations of Indo-Iranian culture was inherent within Iranian nationalism's inter-war political history and was also an unresolved contradiction found within Tagore's own political and ideological message. His calls for an "Asian cultural revival" had always been interpreted in mutually exclusive ways as both a call for a liberal, inclusive, and cosmopolitan conception of Pan-Asianism, and as a conservative and illiberal assertion of national identity. Tagore had seen the same contradictory readings of his ideas during his travels to China in 1924 and 1928 and to Japan in 1916, 1924, and 1929, where political and cultural conservatives in both countries had mocked his liberal-cosmopolitan vision of Asian politics. Tagore also had similar political conflicts with Hindu chauvinists, in particular with the Greater India Society, whose members sought to appropriate his ideas for their own more narrowly conceived version of Indian nationalism. These same tensions followed Tagore to Iran, where the Pahlavi state's Neo-Zoroastrian project of Iranian nationalism sometimes contradicted his message of Indo-Iranian cultural affinity as part of a broader Pan-Asian cosmopolitanism.

INTRODUCING TAGORE TO IRAN

The nature of the contested symbolism of Tagore's visit to Iran became clear during the course of his four-week visit to Iran. The public events and officially staged ceremonies that occurred as he traveled from Bushehr to Shiraz, Isfahan, Tehran, and points in between were all covered with much detail and great fanfare in the Iranian press. The public ceremonies and events, and their prolific press coverage inside Iran, introduced Tagore to the Iranian public as a living personification of an Indo-Iranian civilizational ideal. That ideal and its grounding in the pre-Islamic cultural memory of Iranian nationalism served as the focus of much of the Pahlavi state's cultural policy during the interwar period, including through means of education, public commemorations, the promotion of archaeology, the construction of public sites in neoclassical architectural style, and other forms of cultural production.

Situating Tagore as a symbolic personification of that Indo-Iranian and pre-Islamic civilizational ideal, however, required a certain amount of work on the part of his Iranian hosts. Prior to the 1932 visit, Tagore was largely unknown to Persian readers inside Iran. Beyond a select group of Iranian literati who were familiar with his writing—not in its original Bengali, but through German, French, and English translations—Tagore remained largely obscure. Tagore was himself aware of this dearth of public awareness of his literary work and wondered how it would affect his reception during his trip to Iran; how would he be perceived, he wrote in his travelogue of his journey, "in a land where I have no readers."[35] Available Persian-language translations of his poetry, plays, and essays were minimal in 1932; such translations as were available were made entirely from translations rendered originally into European languages rather than directly from the Bengali. The most important of these early Persian-language translations of Tagore's poetry were those serialized in the newspaper *Parvaresh* by the important Iranian writer and intellectual Bozorg Alavi.[36] Colonel Mohammad Taqi Khan Pasyan, the gendarme commander and nationalist rival of Reza Khan, also translated selections of Tagore's poetry into Persian during his years in Berlin between 1918 and 1920.[37] Another important early Persian text that introduced Tagore to an Iranian audience was the short booklet written by the historian and literary critic Mohammad Mohit Tabataba'i, *Rabindranat Tagur: Sha'er va Filsuf-e Bozorg-e Hend*, published in 1932.[38] It was only after Tagore's visit to Iran that the work of translating his oeuvre into Persian began, most importantly with the 1935 publication of *Sad Band-e Tagur*, a specially commissioned collection of one hundred poems, including numerous poems from his most famous work, the *Gitanjali* (1910), translated collaboratively from the original Bengali by Ebrahim Purdavud and Mulvi Zia al-Din at the Visva-Bharati Academy.[39]

To compensate for the relative obscurity of Tagore as a public and literary figure, his Iranian hosts used the press to publicize his significance and to situate him within the ideological parameters of Pahlavi nationalism. In the days and weeks before his arrival in Iran, and during the trip as well, Iranian newspapers carried summaries, descriptions, and assessments of Tagore's literary and political work. The April 20, 1932, issue of the leading Tehran daily, *Ettela'at*, introduced Tagore to the public and explained why his presence was so important. "Our dear readers," the article began, "may wish to acquaint themselves more fully with the ideas and thought of the poet and philosopher from India who is our new guest."[40] He was not just another poet, but a poet and sage "whose writings have been translated from Bengali, which is his mother tongue, to many foreign languages and have been published all over the world, placing his poetry and thought in the lofty garden of world literature."[41] Articles lauding Tagore's poetry and his stature as a cultural icon continued to appear during the whole of his four-week stay in Iran.

The April 28, 1932, issue of *Ettela'at* contained an article that was particularly important in conveying the cultural symbolism of a national revival associated with the visit. The article placed Tagore—"the famous Bengali sage and poet who is one of the most famous luminaries of the present age"[42]—and his visit in the broader context of the cultural history tying Iran and India together. "The people of any nation have a specific destiny," it read, "and the destiny of the Iranian nation is to have a very close relationship with the destiny of the nation of India."[43] The connection between Iranian national authenticity and the classical heritage of India was a common and consistent theme of Iranian nationalism during this period, and Tagore's visit was yet another opportunity to popularize the theme. The article went on to say that

> six thousand years ago our fathers were brothers with the Indians and lived together as one nation. Afterwards these two brothers were separated from one another, and our ancestors came to the Iran of today by way of Transoxiana and the River Oxus. However, during this voyage they brought with them the essence of Indian culture. Even today names such as Jamsheed, Fereydun, Kyumars, and others that are repeated in our language and are part of our mythology have not been separated from the mythology of India, and these names are the same words that our forefathers brought with them.[44]

The article described in detail the elements of cultural continuity that continued to link Iran and India. Just as elements of Iranian culture could be found in Central Asian cities such as Samarqand, Balkh, Bokhara, Kabul, and Herat, so too they could be found in South Asian cities and regions such as the Punjab, Lahore, and Sindh. "In no way is there any distinction between these people in terms of race, culture, literature, opinion, ways of thinking, or material life,"[45] the article stated. Persian poetry was still recited by India's poets, and the Persian language was known by anyone who claimed to have literacy. "Even down to the present day the non-Muslim population of India uses the divan of Hafez in religious ceremonies and on Fridays gather to pay homage to the spirit of Hafez."[46]

Iran and India were thus presented as part of a single national culture. The article suggested that circumstances of history had separated the two, but at their core they continued to share a common authenticity. The implication was that the separation had been affected during the Islamic period, and with the renaissance of national culture then under way, this "unnatural" condition of segregation could be remedied. The author's references to the traces of cultural continuity linking Iran and India were attempts to find and highlight those remnants of "authenticity" that remained and to begin the work of rekindling them. The promotion of this sentiment in the public's mind established the framework in which Tagore's presence in Iran was perceived. The article of April 28 concluded, next to a front-page portrait of a saintly figured Tagore: "The arrival of Rabindranath Tagore in our country is like the arrival of an elder in the land of his forefathers. With total happiness we Iranians will show hospitality to this brother."[47]

Tagore himself was well aware of the symbolism that surrounded the trip. During his three days in Bushehr, he was presented to the local public through a series of receptions and welcoming ceremonies. His official host was the governor of the province, along with Iran's consul-general to Bombay, Jalal al-Din Kayhan, who arrived to guide Tagore and his entourage during the trip. Also arriving in Bushehr was a Parsi delegation led by Dinshah Irani, who had likewise made the journey from Bombay to accompany the poet. As his hosts led Tagore and his Parsi entourage from one public reception to another, Tagore perceptively recorded in his travelogue his impressions of how he was being received by the people of the city:

> Who or what am I to these . . . crowds? . . . When I had been
> to Europe, the people there know something of me as a poet,
> and so could judge me on materials before them. These
> people [Iranians] also believe me to be a poet, but solely by
> force of imagination. To them I am a poet, not of this or that
> kind, but in the abstract; so that nothing stands in the way of
> their clothing me with their own idea of what a poet should
> be. Persians have a passion for poetry, a genuine affection
> for their poets; and I have obtained a share of this affection
> without having to show anything for it in return.[48]

The "force of imagination" that Tagore perceived was the Indo-Iranian civilizational ideal forming the basis of interwar Iranian nationalism.

It was this ideological background that conditioned Tagore's presence in Iran, and he was in effect placed on display as a living personification of Indo-Iranian authenticity. He went on to compare the receptions he received in other countries that he had visited with the welcome he experienced in Iran. "I am reminded of what happened when I was in Egypt,"[49] he wrote; "They [Egyptians] evidently looked on me not only as a poet, but an Oriental Poet, and must have felt that their country was sharing in the honor which was being shown to me."[50] In Iran, he continued, the cultural bonds were even closer:

> Coming to think of it, my relations with Persia are even more intimate, for am I not an Indo-Aryan! Persians have throughout their history taken pride in their Aryan descent, and that feeling is gaining strength under the present regime. So they are looking on me as a blood relation . . . in thus feeling me to be their own, they have made no mistake, for I too feel quite close to them.[51]

The racial vocabulary was a very important element of the Indo-Iranian civilizational ideal, which both Tagore and his Iranian hosts made consistent reference to during the trip.

Since the discovery of the Indo-European language family in the nineteenth century, philologists and anthropologists had theorized about its various branches.[52] Indian and Iranian intellectuals were pleased to discover that the authority of European science had placed their nations among those with the most "advanced" racial stock. By the interwar period, and especially during the time of Tagore's visit to Iran, the Indo-European theory—and the associated cult of Aryanism—had reached its "scientific" and ideological peak, not only in Germany, but also in Iran and India. One of Tagore's travel companions, Kedar Nath Chatterji, who accompanied the poet during the trip to Iran as the official correspondent for the Calcutta-based *Modern Review*, observed the Aryan symbolism that followed Tagore during the trip:

> Firstly, there is the Aryan movement. There is now a very strong feeling amongst all the intellectuals—and with the lead of His Majesty the Shah, amongst all young Iranians—that Iranian means pre-dominantly Aryan. This has now completely superseded the Pan-Islamic movement and the pride

of the intellectuals and the younger generation in the cultural achievements of Aryan Iran is growing fast. This has awakened a feeling of kinship with Indians and as such intellectual Iran feels proud at the fame of a brother Aryan—the Poet.[53]

The references to Aryanism employed during the trip were part of the larger project of defining the historical genealogy of Indo-Iranian civilization. Interwar Iranian nationalism was in the process of defining a new ideal of national "authenticity" rooted in the classical history of pre-Islamic Iran's Zoroastrian religious-cultural heritage. Aryanism and the idea of Indo-Iranian civilization were important elements of that heritage, and became new cultural markers that now defined Iranian authenticity.

CONVERSATIONS WITH ALI DASHTI

In Bushehr, Tagore also met with Ali Dashti (1894–1982), the Iranian Majles deputy then representing the region. In addition to his work as a Majles deputy, and later as a senator, Dashti was a key figure in modern Iranian intellectual history. His prolific writing in newspapers and literary journals, as well as numerous monographs and novels, spanned an impressive array of topics from poetry and religion to politics and social reform. Over the course of his long career as a writer, his intellectual iconoclasm drew harassment, censorship, and periodic imprisonment by the authorities, first during the Reza Shah period and then to his ultimate demise following the Islamic revolution of 1979.[54] Dashti met Tagore on at least two occasions during the poet's time in Iran, first in Bushehr and again, later in the poet's journey, at Dashti's home in Tehran where he introduced Tagore to a circle of young Iranian intellectuals.[55] Their conversations, which were eventually published as interviews in the newspaper founded by Dashti, *Shafaq-e Sorkh*, reveal how Tagore and his Iranian hosts were thinking about the idea of national authenticity and cultural change.

During their first meeting in Bushehr, Tagore commented to Dashti that part of his intention in coming to Iran was to "make acquaintance with the real Persia."[56] In referencing this comment in their later conversation, Dashti replied:

You told me in Bushehr that you have come to us in Persia to discover the old India. Quite true, our real spirit is old

Indian; it comes from a past when we shared a common culture. Even now an inner affinity persists, and it is this that makes you feel at home with us.[57]

Tagore confirmed the Indo-Iranian cultural bond that Dashti referred to. Echoing a common sentiment that he repeated to a number of interviewers and correspondents during the course of the trip, Tagore referred to the Indo-Iranian and Persianate culture of his childhood in the Jorasanko district of northern Calcutta:

The path was open for me before I was born. As a matter of fact, in our home in Bengal the spirit of Iran was a living influence when I was a child. My revered father and my elder brothers were deeply attached to Persian mystical literature and art. Going back further one discovers that at one time the Bengali language freely borrowed words from your vocabulary, which we use now without knowing their origin. When you find this, you must know that something of your culture flows through our daily life; for words are merely symbols of thoughts and attitudes, which they represent. Even before the Mohammadan rule in India there was an active cultural interchange between India and Iran; in our classical art and literature direct traces of this are to be discovered.[58]

From this common cultural background their conversation then proceeded to discuss changes in art, literature, and music then taking place in both Iran and India. The question of cultural adaptation to new and modern influences—especially influences from European and American culture—was another major preoccupation for Tagore, and found its way into his conversation with Dashti. In discussing music, Tagore referred to the "unquestionable greatness" of European composers such as Beethoven and commented, "without doubt our own music would be all the richer if it can absorb, into its living texture, creative influences from European music."[59] Tagore continued, however—echoing another prominent theme that runs throughout his writing—by cautioning that Iranians and Indians "must ponder seriously before we go in for hasty imitation of Western life in its totality."[60]

Tagore had a long history of arguing this point in Asian societies he visited. As early as 1916 he lectured in Japan regarding the danger of the "material" culture of the West threatening to devour the "spiritual" culture of Asia.[61] The response of the Japanese intelligentsia in attendance at Tagore's lecture at Tokyo's Imperial University, where he delivered his speech "The Message of India to Japan," was just as skeptical as that of Ali Dashti and his salon of young Iranian intellectuals in Tehran in May of 1932. In his response to Tagore's warning, Dashti challenged the poet by saying that the process of cultural change is impossible to manage and may require bold efforts of innovation. Dashti stated:

> I am not afraid of foreign influence. . . . Our soul accepts
> what it may; we cannot determine consciously how much to
> receive or reject exactly. The whole process of assimilation
> is a subconscious one so that there is no fear of only outside
> influence totally submerging or exterminating the basic
> character of our civilization. . . . Greek ideals, for example,
> have left their legacy in the great architecture and sculpture
> of India; but at the beginning of Greek influence we would
> probably have feared that India was doing harm to its tradi-
> tions by accepting Greek motifs and technique. . . . In Persia
> similarly, we have had periods of extraneous influence but
> this has only vitalized our Persian genius. We have quickly
> shaken off the imitative phase and retained something from it
> which has helped us.[62]

Dashti's impatience for modern reform, like that of the Japanese intellectuals whom Tagore encountered in Tokyo, troubled the poet. On more than one occasion he cautioned Dashti and others regarding the dangers of too rapid cultural change. Those dangers included losing the "native genius" of the culture, as well as rousing the opposition of what he described as—comparing Iran with India—"rigidly pious mullahs corresponding to our Hindu priests."[63] Tagore's concern regarding the dangers of conservative orthodoxy and narrow sectarianism was another of the central themes emphasized throughout his writing. It was also a central issue discussed with many of his hosts during the trip to Iran. His own experience in India had shown him that conservative Muslims and conservative Hindus could prevent the deeper cultural universalism that he envisioned tying India and Iran together. Tagore's own father, the Maharishi Debendranath Tagore (1817–1905), a major figure in nine-teenth-century Indian religious and cultural reform, had been an early founder of the Brahmo Samaj movement, which was seen with suspicion by orthodox Hindus. Also, according to commonly known tradition, the Tagore family's ancestry was derived from the Pirali Brahmins who had been ostracized by orthodox Hindus after they became tainted by contact with Muslims in the eighteenth century, rendering them by writ of conservative Hinduism as unworthy of marriage.[64]

The suspicion of Hindu conservatives no doubt reminded Tagore of the conservative Muslim clerics whom he also encountered in Iran, such as those who greeted him at the Masjed-i Shah in Isfahan:

> Everyone I saw inside the mosque was dressed like a mullah, and from their disapproving countenance we were apparently not very welcome there. . . . Which did not surprise me, because I am not sure if . . . outcasts like me will be allowed to enter the Jagannath temple in Puri!"[65]

Elsewhere he described "the asphyxiating domination of the mullahs" as a danger to "progress."[66] Despite his seemingly prophetic warnings concerning the dangers of religio-cultural conservatism, Tagore's overarching mission during the trip to Iran was to emphasize the threads of a common Indo-Iranian culture that could overcome the dangers of narrowly conceived orthodoxy and instead serve as the moral-aesthetic and civilizational basis for a modern, liberal, and religiously pluralistic identity rooted in a shared authenticity.

TAGORE IN SHIRAZ

During the next leg of his journey to Iran, in Shiraz, Tagore continued to emphasize the theme of a broadly shared Indo-Iranian authenticity. Arriving in Shiraz by way of Kazerun on April 16 after an arduous drive along what he described as "the rough, desolate road"[67] from Bushehr, Tagore's five-car motorcade was greeted by a military escort and welcomed into the center of the city. At a specially prepared garden reception, citizens, dignitaries, and representatives from various local organizations were assembled to welcome Tagore to Iran's most famous "city of poets." Also present at the Shiraz welcoming reception were three eminent figures of interwar Iranian cultural and intellectual history: Hasan Foruqi, the scholar, diplomat, and brother of Prime Minister Mohammad Ali Foruqi; Arbab Kaykhosrow Shahrokh, the official representative of Iran's Zoroastrian community in the Majles; and

Mohammad-Taqi Bahar, the most renowned and respected Persian poet of the time.[68] All three were key figures in shaping the cultural policy of the Pahlavi state during the 1920s and 1930s and were well aware of the important symbolism of Tagore's presence in Shiraz.

The ceremony began with the governor of Fars thanking Tagore for making the journey. Next, an official welcome message was read aloud by a citizen of the city:

> The town of Shiraz is proud of its two immortal and glorious sons [Sa'di and Hafez]. The sweep of their genius is akin to yours. The fountain of inspiration that nourished the flowering of our two great poets is the same as the source of your inspiration. The spirit of the poet Sa'di whose resting place has for centuries sanctified our city is now watching over us. Hafez's delight is reflected in the joyous mood of our countrymen celebrating your presence here.[69]

From the beginning of Tagore's visit to Shiraz, he was presented as a living heir to the poetic tradition of Sa'di and Hafez. In responding to the welcome message, Tagore, speaking to the assembled crowd in English with translation into Persian, continued the symbolic comparison of himself with the famous poets of Shiraz:

> Ages ago the then ruler of Bengal had invited the poet Hafez to visit Bengal, but he could not make it. But I, a poet from Bengal, received an invitation from the ruler of Persia, and in response to that I am now personally amongst you. This gives me the privilege and pleasure of conveying my greetings and good wishes in person to you in Persia.[70]

Tagore was referring to the story of Ghiyas al-Din Azam Shah (r. 1390–1411) of Bengal, who according to literary legend traded hemistichs with Hafez and reputedly invited him to the court of the Ilyas Shahi dynasty in Pandua.[71] While there is much reason to question the historicity of this story, Tagore's well-placed referencing of the legend suggests a shared oral and written tradition of myths, legends, and literary-biographical anecdotes that were part of a unified Persianate literary tradition spanning Indo-Iranian culture. While in Shiraz, Tagore in fact consistently emphasized to his hosts and interviewers the presence of

Persian poetry—in particular the influence of Hafez—in the subcontinent and the effect that it had on his own poetic sensibility.[72] As the court language during the Mughal period, Persian was the *lingua franca* of the political and literary elite of India for several centuries. Tagore's father, the Maharishi Debendranath Tagore, who was perhaps the most important influence on Tagore's life, was fluent in Persian, and, as he writes in his own autobiography, had a special affection for the poetry of Hafez.[73] Tagore, while himself not proficient in Persian, recounts on numerous occasions that his father would recite the poetry of Hafez to him as a child.[74]

Tagore's referencing of the Hafez legend is important for yet another reason. Implicit in the story is the theme of travel and migration between India and Iran. Travel and migration were key elements in the culture of premodern Indo-Iranian civilization. The obsessive territoriality of modern nation-states obscured the transnational, transterritorial, and considerably deterritorialized understanding of culture that existed in the premodern period. The long history of Indo-Iranian religious, artistic, and literary contact as expressed through not only the medium of poetry but also the vast record of early modern travel writing between Iran and India suggests—as Muzaffar Alam and Sanjay Subrahmanyam have suggested—that there existed an "Indo-Persian republic of letters"[75] that stretched across the *fuzzy boundaries* of the Iranian plateau, Central Asia, the subcontinent, and the greater Indian Ocean cultural universe. Standing before the admiring crowd at the garden reception in the city of Shiraz, having made the long journey from Calcutta, Tagore's spectral presence now reminded his Iranian audience of this dimly remnant transnational cultural ideal.[76]

The visits to the burial sites of Sa'di and Hafez reinforced this idea even further. Among the projects carried out by the Pahlavi state beginning in the interwar period was the rebuilding and embellishing of the tombs of the great poets of Persian literature, including those of Khayam, Ferdowsi, Sa'di, and Hafez into suitable sites of national memory.[77] Tagore's visits to the tombs of Sa'di and Hafez took place before the final transformation of the sites into national monuments, but nevertheless underscored their status as important to the project of Pahlavi nationalism. At a reception held in the courtyard adjacent to Sa'di's tomb, Tagore was presented, with some fanfare and before another assembled crowd, with an illuminated manuscript of Sa'di's *Golestan*.[78] The following day, April 18, Tagore visited the mausoleum of Hafez. As with the tomb of Saʻdi, the famous Hafeziyeh had not yet been rebuilt at the time of Tagore's visit in 1932 into the much-better-known structure that it became after 1935 when the French archaeologist André Godard and his Iranian associates, Ali Riazi and Ali Sami, designed and built the new neoclassical columned edifice to honor Hafez.[79] The structure, as it existed at the time of Tagore's visit, was an enclosed edifice composed of iron, more typical of Qajar-era religious shrines. Tagore's description of the tomb perhaps anticipated the soon-to-be-initiated rebuilding of the structure; the Hafeziyeh consisted of, he wrote, "a machine cast pavilion with grilled rails [that] had been erected atop the old tomb, which to me did not at all fit in with the spirit of Hafez's poetry."[80] Approaching the tomb, his hosts next allowed Tagore and some of the Parsi members of his entourage, including Dinshah Irani, to enter the railed enclosure and sit beside the stone slab marking the grave of Hafez. Accounts indicate that Tagore sat momentarily in deep contemplation. As he writes in his travelogue, he was clearly moved by the experience:

> Sitting near the tomb a signal flashed through my mind, a signal from the bright and smiling eyes of the poet on a long past spring day—akin to the spring time sunshine of today. We were, as it were, companions in the same tavern savoring together many cups of many flavors … I had the distinct feeling that after a lapse of many centuries, across the span of many deaths and births, sitting near this tomb was another wayfarer who had found a bond with Hafez.[81]

Tagore's communion with Hafez was more than simple histrionics: it was rather important as a symbolic expression of yet another common strand of Indo-Iranian culture that Tagore and his Iranian hosts were trying to emphasize during the course of Tagore's visit to Iran. Significantly, in the case of Tagore's visit to the Hafeziyeh, the shared national authenticity of Indo-Iranian civilization was now expressed through an appreciation of Persian mystical poetry. Much of the rest of the symbolism tied to Tagore's trip to Iran emphasized the pre-Islamic history of Indo-Iranian civilization, whether it be through the invocation of racial and linguistic themes or the referencing of Indo-Iranian cultural ties as expressed through the ancient Avestan and Vedic Zoroastrian and Hindu traditions. Tagore's expressions of affection for Hafez, however, seemed to suggest that the Indo-Iranian bonds of national authenticity

Tagore in Shiraz with Dinshah Iran and others, inside the Hafeziyeh, 1932.
Bokhara, *Tehran, 2005.*

were not exclusive to the pre-Islamic period, but extended—through the medium of classical Persian poetry—into the Islamic era as well; as Sugata Bose has commented, the "shades of Aryanism" invoked by Tagore in this case came to intermingle with the "depths of Sufism."[82]

The idea that the great poets of the medieval Persian mystical tradition were expressing *national sentiments* beneath the guise of Islamicate Sufi poetry was increasing in circulation in the interwar period.[83] In much of the interwar debates regarding Iranian *national literature*, figures such as Ferdowsi and Hafez were increasingly depicted as using the language of poetry to express deeper Iranian sentiments, including Zoroastrian ideas that could be associated with a perennialist Aryan mysticism. According to this reading, the expressions of mystical insight in the poetry of Hafez, for example, were not tied to a liberal-ecumenical mysticism connecting Zoroastrianism and Islam, but were instead articulations of an Indo-Iranian Aryan metaphysics that was in fact resisting Islamicate cultural hegemony. It was precisely this idea that had inspired the Pahlavi state to commission the rebuilding of the tombs of the great Persian poets of the tenth to fourteenth centuries, as a way to physically embody the idea of the *Iranianness* of Hafez, Sa'di, and the entire literary canon of Persianate belle-lettres. Both Iranian and Indian nationalist intellectuals were making the case that Persian Sufi poetry was in fact the expression of a much deeper tradition of *Indo-Iranian spirituality* that stretched back into the earliest stages of the pre-Islamic period. The great Indian philologist, member of the Greater India Society, and close associate of Tagore's, Suniti Kumar Chatterji, wrote evocatively in describing Tagore as the heir to this tradition that began in the pre-Islamic past and which found its later cultural expression in Iranian Sufism:

> *Tasavvof* as a perfected system went from Iran to India after Northern India was conquered by the Turks from Afghanistan and Central Asia in the 11th–12th centuries. . . . *Tasavvof* became one of the common platforms on which the seekers of Truth in both Muslim Iran and Central Asia on the one hand and Hindu or Brahmanical India on the other could meet and enrich each other's minds. . . . We need not go into the details of this international fellowship in the domain of mysticism. The history certainly requires to be fully investigated, and the beginnings of it go to the earliest Indo-Iranian times, when the two immediate sections of the Aryan or Indo-Iranian branch of the Indo-European language-culture group, in Iran and in India, started adventuring in the domain of spiritual intuition and realization. . . . And we are happy to find that the great Rabindranath Tagore himself formed a golden link during this century in the chain of spiritual friendship binding up India and Iran.[84]

Suniti Chatterji's invocation of the deep Indo-Iranian spiritual roots of later Sufi traditions is similar to the ideas of the Iranian scholar and intellectual Sadeq Rezazadeh-Shafaq. In discussing one of Tagore's more famous essays, "The Religion of Man" (1931), Rezazadeh-Shafaq explains that Tagore's discussion of Zoroastrianism emphasizes the idea of ethical universalism. As seen from Tagore's viewpoint, wrote Rezazadeh-Shafaq, Zoroastrianism was among the earliest world religions to combine spirituality and ethics as the basis of a universal teaching. According to Rezazadeh-Shafaq, the later arrival of the universalism of Islam to

Iran thus had a precedent in earlier Iranian history, helping to explain why Islam found fertile ground in Iran after the seventh century.[85] As Rezazadeh-Shafaq writes, the distinctions between particular religious traditions—in this case between the pre-Islamic and Islamic religious traditions of Iran—work to obscure the underlying spiritual continuity expressed in what he describes as the "Iranian spirit" (*rūh-e Īrānī*):

> It was the Iranian spirit, and the truths of Zoroastrianism and the sacred religion of Islam, that once again gave voice to this universalist teaching through the beautiful and supple forms of the philosophy of Iranian 'erfān.[86]

Rezazadeh-Shafaq, like Suniti Chatterji, was situating Iran's mystical tradition within a larger tradition of national culture. The medieval tradition of Persianate literary mysticism was thus rearticulated as the moral-aesthetic expression of Iran's national spirit. From this reading of Indo-Iranian history, at its roots the religious dimension of this national spirit transcended the particular religio-spiritual boundaries of Zoroastrianism, Hinduism, and Islam, and instead approached what was now understood as an ecumenical monism that in the later medieval period became manifest through the language of Persian Sufi poetry. As Chatterji and Rezazadeh-Shafaq argue—following Tagore—the traditions of *tasavvof*, *'erfān*, and the poetry of Hafez were thus rooted within a repositioned civilizational genealogy that was enframed as Indo-Iranian spirituality.[87] Tagore's presence in Shiraz, and his public displays at the mausoleum of Hafez, thus came to further symbolize and personify the idea of a common religio-spiritual essence tying Iran and India together.

FROM SHIRAZ TO TEHRAN

After setting out from Shiraz on April 22, Tagore's five-car caravan next trekked along the "comparatively wide and smooth"[88] road linking Shiraz, Isfahan, and Tehran. His first stop was at the ruins of the ancient Achaeminid Empire at Persepolis, outside of Shiraz, where he and members of his Parsi entourage were given a tour of the site by Ernst Herzfeld, the German-born archaeologist who was then conducting the first systematic excavation of the site under the sponsorship of the University of Chicago's Oriental Institute.[89] Like his visit to Shiraz and the Hafeziyeh, Tagore's visit to Persepolis was again underscored with grand symbolism.[90] Tagore described his ascendance of the

Apadana staircase of the palace complex of Darius I and his meeting with Herzfeld:

> I was carried up the stone steps on a chair. Hills behind me, the infinite sky above me, and down below the vast expanse of a desolate countryside. At one end stood the frozen-in-time stone monuments bearing silent witness to the glories of the past. Here I met the famous German archaeologist Dr. Herzfeld, who was in charge of excavating and bringing to light the relics of the ancient achievements.[91]

Tagore's meeting with Herzfeld—whom he describes as "in high spirits!"[92]—was a remarkable encounter that was covered in his travelogue in some detail. The two men, in fact, had a great deal in common, having met once before in Berlin in 1921 when Herzfeld, then a professor of Near Eastern archaeology at the University of Berlin, had gone to hear Tagore speak during one of the famed Nobel laureate's numerous lecture tours through Europe. Both men shared a keen interest in the large-scale evolution of the cultures and societies of the ancient period and did not shy away from making broad civilizational speculations.

Tagore recounts in his travelogue that as the two were strolling through the grounds of the site, Herzfeld pointed out the many connections between the relics found at Persepolis and the archaeological record of India. Among these connections was suggestive evidence from the physical structure of the palace complex itself; Tagore writes that "from the available record it appeared that Indian teakwood was also employed for roof construction."[93] Tagore was particularly interested to learn from Herzfeld about the physical remnants of an ancient Indo-Iranian civilization. In recounting another point of their conversation, he described an object collected by Herzfeld and presented for his consideration:

> The German professor showed me one of these exhibits, an egg shell cup with etched designs on it, and he remarked that these designs were of the same family as those found in Mohenjodaro. Sir Aurel Stein had found many specimens in Central Asia which could be identified with Mohenjodaro culture. From the evidence of these far-flung findings one is tempted to conclude that an earlier major civilization

preceded the known modern civilizations, and having spread its wings was now extinct.[94]

His remark regarding relics at the city of Mohenjodaro is a reference to the Indus Valley civilization of the second and third millennium BC, which had only recently been discovered in the Sindh region and was, like Persepolis, receiving its first extensive excavation in the 1920s and 1930s, in this case by the Indian Archaeological Survey.[95] Similarly, his reference to the work of Sir Aurel Stein (1862–1943) indicates Tagore's up-to-date knowledge of the latest archaeological discoveries in India, Iran, and Central Asia in the early twentieth century. Stein, a Hungarian-born British subject, was—like Herzfeld—another key figure in late nineteenth- and early twentieth-century archaeology. His excavations in eastern Iran, central Asia, northern India, and western China received wide publicity and brought to light a great deal of information relevant to understanding the Buddhist cultural and religious history of Asia, earning him, like Tagore, a knighthood from George V of Britain.[96] Tagore, like many Iranian and Indian nationalist intellectuals of the interwar period, followed with great fascination the latest scientific discoveries of European anthropology and archaeology. Based on this knowledge, and inspired by the archaeological remains he saw all around him at Persepolis, Tagore speculated about the civilizational genealogy of Indo-Iranian culture:

> Sometime in the distant past a breakaway group of Aryans took shelter on the high tableau of Persia . . . it is possible that these people were contemporaries of the Mohenjodaro era.[97]

While Tagore's speculation regarding the historical sequencing of the Aryan migration to Iran and the Mohenjodaro civilization is dubious, what is more interesting is that Tagore, like his Iranian hosts, was intellectually tantalized by the suggestions of Indo-Iranian cultural continuity stretching back to the most remote past. Beyond references to archaeology, Tagore went on to make continuous observations throughout the trip of similarities between Indian and Iranian religion, mythology, music, art, and literature. In thinking about religion in the Achaeminid period, for example, Tagore writes—again following the thinking of many Indian and Iranian nationalists of the early and middle twentieth century—that "the ruling deity of this heroic dynasty was

Ahura Mazda. One finds some similarity with the Aryan god Varuna of India."[98]

In all of these cases it was an idealized classical past that most inspired Tagore and his Iranian hosts. The symbolism of Tagore and his Parsi associates touring the grounds of the ancient Achaeminid capital allowed the Pahlavi state to underscore one of its main ideological projects of the interwar period. Neoclassicism had become a central motif of Iranian nationalism by the 1930s, enabling the cultural and political project of the Pahlavi state. By associating modern Iranian culture with the classical phase of Indo-Iranian civilization, the Pahlavi state was repositioning Iran within the civilizational discourse of the early twentieth century. By the interwar period, the global legal-political discourse of nationalism simultaneously conceived of individual nation-states as politically sovereign and defined within strict territorial parameters, but at the same time, individual nations were also conceived as being part of larger networks of cultural alignments and civilizational blocs. These cultural and civilizational alignments worked to strengthen the moral and political authority of individual states within the larger international system. Iranian nationalism's ideological project of interwar neoclassicism thus worked to simultaneously emphasize Iran's political and territorial sovereignty while also situating Iran within the deeper civilizational parameters of an Indo-Iranian culture. Tagore's presence at Persepolis, as with the symbolism throughout his journey to Iran, bestowed the moral authority of *Indo-Iranian civilization* onto the Iranian nation-state.

It was during his time in Tehran that this symbolism reached its ideological peak. Tagore arrived in Tehran on April 29 and spent the next two weeks in the capital city. His itinerary during this, the final portion of his trip, was filled with an almost continuous series of receptions, ceremonies, meetings, and lectures before a variety of local audiences.[99] Isa Sadiq, chancellor of the Teacher's College and an important player in the cultural life of Iran during the Reza Shah years, spent considerable time with Tagore during the Tehran portion of his trip. Sadiq's memoir invokes an image of Tagore that reflects how his Tehran hosts perceived the visiting poet:

> Tagore had a tall, lanky stature and wore a long, simple cloak
> that only increased his lankiness. With his tousled white
> and silvery hair and long forehead, an open and elongated

Rabindranath Tagore (1861–1941). Wikimedia Commons.

countenance, penetrating and engrossing eyes, long and delicate beard, a voice which was mild and pleasing, speech that was measured and deliberate, and movements that were supple and graceful, Tagore exuded a very noticeable and effective presence.[100]

Sadiq went on to say that this impressive appearance "reminded one of the mystics and ancient prophets."[101] There was a great deal of interest in Tagore's physical appearance during the Tehran portion of the trip. The daily *Ettelaʿat* included numerous references and descriptions of Tagore, including a detailed article with a headline in the May 5 issue of the newspaper that read "The Visage [Qiyafeh] of Tagore."[102] Tagore's statements, activities, and physical presence reinforced the impression of him as an ideal-type sage personifying a notion of Indo-Iranian authenticity.

The symbolism of Tagore's presence in Iran was also conveyed during the speeches and ceremonies that he participated in during his two weeks in Tehran. Tagore gave two formal speeches during his stay in Tehran, one at the Ministry of Education on May 5 and the other at the Literary Society on May 9. Both speeches attracted great interest on the part of the political and literary elite of Iran and were widely covered in the local press. Tagore also had at least one private reception with Reza Shah on May 2 at the Sa'dabad Palace, accompanied by his Parsi companions. The meeting with Reza Shah also received wide coverage in the media.

At the meeting with the Shah, Tagore and his Parsi entourage presented the monarch with two paintings. The first was a portrait of Reza Shah produced by the renowned Parsi salon artist M. F. Pithawala (1872–1937).[103] The portrait was presented to the monarch as a gift from the Parsi community. The second painting was from Tagore himself and was an example of one of his famous "poem-paintings." Tagore's "poem-paintings" combined poems written on canvas against a backdrop of an abstract image usually composed in watercolor. Tagore composed numerous such "poem-paintings" during his career as one of his favorite creative forms, allowing him to combine his love of poetry with the visual arts.[104] In an interview with *Ettela'at* several days following the meeting with Reza Shah, Tagore explained the symbolism of the central motif in the abstract painting. It included, according to Tagore, a figure intended to represent Reza Shah kindling a small flame, which in turn represented "the light of Iran."[105] A figure representing Tagore was also drawn, approaching the central figure to help light the flame.[106] The imagery captured the symbolism of the Indo-Iranian cultural revival intended by Tagore's trip to Iran. Tagore, as the symbol of Indo-Iranian authenticity, was portrayed as returning to Iran to help Reza Shah revive that authenticity after centuries in which that sense of national culture had been diminished.

Tagore also made reference to the painting during his speeches at the Ministry of Education and the Literary Society, which attracted approximately one thousand audience members according to contemporary and newspaper accounts.[107] Both speeches were given in English but translated into Persian by Mohsen Asadi, a professor of English and former member of the Iranian Foreign Service. Coverage of the speeches, accompanied by excerpted translations, were included in the press coverage. Tagore elaborated on the painting and his trip to Iran by saying:

I am an Iranian and my ancestors passed through this land
and went to India. I am therefore pleased to be returning to
my homeland. I realize that the kindness shown to me here
is because of this unity of race and culture. And the reason
for my trip, despite the difficulty of the journey, is precisely to
show the sense of unity and affection that I have for Iran.[108]

After referring to the cultural, historical, and racial ties between Iran
and India, he alluded to the painting more directly. "War and disease,"
he said, had ravaged the "civilization" of Asia, and Iran, like India and
China, had fallen "into the shadows":[109]

In Iran, however, the light entered into Reza Shah's hand. I
was in a far corner of India when I saw this new light on the
distant horizon. And so I came here on behalf of India and
all of Asia to salute him and to witness his great deeds, which
are a source of pride and strength for all of Asia.[110]

In these speeches, as elsewhere during his Iran tour, Tagore once again
invoked the idea of Iran and India as part of a larger Asian ideal of civilization. His speeches and interviews in Iran, and the ceremonies and
activities in which he participated, underscored these metaphors of
national renewal and Indo-Iranian cultural solidarity.

Reza Shah himself emphasized this theme during a private meeting
with Tagore and his entourage. During this meeting, Reza Shah made
his goals for Indo-Iranian relations very clear to Tagore and his Parsi
associates. As Rustam Masani, who along with Dinshah Irani was one
of the Parsi civic leaders who accompanied Tagore during the Iran tour,
later recalled:

His majesty's message to us was simple and straightfor-
ward. He expressed his regret that the descendants of the
ancient Iranians had very little contact with their fatherland.
He wished to see more of them. He did not ask that they
should take their money with them from Hindustan to Iran,
although he was anxious to see the resources of Iran developed and the Parsis taking a hand in it. "Come in small numbers," he [Reza Shah] said, "see things with your own eyes;

Tagore in Tehran, with members of the Iranian Literary Society (anjoman-e adabi*),
May 1932. Seated, left to right: Ali Dashti, Tagore, Mohammad-Taqi Bahar, Dinshah
Irani. Standing, third to sixth, left to right: Nasrollah Falsafi, Saʿid Nafisi, Abbas Eqbal
Ashtiani, Gholamreza Rashid-Yasemi. Dinshah J. Irani, ed.,* Poets of the Pahlavi
Regime, *Bombay, 1933.*

wait and watch and then decide for yourselves whether some
of you should settle down in the country of your ancestors.
We will welcome you with arms outstretched."[111]

Reza Shah's interest in encouraging renewed contact between the Parsi
community of India and Iran was both pragmatic and ideological. The
wealth of the Bombay Parsi community was seen as a potential source
of investment in Iran's social and economic development. At least as
importantly, the ideological interest was to identify the Parsi community of Bombay as the embodiment of Iranian authenticity and as a
model of modern Iranian national identity. To promote both of these
interests, during their private meeting, Tagore and Reza Shah also discussed the Iranian state's decision to establish an endowment at Tagore's
Visva-Bharati Academy at Santineketan for the study of Zoroastrianism
and ancient Iranian culture.[112]

In addition to his formal speeches at the Ministry of Education and the Literary Society and his private meeting with Reza Shah, Tagore also visited Alborz College in Tehran, the Majles, the newly established College of Music, and met with members of the Baha'i, Zoroastrian, and Armenian communities of Tehran.[113] Kaykhosrow Shahrokh, the Zoroastrian member of the Iranian Majles who had accompanied Tagore during much of the poet's trip to Iran, also gave Tagore a special tour of the newly founded Firuz Bahram Zoroastrian School in Tehran. Tagore was given the honor of laying the foundation stone of the school.[114] Later the same day he was honored as the special guest at a play at the school, which was inspired by a story from the *Shahnameh* and performed, as he describes, "with a large dose of patriotic ardor."[115]

Tagore's stay in Tehran also coincided with the celebration of his seventy-first birthday, which was held in the streets of the capital in a large, state-sponsored public ceremony.[116] The celebrations concluded with Tagore reading to the assembled crowd a poem he had composed for the occasion. The poem was translated into Persian and published prominently in the newspapers on the following day, along with details of the public event.[117] When Tagore finally departed Iran on May 15, 1932, and headed toward Baghdad for a visit to the soon-to-be-independent Hashemite Kingdom of Iraq, he sent a telegram thanking his Iranian hosts:

> I am deeply grateful to His Majesty the Shah of Iran for giving me the opportunity to visit the ancient country of Iran. I am also deeply grateful for the kindness and hospitality you have shown me. Your gracious invitation to a poet from India shows how close our two nations are. Our nations, which at the beginning of history were one nation . . . and which spoke the language of a common civilization . . . but which subsequently became divided from one another. . . . I am hopeful that today, in which both have awakened from a deep sleep, that the two will once again move towards the future as brothers.[118]

The telegram, the Persian translation of which was also prominently published in *Ettela'at*, captured both the political and cultural message that Tagore's visit conveyed during the four-week official visit. The diplomatic ceremonies and official displays of friendship were intended to strengthen political relations between the new Pahlavi state of Iran and the emerging national movement in India. Central to this political objective was the articulation of the ideological message of the trip to reinforce an Indo-Iranian cultural ideal as the civilizational basis of Iranian nationalism.

TAGORE'S CRITICS

Not everyone was convinced by the political and ideological implications of the symbolism surrounding Tagore's visit to Iran. From the point of view of a host of contemporaneous critics, the invocation of an Indo-Iranian neoclassicism conveyed not only an idealized revival of the Vedic, Avestan, and "Aryan" heritage connecting India and Iran but also a simultaneous revaluation and denigration of the Abrahamic-Islamic heritage that Iran and India also shared. In the context of the global rise of Nazi ideology during the interwar period, these political and ideological implications were difficult to ignore. A host of critics, from the Muslim-Indian poet, intellectual, and activist Muhammad Iqbal (1877–1938) to the dissident Parsi scholar G. K. Nariman (1873–1933) and the Iranian-Tajiki Persian poet and socialist revolutionary Abolqasem Lahuti (1887–1957), all went on record to express their disapproval of Tagore's decision to allow his personal cultural-political capital to be used by Indo-Iranian nationalists in this way. As Farzin Vejdani has observed, the concern of Iqbal and Nariman in particular was that "extreme Hindus, Parsis, and Iranian nationalists were making common cause against Indian Muslims through the anachronistic glorification of a shared 'Aryan' past."[119] The symbolism surrounding Tagore's visit to Iran, they argued, only reinforced what Vejdani has described as a "shared anti-Islamic agenda"[120] common to many nationalists in both Iran and India.

Iqbal went so far as to claim that the real intention of what he described as an emerging Hindu-Iranian alliance was to displace Islam and establish the preconditions necessary to reconvert Iranians to their original Zoroastrian faith. "Tagore's trip to Iran has revealed itself to be an effort to promote and strengthen Aryan connections between Hindus and Iranians," Iqbal wrote in a June 27, 1932, letter to an Iranian diplomat in India.[121] The goal of this effort, he continued, was to promote "propaganda suggesting Iran's readiness for a return to the religion of Zoroaster."[122] Pursuing this policy, Iqbal warned, "will produce immeasurable political damage for Iran."[123] G. K. Nariman, the iconoclastic Parsi scholar who frequently demurred from the prevailing orthodoxies of the Parsi scholarly community, echoed Iqbal's criticisms. "Tagore's visit to Persia was a farce," Nariman wrote in a letter to Iqbal, dated July 11, 1932. The culprits, he suggested, were not only Tagore and his Iranian nationalist hosts, but also the "Parsi bigots" eager to see a Zoroastrian resurgence inside Iran. The Iranians were eager to encourage this thinking among the Parsis, Nariman argued:

> In order to induce the Parsis to migrate to Persia, of course with their capital, it was suggested to them that Persia was ripe to re-adopt Zoroastrianism and that the return of the Parsis would see the conversion of mosques into fire-temples. Nay there are rumors, and a number of Parsis believe, that Reza Shah is going to put on the sudreh and kusti, the outward symbols of Zoroastrianism![124]

For both Iqbal and Nariman, the tensions inherent in the symbolism surrounding Tagore's visit to Iran were stark. Tagore's self-professed Pan-Asian ecumenism seemed to invoke a liberal, pluralist, and inclusive ideal, and yet the racial logic of Aryanism and Indo-Iranian neoclassicism seemed to imply that there was little room for Iran and India's Islamic heritage within that ecumenical vision. Writing from within the assumptions of an enduring early modern Persianate and Islamicate cultural system that made its own claims to religio-cultural pluralism, Iqbal and Nariman were quick to point out the contradiction inherent in Tagore's infatuation with the more illiberal strands of Indo-Iranian neoclassicism.

Also critical of Tagore's visit to Iran was Abolqasem Lahuti, the poet and activist originally from Kermanshah, who became an early member of Iran's Communist movement. Following the consolidation of the Pahlavi state in the early 1920s, Lahuti left Iran and spent the most productive years of his life in the Soviet Socialist Republic of Tajikistan. From Dushanbe, Lahuti watched with grave concern as Tagore prepared to make his much-publicized journey to Iran in the spring of 1932. Like Iqbal and Nariman, Lahuti was critical of the political symbolism surrounding Tagore's trip. Unlike his contemporaries, however, Lahuti's criticisms focused on the class politics surrounding the visit. His criticism took the form of an open letter addressed directly to Tagore and published in the Berlin-based Persian-language Socialist newspaper, *Paykar*. "Since the Indian newspapers bring us reports that the government of Reza Shah has . . . invited you to visit Iran," Lahuti's letter began, "I consider it my revolutionary duty to bring to your attention some of the conditions that exist in today's Iran."[125] The letter goes on to give a scathing critique of Reza Shah's government and admonishes Tagore for participating in an official visit that only served to give tacit support to the Pahlavi state:

> The reactionary and oppressive government of Reza Shah,
> which has suppressed the movement of the peasants and the
> workers with swords and fire, and has again brought the tyr-
> anny of Zahak to Iran, does not enjoy the trust or respect of
> Iran's public, and is, in fact, to an extreme degree the object of
> hatred and scorn by the masses [*tudeh*] of the Iranian nation.
> . . . Therefore, the principal objective of the government of
> Reza Shah for inviting you to Iran is to make use of [*su'es-
> tefādegī*] your good name and global reputation. . . . It is not
> proper for a progressive poet like yourself to allow yourself to
> be used . . . as a source for promoting the moral authority of
> an oppressive and tyrannical government. The toiling nation
> of Iran will one day issue to you an invitation, and will again
> warmly welcome you to Iran. However, that day will be the
> day when the flag of the peasants and the workers will glori-
> ously wave in the courtyard [of the National Assembly].[126]

The letter's critique of Tagore suggests that there was also a coherent cultural-political language emanating from the Soviet Union by 1932. This new *Soviet ecumene* was espousing its own quasi-civilizational claims rooted in both a socio-economic and moral-political ethos. This ethos enabled the insurgent "Soviet ecumene" to claim its own authority as a civilization and gave it the ability to contest the political and cultural geography of Asia on equal terms with its Indo-Iranian and Islamicate civilizational rivals.[127] Just as Iqbal and Nariman had critiqued Tagore's Indo-Iranian civilizational language on the basis of his neglect of Abrahamic-Islamicate civilization, so too did Lahuti contest the implicit class contradictions inherent in Tagore's journey to Iran. Lahuti's critique of Tagore implied that there was room for the Persian language—and its poetic and political heritage—within the emerging cultural-political system of the Soviet ecumene. Despite these trenchant critiques, Lahuti's open letter to Tagore, like Iqbal and Nariman's private correspondence, ultimately passed largely unheard outside of the marginal and periph-eral zones of dissent to the consolidation of the nation-state system in Iran and India.

CONCLUSION

Tagore's four-week visit to Iran in April and May of 1932 was just one example of the Pahlavi state's effort to emphasize the Indo-Iranian and Zoroastrian cultural heritage of Iran as the basis of its modern national identity. Other efforts in this regard included the dissemination of a nationalist culture through the curriculum of the expanding school sys-tem; the promotion of archaeology and the building of museums for the public display of *national objects*; the construction of monuments, statues, and mausoleums designed to select and emphasize certain parts of Iranian national culture; and the appearance of a new officially sanc-tioned visual style of neoclassical architecture that increasingly came to dominate the public life of Iran's urban spaces. Tagore's visit to Iran can be understood in part as one component within this larger context of state-led cultural production during the interwar period.

What made Tagore's trip unique was the transnational context of the visit and the important role played by the Parsi community of Bombay in both organizing the visit and helping to choreograph much of its intended symbolism. While Zoroastrian figures such as Dinshah Irani, Hormusji Adenwalla, Rustam Masani, and Kaykhosrow Shahrokh played important but mostly behind-the-scenes roles in planning the trip, their presence during the four-week journey as part of Tagore's official entourage—as he traveled from city to city inside Iran—made it clear that the Zoroastrian element was a key role in the renewed effort to build connections between Iran and India. The Parsi community's increasingly visible and important role in building ties between Iran and India had implications that were both pragmatic and ideological.

Pragmatically, the Parsi community had by 1932 invested consid-erable time, effort, and resources—over the course of several genera-tions—in building institutions of exchange between the Zoroastrian communities of India and Iran. Since the mid-nineteenth century, Bom-bay-based Zoroastrian organizations had devoted extensive charity and philanthropic efforts to building schools and orphanages for Zoroas-trian communities inside Iran, and had likewise provided other fund-ing for cultural and educational initiatives promoting ties between the Zoroastrian communities of India and Iran. By 1932 these efforts had acquired substantial momentum. The Parsi role in helping to arrange Tagore's 1932 trip to Iran grew out of these already established connections. In a practical and pragmatic sense, by 1932 the Parsis of India had therefore come to see themselves as the indispensable, natural, and logical intermediaries between Indians and Iranians.

In an ideological sense, Tagore's trip to Iran also reinforced the goals of both the Parsis and the Pahlavi state. The ideological goal of the Pahlavi state to promote Iran's ancient history and Zoroastrian culture at the expense of its Islamic heritage coincided with Parsi interests of promoting a revival of Zoroastrian culture inside Iran, as well as of improving the status of Iran's Zoroastrian communities after generations of marginalization, misunderstanding, and, in many cases, mistreatment.[128] Tagore's endorsement of Zoroastrianism and ancient Iranian culture during his tour of Iran, as part of his larger invocation of an idealized Indo-Iranian civilization, reinforced both of these ideological goals.

What remained unresolved at the time of Tagore's visit to Iran in 1932, however, was the growing tension between the liberal and cosmopolitan political project of Tagore's invocation of Indo-Iranian civilization as part of a broader Pan-Asian solidarity on the one hand, and on the other hand the more narrowly essentialist and exclusionary politics that increasingly defined the ideological basis of the Pahlavi project of Iranian nationalism. Central to this ideological tension was the way in which the Parsis, Tagore, and the Pahlavi state made use of the discourse of "civilization" as it existed during the early decades of the twentieth century. By the 1920s and 1930s this discourse was changing in important ways that came to shape how emerging nation-states viewed themselves on a rapidly crystallizing world stage. The older nineteenth-century meaning—in which a singular notion of "civilization" was contrasted to "barbarism"—was giving way to a new cultural mapping of the world in which distinct civilizational blocs stood alongside one another, with each characterized by a distinct moral-aesthetic essence. This new civilizational discourse followed the political logic of post–World War I liberal internationalism and the new Wilsonian doctrine of "national sovereignty." The civilizational blocs of this new cultural mapping of the world were rooted in an understanding of the "moral equivalence" of distinct civilizations, which in turn was understood as parallel with the legal and political rights of emerging sovereign nation-states.

The unresolved ideological tension inherent in Tagore's 1932 visit to Iran grew out of this changing understanding of the concept of "civilization" during the interwar period. Tagore's visit was part of the Pahlavi state's project of aligning Iran's cultural-political genealogy with the moral authority of Zoroastrianism and the neoclassical idea of an Indo-Iranian civilization. What it also meant was that the Pahlavi state was increasingly contesting the Abrahamic-Islamicate civilizational affiliation, which was also a key element of Iran's cultural heritage. From the point of view of Tagore's cosmopolitan understanding of Pan-Asian solidarity, the Indo-Iranian and Abrahamic-Islamicate civilizational affiliations were not mutually exclusive. From the point of view of Iran's project of interwar Pahlavi nationalism, their mutual coexistence and compatibility was considerably more problematic. While the Pahlavi state's Zoroastrian and Indo-Iranian project of neoclassicism successfully aligned the ideological basis of Iranian nationalism within the interwar cultural-political discourse of nationalism, it did so without the liberal and cosmopolitan ethos that Tagore's understanding implied. As a result, while the Pahlavi state's Indo-Iranian project of neoclassicism became increasingly consolidated during the interwar period, the unresolved tension within this discursive realignment would over time go on to produce further cultural, ideological, and political contestations.

For their part, the Parsis found themselves caught between Tagore's liberal-cosmopolitan understanding of Indo-Iranian civilization and the Neo-Zoroastrian version of Iranian nationalism increasingly invoked by the Pahlavi state. While by temperament the Parsis were generally more inclined to follow Tagore's more inclusive political-historical reading of Indo-Iranian culture, they were also aware of the potential benefits that an ascendant Iranian nationalism rooted in Zoroastrian culture might have for their own fortunes, especially as their own future in a post-independence India was being increasingly called into question. By the time of Tagore's 1932 visit to Iran, while these political and ideological tensions were yet unresolved, the contours of their inherent contradictions were becoming increasingly clear.

CHAPTER 4

EBRAHIM PURDAVUD AND HIS INTERLOCUTORS

Parsi Patronage and the Making of the Vernacular Avesta

The meeting between Madame Bhikaiji Rustom Cama (1861–1936) and Ebrahim Purdavud (1886–1968) took place at Madame Cama's apartment in central Paris, at 25 Rue de Panthieu.[1] The invitation to what became a historic afternoon tea took place sometime after Purdavud's arrival in Paris in the late summer of 1910. The serious and impressionable twenty-four-year-old Purdavud had come to the French capital ostensibly to pursue the study of law after having completed his primary education in his native city of Rasht, as well as additional study in Tehran and several years of further schooling at the French Laique School in Beirut.[2] Once in Paris, however, Purdavud soon found himself drawn to the literary cafés and political salons of the Parisian Belle Époque. The cafés that Purdavud frequented during his five years of residence in the city, between 1910 and 1915—such as Le Café Soufflet and La Closerie de Lilas—were in the Latin Quarter of the Left Bank, along the Boulevard Saint-Michel, adjacent to the University of Paris.[3] The patrons who frequented these cafés during the years preceding the First World War were not only among the more familiar names of early twentieth-century avant-garde literary and artistic modernism, such as Jean Cocteau, Marcel Proust, Pablo Picasso, and Amedeo Modigliani, but also a substantial number of Anarchist activists, Marxist revolutionaries, and a sizable contingent of Iranian, Egyptian, Turkish, and Indian nationalists.[4] These exiles, expatriates, and dissidents—people like Madame Cama—had come to Paris to organize opposition to the waning imperial states of Czarist Russia and the British

Madame Cama (1861–1936) with the cofounder of the Paris Indian Society, S. R. Rana (1870–1957), at the Stuttgart Congress of the Second International, 1907. International Institute for Social History (Amsterdam).

Raj, as well as the feeble yet repressive monarchies still ruling the Ottoman Empire and Qajar Iran.

By 1910, Madame Cama, as she was called by her many admirers—or, just as often, by her equally familiar appellation of "India's Joan of Arc"[5]—was in many ways the political impresario of this community of proto–Third Worldist activists and intellectuals in Paris. A scion of a wealthy Parsi family from Bombay and the daughter-in-law of the revered Parsi scholar and Zoroastrian reformer Kharshedji Rustomji Cama (1831–1909), Madame Cama had moved to Paris in 1909 after living in London since her departure from India in 1902.[6] In London she had quickly become politicized to the cause of India's independence, first working for the London-based Parsi politician Dadabhai Naoroji (1825–1917) and the London branch of the India Home Rule Society, and later helping to establish more radical independence groups such as the Free India Society and the Young India Society.[7] The scrutiny caused by her growing activism in London led her to relocate to the relatively more secure base of Paris, where she continued her work as an activist, agitator, and anticolonial revolutionary. In Paris she cofounded the "Paris India Society" and became one of the principal writers, editors,

Ebrahim Purdavud in Paris, 1915.
Mohammad Mo'in, ed., Yadnameh-ye
Purdavud, *Tehran, 1946.*

and patrons of the Indian nationalist English-language newspaper *Bande Mataram*.[8] She also continued her efforts to network and build alliances of solidarity with the large expatriate communities of activists and intellectuals who had likewise settled in Paris from many parts of the world. The associations that she built with these Irish, Egyptian, Turkish, German, Russian, and Iranian activists during these years earned her a reputation as one of the principal figures working to organize a global movement for independence and social justice on the eve of the First World War.[9]

It was in this context that Madame Cama first came into contact with the young Ebrahim Purdavud. The two initially met at one of the literary salons organized by the small community of Iranian intellectuals residing in Paris at that time.[10] Upon his arrival in the city in 1910, Purdavud had quickly befriended the longtime Iranian denizen of Paris and renowned scholar Mohammad Qazvini (1877–1949) and other Iranians in the city who would also go on to become notable scholars and intellectuals, such as Hossein Kazemzadeh-Iranshahr (1884–1962).[11] This trio of Parisian Iranians soon established the "Iranian Literary and Scientific Society of Paris," which held regular meetings at various cafés in the Latin Quarter, open to both Iranians and non-Iranians, to discuss cultural and literary matters as well as current events. Madame Cama attended some of these meetings, and was so impressed with the young Ebrahim Purdavud that she invited him to tea.[12]

Many years later, in 1934, Purdavud recalled how important this initial encounter with Madame Cama had been for his personal and intellectual development. At a gathering of Parsi dignitaries and patrons in Bombay held to honor him for his many years of scholarly labor in translating the corpus of Zoroastrian literature into the modern Persian language, Purdavud recalled the meeting at Madame Cama's Parisian home some twenty-four years earlier. He described for his audience the patience with which Madame Cama introduced him to the ritual and theological subtleties of the Zoroastrian faith, such as the Navjote initiation ceremony and the meaning of the Sedreh and Kushti garments. As Purdavud recalled in 1934, after this initial encounter with Madame Cama, he went on to become "a constant visitor to her place, and was deeply impressed by that Zoroastrian lady's pure, intelligent, and active life."[13]

His friendship with Madame Cama was just one of the many important relationships that Ebrahim Purdavud established with members of the Parsi community over the course of his long career. Other Parsis with whom he had personal and professional collaborations included the Zoroastrian lay intellectual and civic leader Dinshah J. Irani (1881–1938), the community benefactor and major Parsi financial patron Peshotanji Dossabhai Marker (1871–1965), as well as a large group of Parsi priests and scholars in India for whose erudition Purdavud acknowledged his abiding intellectual debt. These figures included such important intellectual luminaries of the nineteenth- and early twentieth-century Zoroastrian reform movement as Bahramgore Tahmuras Anklesaria (1873–1944),[14] Gushtaspshah Kaikhushro Nariman (1873–1933),[15] Jivanji Jamshedji Modi (1854–1933),[16] Darab Dastur Peshotan Sanjana (1857–1931),[17] Irach J. S. Taraporewalla (1884–1956),[18] and numerous others. These priests and scholars of the Parsi community—figures who can be described as Purdavud's Parsi interlocutors—greatly shaped not only Purdavud's own understanding of Zoroastrianism, but also, through Purdavud's published writings, an understanding of Iranian history, culture, and national identity that would shape much of Iran's twentieth-century history. Through their example and encouragement, as well as the intellectual support and financial sponsorship of these Parsi interlocutors—in particular the work initiated through the efforts of the Bombay-based Iranian Zoroastrian Anjoman and the Iran

League—Ebrahim Purdavud was able to produce no fewer than nine substantial volumes of modern Persian translations of the Zoroastrian literary-religious corpus from their original Avestan. He also wrote extensive annotations and commentaries based on the most recent findings of European orientalist scholarship and the writings of reformist Parsi priests and scholars in India.

Purdavud's work in translating these Zoroastrian texts into modern Persian—his three editions of the *Gatha*,[19] two volumes of the *Yashtha*,[20] two volumes of the *Yasna*,[21] the *Khordeh Avesta*,[22] and the *Visperad*[23]—and making these texts available to an emerging reading public inside Iran has long been acknowledged as one of the major achievements of Iran's twentieth-century intellectual history. His other more concise, popular, and accessible writings on Iran's pre-Islamic Zoroastrian heritage has also been recognized for their contributions toward popularizing Iran's twentieth-century culture of neoclassicism.[24] What is less often acknowledged, much less critically assessed, is the key role that the Parsi community of India played in bringing Purdavud's scholarly oeuvre to fruition. From the earliest stages of his life in Rasht, Tehran, and Beirut to his encounter with Madame Cama in Paris, his years of study in Berlin, and his subsequent engagement with the Parsis in Bombay and western India, Purdavud's understanding of Zoroastrianism was consistently mediated through Parsi sources and institutions of knowledge. Accounting for this history of cultural mediation, and assessing the cultural politics of its intellectual history, is important for understanding the complexities of Iran's larger twentieth-century history of modernity and nationalism.

The nature of this Parsi mediation is important for a number of reasons. In the broadest sense, it was through the efforts of Purdavud's Parsi interlocutors that the Zoroastrian sacred texts became available for the first time to readers of Iran's vernacular language. Prior to Purdavud's New Persian translations, the Avestan and Pahlavi-language Zoroastrian scriptures held the status of liturgical texts that were circumscribed narrowly within the religious culture of Iran's small Zoroastrian community, largely located in Kerman and Yazd. These Zoroastrian texts were either shrouded in mystery and misunderstanding, or were entirely unknown to non-Zoroastrian Iranians, and were certainly never considered to be textual artifacts of an Iranian *national* heritage. Purdavud's translations—with their accompanying annotations and commentaries—began the process of reinscribing the meaning and significance of these texts for an audience of both Zoroastrian and non-Zoroastrian Iranian readers. In doing so, Purdavud's translations and commentaries also carried with them important traces of the modernist intellectual reconstruction of the Zoroastrian faith that had been undertaken by India's community of Parsi priests and scholars since at least the middle decades of the nineteenth century. From the Parsi point of view, Purdavud's labors of translation not only made the *Avesta* available in the vernacular language of modern Iranians, but those translations and commentaries also promised to do the work of popularizing a Parsi modernist understanding of Zoroastrianism among Iranians, or as Monica Ringer has argued, of "transplanting religious reform" from its South Asian Zoroastrian milieu to the heartland of the Iranian plateau.[25] Daniel Sheffield has similarly documented the evolution of new trends in Zoroastrian thought, tracing their roots even further to early modern projects of religious reformation, projects that by the high-colonial period of the late nineteenth century produced a Zoroastrianism defined by a distinctly modern and "cosmopolitan" religious and cultural ethos.[26]

Both Ringer and Sheffield identify the cultural and religious climate of colonial India as an important context for this reconstruction of Zoroastrianism from its classical and medieval forms to a modern faith comparable to the post-reformation interpretations of the Judeo-Christian tradition. Like these other religious reform projects of the modern era, the post-reformation understanding of Zoroastrianism came to emphasize its essential monotheism, its spiritual and antinomian elements, as well as the importance of broadly ethical qualities defining Zoroastrian religious praxis. This modernized, reformed, and cosmopolitan understanding of Zoroastrianism not only brought the faith into conversation with changes underway in other religious traditions of the early modern and modern eras, but also worked to bring to the surface elements of the Zoroastrian tradition that were congruent with the social, political, and commercial mores of a multiconfessional colonial modernity administered by the British Raj. The great nineteenth-century Zoroastrian religious reform movements—like so many other reform movements also underway in nineteenth-century India, and the larger global religious reformations of the early modern and modern eras—emerged in the context of an encroaching modernity brought to bear by the new age of globalization and the authority of empire.[27]

What is less clear—and requires additional investigation—is the manner in which Purdavud's Zoroastrian revival unfolded inside the cultural and political context of Pahlavi Iran. While encouraging the emergence of a cosmopolitan and reform-minded Zoroastrianism to serve the role of a surrogate Protestantism for Iran's project of modernity was part of the implicit goal of Purdavud's—and the Parsis'—translation efforts, the social, cultural, and political terrain on which those efforts unfolded inside Iran was very different from that found in British India. Inside noncolonized Iran, the promotion of a reform-minded Zoroastrianism not only brought with it the promise of a dialogue between Iranian culture and a perceived utopian and universal modernity, but also, and just as significantly, it connoted a cultural politics of reasserting long-suppressed narratives of religion and history that could be understood as provocative acts of cultural contestation challenging long-dominant premodern Islamic civilizational narratives, or what Reza Zia-Ebrahimi has described as Iranian modernity's incendiary logic of precipitating a "dislocative" nationalism.[28] It is the contrasting political terrains of late nineteenth- and early twentieth-century Iran and India that help to explain what became of these alternative cultural, political, and ideological trajectories of reformist Zoroastrianism in these two arenas of nationalization. Detailing the evolution of Ebrahim Purdavud's life and work helps to explain how these contrasting political terrains worked to set in place what became an ultimately irresolvable tension within the later political history of Iranian nationalism.

EARLY LIFE

Ebrahim Purdavud's early life was in many ways typical of someone born into a prosperous Iranian family in the late nineteenth century. He was born in March of 1886 in the town of Rasht, a growing region near the Caspian coast in Iran's Gilan province.[29] By the time of his birth, the commercial and agricultural economy of the region was feeling the economic effects of globalization, especially the growing presence of the Russian empire to the north. The nearby port city of Bandar-e Anzali had already become an important transit point for people and goods moving between Iran and important industrial cities in the southern Caucasus such as Baku. Additionally, the proximity of Rasht to Tehran—approximately two hundred miles—also made the city an important link for travelers moving between the Russian Caucasus and Iran's capital city.

Ebrahim Purdavud was born into a family with deep ties to Rasht and the Gilan region. His father, Haji Davud, a pious Shi'ite Muslim who had the means to ensure that his children received a proper *maktab* education, was both a successful merchant in the local bazaar and a landowner with holdings that had been passed down for at least three generations.[30] The expansion of cash-crop agriculture during this period made land ownership a source of considerable wealth, and the fortunes of Haji Davud and his family rose around the time of Ebrahim's birth. Haji Davud also married the daughter of a prominent local mujtahid of the Gilan region, confirming the social and economic bonds that traditionally linked prosperous merchants and landowners to 'ulama families in the Qajar era. By the time of Ebrahim's birth, his father was wealthy enough not only to make the pilgrimage to Mecca, but also to bring back a wet nurse to attend to the needs of his young children.[31]

Haji Davud was also wealthy enough to endow the construction of a small maktab school near the Sabz-e Maydan town square in Rasht for the education of Ebrahim and his brother, Soleyman. Today the small structure functions as the family mausoleum, but when it was built in 1892 it served as the one-room schoolhouse where Ebrahim and his brother received their foundational religious education, as well as their instruction in Persian literature and Arabic grammar. Their principal teacher during their early education was a minor local cleric—Mirza Mohammad-Ali Khalkhali—with whom Purdavud would maintain contact until Khalkhali's death in Tehran in 1942. The Purdavud brothers began their studies with Mirza Mohammad-Ali when Ebrahim was six years of age. Ebrahim quickly displayed a talent for both grammar and poetry.[32] In a brief account of his early education, written in 1928 as part of the introduction to a collection of his poetry, the *Purandokht-Nameh*, Purdavud recalled his early fascination with language: "From my childhood years I had a taste for rhythmic language . . . and I would combine words together in such a way that was neither poetry nor prose."[33] Purdavud noted that his early religious education and linguistic talents gained him notice in Rasht as a poetic prodigy when, while still very young, he began composing and reciting *marsiyas*, religious elegies sung as part of traditional Shi'ite mourning practices.[34] This early education and poetic talent would later serve Purdavud in his efforts to translate the Zoroastrian religious texts. While still in Rasht, however, his knowledge of Zoroastrianism, like that of the vast majority of Iranians at that time, remained very limited.

It was only when he moved to Tehran on the eve of the Constitutional Revolution of 1905 that he first came into contact with a new world of ideas. His move from Rasht to Tehran was ostensibly to continue his education. Along with his brother, Soleyman, and Mirza Mohammad-Ali Khalkhali, the educational custodian hired by his father, Purdavud traveled to Tehran to begin the study of medicine and to pursue a career as a medical doctor, a worthy profession for the son of a prosperous landowner and merchant of the late Qajar era.[35] Purdavud spent approximately two years studying traditional medicine in Tehran, including the standard curriculum of the medical texts of Ibn Sina, with the noted local authority Mohammad Hossein Khan Sultan al-Falsafa.[36]

Once in Tehran, however, Purdavud's curiosities began to steer him in new directions. He began his study of French in this period, enrolling in the capital city's Alliance Français academy as a supplement to his medical education. He also began to show a more serious interest in the history of Zoroastrianism and the Persian language. In one of his fragmentary memoirs, delivered as a lecture to an audience of Parsis in Bombay many years later, he recalled the first time he met a member of the Zoroastrian faith. While strolling down Tehran's then-fashionable Lalehzar Street sometime between 1905 and 1907 in conversation with a friend about the etymology of a certain Persian word, Purdavud's friend introduced him to a local Zoroastrian to help resolve the etymology in question. This first encounter with a Zoroastrian led to others.[37] His budding curiosity about pre-Islamic Iran and the history of the Persian language also led him to draft a letter to the Zoroastrian Anjoman in Yazd with "a long list of words" whose meanings and etymologies he likewise hoped could be explained. As he later recalled, the Zoroastrian Anjoman did reply to his query, but the etymological explanations that were offered "were very unsatisfactory."[38] Despite these frustrations, it is clear that from an early age his interests and curiosities were already turning toward questions of language, pre-Islamic history, and Iran's Zoroastrian heritage.

His two years in the Iranian capital city were defined as well by the politics of the constitutional revolution. Notably, Purdavud was not an active member of the revolutionary movement in this period, although his political activities increased significantly in the following years. Nevertheless, like others of the generation of 1905, he experienced the constitutional revolution as a politically defining moment. Purdavud was steeped in the constitutional literature of the movement and followed the press of the era very closely. He also described the constitutional movement as a patriotic cause, and remembered being part of the broad coalition of participants who helped bring about the signing

of the royal proclamation in August of 1906 that authorized the establishment of the majles.[39] In describing those events, he recalled joining
with the progressive forces of the era, including pro-constitutionalist
'ulema, writing, "I was in Tehran during the establishment of the constitution, and on numerous occasions I marched in line behind Nuri,
Behbehani, and Tabataba'i."[40]

Despite his participation during the early stages of the struggle for
the constitution, Purdavud did not remain in Tehran to participate in
the later and more divisive stages of the revolution of 1905–1911. By
1907 he had once again decided to relocate—this time to Beirut—to
pursue new educational opportunities.[41] At this point he also set aside
his pursuit of medicine, and perhaps in part because of his early experience as a participant in the constitutional revolution, he now decided
to begin the study of law. His move to Beirut was designed to focus his
energies on improving his proficiency in French, and he enrolled in the
Beirut Laique School between 1907 and 1910 as the first step toward
moving to France for more formal legal education.[42]

By 1907, Beirut had become an important city for many Iranian
students pursuing modern learning. The Syrian Protestant College
(after 1920, the American University of Beirut) and the numerous
French institutions of secondary and postsecondary education provided relatively accessible educational opportunities for students traveling from Iran. When Purdavud arrived in Beirut in January of 1907,
he joined a small but growing community of other Iranian students
in the city.[43] Mohammad-Ali Jamalzadeh (1892–1997), the modernist
literary figure who would later be credited with establishing the genre
of the twentieth-century Persian short story, was also in Beirut during
Purdavud's three-year stay in the city from 1907 to 1910. In an obituary for Purdavud published in 1968, Jamalzadeh recalled Purdavud's
commanding presence among the Iranian students in Beirut at that
time; he described Purdavud as "the best dressed [*chic-push*] among
the [Iranian] students in Beirut."[44] He also recalled that Purdavud's
father was able to send a substantial allowance to his son on a regular
basis, thus allowing Purdavud to enjoy more comfortable accommodations in the city. "The apartment that Purdavud had in Beirut was
much nicer than that of the rest of us," Jamalzadeh recalled.[45] This
apartment also seems to have become an important gathering place
for the community of Iranian students in the city during those years.
Jamalzadeh recalled the social gatherings that Pardavud would host,

describing his generosity to the other Iranian students in the tight-knit community: "in hosting these gatherings of friends," he wrote, "[Purdavud] was always pleasant and would graciously welcome other young compatriots."[46]

Purdavud's Beirut apartment also served as an intellectual hub for the young Iranians gathered in the city. In addition to following—from the distance of Beirut—the latest updates of the still-unfolding struggle of the constitutional movement inside Iran, Purdavud had his second significant encounter with Iran's Zoroastrian tradition within the social and intellectual climate of the expatriate community of Iranians in Beirut. At one of the social gatherings held at his Beirut apartment, Purdavud was introduced for the first time to the text of the *Dasatir-e Aseman* by a fellow Iranian student.[47] The *Dasatir* text has long since been identified as a fabricated Neo-Zoroastrian text produced originally by the Azar Kayvan Zoroastrian sect in the sixteenth century.[48] The text purports to convey episodes of a lost history of pre-Islamic Iran, including stories of forgotten kings and sages that are not referenced in any other textual source. The language of the *Dasatir* text also purports to be an archaic and original form of the Persian language, which likewise is not found in any other textual tradition of the Persian language. The original production of the text in the sixteenth century was likely shaped by the culturally and religiously syncretic environment unfolding in Akbar's India and Safavid Iran. The audience of the *Dasatir* was likely limited to small groups of readers within the Azar Kayvan Zoroastrian movement and others whose interests in this speculative text were similarly circumscribed within an early modern Persianate cultural and religious landscape.

By the nineteenth and early twentieth century, however, the *Dasatir*—and other texts produced by the Kayvani sect—found their way into the hands of new readers who approached the text with entirely new hermeneutical demands. From the vantage point of nineteenth and early twentieth century Iranian modernist readers, the speculative history contained in the *Dasatir* was seen as a mysterious link to a lost pre-Islamic Iranian national heritage. Ebrahim Purdavud, like many other Iranian modernist intellectuals of his generation, found the text compelling, and was naively convinced of its historicity and cultural significance. Purdavud himself details his initial discovery of this text. In 1940, for an article that was originally published in the newspaper *Iran-e Emruz*, Purdavud writes:

> Thirty-three years ago [1907] when I was a student in Beirut,
> an Iranian friend ... who knew that I was interested in old
> Persian words and curious about ancient stories, gave me
> a book to read. That book, which until that day I had not
> heard of, was the *Dasatir*. ... What I read in it, I committed
> to memory, and considered myself lucky to be the fortuitous
> recipient of a divine gift, since I felt that I had discovered
> what I had been seeking.[49]

He goes on to detail his early fascination with the *Dasatir*, as well as his later disappointment when, after his introduction to orientalist scholarship, he belatedly learned that "this book is from top to bottom an invention, and neither does the content have anything to do with the Zoroastrian faith, nor does its language have any relationship to ancient languages."[50]

Purdavud's initial fascination and subsequent disappointment with the *Dasatir* helps to illustrate an important dimension of his own intellectual development, as well as the larger evolution of Iranian Neo-Zoroastrianism and neoclassicism at the turn of the twentieth century. Within the context of Purdavud's personal evolution, his discovery of the *Dasatir* not only illustrates his increasingly serious fascination with Iran's pre-Islamic history and Zoroastrian heritage, but also suggests that—as of 1907—his knowledge of that history and heritage remained very superficial. European orientalist scholarship on Zoroastrianism had long since debunked the authenticity of the *Dasatir*, despite the early enthusiasm shown for it by such prominent figures as William Jones and John Malcolm.[51] The Parsi scholarly community of India, despite their own initial enthusiasm for the text upon its initial "discovery" by Mulla Firuz in the early nineteenth century, had likewise concluded that the *Dasatir* was not a lost ancient text, but rather an early modern forgery produced to serve the interests of sectarian considerations of the religiously fertile sixteenth century.[52] Purdavud's own youthful indiscretion with the text suggests that during his student days in Beirut he was eager—like other Iranian nationalists of the era—to discover the mysteries of Iran's classical past, yet remained entirely ignorant of the scholarly consensus regarding the *Dasatir's* implausibility.

PURDAVUD'S PARIS

It was only after his journey to Paris and what became the next important stage in his intellectual development that Purdavud began to more fully immerse himself in the study of Zoroastrianism and pre-Islamic Iranian history. His stay in the city between August of 1910 and the spring of 1915 coincided with the tumultuous years leading to the dissolution of the constitutional movement in Iran and the outbreak of World War I in Europe. Purdavud had come to France to continue his study of law, briefly residing in the town of Beauvais to complete his undergraduate education and then transferring to the Sorbonne Law School at the University of Paris.[53] Once in the city, however, his intellectual curiosities in the areas of language, literature, history, and politics quickly became his primary preoccupation. His apartment in Paris at 81 Rue Saint-Louis en l'Ile, in the fourth arrondissement, became, like his apartment in Beirut, a convenient location from which to build connections with a wide range of Parisian activists and intellectuals and to explore the cultural life of the city.[54]

In addition to the important friendship he built with Madame Cama during this period, the other key personality who played an important role in shaping Purdavud's intellectual development in Paris was Mohammad Qazvini. Purdavud and Qazvini began a long-term friendship soon after Purdavud arrived in the city, ending only with Qazvini's death in 1949.[55] Although they would not always agree on certain questions of Iranian history and culture, such as, for example, the suitability of the Arabic script for use in the written form of the Persian language,[56] the intellectual mentorship of Qazvini nevertheless became one of the most important factors in defining the direction of the twenty-four-year-old Purdavud's intellectual curiosities. Qazvini was approximately ten years older than Purdavud and had come to Paris as early as 1904 after receiving a thorough education in the Islamic sciences, Arabic grammar, and the Persian literary tradition while still in Iran, as well as achieving proficiency in French through study at the Alliance Academy in Tehran.[57] Despite a parsimonious scholarly output, Qazvini quickly gained a reputation among early twentieth-century Iranian intellectuals as a polymath in the fields of medieval history, literature, and religious studies. He also garnered the deep respect of numerous European orientalists in Britain, France, and Germany, most especially

Edward G. Browne, with whom he worked on a number of important manuscript projects.[58]

It was Qazvini who dispelled Purdavud of his naïve infatuation with the *Dasatir* during one of their conversations in Paris. Purdavud relates the story of this conversation in the context of explaining his rapidly expanding intellectual horizons during his early years in the French capital. In keeping with his wide range of interests and talents, Purdavud had continued to compose poetry throughout his travels from Tehran to Beirut and now in Paris. As he recalled, the impression that the mysterious language of the *Dasatir* had left on him encouraged him to use some vocabulary from the text to occasionally embellish his own budding poetic oeuvre: "I would proclaim the value of the words of the *Dasatir* like a drum-major to this person and that person, and sometimes I would decorate my own poetry with those words as well."[59] Purdavud's poetry embellished with the invented vocabulary of the *Dasatir* was, as he explained, published in a small literary journal, *Peyk-e Dohol*, that he began to publish with like-minded literary friends in Paris.[60] In Purdavud's telling of the story, when he showed this poetry to Mohammad Qazvini it became clear that the mysterious vocabulary of the *Dasatir* was not an ancient form of the Persian language, but was instead nothing more than the invented neologisms of the Kayvani sect. Purdavud recalled Qazvini commenting:

> One day he [Qazvini] said to me that I hope these words
> are not from Mulla Firuz. I [Purdavud] replied "yes, they
> are words from the *Dasatir-e Aseman* and from the Iranian
> prophets, which Mulla Firuz has published." He [Qazvini]
> then explained that both the language and the subject matter
> of this text are the product of an unknown forger.[61]

Purdavud said that Qazvini's critical reading of the *Dasatir* "weighed heavily on me, since I learned that something that I had invested myself in can easily be dispelled."[62] This realization of his intellectual immaturity led him to immerse himself in the available scholarly literature on Zoroastrianism and renewed his commitment to the study of philology. This critical turning point also led to his growing aversion to the study of law. As he described, "in Paris I studied law, but my heart was not committed to it."[63] More of his time was now devoted to exploring the secondary literature available in Paris on Zoroastrianism and ancient

Iranian history. As Purdavud's reading in these subjects expanded, he came to understand that Qazvini's assessment of the *Dasatir* was based on an already well-established scholarly consensus. In describing his reading in this area, Purdavud paid special attention to the writing of Parsi scholars, in particular the work of Sheriarji Dadabhai Bharucha, whose article, "*Dasatir*, Being a Paper Prepared for the Tenth International Congress of Orientalists held at Geneva in 1894 A.C.," published in 1907, gave perhaps the most comprehensive critical assessment of the text among the scholarship produced during the late nineteenth and early twentieth century. As Purdavud concluded, comparing Qazvini's assessment of the text to Bharucha's reading, "in his [Bharucha's] own research he has reached the same conclusion."[64]

The four years that Purdavud spent in Paris were full of other important personal and intellectual transformations as well. It is unclear at what point in his life he began a more serious study of the Avestan and Pahlavi languages, but it may have started as early as his time in Paris. The encouragement to devote himself to this task may have been another example of the intellectual mentorship that Qazvini bequeathed to his younger colleague. Despite what became his clear mastery of these languages, it is also unclear if Purdavud ever had any formal training in Avestan or Pahlavi. He remained enrolled at the Sorbonne Law School, and his official intentions during his years in Paris remained to advance his legal education. His study of Avestan and Pahlavi, if they began as early as his time in Paris, were almost certainly the result of an autodidacticism born of a newfound intellectual vocation.

What is more clear about his years in Paris is that Purdavud became—as he had been in Beirut—an energetic figure in the literary and intellectual community of expatriate Iranians in the city. Purdavud, along with Mohammad Qazvini and Hossein Kazemzadeh-Iranshahr, began to hold informal discussion sessions in the cafés of the Left Bank.[65] There was a lively café culture in Paris during this time, catering to avant-garde modernist artists, Marxist revolutionaries, anarchists, and expatriate nationalist intellectuals from all over the world. Purdavud took the lead in organizing the Iranian intellectuals in the city and formed the "Iranian Literary and Scientific Society of Paris."[66] The group met regularly at Café Soufflet, La Closerie des Lilas, and other legendary establishments of the Latin Quarter that catered to artists, activists, and intellectuals of Belle Époque French modernism. In addition to the public spaces of the cafés' main rooms

Café Soufflet, Paris, 1920. Postcard, author's personal collection.

or in their gardens or sidewalk spaces, many of the cafés of Paris also rented rooms to hold private meetings. It was in the private rooms— or the *"salon-e makhsus"*—that Purdavud, Qazvini, and Kazemzadeh-Iranshahr held regular gatherings of the approximately thirty to forty members of the Society.[67]

Isa Sadiq (1894–1978), the founder of Iran's modern educational system and a contemporary of Purdavud, remembered attending one of the literary salons organized by Purdavud in Paris, sometime in the early part of 1912. As Sadiq wrote in a memorial essay in 1974 on the sixth anniversary of Purdavud's death, "I became acquainted with this great man from the beginning of my youth."[68] Sadiq recalled that soon after he had arrived in France to pursue his own education, he received an invitation by mail to attend a meeting of the Iranian Literary Society. The meeting took place in the context of the Russian occupation of northern Iran. At the meeting, held in a private room at La Closerie des Lilas, Sadiq wrote that "Purdavud, who at that time was approximately twenty-five years old, and on this evening was wearing an Iranian hat [*kolah*], rose from his chair and with an excited voice recited a poem."[69] It was one of the same poems that E. G. Browne eventually included in his *Press and Poetry in Modern Persia* as a literary specimen of the new themes of nationalism and neoclassicism that Browne identified as emerging among a new cohort of modern Iranian poets:

If the fire-temple has been extinguished through the tyranny
   of fate,
I will kindle in the chamber of the heart the alter of the
   Avesta . . .

From the direction of Persia every moment there reaches the
   ear
A voice which causes this blue vault of heaven to tremble . . .

Through the tyranny of evil men the kingdom of Jamshid and
   Kay hath been made desolate
Behold Persia, once exalted to heaven, now a ruin haunted by
   owls.

The lion of the Kayannians is hidden; it is the time of the
   jackal's prowling
Humiliation hath succeeded the splendor and glory of
   Darius.

King Nushirvan slumbers in the dark tomb, while the bear
   stands over his place.
Behold the tricks of fate . . .'[70]

The poem that Purdavud recited before the members of the Iranian Literary Society of Paris on that evening reflected not only the political urgency of the immediate post-constitutional era but also Purdavud's growing turn toward Iran's pre-Islamic heritage as a reservoir for both poetic and political inspiration. Purdavud's time in Paris—like his time in Beirut—had led to a new stage in his intellectual maturity, which brought together his political commitment to encourage Iran's independence with his newfound exploration of Iran's ancient history. Those in attendance on that night in Paris were struck by the power of his words. As Sadiq recalled, the lines of poetry that Purdavud recited "from a distance of several thousand kilometers from the homeland . . . set off a tremendous uproar (che ghugha'i be pa kard)."[71]

The cultural activities of the Iranian community in Paris on the eve of World War I were not limited to poetry readings. Hossein Kazemzadeh, one of Purdavud's close collaborators in organizing the Literary Society of Paris, described in his own memoir the efforts led by "a few

Iranian students" to stage a small production of the tragedy of Rustam and Sohrab, as adapted from Ferdowsi's *Shahnameh*.[72] This musical adaptation, which gained some notice at the time among commentators and theatergoers—and was supported by the pioneering French dramatist Léon Poirier (1884–1968)—was first performed at the Theatre des Champs Élysées in December of 1913.[73] The cast included the famous dancer, actress, and libertine Armen Ohanian (1887–1976), an Armenian-Iranian whose talent and stage presence had earned her an international reputation in the early years of the twentieth century.[74] As Kazemzadeh recalled, "At that time Madame Ohanian had gained much fame and respect in the cultural centers of Paris for her spiritual dances."[75] In the production, Ohanian played the role of Sohrab's mother, Tahmineh. The production had a short but notable run from December of 1913 to January of 1914.[76]

Perhaps most important, however, was the publication of the *Iranshahr* newspaper in the spring of 1914, the most significant achievement of Purdavud and the Parisian-Iranian community on the eve of World War I. The *Iranshahr* published in Paris between April and June of 1914 should not be confused with its eponymous counterpart published in Berlin between 1922 to 1927.[77] The two periodicals were in many ways similarly conceived as historical and literary journals that would also make connections to contemporary events pertaining to Iran and its place in global politics. The connection between them is also demonstrated by the involvement of Hossein Kazemzadeh in both the Paris and Berlin incarnations of the journal.[78] Kazemzadeh became the founder, editor, and a major contributor to the Berlin edition of *Iranshahr*. He also played an important early role in the Paris edition, although he left Paris before the publication of its first issue to begin work as an instructor of Persian at Cambridge University, where he also began an important collaboration with E. G. Browne.[79]

Purdavud, however, was by all accounts the principal figure who initiated the effort to publish the Paris edition of *Iranshahr*.[80] Despite its short print run of two months—printing only three issues before being curtailed by the beginning of World War I—the newspaper served as an important publishing template for not only the eponymously titled Berlin-edition published by Kazemzadeh, but also the other key nationalist periodical produced in Berlin between 1916 and 1919, *Kaveh*. While much has been written about *Kaveh*, its connection to the Paris-based *Iranshahr*—as its most important periodical precursor—has generally been overlooked. Purdavud's own efforts would extend to both newspapers, but it was as early as 1912, soon after the establishment of the Iranian Literary Society, that he began to conceive of the idea of publishing a newspaper in Paris.[81]

In a letter written on August 12, 1912, to Hasan Taqizadeh, the main activist and intellectual who was then organizing the Iranian constitutionalist and nationalist expatriate communities in Europe, and would become the future principal editor of *Kaveh*, Purdavud described the activities of the recently established Literary Society, including holding regular meetings and building alliances with other activist groups in the city. He then states, "In a recent conversation with Haydar Khan and Kazemzadeh we discussed the idea that we should establish a newspaper in Paris, in half-French and half-Persian."[82] He went on in the letter to consider the feasibility of such an enterprise in terms of printing expenses and the paper's potential readership. What convinced him that the newspaper would be a worthwhile project—despite the fact that, as he states, "we do not have the resources"[83]—was the newspaper's potential to make the case for Iran's political independence to the French-reading political class of Paris. In particular, Purdavud mentions the International League for Defending the Rights of People (Ligue internationale pour la défense du droit des peoples), a political solidarity organization that Madame Cama also supported.[84] The League's mission was to organize proto-nationalist movements, and other progressive forces in Europe, in support of social justice, anti-imperialism, and political independence in Asia and Africa. Purdavud and his Iranian colleagues in Paris had already started to attend meetings of the League.[85] His hope for *Iranshahr* was that it would raise the profile of the Iranian nationalist movement within the platform and agenda of the League, especially during a time when Russian imperial designs on northern Iran seemed increasingly ominous. As he conveyed to the then Istanbul-based Taqizadeh, the publication of *Iranshahr* "would reach the most important people in Europe. We must strive to make sure that news always and consistently reaches the League. . . . All of this, however, depends on your esteemed good offices."[86] Purdavud then inquired about the possibility of finding financial supporters to help launch the newspaper, analogous to the help received from Iranian donors in the merchant community of Istanbul associated with the Anjoman-e Saʿadat (The Society of Felicity) who were then supporting the constitutional movement.[87] As the de facto political leader of the expatriate dissident

Iranians, Taqizadeh would have been in a position to muster resources for such an endeavor.

The result of this effort was the short-lived publication of Purdavud's *Iranshahr* between April and June of 1914. The newspaper's title is another indication of Purdavud's growing fixation with Iran's pre-Islamic history as the cultural basis for modern Iranian nationalism. The term was originally used in late antique Pahlavi sources to refer to the greater territorial domains of the Sassanian imperium. By the early twentieth century it had also become the subject of important orientalist scholarship. The term is most commonly associated with the descriptive Pahlavi text *Shahrestanha-ye Iranshahr* (*The Cities of Iranshahr*), which—like the *Dasatir*—was gaining new readers in the late nineteenth and early twentieth centuries among those Iranians who were looking for textual threads to forge an Iranian national identity defined by neoclassicism. Additionally, *Iranshahr* was also the title of a monumental historical and geographical survey of Sassanian Iran published in 1901 by the German orientalist Josef Markwart (1864–1930).[88] Purdavud referred to Markwart as his most important European scholarly influence: "his [Markwart's] knowledge and understanding was extraordinary and make Markwart an unrivaled and most significant orientalist in the field of Iranian studies."[89] Purdavud went on to work with Markwart in Berlin between 1916 and 1924, and maintained a correspondence with him until Markwart's death in 1930. Given the pace of Purdavud's reading during his years in Paris and the importance that he places on Markwart's influence on his own intellectual development, it is likely that Purdavud was already aware of Markwart's *Iranshahr* by the time he selected the term for the title of the Iranian Literary Society of Paris's newspaper.[90]

It is not entirely clear where the money and logistical support for *Iranshahr* ultimately came from. Purdavud's inquiry to Taqizadeh for financial support from the Iranian merchant community in Istanbul may have borne fruit. The historian Nassredin Parvin suggests that the French Foreign Ministry may have also seen some benefit in sponsoring a journal such as *Iranshahr*.[91] Wherever the resources came from, Purdavud's request to Taqizadeh suggests that the search for financial backing in support of their political and cultural efforts was never far removed from their concerns. In the end, modest sums were procured to publish what became the short-lived Persian and French bilingual newspaper that combined an Iranian nationalist perspective on international relations on the eve of the First World War with literary and historical content about Iran. It is noteworthy that the newspaper also gives some additional details relating to the cooperation between Iranian expatriate nationalists in Paris and French intellectuals and activists who were also involved in the work of the Literary Society.

In the inaugural issue of the journal there is a printed calendar that lists the dates of meetings along with the names of speakers and topics presented at the meetings of the Society from early 1912 to the publication of *Iranshahr*'s first issue.[92] As the unsigned editorial—most likely penned by Purdavud—states, "at the beginning the talks were exclusively in Persian," but that changed when "several of our French friends" also wished to attend the meetings.[93] As a result, the meetings—like the journal itself—sought to become bilingual. Lucien Bouvat (1872–1942), the French historian of the Mongol and Timurid periods, for example, is listed on the calendar as giving a talk to the Society. M. Paul Cassanova (1861–1926), another French historian and anthropologist, also gave a talk titled "Arabes et Persans aux premiere siècles de l'hégire." Contemporary topics were also covered at the meetings and in the pages of the journal, such as an article by Marylie Markovitch (1866–1926), a French progressive and suffragette activist who regularly commented and wrote on the politics of Russia and Iran. Her contribution was titled "L'émancipation de la femme Persane." The topics presented in Persian likewise covered a broad range of topics, from a farsighted article by Musa Cheybani on reforming the land tax system in Iran to an article by Purdavud on Ferdowsi's life and work. Purdavud's original poetry was also a major component of the society's meetings as well as the Persian section of *Iranshahr*. Hossein Kazemzadeh is also well represented in the journal, with several talks listed covering topics relating to ancient Iran. One such talk by Kazemzadeh, divided into two parts, titled "I: Etude historique sur l'espirit iranien avant la conquète arabe; and II: Etude historique sur l'espirit Iranian après la conquète arabe," was a herald of the central theme of much Iranian nationalist thought that was then steadily fermenting among the expatriate intellectuals in Paris and elsewhere in Europe.[94] Purdavud himself devoted his efforts to organizing the meetings of the Society and editing the newspaper. His other contributions, despite his talk on Ferdowsi, were limited to his poetic contributions. Although he steeped himself in the study of pre-Islamic Iran and Zoroastrian studies during his years in Paris, Purdavud still considered himself to be primarily a poet and, increasingly, an activist.

It would take more years of study, until the early 1920s, and relocating from Paris to Berlin for Purdavud to begin making the transition from constitutional-era poet and activist to scholar and translator of Zoroastrian literature.

MISSION TO BAGHDAD

Iranshahr's Paris print run was cut short by the outbreak of World War I. Shortly after the publication of the June 1914 issue of the newspaper, the assassination of the Austrian Archduke Ferdinand in Sarajevo set in motion a series of events leading to war between the European powers. From the vantage point of the expatriate Iranian community, the conflict meant that the political status of Iran would now become even more precarious. In the midst of the rapidly unfolding events in the spring, summer, and fall of 1914, the de facto leader of the Iranian expatriates in Europe—Hasan Taqizadeh—quickly began to forge alliances with potential political allies and rallied the resources of like-minded Iranians. Purdavud—along with a cohort of other young Iranian students, intellectuals, and activists—was among the first to be recruited by Taqizadeh to form the newly established "Iranian National Committee."[95]

Taqizadeh had already traveled to New York City eighteen months earlier in anticipation of the beginning of the war and found the neutral ground of the United States to be a useful base from which to find a broader network of allies and resources to help secure the work of the national committee. His contacts in the summer and fall of 1914 with the well-organized Indian independence movement based in the United States, including associates of the revolutionary Ghadar Party, led to additional contacts with German Foreign Ministry officials in New York City.[96] On the eve of World War I, the German government had established a well-organized campaign to recruit anti-British and anti-Russian activists from throughout the Middle East and Central and South Asia in the hopes of stirring up internal unrest within the British and Russian empires. The German organization established for this purpose—the German Foreign Ministry's "Information Bureau of the East"—was particularly focused on promoting nationalist newspapers, written in vernacular languages, which would circulate among local communities inside Iran and India.[97] This German plan, which was the mastermind of the German orientalist Max von Oppenheimer, was also exceptionally well-funded; as Taqizadeh recalled in his memoir of this time, "the Germans freely gave money."[98] In his memoir, Taqizadeh also described meeting with Oppenheimer in Berlin in January of 1915 after being sent to the German capital by his Foreign Ministry contacts in New York City. Also at the Berlin meeting was Friedrich von Pourtalès, the German ambassador to Russia and another of the principal planners of the German strategy to foment internal rebellion in India, Iran, and Central Asia.[99]

The result of Taqizadeh's meetings with the Germans was the decision to establish a base of operations for the Iranian National Committee in the Charlottenburg neighborhood of Berlin, not far from the headquarters of Oppenheimer's Information Bureau of the East. From this base, the committee began publishing the pro-German Iranian nationalist newspaper *Kaveh* in January of 1916. The Germans provided the committee with a monthly stipend as well as access to the exceptionally well-engineered "Kaviani" printing press from which both *Kaveh* and a host of other Persian-language books, pamphlets, journals, and newspapers would be produced in Berlin over the course of the next decade. In addition to the publication of *Kaveh*, the committee's other mission in 1915 was to dispatch teams of agents to the contested regions of the war zone—both inside and adjacent to Iran—with the goal of producing and disseminating additional war propaganda.

The first team dispatched by Taqizadeh and the National Committee was sent to Baghdad, where it was led by Ebrahim Purdavud. Like the other members of the committee, Purdavud had received an invitation to join Taqizadeh in Berlin. Upon receiving the invitation, he traveled from Paris to the German capital sometime in February or early March of 1915, staying briefly in the city before embarking on his mission to Baghdad in the early spring. The clandestine journey took Purdavud from Berlin through Austria, Romania, and Bulgaria to Istanbul and Aleppo, followed by an eighteen-day riverboat journey down the Euphrates to Fallujah, and ultimately to Baghdad.[100]

By August of 1915, Purdavud and the members of his approximately ten-member team—which also included Mohammad-Ali Jamalzadeh— had successfully ensconced themselves in the Kazemin neighborhood of Baghdad. The predominantly Shi'ite neighborhood with a large Persian-speaking population had already earned a reputation as a center of anti-British resistance during the early stages of the war.[101] From Kazemin, Purdavud and his colleagues began to publish *Rastakhiz* (Resurrection) as a Persian-language newspaper advocating for the maintenance of Iran's independence and characterized by a strong Iranian nationalist

tone.[102] The newspaper circulated among the Persian-speaking populations of Baghdad and the Ottoman-Iranian borderland region. It also
consciously reflected many of the pre-Islamic themes that were becoming increasingly central in Purdavud's writing. In addition to rallying
against the Russian and British threats to Iran's independence and
extolling Iranians to defend their homeland, Purdavud invoked the historical memory of ancient Iran. In one poem published in *Rastakhiz* in
the fall of 1915, he wrote:

> This land of ours in ancient times, had a nation free and
>   famous
> Through the might of the arms of the valiant heroes
> Awake, Awake, O Iranians.

> Bring back to your mind those ancient days
> Bring back to your mind the glory of your armies
> Bring back to your mind your world-famous emperors
> Awake, Awake, O Iranians.

> Where indeed are your Jamsheed, Sam, and Zab? Tahmuras
>   and Darab?
> Where is Eraj, the Peshdadian of yore?
> Awake, Awake, O Iranians.

> Where is Cyrus and where is Cambyses?
> Where is the Great Ardeshir and his glory?
> Where is Kaikhosraw, the Great Kayanian?
> Awake, Awake, O Iranians . . .

> We are asleep, alas!
> And the enemy is ready to attack us with eyes and heart full
>   of hatred and greed
> Beware of Ahrimans.
> Awake, Awake, O Iranians.

> The ugly evil-natured Russian bear, without the slightest
>   excuse
> Thinks that Gilan, Azerbaijan are all its own
> Awake, Awake, O Iranians.

Now is the time to fight and give battle
The trumpet of Resurrection is blown
Rise with the cry of battle, ye old and young
Awake, Awake, O Iranians[103]

Approximately twenty-five issues of *Rastakhiz* reflecting these themes of political resistance and nationalist renaissance were published between August of 1915 and April of 1916.[104] Mohammad-Ali Jamalzadeh, one of Purdavud's earliest friends from their days in Beirut as well as a fellow member of the National Committee's mission to Baghdad, later wrote about the great effort that Purdavud put into *Rastakhiz*: "he sweated and labored, and wrote articles, and took them to the printer, and would correct the errors, and would do hundreds of other things with great skill and enthusiasm."[105]

The efforts of Purdavud and his team to publish *Rastakhiz* were interrupted on several occasions by the shifting fortunes of the war. The British advance from the south toward Baghdad in the fall of 1915 forced Purdavud to move his operation to the Iranian city of Kermanshah, where he continued to publish *Rastakhiz* during the fall and winter.[106] As the Russians next advanced toward Kermanshah from the north, he was forced to flee once again, this time moving his team to the more remote Kurdish-speaking ancient town of Qasr-e Shirin.[107] Following the Ottoman army's successful siege of the British forces in the city of Kut in the early part of 1916, Purdavud was able to return with his team to Baghdad and resume publication of *Rastakhiz*.[108]

Despite the temporary Ottoman victory at the Battle of Kut and Purdavud's ability to return to Baghdad to resume publishing *Rastakhiz*, the Ottoman authorities now began to exert pressure on Purdavud to modify the editorial tone of the newspaper. The Ottoman-German strategy of defeating the Allies had come to focus on appealing to a Pan-Islamic solidarity to unify the Sunni and Shi'ite worlds against the Russian and British empires. This so-called *jihadist* strategy had been conceived as early as 1914 and had become a major component of the Ottoman-German plan for victory in the Middle East and Central and South Asia.[109] After reasserting their control over Baghdad, the Ottoman authorities realized that Purdavud's *Rastakhiz* had diverted from the Pan-Islamist editorial content and was instead pursuing a much narrower Iranian nationalist editorial policy grounded in a language intended to revive—or resurrect—Iran's pre-Islamic cultural memory.

As a result, the Ottoman authorities gave Purdavud an ultimatum to either alter the content of *Rastakhiz* to conform to the Pan-Islamist rhetoric or cease publication. As Purdavud recalled some years later, the decision was an easy one to make: "The Turks no longer gave me permission to publish *Rastakhiz* because I refused to support Islamic unity, which was nothing more than a trap based on illusions."[110]

The abrupt end of *Rastakhiz* in April of 1916 also marked an important turning point in Purdavud's own personal evolution. The experience of his mission to Baghdad had helped to ally his political commitment to the cause of Iran's independence, and to a nascent ideology of Iranian nationalism grounded in an invocation of pre-Islamic cultural memory. The Ottoman-German *jihad* strategy now caused him great disappointment and became the source of his disillusionment with conventional politics. As he wrote, after this "bitter experience, I realized that the Germans had deceived us, and that there was no hope of real help from them, and that they only wanted to handle us Iranians as tools to carry out their own plans."[111] It seems likely that one result of Purdavud's experience during his mission to Baghdad, and his consequent disillusionment with the war effort, was to turn away from conventional politics and instead begin a period during which he redoubled his commitment to his studies of Zoroastrianism and pre-Islamic Iranian history. After some additional months in Baghdad and Istanbul, he managed to return to Berlin in the fall of 1916 and rejoin his comrades of the Iranian National Committee. He also began his total commitment to the study of the languages, history, and religion of pre-Islamic Iran.

THE BERLIN YEARS

Purdavud's relocation to Berlin began the next and most intellectually productive phase of his life. From 1916, when he managed to make his way to Berlin from Baghdad—while the war was still at a critical stage—until 1938 when he would permanently repatriate himself and his family to Iran, Purdavud came to live, work, study, and write in the German capital alongside his fellow Berliners. Despite an important three-year interlude between 1924 and 1927, and another between 1933 and 1934, when he would travel to India to study with Parsi scholars, Purdavud lived in Berlin during the tumultuous years of the German defeat in 1918, the rise and fall of the Weimar Republic, the takeover of the German state by the Nazi Party, and the subsequent approach of another European war.

Upon his arrival in Berlin, Purdavud's initial effort was to rejoin his comrades in the National Committee and to help in the publication of *Kaveh*, which had commenced during the time of Purdavud's mission to Baghdad and grown to become the major preoccupation of the National Committee. The newspaper was published in two stages. During the war years of 1916 to 1918, it combined pro-German political coverage of the war with more substantive historical and literary articles focusing on Iranian culture. In this initial stage of its publication, *Kaveh*'s editorial team received technical assistance and a monthly stipend from the German government to produce the newspaper. A second, "new series" (*dowreh-ye jadid*) of *Kaveh* began in 1919. With the war ended, the Germans terminated the paper's subsidy but bequeathed the "Kaviani" press on which *Kaveh* had been produced to the members of the National Committee. The committee, led by Taqizadeh, tried to continue *Kaveh* through financial support from sales and subscriptions of the newspaper. By the early part of 1922, for both logistical and financial reasons, the newspaper ceased publication.[112]

Purdavud's contributions to *Kaveh* between 1916 and 1922 are not specifically delineated. Neither his given name nor his pen name of "*gol*" (flower) that he had periodically used in his poetic writings appear in the pages of *Kaveh*.[113] The most important editorials and substantive articles of the periodical were written by Taqizadeh, but these were either unsigned, or signed with Taqizadeh's pen-name of "*mohasel*" (student). Other articles that were either extracted or serialized literary works—such as Mohammad-Ali Jamalzadeh's famous "*farsi shekar ast*" (Persian is sugar)—did on occasion carry an authorial appellation. In most cases, however, the articles in *Kaveh* were unsigned and unattributed. The lack of designated authorship may have reflected the collective efforts of the editorial team in producing the individual articles. The offices of *Kaveh*, at 64 Leibnizstrasse in the Charlottenburg district of central Berlin, had in fact quickly evolved to become a gathering place for the expatriate intellectuals of the National Committee. The site became an intellectual clubhouse where figures such as Taqizadeh, Qazvini, Jamalzadeh, Purdavud, and others—including visiting German orientalists—shared, discussed, debated, and collectively produced a concentrated and staggering amount of scholarship on Iran's history and culture during the short period of the newspaper's life.[114]

Purdavud was an active participant in this collective effort. At this stage in his intellectual development, Taqizadeh and Qazvini remained his scholarly elders. Purdavud's Berlin years, however, represented a period of rapid intellectual growth, and in the fields of Zoroastrian studies and Sassanian history his range and depth of knowledge quickly surpassed that of any of his Iranian contemporaries. With the help of the small monthly subsidy provided by the German government, Purdavud was now able to fully devote himself to the study of pre-Islamic Iran. In a manner similar to what Mohammad Qazvini had done in Paris at the Bibliothèque Nationale, Purdavud now became a fixture at the libraries, universities, and museums of Berlin. He spent considerable time at the University of Berlin, as well as at the Berlin State Library (Staatsbibliothek zu Berlin), the Kaiser Friedrich Museum (Bode Museum), and Berlin's Pergamon Museum of Antiquities.[115] He also became closely associated with a number of senior scholars in the tradition of German orientalist scholarship on ancient Iran. Although never formally enrolled in a doctoral program at the University of Berlin, he was able to build a number of important and enduring personal and professional relationships with faculty there.

By his own account, the most important German scholarly figure who informally helped to direct his intellectual efforts during this period was Josef Markwart.[116] While still in Paris, Purdavud had already encountered Markwart's monumental work, the *Eranshahr* (1901), a historical and geographic account of "greater Iran" during the Sassanian period. Markwart had settled into a faculty position as professor of Iranian and Armenian philology at the Humboldt University of Berlin in 1912, where he remained until the end of his life in 1930. Markwart was aware of and supported the work of the Iranian National Committee, and it was through this means that he and Purdavud began their friendship and collaboration.[117] Some years later when writing the introduction to his second volume of translations and commentary on the *Yashts*, published in 1931, Purdavud acknowledged the intellectual debt that he owed to Markwart. He wrote, "All orientalists and Iranians owe this great scholar a debt, especially myself, since Markwart was a great help to me during the course of writing this book [*Yashtha*]. Many times, I had difficulties that were solved by discussions with him."[118]

Markwart's scholarship was also deeply imbued with many of the prevailing assumptions of nineteenth- and early twentieth-century orientalism and nationalism. Among those assumptions was a racialized understanding of ancient and medieval history and a particularly visceral dislike for Arabs and Turks. According to Purdavud,

Josef Markwart (1864–1930). Wikimedia Commons.

Markwart—whom he describes as "a friend of Iran" and compares to E. G. Browne in that regard—believed that Arab and Turkish influence had "brought calamity to Iranian civilization."[119] Markwart's scholarship, however, went beyond trite expressions of the casual racialism that was endemic to a broad range of orientalist scholarship of the era; there was, in fact, nothing sterile or pedantic about his orientalism. Markwart's close engagement with Purdavud and his association with the Iranian National Committee in Berlin allowed his work to serve as a template for transforming the raw scholarship of German orientalism into the more refined ideology of Iranian proto-nationalism. As Purdavud was clear to point out, Markwart's ideas were prescriptive: "He wanted the entirety of ancient Iran to once again be part of Iran's dominion, and for Iranians to revert to the ways of their forefathers and ancestors."[120] In the area of reviving Iranian national memory, Markwart's advocacy of an Iranian neoclassical revival can be described as not only prescriptive, but also prophetic; Purdavud writes, "He hoped that the tomb of Cyrus would become a place of pilgrimage for Iranians."[121] Similarly, Markwart was also among the first to advocate for replacing the Islamic Hijri calendar with an Iranian "national" one. Markwart's ideas also extended to Iran's language policy. Purdavud recalled Markwart's advocacy that "the Persian language should be rid of foreign words, and the Arab script should be replaced with the Avestan alphabet."[122] In this regard Markwart's influence was also decisive for Purdavud, who in later years would for a time be one of the most vocal Iranian advocates for the "purification" of the Persian language.[123]

Purdavud's years in Berlin also led him to cross paths with a host of other scholars specializing in Iranian and Islamic history. His reading in early Islamic history, for example, was informed by the work of the German Arabist Joseph Hell (1875–1950). Hell's 1909 work, *Die Kulter der Araber*, was a concise and synthetic treatment of early Islamic history, and served as a useful primer for Purdavud's rapidly expanding historiographic knowledge.[124] Purdavud also crossed paths with the important German-Jewish medievalist Eugen Mittwoch (1876–1942). Mittwoch had been an associate of Max Oppenheimer and had, like Purdavud, worked with the German Information Bureau of the East during World War I. With the ascendency of the Nazi Party in Germany, Mittwoch managed to retain his academic position—despite his Jewish background—as late as 1938, before immigrating to London on the eve of the Second World War. Wittwoch had also spent time in Palestine and was one of the founders of the Department of Semitic Studies at the Hebrew University of Jerusalem.[125] Purdavud's Berlin associates also included another German-Jewish scholar who would become a victim of the Nazi rise to power, the great scholar of Persian literature Fritz Wolff (1880–1944). Before perishing in the Holocaust, Wolff—who had been a scholar of Sanskrit and Avestan, as well as of New Persian literature—had made extensive use of Christian Bartholomae's (1855–1925) pioneering lexigraphical work, the *Altiranischer Wörterbuch* (1904), to produce his own German translation of the *Avesta* in 1910. Wolff's German translation of the main corpus of Avestan texts, like Bartholomae's German translation of the *Gatha* and James Darmesteter's three-volume French translations of 1892–1893, came to serve as the most immediate orientalist models for what became Purdavud's own work of bringing a translation and commentary of the *Avesta* into the modern Persian intellectual and literary tradition.[126] Other scholars in Berlin with whom Purdavud worked, studied, and built personal relationships included the pioneering German scholar of cuneiform tablets Carl Frank (1881–1945), the philologist and scholar of Manichaean and Zoroastrian studies Hans Heinrich Schraeder (1896–1957), and the Kurdish and Persian linguist Oskar Mann (1867–1917).[127] Mann, in particular, worked closely with the Iranian National Committee during its first year in Berlin and is credited with authoring the article in *Kaveh* detailing the legend of Kaveh's flag (Derafsh-e Kavianeh) as told in the *Shahnameh*.[128]

The mix of scholarly influences that Purdavud encountered in Berlin made his time in the city one of the most personally transformative and intellectually productive periods of his life. By the early 1920s he had largely set aside his earlier life as a poet and activist and instead settled into the more serious and mature life of an independent scholar. Although his German subsidy had been terminated, he managed to support his continuing studies of Zoroastrianism and ancient Iranian history through funds that he now regularly received from his family's estate in Iran. Also contributing to his newfound personal stability was his marriage in 1920 to Erna Haase, a German woman from Stettin, a port city on the Baltic Sea in the German-Polish border region.[129] By 1922 the young family had grown to include a daughter, Purandokht.[130] In addition to support from his parents' estate, the young Purdavud family also received financial support from Erna's father, a prominent doctor and property owner in Stettin.[131] This newfound domestic and financial stability—combined with the intellectually creative environment of Weimar Berlin—enabled Purdavud to make rapid progress as a scholar. In late 1922 he published the first of what became a remarkably prolific series of essays, translations, and commentaries on the corpus of Zoroastrian literature.

Purdavud's first publication reflecting the growing breadth of his intellectual influences as well as the depth of his newfound historical knowledge appeared in the Berlin-based journal *Iranshahr*. The journal was edited by Hossein Kazemzadeh, who had known Purdavud from their time together in prewar Paris. Along with Mohammad Qazvini, Kazemzadeh and Purdavud had organized the "Persian Literary Society of Paris" between 1910 and 1914, and had similarly worked together to publish the short-lived Paris edition of *Iranshahr* between April and June of 1914. After spending a number of years working with E. G. Browne as a research assistant and instructor of Persian at Cambridge University, Kazemzadeh, like many other Iranian expatriate nationalists, had settled in Berlin by 1922 and begun a career as a bookseller and publisher.[132] The bookstore that Kazemzadeh founded, also called "Iranshahr," became a meeting place for intellectually engaged Iranians as well as the most successful bookseller, publisher, and distributor of Persian books in Europe. Kazemzadeh also used the offices of the bookstore as the head-quarters for the Berlin-based edition of *Iranshahr*. The biweekly jour-nal remained in publication from 1922 until 1927 and circulated widely among Persian readers in Europe, Iran, India, and the United States.[133] In many respects, *Iranshahr* was the successor to *Kaveh* and continued the mission of producing a Persian-language periodical in Berlin that kept abreast of the most recent findings of orientalist knowledge while also advocating for the cause of Iran's cultural and political revival.

Purdavud published two articles in Kazemzadeh's *Iranshahr*. The first appeared in the October 25, 1922, issue of the journal (vol. 1, no. 5) and the second in the June 15, 1923, issue (vol. 1, no. 12). Both articles reflected the impressive range of Purdavud's reading over the course of his several years in Berlin. The first of the articles, "The Letter of Yazdegerd II to the Christian Armenians,"[134] gives a detailed account of one of the lesser-known episodes in the history of the religious wars of late antiquity. The status of Armenia and the role of Zoroastrianism in Sassanian imperial ideology had been one of the contested issues dividing the Byzantine and Sassanian empires during the fourth and fifth centuries CE. Purdavud's assessment of Yazdegerd's efforts to assert Zoroastrianism in Armenia, and the Armenian resistance to these efforts, displays an impressive command of sources drawn from Greek and Armenian historiography, including the fourth- and fifth-century writings of Bishop Theodoretus of Cyrrhus, Lazar of Pharp, and the Armenian historian Elisaeus.[135] By the nineteenth century these sources had been translated into French, German, and English and were readily available to Purdavud in Berlin. In addition to giving some historio-graphic background to the status of Armenia in the Perso-Byzantine wars, Purdavud also provides a Persian translation of the letter writ-ten by Yazdegerd to the Armenians. As Purdavud explains, the text of Yazdegerd's letter was derived from the histories of Elisaeus and Lazar, which he then translated into Persian from the available German and English editions of the Armenian version.[136]

The resulting article is an impressive debut for what became Purdavud's long and prolific career of producing Persian-language translations and scholarship on pre-Islamic Iran for an audience of lay readers with modern Iranian nationalist sensibilities. Kazemzadeh himself underscored this fact when he included an unconventional editorial preface to Purdavud's article. In a preface to Purdavud's October 25, 1922, article, Kazemzadeh seemed to take some pride in introducing Purdavud to the readers of *Iranshahr*. He wrote:

> The following article was written by Mr. Purdavud, who is a studious, serious, and brilliant young man who for some time has been living in Berlin, and studying and researching the history, language, and civilization of ancient Iran.[137]

Kazemzadeh went on to ask his readers to pay particular attention to Purdavud's prose style, which he described as "simple and sweet" and "to the extent possible is devoid of Arabic vocabulary."[138] Kazemzadeh's introduction worked to define how Purdavud would come to be perceived throughout his career. From this 1922 publication debut, Purdavud became defined as a scholar of ancient Iran whose primary intellectual mission was a public one of reviving Iranian national identity through his use of language and his contributions to popularizing a nationalist version of pre-Islamic Iranian history.

The second of the two articles, published by Purdavud in the June 15, 1923, issue of *Iranshahr*, was a religious and historical examination of the sixth-century CE Zoroastrian apocalyptic text known as the *Bahman Yasht*.[139] The extant Pahlavi text contains a dialogue between Ahuramazda and Zoroaster as well as a series of prophesies describing the great calamities—and ultimate redemption—that Iranian civilization would experience over the course of several millennia. The text had already become the subject of modern scholarship, both within the European orientalist tradition and among reformist Parsi scholars in India.[140] Purdavud's assessment of this text begins by considering its historicity, such as the possibility that the tenth-century Pahlavi text may have a genealogy descending back to a now lost Avestan original that was part of an earlier corpus of Zoroastrian literature. In this respect, Purdavud was following the argument of modern orientalist and Parsi scholarship on the historicity of the *Bahman Yasht*. Without citing a specific source, Purdavud conveys to his readers that "the Parsis are of the opinion that in the past, each of the Ameshaspands had their own *yasht*, which have now been lost from the remaining portions of the Avesta."[141] He then discusses fragments of texts that, he speculates, give partial accounts of the Ameshaspands, such as the *yashts* describing the divine attributes of Ardibehesht and Khordad. Purdavud then concludes by saying, "Of the existence of the *Bahman Yasht*, we can say that the views of the Parsis is correct, and that other Ameshaspands . . . also exist."[142] Purdavud's assessment of the *Bahman Yasht*'s historicity is speculative, but nevertheless still remains within the parameters of orientalist and Parsi scholarship.

Purdavud, however, goes on to consider even bolder implications regarding the meaning and significance of the *Bahman Yasht*. Beyond tracing its historicity and textual genealogy, Purdavud reads the text as a genuinely apocalyptic document whose historical prophesies of Iran's fall have in fact already come to pass. As he writes—for his audience of Iranian readers—the topics discussed in the *Bahman Yasht* "are the prophesies (*pīshgū'ī*) which Ahuramazda conveyed to his prophet Zoroaster."[143] These prophesies, Purdavud argues, have striking parallels to the existing historical record of Iran's evolution in the late antique and medieval periods. He continues, "One of these prophesies very clearly reminds one of the tumult of the Mongols, which came to pass six hundred years after the writing of the *Bahman Yasht*."[144] Purdavud goes on to describe the great destruction caused by the Mongol conquest and states, "Yes, that which the *Bahman Yasht* prophesied came to pass. The dark devils of the Mongol race inflicted such harm to Iran that it would come as no surprise that Iran will not be able rise up and regain its consciousness until the day of resurrection."[145] In taking the prophesies of the *Bahman Yasht* seriously, Purdavud's hermeneutical approach to the text moves beyond the conventions of traditional orientalist science. For Purdavud, the *Bahman Yasht* was not a text meant to be understood merely within the conventions of modern historicism. Rather, for Purdavud, the corpus of Zoroastrian scripture was understood as part of the living tradition of Zoroastrianism's mytho-religious imagination. His determination to read the *Bahman Yasht* on its own terms, in order to extract its *truth* for a broader understanding of Iranian history, moves Purdavud's hermeneutical method beyond the tradition of orientalism and brings his approach to the text to one combining a premodern mytho-religious consciousness with modern nationalist ideology. His earlier attempt—while still a young man in Beirut in 1908—to approach the *Dasatir* in this same way proved, by his own account, to have failed.

Fifteen years later, however—now in 1923—the intellectual tools at his command had matured, and from this point onward he remained committed to using his growing knowledge of the Zoroastrian tradition, as well as the methods of modern orientalism and Parsi scholarship, to help shape the ongoing revival of Iranian national identity.

We see this again in the way Purdavud assesses the implications of the Arab-Muslim conquest of Iran. In the *Bahman Yasht* article, Purdavud spends considerable time detailing a broader outline of a nationalist narrative of Iranian history that places great importance on not only the thirteenth-century Mongol conquest but also the seventh-century fall of the Sassanian Empire. This narrative, which had already taken its essential form during the course of the nineteenth century—and which had begun the project of contesting the Islamicate notion of pre-Islamic *jahaliyya*—saw the fall of the Sassanian Empire as the end of a classical "golden age" of Iranian civilization and the beginning of a long period of decline. In expanding on this narrative, Purdavud fully embraced what was then the increasingly common Iranian nationalist tone of derision when referring to the Arab conquerors of Iran. The "bare-footed"[146] Arabs, whom he also describes as "savages" (*vahshi*), came to Iran and "consumed the kingdom."[147] The result of this calamity, according to Purdavud, was that "Iran became one of the provinces of the caliphate . . . and desperation spread throughout the fertile Iranian soil."[148] He then laments the loss of the Pahlavi language and the increasing spread of Arab manners and mores throughout the lands of the Iranian plateau following its absorption into the Islamic Caliphate: "these two centuries [following the Arab-Muslim conquest]," he states, "can be described as the darkest days in our history."[149]

Purdavud's tone of derision toward the Arabs and Islamic civilization may sound trite from the vantage point of almost a century in which the Pahlavi dynasty adopted this narrative as Iran's official nationalism. Within the immediate context of his time, however, there was nothing stale, tedious, or belabored about Purdavud's pronouncements. To the contrary, in the context of the early twentieth century, his reassessment of Iranian history could be described as iconoclastic. Purdavud's radical assessment of the fall of the Sassanian Empire, like his comments on the Mongol conquest, was novel in its competent straddling of the hermeneutical divide between the "science" of orientalism and the ideology of nationalism. His critique of the Arab-Muslim conquest of Iran was not merely the result of a callous or base ethnocentrism. His writing—more so than that of any of his Iranian contemporaries—was deeply engaged with both the scholarly tradition of European orientalism and the mytho-religious imagination of Zoroastrianism. His radical judgments regarding Iran's history drew emphatically from both of these traditions. Purdavud's ultimate conclusion that the text of the *Bahman Yasht* represents a *true* prophecy that could be productively read to understand the course of Iran's history was in fact born of his stubborn refusal to merely order, decode, and situate the *Bahman Yasht* within conventional orientalist textual taxonomies. His hermeneutical goal was to engage— but also to transcend—those conventions and to ultimately approach the text from the vantage point of its own truth-claims as they were understood by those within the tradition. For Purdavud and other nationalists of his generation, the truth-claims contained within these rediscovered texts transcended both ethnocentrism and orientalist "science" and ultimately bore the promise of utopian possibilities. Purdavud's reading of the *Bahman Yasht*, like the approach that will be represented in all of his subsequent Persian-language writing, was revolutionary in this regard.

INVITATION TO BOMBAY

Purdavud's first published articles are important for more than their demonstrations of textual, hermeneutical, or methodological dexterity. They also publicized the arrival of a new Iranian nationalist intellectual with complete command of both modern European and classical languages as well as a deep understanding of the philological and historiographic tradition of European orientalism. In the early 1920s, Purdavud was still unique among Iranian intellectuals in possessing both of these sets of skills. While there were numerous Iranian intellectuals who could be described as dilettante orientalists with some knowledge of classical history and European languages, there were as yet none who had also acquired knowledge of Pahlavi and Avestan. Conversely, while there were substantial numbers of Parsis (and Europeans) who had acquired knowledge of Pahlavi and Avestan, there were few among them who could claim high proficiency in New Persian. Purdavud alone was proficient in Avestan and Pahlavi as well as the major European scholarly languages (French, German, and English), while also having native command of Persian. There was also one additional quality that made Purdavud unique: he was an accomplished poet of the Persian language, having written and published poetry since the immediate post-constitutionalist era.

These unique attributes made Purdavud ideally suited to embark on the project that would ultimately define his professional career and secure his posthumous reputation: the translation of the Zoroastrian corpus of religious literature into the idiom of the modern Persian language. The idea of making these texts available to readers of modern Persian had been conceived by Parsi scholars, activists, and benefactors going back to the time of Manekji Limji Hataria in the mid-nineteenth century. Some notable early achievements in this regard included an 1882 New Persian translation of the Zoroastrian book of common prayer, the *Khordeh Avesta*.[150] By the early twentieth century a Persian-language reformist literature regarding Zoroastrianism had also emerged that produced collections of short essays designed to introduce the Parsi modernist understanding of the Zoroastrian faith to Persian-language Iranian readers. The writing of Kaykhosrow Shahrokh, for example, as early as 1907 consisted of introductory essays on Zoroastrianism written in Persian and intended to define the faith in terms of its progressive qualities.[151] Ebrahim Purdavud had himself paid very close attention to these initial modernist Persian texts on Zoroastrianism. In Shahrokh's memoir, for example, he describes his association with Purdavud and recalls a meeting with him in Berlin after Purdavud had published his translations and commentary of the *Gathas*. Shahrokh, like Kazemzadeh before him, recalled with some pride:

> Mr. Purdavud, who has rendered a tremendous service in translating the Zoroastrian books, conveyed to me one day in Berlin, that the inspiration which led him to pursue and acquire his knowledge of the Zoroastrian faith . . . were my books.[152]

Others have also been suggested as possible inspirations for what became Purdavud's translation work. In his *Farzanegan-e Zartoshti* (1951), Iranian historian Rashid Shahmardan suggests that Ardashir Reporter was the person who initially conceived of the project of translating the Zoroastrian texts and who set out to find a suitable translator.[153] Kaykhosrow Shahrokh himself also claims to have had the requisite linguistic skills, and the intention, to translate the Zoroastrian texts into New Persian. He claims he was too consumed with his government work as a representative in the Majles, as well as his philanthropic work for the Iranian Zoroastrian community, to devote himself to this task.[154] The same can be said for Dinshah Irani, who was perhaps the most linguistically accomplished Indian Zoroastrian with command of Persian. The Bombay-based lawyer and civic leader's partial translations of the *Gathas* ultimately made their way only into English,[155] but his personal hope of seeing a Persian translation were realized, not through his own Persian translation, but through his collaboration with Purdavud. None of these earlier attempts to initiate a translation of the Zoroastrian texts into modern Persian gained much momentum. It was only when Ebrahim Purdavud's reputation began to circulate—following the publication of his two articles in *Iranshahr* in October of 1922 and June of 1923—that the goal of finding a translator with the requisite linguistic and scholarly skills became realized.

It was not long after the publication of these two articles that Purdavud was contacted by Parsi intermediaries and invited to Bombay for what became an extended period of collaboration with Parsi priests and scholars. The ultimate product of this collaboration became a series of translations into New Persian of the major Zoroastrian religious texts. These translations, along with extensive commentary, were sponsored by the Parsi philanthropist Peshotanji Marker and were published in what became known as the "Marker Avestan Series."[156] The first publication in this series was Purdavud's 1927 translation and commentary of the *Gathas*, with additional publications appearing until the outbreak of World War II. Despite Purdavud's unique set of linguistic skills, he had not previously expressed any intention of undertaking a translation project of this scale. His effort to begin this translation project in the mid-1920s was likely a product of the initiative and patronage of his newfound Parsi benefactors.

Purdavud in fact set out not for India, but for Iran in the spring of 1924. His travel back to Iran represented his first trip home since leaving for Beirut in 1907. Accompanied by his wife and daughter, he traveled from Berlin to Riga, Moscow, and Baku before arriving in Rasht.[157] For the next fourteen months, Purdavud visited family, friends, and collaborators in Rasht and Tehran and continued his studies in the Shemiran district north of the capital. It is unclear exactly at what point the Parsis contacted him to issue the invitation to travel to India. The invitation likely came while he was still in Berlin. Purdavud's reputation as a multilingual intellectual with a keen interest in Iran's pre-Islamic history and Zoroastrian heritage had already begun to circulate among Zoroastrians in Europe, Iran, and India. The suggestion that Purdavud would be an ideal candidate to undertake a translation project of this sort may have also come from Mohammad Qazvini. From his apartment in Paris, Qazvini maintained a wide-ranging correspondence with a broad network of scholars and intellectuals, including Dinshah Irani, the president of the Iran League and Iranian Zoroastrian Anjoman and the person who ultimately made the formal invitation for Purdauvd to travel to India.[158] The time that Purdavud spent in Tehran—between the summer of 1924 and the fall of 1925—may have also helped him to establish contacts with Iranian Zoroastrians living in the capital city who knew Parsis in Bombay. Both Kaykhosrow Shahrokh and Ardeshir Reporter were living and working in Tehran at this time, and both had already served as important intermediaries between Parsis and Iranians.[159] Dinshah Irani also made the first of his three visits to Iran sometime in 1924, and may have communicated with Reporter, Shahrokh, and perhaps even Purdavud about the translation project during this trip.[160] Like Qazvini, both Shahrokh and Reporter were also in intermittent contact with Dinshah Irani. Whatever the exact mechanism for the invitation, it was ultimately Dinshah Irani who issued the formal written invitation to sponsor Purdavud and his family's travel to India in 1925.[161]

PURDAVUD AND THE PARSI SCHOLARS

Purdavud set out for India in October of 1925, traveling by road and rail from Tehran to Baghdad, and then by riverboat to the port at Basra, where he and his family boarded a steamship to Bombay.[162] While these modalities of travel may seem cumbersome by later standards, the infrastructure of rail and steam-powered transportation had in fact progressed to the point that Purdavud's trip from Tehran to Bombay was accomplished in a relatively efficient span of several days. Upon his arrival in Bombay, Purdavud recorded his first impressions of his new surroundings and of his Parsi hosts, commenting on the "harsh air of India" that, he observed, "renders lifeless most of the people of that land."[163] Despite his stark initial reaction to the stifling environment, Purdavud also recorded that he immediately recognized something very familiar when he was greeted by his Parsi hosts. The Parsis, he quickly concluded, had preserved something essential of their pre-Islamic Iranian heritage. The centuries of displacement and exile, he observed, "had not been able to conquer the faith of the Avesta . . . and the strength of will, struggle, and perseverance of the believers who follow the commands of the Iranian

Purdavud arriving at port of Bombay, with Dinshah Irani, P. D. Marker, and others.
Iran League Quarterly, *Bombay, 1932.*

prophet has not weakened. . . . Amidst the Parsis, I recognized that the spirit of ancient Iran remains."[164]

Purdavud's principal host and guide during the course of his subsequent two-and-a-half-year sojourn in India was Dinshah Irani, the founding president of Bombay's Iran League and Iranian Zoroastrian Anjoman. Irani was a fluent speaker of Persian, and along with his Iranian assistant, Abdol-Hosayn Sepanta, was able to communicate with Purdavud in personal and informal terms.[165] By 1925 most of the Parsis of India, including members of the scholarly community, no longer used Persian as a vernacular language. Nevertheless, through the help of Irani, Sepanta, and others, Purdavud managed to cultivate associations, intellectual exchanges, and personal friendships with a large cohort of Parsi priests and scholars. Among those Purdavud subsequently acknowledged or who later wrote about him were such eminent Parsi figures of the reformist tradition of modern Zoroastrian studies as Jivanji Jamshedji Modi, Gushtaspshah Kaikhushro Nariman, Bahmanji Nasarvanji Dhabhar (1869–1952), Behramgore Tehmuras Anklesaria, Dhalla Maneckji Nusserwaji (1875–1956), Sohrab Jamshedji Bulsara

(1877–1945), Iraj Jahangir Sohrabji Taraporewalla (1884–1956), and numerous others.

Purdavud spent the next two and a half years immersed inside this community of Parsi priests and scholars. His Bombay sojourn can in this way be compared to his Berlin years in terms of how important that time was for shaping the direction of his subsequent work. In his later writings, Purdavud acknowledged the importance of his time in Bombay and was careful to recognize his Parsi collaborators. Of J. J. Modi, for example, Purdavud wrote in the introduction to his Persian translation of the *Yashtha* that "the famous Parsi scholar Dr. Jijanji Jamshidji Modi Shams al-Ulama always generously granted my requests for books that I needed . . . and arranged for approximately twenty volumes of fine books relating to Zoroastrianism, published by the Parsi Panchayet, to be gifted to me."[166] Purdavud also recognized the importance of G. K. Nariman, the independent-minded historian and linguistic polymath who did not always agree with the new historiographic orthodoxies of the Parsi modernist scholars.[167] Purdavud described Nariman as "a great man who has spent his entire life propagating knowledge."[168] He also noted the assistance he received from B. N. Dhabhar in the preparation of his translation of the *yashts* in parallel Avestan and Persian text. Dhabhar, Purdavud remembered, "carefully examined, with great scholarly precision, which is his characteristic, the entire Avestan text of this book [*Yashtha*, vol. 1]. He also examined the Persian section and informed me of some of my errors."[169]

Perhaps his closest scholarly collaboration in India—aside from his friend and host, Dinshah Irani—was with the Parsi scholar Bahramgore Tahmuras Anklesaria.[170] Like numerous other Parsi scholars and reformers of the era, Anklesaria had descended from a family of Parsi priests. His father, Tahmuras Dinshah Anklesaria (1843–1903), was one of the pioneering reformers of the Parsi priestly tradition. The younger Anklesaria followed his father's footsteps and became one of the most active and productive scholars of his generation, especially with respect to translating, editing, and publishing important Pahlavi texts. The Anklesaria family had also founded one of the most prolific publishing houses of Zoroastrian books in India. The Fort Printing Press was established by the elder Anklesaria in the nineteenth century, and by the 1920s and 1930s it was under the direction of Bahramgore and his brother Hushang.[171] Fort published all of Purdavud's Persian-language

Bahramgore Tahmuras Anklesaria (1873– 1944). Iran League Quarterly, *Bombay, 1931.*

translations of the Avestan literature as part of what became the Marker Avestan Series. The press also published many of Purdavud's other more general works that emerged out of his collaboration with Dinshah Irani and the Parsis between 1925 and 1939.[172] Anklesaria's collaboration with Iranian intellectuals extended beyond his association with Ebrahim Purdavud. The other key figure with whom Anklesaria served as an important Parsi interlocutor was the Iranian novelist and nationalist intellectual Sadeq Hedayat (1903–1951).[173] Anklesaria served as a teacher of Pahlavi to Hedayat during the latter's stay in Bombay between 1936 and 1937, assisting him in the translation and commentary of a number of Pahlavi texts.[174] Purdavud's own association with Anklesaria was so important that upon Anklesaria's death in 1944, Purdavud—who by then was living in Iran and had become a professor of Iranian Studies at the University of Tehran—arranged for a memorial service at the Parsi-founded Firuz Bahram High School in Tehran. Purdavud gave a eulogy for his former Parsi interlocator, which was later published in the Tehran-based journal *Sokhan,* in which he recalled,

During my first trip to India in October 1925, I became
acquainted and developed a friendship with Bahramgore
Anklesaria, and I greatly benefited from this relationship.
Even though his home was sixty kilometers south of Bombay,
in Santa Cruz, every day he would make the arduous effort
of taking the train, and would come to my residence so that I
could benefit from his presence.[175]

The relationships that Purdavud developed with Parsi scholars during
his first visit to India—like the one that he describes in his eulogy for
Anklesaria—left a lasting impression on him. These impressions were
not only of a personal kind but also helped Purdavud to gain a vivid
understanding of modern Zoroastrianism as a living tradition. His
experience as a student of ancient Iran during his years in Berlin had
not, by contrast, afforded him this same perspective.

In his later recounting of his associations and experiences during
his time in India, Purdavud described one experience that stood out for
him as a particularly meaningful and intimate encounter with Zoroastrianism. As he writes in his collection of essays published in the 1926
work *Khorramshah*, Purdavud was granted the rare opportunity to witness the Zoroastrian Yasna ceremony, which is the most sacred ritual of
the Zoroastrian faith.[176] It is performed daily by two to four priests in
the inner sanctum of a Zoroastrian fire temple and includes a recitation
of the Yasna liturgy and the performance of ritual acts by which, it was
understood, according to Mary Boyce, "the seven creations were sustained and blessed."[177] The Yasna ceremony is also considered a "closed
ritual" that only Zoroastrians may witness. In the more traditional practice of the faith, even the Zoroastrian laity are sometimes excluded from
its performance and instead contribute their tithe to sustain the work
of the priests in the ritual's regular observance.[178] In the history of the
faith there have only been four known exceptions to the prohibition of
non-Zoroastrian observance of the Yasna ceremony. These exceptions
include the German scholar Martin Haug (1827–1876), the French
scholar Delphine Menant (1850–?), the American scholar A. V. Jackson
(1862–1937), and Ebrahim Purdavud.[179]

Purdavud's opportunity to witness the Yasna ceremony came in
December of 1925 during his visit to the historic Atash Bahram fire
temple in the coastal Gujarat town of Udvada. The visit, like so many of
the rest of Purdavud's activities during his two-and-a-half-year visit to

The Zoroastrian fire temple in Udvada. National Geographic, *1905.*

Interior of Zoroastrian fire temple. National Geographic, *1905.*

India, was arranged by Dinshah Irani through contacts Irani had with the two Zoroastrian priests then administering the Udvada Atash Bahram.[180] Purdavud was well aware of how rare the opportunity to witness the Yasna ceremony was for a non-Zoroastrian. In his 1926 essay recounting the experience, he commented that very few others had been afforded this special honor, stating that "even the famous French orientalist Darmesteter, despite his long period of residence in India was unsuccessful in seeing it."[181] In recounting his observation of the ceremony, Purdavud was also aware that witnessing the living experience of Zoroastrianism added a new and much-desired dimension to his own understanding of the faith that went beyond the limited parameters afforded by orientalist science: "I witnessed here at the center of the Zoroastrian priesthood the thing which for many years I had read about in books, and which I was eager to see."[182] In describing the importance of witnessing the Yasna ceremony, Purdavud stated, "I became very pleased to hear the songs of the Avesta, whose rhymes and rhythms were uttered by the Iranian prophet Zarathustra."[183] Hearing these verses was more than an ethnographic exercise. As he described it, his participation in the ceremony clearly produced an emotional effect, which he was also careful to document: "during the one hour in which it took to complete the elements of the ceremony, the vicissitudes of Iran's past, from the era of Cyrus the Great to the dark day of Yazdegird III, one by one, passed before my eyes."[184] The exclusive invitation of witnessing the ceremony, combined with the emotional experience that he describes, reinforced the ultimate goal of Purdavud's visit to India, which was to cultivate a personal connection to a living tradition of Zoroastrianism. Experiencing this personal connection with the Parsi community of India, it was hoped, would inspire him in what was now his mission of bringing the Zoroastrian texts into an intelligible and vividly poetic idiom of the Persian language for an audience of modern Iranians.

PURDAVUD'S BOMBAY BOOKS

The first text that was published following Purdavud's experience of witnessing the Yasna ceremony was his 1926 book *Iranshah*, a short Persian-language pamphlet of approximately one hundred pages, named after the sacred fire of Atash Bahram at Udvada.[185] The slim volume was a general history intended for a broad audience of Iranian readers. It contained Purdavud's discussion of the Zoroastrian exodus from Iran following the seventh-century Arab-Muslim conquest of the plateau and the Zoroastrian migration to the coast of western India. By the 1920s, most Iranians were only beginning to learn of the Bombay-Parsi community's existence and had very little detailed knowledge of the history of Zoroastrianism or a feeling of shared history with the Parsis. Purdavud's *Iranshah* was therefore carefully selected as a suitable initial text that worked to introduce Parsis to the Iranians.

The text of Purdavud's *Iranshah* begins, suitably, with his dedication of the work "to my dear friend and scholar Mr. Dinshah Jijibhoy Irani."[186] Later in the text, Purdavud again shows his gratitude to Irani and the Bombay charitable groups that supported the social services, schools, and hospitals the Parsis had established in Kerman and Yazd since the mid-nineteenth century. He writes:

> In these last two centuries the Zoroastrian population [in Iran] has gone from one hundred thousand to nine thousand and maybe this nine thousand would have become nonexistent by now if no one had heard their screams and come to their aid ... two anjomans ... have been of great service to Iran. One is the Iran League ... and the other is known by the name of the Iranian Zoroastrian Anjoman under the leadership of Dinshah Irani.[187]

This would not be the last time that Purdavud acknowledged Irani and the Parsi charitable foundations. Purdavud and Irani in fact made occasional references to one another in their various writings. It is clear why Purdavud dedicated the text of the *Iranshah* to Irani; not only had Dinshah facilitated his travel to Bombay in the previous year and financially sponsored the publication of the pamphlet, but also the subject matter of the *Iranshah* echoed much of Purdavud and Irani's shared objective of reviving the historical memory of Indo-Iranian classicism.

The main narrative of Purdavud's *Iranshah* begins with what in the later twentieth century would seem a rather conventional Persian-language prose rendering of the Islamic conquest of Iran, describing the invasion of the Arab-Muslim armies, for example, in terms of a military conquest in which "the Kiyanid flag fell to the enemies."[188] The decisive Arab-Muslim victory at the 636 CE battle of Qadisiah is likewise described as "a dark day for the kingdom."[189] Purdavud's account of the immediate post-conquest history of Islamic Iran then emphasizes the movements of resistance on the part of Iranian Zoroastrians in the face of the Arab-Muslim conquerors, and the internal migrations to remote regions and mountainous zones within Iran in order for the Iranian Zoroastrians to find refuge and "preserve their ancient faith."[190] These internal migrations continued for a century, until, as Purdavud states,

> that time when this refuge also came into the clutches of the enemy and in desperation they [Iranian Zoroastrians] were forced to flee once again. A group of them found their way to the island of Hormuz on the Persian Gulf. Since even there the enemy would not grant them safety they were forced to say goodbye to Iran and their ancestral homeland and set out for India.[191]

Purdavud goes on to describe the sources that are used for narrating this history. Most importantly, he describes in some detail the *Qesseh-ye Sanjan*, the sixteenth-century Persian text written in India that is believed to be the first written account of the Zoroastrian exodus from Iran.[192] Purdavud is careful to closely evaluate the historicity of this text. He compares the account narrated in the *Qesseh-ye Sanjan* with details found in other sources describing the same period, such as the histories of Mas'udi and Tabari.[193] Purdavud also shows a very detailed knowledge of both the Parsi and European scholarship on the *Qesseh-ye Sanjan* and the Zoroastrian exodus generally, citing sources with which he came into contact during his stay in Bombay, such as Dosabhai Framji Karaka's *History of the Parsis* (1884), Jivanji Jamshedji Modi's *A Few Events in the Early History of the Parsis* (1905), and key European texts on the early history of the Parsis by such scholars as Menant, Jackson, Wilhelm Geiger, and Ernst Kuhn.[194] What is most interesting in Purdavud's rendering of this history is how he combines a detailed scholarly knowledge of the modern historiography with his own telling of this history that is clearly shaped by the demands of Iranian nationalist ideology. The ultimate goal of the books Purdavud published in Bombay was not to produce a detached humanistic project of historical research, but rather to revive a lost Zoroastrian identity and a shared Indo-Iranian classical heritage.

This shared heritage was also brought to life in the *Iranshah* with more than fifty pages of photographs, which visually represented the principal figures and key institutions of the Parsi community of Bombay. These photos include not only portraits of Parsi benefactors—such as Dinshaw Petit, Dorab Jamshedji Tata, and Peshotanji Dossabhai

Marker—but also photographs of key Parsi institutions, such as fire temples in Bombay, the "Iranshah" Atash Bahram in Udvada, and an architectural rendering of the "Sanjan Column" which had been erected in 1914 in Gujarat to memorialize the assumed original landing site of the Iranian Zoroastrians in India. There are also photographs of hospitals, schools, hotels, charitable institutes, and factories, all of which had been built through the efforts of the Bombay Parsi community.[195] This visual referencing of the Parsis, and in particular of the great prosperity achieved by the Parsis in India, followed Purdavud and Irani's larger aim of introducing Iranian readers to what was now portrayed as their national compatriots.

Following the publication of the *Iranshah*, Purdavud went on to produce at a brisk pace a series of Persian translations of the main corpus of Zoroastrian scripture. In 1927 the first of his three revised translations of the *Gathas* appeared, followed in 1928 by the first volume of the *Yashtha*. A second volume of the *Yashtha* was published in 1931. Also appearing in 1931 was Purdavud's own Persian translation of the *Khordeh Avesta*. While still in Bombay, he also began work on a complete translation of the *Yasna*, the first volume of which appeared in 1938. A planned second volume was completed but was delayed until the 1950s by the Second World War as well as a fire at the Fort Printing Press.[196] All of the translations published as a result of the collaboration between Purdavud and Irani between 1926 and 1938 were produced under the auspices of the Iran League and the Iranian Zoroastrian Anjoman through the endowment established by P. D. Marker, and printed at the Fort Printing Press in Bombay.

These translations marked a major achievement in making the Zoroastrian texts available to modern Iranians. The texts had long been neglected and inaccessible to modern Iranians because they were written in the forgotten language of Avestan. Purdavud's new translations—accompanied by extensive commentary—suddenly made the Zoroastrian scriptures available for the first time in a modern Persian translation that not only rendered the religious content of the original scriptures but also produced a text that lyrically conformed to a Persian poetic sensibility. Purdavud's talent as a poet made him the ideal translator of these texts. The synthesis of his linguistic skills in Avestan and Pahlavi with his poetic talents in New Persian and his scholarly annotations of the text made his translations foundational texts in Iran's twentieth-century pre-Islamic revival.

Purdavud in Bombay, India. Iran League Quarterly, *Bombay, 1932.*

Dinshah Irani's role in these translation efforts was central to their success. The close-knit community of Parsi scholars in Bombay was an important resource for Purdavud in producing his translations. Dinshah Irani facilitated Purdavud's engagement with Parsi scholars, whose work Purdavud cites extensively in these books. Irani also made a personal financial contribution toward the publication of Purdavud's books.[197] Purdavud was in fact effusive in expressing his gratitude to Irani for helping to make the publication of his translations possible: "If I had not the good fortune of encountering this man [Irani] I would never have reached my goal and would not have been able to over-come the obstacles to publish this work,"[198] he states in the introduction to the second volume of the *Yashtha*. Purdavud's gratitude to Irani was due not only to Irani's efforts in facilitating his encounter with the Parsi scholarly community and securing financial sponsorship for the publications, but also to his larger efforts in bringing to fruition their common goal of introducing Iranian readers to the heritage of Iran's pre-Islamic past. In the most direct expression of his gratitude, Purdavud writes:

> If our fellow countrymen have come to know the Avesta and
> have access to thousand-year old texts, and if they come to
> know the religion of their ancestors in a way contrary to that
> posed by enemies and impostors, and if the followers of this
> ancient faith in Iran and those who like the texts of their
> forebears to appear after a thousand years in their own native
> vernacular language in a few volumes dealing with Zoroastri-
> anism, then these people are indebted to the work and labor
> of this great man [Irani]. It is clear that anyone who likes
> knowledge and learning as well as the glory and greatness of
> ancient Iran is grateful to Dinshah Irani for publishing and
> bringing to life the lost past of our nation.[199]

Purdavud's acknowledgment of Dinshah Irani is an indication of the
importance of not only Irani but also the broader network of textual and
intellectual exchange that became possible between Iranians and Parsis
by the 1920s and 1930s.

CONCLUSION

Despite Purdavud and Irani's seeming unity of purpose in working to
produce modern Persian editions of the Zoroastrian religious texts, there
was also an unacknowledged tension at work in their collaboration. This
tension grew out of what were ultimately their contrasting objectives
when it came to defining the meaning of the pre-Islamic revival in the
context of Iran's twentieth-century national politics.

The goals of the Bombay-based Parsi community were never simply
to revive the Zoroastrian faith inside Iran, but to do so with the intention
of helping to foster an inclusive and religiously pluralistic Iranian polity.
This goal was compelled by a Parsi awareness of the poor social conditions experienced by the Zoroastrians inside Iran, as well as by the anxieties they expressed for the Iranian Zoroastrian community's minority
status. As the Parsis of Bombay understood it, the poor social conditions
for Zoroastrians inside Iran were to a large extent caused by the persecution the community suffered as a result of their status as non-Muslims
living within a majority Muslim-Shi'ite polity. Helping to foster an
enlightened and progressive political order inside Iran that would recognize the cultural status and religious rights of non-Muslim communities would, they believed, help to alleviate the Iranian Zoroastrian
community's poor social, political, and economic standing inside Iran.

From the Parsi point of view, the goal of Purdavud's translations was therefore to help promote new understandings of Zoroastrianism that would help to dispel age-old religious misgivings and misunderstandings of the faith, and to situate Zoroastrianism within Iran's national heritage. This goal of religio-cultural pluralism was likely an ideal drawn from the Parsis' own experience as a historic minority community in a multicultural India during the premodern era and then as a privileged community within the liberal empire of the British Raj. The Parsis were convinced that the remarkable social and economic prosperity that they had achieved by the nineteenth century had grown out of the possibilities enabled by both of these contexts. It was ultimately this model of religio-cultural pluralism that the Parsis believed they were promoting with all of their charity work inside Iran, including their sponsorship of Purdavud's translations. Dinshah Irani, in his 1927 foreword to Purdavud's *Gathas*—the first of the series of translations produced under Parsi sponsorship—defined the goals of the Parsi sponsorship of Purdavud's translations in precisely these terms:

> Like the Sufis of yore, we believe that all great religions lead to the One Great Truth, and that fanaticism so prevalent all over the world is a disease of the mind only, due to ignorance. As a step towards the goal of knowledge, we humbly believe that such a translation [of the *Gathas*] would be welcomed by all cultured Iranians, to whatever creed they might belong.[200]

This theme of promoting religio-cultural pluralism inside Iran through the introduction of modern understandings of Zoroastrianism was a consistent theme in Parsi descriptions of their intentions toward Iran.

From the Iranian point of view, however, the goals of making the heritage of Iranian Zoroastrianism known to the Persian-reading public were never quite as clear. The liberal ideals of Indian multiculturalism—whether defined by the traditional politics of the Mughal Empire or those of the British Raj—were not the ideals that defined Iran's Zoroastrian revival. By the Reza Shah era, the democratic ethos of Iran's constitutional revolution did not serve this purpose either. For Purdavud, as for the Iranian nationalists of the 1920s and 1930s, the Zoroastrian revival was always more about distinguishing the *real* and *authentic* Iranian culture from the layers of *inauthentic* cultural accretions that Iran's national heritage had acquired over the long duration of its history. It was this nationalist logic of distinguishing the *authentic* from the *inauthentic* that came to define the new understanding of Iran's Zoroastrian heritage for the Iranian nationalist intellectuals of Purdavud's generation.

In practice, this meant that the nonclassical elements of Iran's history—in particular the Arab and Turkish elements—were now defined as external ingredients that had been artificially grafted onto Iran's cultural heritage. Rather than being inspired by a politics of inclusion, the political logic of Purdavud's cultural excavation, extraction, and reconstruction of Iran's classical heritage bore the implicit traces of a political project that was in fact illiberal. As he wrote with no small measure of exasperation in his own introductory remarks to his 1927 translation of the *Gathas*, the official tradition of historical knowledge in premodern Iran had been largely erected on a foundation of Arab-Islamic historical categories:

> In historical works Persian authors expressed joy and rendered thanks to the almighty for the fact that the armies of the enemy from Arabia overran Iran and pillaged and made desolate that prosperous land of our forefathers, and took the ladies of the royal Sassanian dynasty into captivity, and bought and sold them as slaves in the marketplace of Medina. They expressed joy at the extinction of the ways and customs of our forefathers whom they called "fire-worshipping geubres."[201]

The entire logic of Purdavud's intellectual evolution—from his coming of age in Beirut, to his intellectual growth in Paris, to his subsequent maturity during his years in Berlin, and to his final personal and emotional discoveries in Bombay—had always been animated by a desire to nurture a cultural *renaissance* of Iran's classical heritage, and to mobilize that heritage to contest what he perceived as the hegemonic edifice of medieval Arab-Islamic-Turkish civilization within Iranian culture. Purdavud never outlined what form of polity he saw as emerging from this articulation of an Iranian renaissance. However, the culturally assertive nature of his intellectual enterprise invariably carried with it the possibility of producing the most illiberal forms of nationalist politics.

While the contrasting objectives of Irani and Purdavud—and of the Parsis and the Iranian nationalists more generally—were always implicit in the course of their respective efforts, in practice this unacknowledged tension never rose to the level of an intractable contradiction. During the years of Purdavud's collaboration with the Parsis, the textual, scholarly, and intellectual nature of their joint projects never required the making of stark political choices. The same was true in the other aspects of the interwar-era Parsi-Iranian collaboration, such as the symbolism surrounding Tagore's 1932 visit to Iran, or the charity and philanthropic work that the Parsis had initiated in Kerman and Yazd. As the interwar period came to a close, however, the classical heritage of Indo-Iranian culture would increasingly become entangled in Nazi conceptions of culture, politics, and ideology. With the approach of the Second World War, the always implicit contradictions between the liberal goals of the Parsis and the more nationalist goals of many Iranians came increasingly to the surface, eventually bringing the interwar-era Parsi-Iranian collaboration to a moment of crisis.

CHAPTER 5

SWORD OF FREEDOM

Abdulrahman Saif Azad and Interwar Iranian Nationalism

The internment camp where Abdulrahman Saif Azad (1884–1971) was housed following his arrest in September of 1939 by British colonial authorities was in a rural district outside of the western Maharastran city of Nashik.[1] Saif Azad had been brought to this camp following his arrest in Bombay, a city approximately one hundred miles to the west of Nashik where he had spent considerable time working as a journalist and activist in the years immediately preceding the outbreak of World War II. The prison camp in Nashik was in fact part of a network of several dozen other internment centers, prisoner-of-war facilities, and jails established by British authorities throughout western and northern India. These camps—including other major facilities in Bombay and the surrounding areas such as at Arthur Road, Byculla, Pune, and Yerwada—were designed to detain agitators, revolutionaries, and others deemed undesirable by a colonial government now increasingly concerned about a restless population demanding India's independence.[2] Saif Azad felt at home alongside his fellow detainees in Nashik. By the time of his arrest he had long since seen the struggle for India's independence as part of a larger global struggle to challenge British imperial hegemony that would also help to bring about the cultural and political revival of societies throughout Asia. In a fragment of a memoir written after the war, following his release in 1946, Saif Azad recalled with some fondness the feeling of camaraderie that he experienced with his fellow prisoners, remarking proudly that he "shared equally day and night [their] struggles and hardships."[3] He also recalled with some bitterness his treatment by the British authorities, describing how he "fell into the foul clutches of these foreign

Abdulrahman Saif Azad (1884–1971), in British custody, 1939. National Archives (United Kingdom).

usurpers in India . . . and although innocent passed seven long years in various Indian prisons."[4]

Saif Azad was in some ways an unusual figure to find in a British-Indian prisoner-of-war camp. While having spent the better part of two years prior to his arrest traveling throughout the subcontinent as a journalist extolling the political and economic progress achieved by local rulers and regional governments in the pages of his bilingual English-Persian magazine *Salar-e Hend* (1937–1939), he was nevertheless only a visitor in India. Born sometime between 1884 and 1891 in Tehran to a family of Shi'ite Muslims of modest means, Saif Azad had no personal ties to India, and at the time of his arrest in September of 1939 he was a citizen and subject of Pahlavi Iran.[5] From the perspective of British colonial officials, however, his activities and associations during his time in India aroused suspicion that he was working as a German agent. In the years leading up to the Second World War, Bombay, Delhi, and Calcutta were, in fact, cities with significant networks of German sympathizers and collaborators.[6] German diplomatic staff working in consulates and cultural organizations were in regular contact with elements of the Indian nationalist movement, as well as others, like Saif Azad, who considered themselves fellow travelers in the cause of bringing about the end of the British Raj. Saif Azad's association with known German agents in Bombay and his regular visits to the Indo-German Cultural Institute brought him under the increased scrutiny of British authorities, who began preparing for his arrest as early as June of 1939.[7]

The British security services had in fact kept a close eye on Saif Azad for some time. He had been the subject of numerous intelligence inquiries dating back to 1921, when he first came to notice as part of a suspicious wave of Iranian and Indian immigrants to Berlin. A British surveillance report monitoring the movement of these immigrants concluded that they were working "under the Germans for the sole purpose of stirring up unrest, sedition, and rebellion in our Eastern Empire."[8] From the time of this initial encounter with British security services upon his arrival in Berlin in February of 1921 until the time of his arrest in Bombay in September of 1939, Saif Azad was under intermittent surveillance by British authorities. They documented his movements and activities, including his journalistic work for Persian, German, Turkish, Arabic, and Urdu newspapers such as the *Azadi-ye Sharq* (1921–1931), a widely influential pro-German, multilingual, and transnational newspaper under his editorship in Berlin. Saif Azad spent a decade in Berlin editing this newspaper, which gained notice—not only from its broad readership on three continents, but also from British authorities—for its advocacy of the political and economic independence of the Middle East as well as South and Central Asia. British authorities also took notice of his connections and correspondence with Afghan nationalists in Berlin and Paris, who after the Third Anglo-Afghan War of 1919 were now asserting their independence under the leadership of Amanullah Khan.[9] British authorities had in fact gone to some pains to document Saif Azad's long association with the cause of Afghanistan's independence, including his participation in the failed Niedermayer-Hentig mission of 1915–1916. One intelligence report described him as "fighting for Austria during the [last] war"[10] and another described him as belonging to "the class of oriental devotees known as *dervishes* . . . [who] served the Central Powers as a spy against Czarist Russia and against England."[11] Also of interest to British security officials was Saif Azad's editorship between 1933 and 1935 of the Tehran-based weekly newspaper *Iran-e Bastan*—the publication for which he is most often remembered within Iranian historiography. This newspaper aroused the suspicion of British security officials, not only because of its connections to Parsi-Zoroastrian sources of funding in Bombay, but also more perniciously because of what became the newspaper's clearly discernible pro-Nazi editorial policy.[12]

Saif Azad's protestations of innocence, written after the war, were therefore disingenuous. He was not simply an innocent bystander mistakenly swept up by British authorities in a Bombay dragnet. In fact, by the time of his arrest on the eve of World War II he had a substantial record of more than two decades of activism, agitation, and resistance to the British Empire. It is precisely on this account that his life is worthy of consideration. Accounting for Saif Azad's role in the history of India's independence movement, and documenting his activism and collaborations with multiple strands of early twentieth-century forms of anti-British politics throughout Europe, the Middle East, Central and South Asia—including his connections to not only Indian but also Iranian, Afghan, Parsi, Turkish, Egyptian, German, Bolshevik, and Islamist politics—helps us to acknowledge one of the still underacknowledged aspects of the early history of Iranian nationalism.

Saif Azad's understanding of Iranian nationalism was one in which Iran's political and cultural history was not seen in isolation from the broader regional and global context of imperial politics. Rather, the style of Iranian nationalism that he advocated was decidedly internationalist in both its form and content. Unlike the views of other nineteenth- and early twentieth-century activists and reformers whose projects of Iranian nationalism were tied to the more patient task of cultural and intellectual excavation, ideological reconstruction, and institutional reform, Saif Azad's vision of Iranian nationalism was, by contrast, rooted in an emerging populist form of transnational anti-imperialism that could be described as a precursor to the Third Worldist movements of the 1950s, 1960s, and 1970s. Iran's political destiny—as he saw it from the vantage point of the first few decades of the twentieth century—was unmistakably tied to the destiny of the larger struggles for independence throughout the world, and in particular to the territories of Iran's immediate neighbors in the Middle East and South Asia. The type of Iranian nationalism that he advocated, and which he worked to promote via his political activism and journalistic writings, was one which, as Mansour Bonakdarian has described, was part of a larger "global solidarity network"[13] of other Asian nationalist movements. For Saif Azad, Iranian nationalism was seen primarily as a movement in solidarity with these other movements, specifically the independence movements within India and Afghanistan, the struggles within the late Ottoman Empire and its successor states, and the political movements that were characterized both by Pan-Islamic solidarities and the ideologies of secular nationalism and Bolshevism. Saif Azad's version of Iranian nationalism did not see itself as ideologically in competition, or in contradiction, with these movements. His own life and work intersected with all of these political-ideological strands of early twentieth-century anti-imperialism.

And yet it was precisely within this same ecumenical network of political collaboration that the ideological tensions inherent within Saif Azad's understanding of Iranian nationalism also came to reveal themselves. In the long run, his understanding of Iranian nationalism as part of a populist form of transnational anti-imperialism stood uncomfortably alongside other political-ideological understandings of the same phenomenon, such as, on the one hand, a moderate, inclusive, and liberal strand of Iranian nationalism born out of the 1905 Iranian Constitutional Revolution, and on the other hand, a rival form of Iranian nationalism that was increasingly drawn toward exclusionary, racialized, fascist, and Nazi forms of ideology and politics. Nowhere is this tension more clearly demonstrated than in Saif Azad's attempt to enlist the Parsi community of India to the cause of Iranian nationalism. While the Parsis came to develop a deep and powerful attachment to their ancestral homeland, and were initially eager to support Saif Azad's efforts to publish his Persian-language *Iran-e Bastan* in order to promote renewed ties between Parsis and Iranians, the rapid transformation of the newspaper into an anti-British and pro-Nazi periodical contradicted both their own understanding of Iranian nationalism and their goals for building ties with Iran. As a result, the Parsis quickly became disillusioned with Saif Azad and withdrew support from *Iran-e Bastan*. His abrupt break with the Parsis is only one example of the numerous moments in his career when the political contradictions inherent in his understanding of Iranian nationalism led to moments of political, ideological, and personal crisis. These moments of crisis resulted from tensions that not only existed within the context of Saif Azad's own personal understanding of Iranian nationalism, but also reflected larger unresolved contradictions within Iranian nationalism's early twentieth-century history.

EARLY LIFE, RECRUITMENT BY GERMAN AGENTS, AND THE MISSION TO KABUL

The earliest period of Saif Azad's life unfolded between the cities of Tehran, Najaf, and Kabul. Documents providing details of his early life are especially rare and give only the most essential facts regarding his background. Biographical information collected during his internment, and details collected from passport records and surviving visa applications, indicate that Saif Azad was born on February 18, 1891, in Tehran.[14] His father's name is given as Hossein, and his earliest place of residence is listed as Nasseriyeh Street, near the bazaar district of central Tehran. The records also indicate that as of 1937 he was divorced and had no children.[15] Documents collected by British authorities also identify him as using a number of different names, including: Abdulrahman Tehrani, Shaikh Abdulrahman, Saif Islam, Saif Effendi, Saif Azad, Shaikh Saif Azad, Abdulrahman Saif Azad, and others.[16] References to him in Persian and German sources also use slightly different iterations of his name.[17] This evolving nomenclature was not itself unusual for the late nineteenth and early twentieth century, but in this case the evolution of descriptive self-identifying names likely indicates an evolution of Saif Azad's personal identity and his political and ideological views. In addition to tracking his various names and aliases, British security personnel were also keen to assess his manner and temperament. On this point there was general agreement that Saif Azad was, as one British official stated, "well educated and of a serious disposition."[18]

Although it is clear that he was born in Tehran, it is not entirely clear at what age he left the city. Biographical details, however, indicate that by 1911 Saif Azad was a seminary student in Najaf.[19] Beginning in the time of Jamal al-Din al-Afghani's Pan-Islamic political activism in the nineteenth century, and accelerating during the early years of the twentieth century, Najaf and Tehran, like many other parts of the Islamic world, were in the midst of great religious and political transformation, which one historian has described as the "years of upheaval."[20] The Constitutional Revolution of 1905–1911 in particular had inaugurated a period of wide-ranging social, cultural, and political contestation inside Iran. The events of the 1905–1911 revolution were clearly a formative part of Saif Azad's personal development, as well as of his political education, while he was a young man in Tehran's bazaar district. We can also surmise that his move to Najaf sometime during this period suggests that his early teachers had already recognized his aptitude for advanced religious study. Although the details of his earliest education are not clear and his precise educational pedigree—both in Tehran and in Najaf—is unknown, his move to the 'Atabat for further religious instruction indicates that he had already distinguished himself intellectually at a relatively young age, and that he had successfully entered into the Shi'a 'ulama's educational and patronage networks linking the cities of Tehran and Najaf.

Najaf, where Saif Azad spent the years between Iran's constitutional revolution and the outbreak of World War I, was more than a simple seminary town devoted to piety, teaching, and scholarship. It was part of a network of cities, towns, and pilgrimage sites across the Islamic world that, as one observer during this period described, formed "hotbeds of intrigue."[21] Thinking of Najaf and Karbala specifically, another observer described a "chain of holy cities"[22] functioning as "nodes"[23] within a much broader transregional religious and political network of pilgrims, spies, seminary students, 'ulama, and activists connecting Istanbul, Damascus, Cairo, Baghdad, and Mecca to cities across Iran, Afghanistan, and northern India.[24] This traditional network of trade and travel became increasingly mobilized in the years before World War I as both regional and international politics led to a perception of impending threat to the Islamic world. In the years following the Iranian Constitutional Revolution of 1905, the Young Turk Revolution of 1908, the Russian territorial encroachment into northern Iran in 1909, the Italian occupation of Libya in 1911, as well as the events leading to World War I, Najaf had grown into its status as an important center of discussion and debate among Muslim activists. Newspapers from all corners of the Islamic world, including Cairo's *al-Manar* and Calcutta's *Habl al-Matin*, circulated among the city's exceptionally literate population.[25] The city itself was the center of a lively print industry with a number of newspapers in both Arabic and Persian that reflected local Shi'ite perspectives as well as broadly pan-Islamist and anti-imperialist orientations.[26] As the region, and the world, moved toward war, Najaf's residents—including young *talebs* like Saif Azad—became embroiled in the debates about war, religion, politics, and empire.

The Shi'a mujtahids residing in the city were also very much embroiled in these debates, with their most significant engagement being their collective endorsement of the fatwa issued by the Ottoman Sultan Mehmed V and the Shaykh al-Islam declaring jihad in November of 1914. The Young Turk leaders in Istanbul—along with their German allies in Berlin—had conceived of a declaration of jihad as a way of mobilizing the Ottoman populace and the broader Islamic world to defend both the empire and Islam against the impending threats posed by the Entente powers.[27] Coterminous with the Sultan's declaration in the Ottoman capital, Young Turk activists and German agents in Najaf encouraged the leading mujtahids of the Shi'ite Islamic world to follow suit in supporting the declaration. The mujtahids agreed, and in the following days issued a collective statement endorsing the declaration of jihad.[28] Both the original fatwa by the Sunni Shaykh al-Islam and its endorsement by the leading Shi'ite mujtahids were couched in broad ecumenical language intended to appeal to believers across the Sunni-Shi'a divide.[29]

It was in this context that Saif Azad entered into the world of political activism. His association with German agents is first documented in the Niedermayer-Hentig mission to Afghanistan of 1915.[30] The goal of the mission—which, in addition to military officer Oskar-Ritter von Niedermayer (1885–1948) and political officer Werner-Otto von Hentig (1886–1984), also involved the equally noteworthy efforts of Wilhelm Wassmuss (1880–1931)—was to lead an overland delegation of German and Turkish political-military personnel, along with representatives of the Indian nationalist movement,[31] from Istanbul through the Ottoman territories, across Iran, and to Kabul. Once in the Afghan capital, the delegation would forge an alliance with the Amir of Afghanistan, Habibullah Khan (r. 1901–1919), and encourage him to declare war against the British Raj, thus opening up a new front in the war. The expectation was that the Ottoman declaration of jihad, along with the appeal of Afghan-Indian anti-British solidarity and the promise of German military and economic assistance, would persuade the Amir to enter into the alliance. This German-Turkish strategy, reportedly conceived by Enver Pasha himself,[32] was analogous to the British "Arab Revolt" plan of forging a military-political alliance with the Bedouin army of the Arab nationalists within the Ottoman Empire. In the case of the German-Turkish-Indian plan, the delegation hoped to encourage the Amir to mobilize the Pashtun tribes under his influence for a military offensive on the Raj from the north down through the Khyber Pass.[33] Unlike the British-inspired "Arab Revolt," however, the German-Turkish-Indian plan was confronted by innumerable challenges, not the least of which was the logistical difficulty of traversing the great distance from the Ottoman territories to Kabul to beseech the Amir to join the anti-British alliance.[34]

The German-Turkish-Indian Mission in Kabul, May 1916. Left to right: Kazim Bey, Werner-Otto von Hentig, Walter Röhr, Raja Mahendra Pratap, Kurt Wagner, Oskar Niedermayer, Günter Voigt, Maulana Barakatullah. Emil Rybitschka, Im gottgegebenen Afghanistan als gäste des emirs, *1927.*

After the Anglo-Russian Agreement of 1907, Iran had been placed under a de facto territorial partition, with the Russians controlling a northern "sphere of influence" and the British controlling a southern sphere. Between the northern and southern spheres was a central zone that remained formally outside of British and Russian jurisdiction. It was in this central Iranian zone that the German presence grew during World War I. As Werner von Hentig stated in a memoir of his experience during the war, "we Germans ruled Middle Persia."[35] Perhaps most important to the German presence in Iran was the German consulate in Isfahan, which in 1915 was described as "the center of German power"[36] in the region linking the Ottoman territories in the west to the Afghan frontier in the east. Accounts of the Niedermayer-Hentig expedition describe the long and difficult trek to Isfahan after setting out from Istanbul in May of 1915 and traversing across Anatolia with a caravan of horse-drawn carriages and one hundred pack animals, then turning south at Karkemish via river barge and proceeding down the Euphrates to Fallujah, before traveling by land to Baghdad, crossing into Iran at Kermanshah, and finally making their way to Isfahan.[37] When the delegation arrived in Isfahan in July after the arduous three-month journey, they rested, regrouped, and readied themselves for the much more difficult journey from Isfahan across the Dasht-e Kavir desert to the Afghan border and onward to Kabul via Herat.[38] At some point during the course of this leg of the expedition between Baghdad and the Afghan border, Saif Azad joined the German-Turkish-Indian mission to Kabul. Multiple sources indicated that once in Isfahan, Niedermayer and Hentig began to recruit local agents as porters to help in conveying the considerable supplies that the mission had brought on the journey, as well as scouts whose job it was to travel ahead of the caravan to help the mission avoid the territories policed by British and Russian patrols.[39] They also recruited couriers whose job it was to help maintain lines of secret communication between the mission in Kabul and the embassy and consulate staff in Iran.[40]

It was in the last of these roles—as courier—that Saif Azad came to serve in 1915. He continued to work for the mission, first as a courier, and later as a guide, through the fall of 1916. The first mention of Saif Azad in the context of the Niedermayer-Hentig mission is made in the memoir of Wipert von Blücher (1883–1963), one of the members of the diplomatic staff at the German legation in Tehran. Blücher describes the arrival at the legation, sometime in the early spring of 1916, of a haggard, bespectacled, and mysterious young man dressed in a traditional Iranian cloak. The young man

> spent some time digging through his cloak with great dexterity . . . and eventually produced a narrow tube inside of which was a finely rolled piece of silk paper. . . . As though he were conjuring a spell, [the young man] pulled out the silk paper and unfurled it on my office desk.[41]

What Blücher described next was looking at the paper to see an extremely small typewritten coded memorandum that was clearly a message written by Niedermayer and Hentig in Kabul. The messenger, who described himself simply as "Abdulrahman,"[42] had been sent from Kabul as a secret courier to convey to the German diplomatic staff a proposal for a formal treaty of friendship between Germany and Afghanistan.[43] A formal military alliance and a declaration of jihad were clearly not forthcoming; a vaguely worded "friendship agreement" seemed to be all that the Niedermayer-Hentig mission had been able to achieve after more than seven months of negotiations with the Amir.[44] It had taken Abdulrahman Saif Azad three months to deliver the message. His secret journey from Kabul to Tehran required traveling through territories patrolled by

Russian and British forces, especially near the Afghanistan-Iranian border regions. The carefully concealed secret message had been sewn into Saif Azad's cloak precisely to avoid detection by these border patrols.

Three months after delivering the message, by May of 1916, the military situation of the war had clearly tilted in favor of the Allies. Renewed concerns over a territorial partition of Iran began to circulate among politically minded Iranians, especially those associated with the pro-German Iranian Democratic Party and the Swedish-trained Iranian military forces known as the Government Gendarmerie.[45] As the military situation changed, pressure increased on the German diplomatic staff in Tehran to evacuate the city.[46] Saif Azad remained involved in the politics of the capital city during this period. After having successfully delivered the secret memo from Kabul in March he had remained in Tehran, residing in his family's residence on Nasseriyeh Street. He also maintained his contacts with the German legation, and by the summer of 1916 he was once again called to service. This time his mission was to serve as part of a small team of scouts and guides to help Oskar von Niedermayer make his way back through Iran to the Ottoman border.[47]

The Niedermayer-Hentig mission had reached the conclusion that it would be unable to complete its goal of bringing the Afghans into the war. Both the war's shifting fortunes and Habibullah Khan's reticence to challenge the Raj had led to the inevitable conclusion that the mission had failed. What remained was for Niedermayer and Hentig to make their way back to Berlin.[48] Hentig chose to avoid the war zone by traveling the long way, going east through Central Asia and China before crossing to North America and back to Europe. Niedermayer instead chose to travel west, essentially retracing the party's route across Iran. In this context, Saif Azad once again entered into the service of the German war effort. The story of Niedermayer's journey from Kabul to Tehran and back to Germany through the Ottoman Empire has grown to become one of the legendary episodes of World War I. Traveling by horse and donkey and using multiple local disguises as he traveled through Russian-controlled Afghan, Turkoman, and Iranian lands, Niedermayer managed to avoid detection to make his way to Tehran by the end of July 1916.[49] Once in the city he managed to make contact with the remaining members of the German diplomatic staff in the capital. The German staff and their Iranian agents immediately began to plan for the next leg of Niedermayer's journey from Tehran to Hamadan and to the Ottoman border through Kermanshah.

The principal Iranian agent working for the Germans in Tehran during this period was Mirza Abolqasem Khan Kahhalzadeh, a long-time secretary at the German legation in the capital. Kahhalzadeh would become the chief planner of Niedermayer's escape from Tehran and safe passage to Kermanshah. Kahhalzadeh's memoirs provide rich detail regarding the clandestine activities of German and Iranian agents during the years of 1914–1918. By the late summer of 1916 most of the German diplomatic staff had already evacuated Tehran as the threat of an Allied victory became a more real possibility and the growing military presence of the Russians in the north and west of Iran suggested an impending occupation of the capital city.[50] The principal German diplomat remaining in the city was Rudolf Sommer, the chargé d'affaires of the legation.[51] When Niedermayer arrived in Tehran at the end of July, it was the task of Sommer and Kahhalzadeh to devise a plan for his transit to the Ottoman border. They were already aware that Niedermayer's presence in the city was likely to be known to Russian and British authorities, who also had their own extensive network of spies and informants. Both the Russians and British were already well aware of the Niedermayer-Hentig mission and were apprehending German agents throughout Iran with some success.[52] Sommer and Kahhalzadeh first chose to place Niedermayer in the protection of a safe house north of the city, in Darband. This temporary location would give them time to plan the next leg of Niedermayer's journey. Niedermayer's physical condition upon arriving in Tehran was also of some concern. He appeared, according to Kahhalzadeh, not only physically exhausted but also malnourished.[53] He soon also contracted a fever, and his survival was itself in doubt.[54] Given the difficult conditions of the month-long journey from Kabul, as Niedermayer himself described, "having drank from every ditch . . . and having slept in every filthy place," it was "a miracle" that he had not contracted anything more serious than a temporary fever.[55]

After two weeks of recuperation at the Darband safe house, Niedermayer was once again fit enough to continue his escape to the Ottoman border. By mid-August Kahhalzadeh had made contact with two agents who would serve as Niedermayer's guides during the final leg of his journey.[56] One of these guides was Saif Azad, who was by now a veteran of the Niedermayer-Hentig mission. The other was Nurallah Mirza Jahanbani, the great grandson of Fathali Shah and a member of the Qajar royal family.[57] Of the two, Jahanbani was clearly the more distinguished figure. As a prince, he had received his education at the royal military academy,

Saif Azad (left), Oskar Niedermayer, in disguise (center), and Nurallah Mirza Jahanbani (right) in Hamadan, September 1916. Mirza Abulqasem Khan Kahhalzadeh, Didehha va Shenidehha, *Tehran, 1984.*

and then had gone on to serve as an officer in the government gendarmerie. Founded initially with the help of Swedish officers, the gendarmerie had grown to become a significant military force in Iran, rivaled only by the Russian-trained Cossack Brigade and the British South Persia Rifles. In contrast to these, however, the government gendarmerie had quickly taken a pro-German stance at the outbreak of the war, and had forged a de facto political alliance with the equally pro-German Iranian Democratic Party.[58] Kahhalzadeh describes the confidence he had in recruiting the two agents for the mission, writing, "like most Iranians, they had inclinations towards the Germans."[59]

Both Kahhalzadeh and Niedermayer's memoirs are more detailed in describing Jahanbani's role than Saif Azad's.[60] Kahhalzadeh, however, describes the plan to meet at 3 a.m. on August 15 at the home of "one of his [Jahanbani's] closest associates" on Nasseriyeh Street, near the alley of "Khodabandehlu."[61] This may have been the Tehran residence of Saif Azad, from where the three set out by donkey on their journey, first to Hamadan, which only days earlier had fallen under Ottoman control. From Hamadan, Niedermayer and his guides received a motorized military escort to Kermanshah, which was more securely under Ottoman military control.[62] The most specific reference to Saif Azad's role in this part of the Niedermayer mission is in the form of a photograph taken in Hamadan that eventually found its way into both Niedermayer and Kahhalzadeh's memoirs. Taken in August of 1916, the photograph serves as the first visual record of Saif Azad. It also shows Niedermayer dressed in disguise, wearing a common Iranian cloak that he had acquired while in Tehran. On one side of Niedermayer in the photograph stands Nurallah Mirza Jahanbani, and on the other side stands Abdulrahman Saif Azad.[63]

THE BERLIN YEARS, 1920-1931

The failure of the Niedermayer-Hentig mission was only one of multiple failures for the Germans and the Ottomans during the final phase of the First World War. The final Allied victory in 1918–1919—along with the famine of 1917–1918, the flu pandemic of the same year, the Russian Revolution, and the Anglo-Persian Agreement of 1919—ushered in a period of uncertainty for the region, and for Iran in particular. For those Iranians like Saif Azad who had actively worked for the German war effort, Iran's immediate political future did not invoke a great deal of optimism. The result was a significant emigration of politically oriented Iranians in the years immediately following the war. Some of these emigrants made their way to Istanbul, where they joined an already well-established Iranian expatriate community. Others, including Saif Azad, made their way to Berlin.

There was already a small Iranian community in Berlin. The city had served as a political center for pro-German Iranians during the war years.[64] Most famously, Hasan Taqizadeh had gathered a committee of activists and intellectuals in Berlin to publish the pro-German newspaper *Kaveh*. In its early phase, the newspaper had received funding directly from the German government's Foreign Ministry. There was also a small merchant and trading community of Iranians in Berlin, along with a growing number of Iranian students who had come to the German capital for higher education.[65]

By 1920 Saif Azad joined this nascent community of Iranians in Berlin. The German government had been generous in providing visa and immigration documents for those Turks, Afghans, Indians, Iranians, and others who had helped in the war effort. Saif Azad's goals after moving to Berlin were uncertain, and his own activities during his early years there suggest that he had multiple objectives without much clarity of direction. Wipert von Blücher, the German diplomat who knew Saif

Azad from his days in Tehran, described the large number of those who had helped in the war effort who were beginning to filter into Weimar Berlin. These "refugees," as Blücher called them, were in a state of "transformation" as they resettled themselves after the seismic political shifts of the war.[66] Saif Azad was one of these refugees seeking to make a new life for himself in Weimar Germany.

Blücher states that upon meeting Saif Azad at the Foreign Ministry office sometime in 1920, he was surprised by the "new appearance" that his old comrade had adopted. No longer dressed in the traditional attire of a Najaf *taleb*, Saif Azad was wearing modern European trousers and a coat. Blücher also documents a new name adopted by his friend. Until that time he had only known Saif Azad by the name of "Abdulrahman" or simply as "the messenger." At this meeting, however, Blücher described his friend as being newly monikered with the name "Saif Islam" (Sword of Islam).[67] Other records from this period indicate his use of multiple variations of his name, including what would become his most permanent moniker: "Saif Azad" (Sword of Freedom).[68] Like the other refugees of the war, Saif Azad was, it seems, evolving and working to create a new identity for himself, the precise contours of which were still taking shape. The other important detail to emerge from Blücher's account of his meeting with Saif Azad in 1920 was his demand for a government subsidy.[69] In his meeting with Blücher, Saif Azad argued that the German government owed him a debt due to the services he had rendered during the war. The subsidy, according to Blücher, was to be used by Saif Azad to pursue a modern education in dentistry.[70] It seems that in 1920 Saif Azad was also considering setting aside his early career as a mujtahid and political activist for a new career as a dentist.

The German government agreed to a three-year subsidy. As Blücher and other sources indicate, however, Saif Azad ultimately did not pursue dentistry as his newfound vocation. Instead he began a career as a small businessman in Berlin, first operating a tobacco kiosk and later a Berlin café.[71] Neither of these business ventures seem to have led to much commercial success, and Saif Azad gradually drifted once again into the world of politics, this time reinventing himself as a journalist and publisher. Blücher followed the stages of Saif Azad's evolution during the early 1920s, describing him as follows:

> Who can see this oriental man's life, who was a messenger
> and courier, to a student of dentistry, tobacco seller, café

owner, publisher of newspapers, who went from being known
as "Abdulrahman" to "the sword of Islam"—and not think of
the story of Shaharazad.[72]

Wipert von Blücher was not the only one to recognize Saif Azad's many
reinventions after his arrival in Berlin. Bozorg Alavi (1904–1997)—
another of the recent arrivals in Berlin—also recalled, in his oral history memoir, the mercurial figure of Saif Azad in Berlin during the
early 1920s. Alavi describes Saif Azad as "a strange man" and "a man of
seven colors" (*haft rang*).[73] In the memoir, Alavi also uses the colloquial
expression "pācheh varmālīdeh"[74]—perhaps best rendered into English
as "scum of the earth"—to describe Saif Azad's character and personality. Morteza Moshfeq-Kazemi—another pioneering Iranian writer
and Berlin denizen in the 1920s—similarly describes unusual encounters with Saif Azad during this period. In his memoir, Moshfeq-Kazemi
writes about a heated argument that took place on one occasion between
Saif Azad and a number of Iranian students in Berlin. Given the still relatively small number of Iranian students in the city, most of the Iranian
expatriates lived and socialized in close proximity with one another, primarily in the Charlottenburg borough of Berlin. During one of these
gatherings, according to Moshfeq-Kazemi, Saif Azad began to argue
with some of the students about the politics and the family background
of the Iranian students in Berlin.[75] Moshfeq-Kazemi writes that the alter-
cation became so heated that it required the intervention of others to
defuse the tension. Incidents like these earned Saif Azad a reputation for
being eccentric and acerbic. Moshfeq-Kazemi, perhaps expressing the
more general view of others among the Iranian community of Berlin,
described Saif Azad as a person who "expressed his opinions and ideas
. . . in a free and reckless manner."[76]

Saif Azad's difficult interactions with the mainstream of the Iranian expatriate community of Berlin is explained not only by his personal temperament, but also by the nature of the larger horizon of his
political and ideological commitments. Like the motivations behind his
earliest involvement in the Afghan mission of 1915–1917, Saif Azad's
engagement in politics during his Berlin years remained tied to the more
expansive global struggle of anti-imperialism. While Iran remained part
of his focus, he nevertheless continuously sought to situate Iran's political evolution within a larger transregional, transnational, and global
political struggle. Therefore, his personal and political associations

during his years in Berlin very quickly moved away from the reformist circles of the Iranian community and toward the new revolutionary
committees that were quickly forming among the Indian, Turkish, and
Egyptian expatriate communities of the German capital.[77] Saif Azad's
British intelligence file records some of these new proto–Third Worldist
associations, such as, for example, his connections, as early as 1921, to
"the League of Oppressed Peoples," an internationalist political organization consisting of European and American progressives in solidarity
with expatriate nationalists from the Middle East and South Asia.[78] His
associations with groups identified as "the Egyptian Association," the
"Egyptian Bolsheviks," the "Irish Party," and "the Hindustan Ghadar
Party" were also noted by surveillance reports dating to 1921.[79] Reports
based on information from informants close to Saif Azad also speculated
about his Bolshevik associations, with one report stating that he was "a
clever and able man . . . [who] would support Bolshevism as he believed
that through Bolshevism alone the downfall of the British Empire in the
East would be achieved."[80]

The politics of Berlin during the early 1920s worked to foster these
new sorts of pan-Asian and internationalist connections. By 1921, Berlin had become the home not only of Iranian students, but of students,
activists, and revolutionaries from throughout the Middle East and South
Asia.[81] The official policy of the Weimar government was to steer a very
different course in its foreign policy than its imperial predecessor, and
to avoid controversial overseas adventures.[82] More informally, however,
Berlin became a safe haven and gathering place for those proto–Third
Worldist activists who had seen the Germans as a political counterweight
to the British and Russian empires. Much of this anti-imperial political
activity had initially been sponsored by the German Foreign Ministry's
News Bureau for the East during the war years.[83] The mission of the
German News Bureau had been to subsidize pro-German propaganda
written in Middle Eastern and South Asian languages. After the war, the
official mission of the Bureau changed to one of promoting economic
opportunities for German industrial companies abroad.[84] Nevertheless,
the line between promoting German industrial and economic interests
and challenging the hegemony of the British Empire in the Middle East
and South Asia became increasingly blurred.

It was in this context that Saif Azad began his journalistic and
publishing career in Berlin. By the end of 1921, Taqizadeh's *Kaveh* was
reaching the end of its print run. The subsidy from the German Foreign

Ministry that had sustained the newspaper between 1916 and 1919 had ceased. In the absence of outside funding, the editorial team had tried to sustain the paper with financial support from the paper's subscribers. When this effort proved unsuccessful, the final issue of the paper was published on March 30, 1922.[85] Despite the demise of *Kaveh*, the press on which it had been produced—the Kaviani press—continued to oper-ate. Having originally been manufactured through the technical and engineering efforts of the German government, the Kaviani press was well regarded for its production of modern Persian and Arabic typo-graphic print of exceptional quality. The *Kaveh* newspaper itself remains notable not only for its outstanding intellectual, literary, and editorial content, but also for its superior production value. When *Kaveh* became privatized at the end of the war, the ownership of its press passed into the hands of Taqizadeh and a small number of his Berlin associates.[86] When the newspaper ultimately ended its print run, most of the owner-ship group chose to sell the press to a new group of investors, now led by a German publisher, Heinrich J. Rost, along with Mirza Abdul Shakur Tabrizi, who remained the only member from the original ownership team.[87] Under the new ownership group the Kaviani press now made its printing services available to a growing number of newspapers, journals, and publishers in Berlin that used Arabic and Persian scripts. [88]

Among the newspapers that were initially printed on this press was Saif Azad's *Azadi-ye Sharq* (Freedom of the East), a bilingual Persian and German newspaper that was published intermittently between 1921 and 1930.[89] The primary focus of this newspaper was to promote political sol-idarity among the Muslim populations of the Middle East and South and Central Asia, and to promote German economic ties to these regions. To convey this focus, the newspaper's masthead included a graphic con-sisting of a globe with eight figures—dressed in regionally distinctive dress—standing alongside one another across a horizon stretching along the Afro-Eurasian landmass. The figures represented in the graphic were depicted as wearing local Iranian, Afghan, Indian, Turkic, Arab, and Chinese dress.[90] Also included in the newspaper's masthead is an invoca-tion in Arabic to Muslim unity, as well as a text from Sa'di's famous *bani adam* (children of Adam) poem, in its original Persian.[91] *Azadi-ye Sharq* can in some sense be seen as the successor of *Kaveh*, not only because it was initially printed on the same press, but more importantly because it preserved the tradition of Iranian political activism as expressed through the medium of a Berlin-based Persian-language newspaper. The

La Liberté d'Orient
Journal
national, politique et
économique
———
Scheich Seif Azad
———
Rédaction :
Berlin W 50
———
Téléphone :
B 4 Bavaria 7030
———
Adresse télégraphique :
„Azadichark" Berlin

Diese Ausgabe wird
in den Orient-Ländern
gratis verteilt.

آزادی شرق
نامه ایت
ملی ، سیاسی و اقتصادی
———
مؤسس و مدیر مسئول ،
سیف آزاد
———
محل اداره ، برلین و ٥٠
———
تلفون ، باواریا ٧٠٣٠
———
عنوان تلگراف ، آزادی شرق

قیمت این شماره
و برای مشترکین « آزادی
شرق » و « صنایع »

Azadi-ye Sharq *masthead*. Azadi-ye Sharq, *Berlin, 1921.*

similarities, however, end there. Saif Azad's *Azadi-ye Sharq* clearly did
not reach the same level of literary, historical, and scholarly achievement
as its predecessor. Its focus remained primarily political and economic.
Another key difference was the newspaper's Pan-Asian focus. While the
issues of *Kaveh* during its first series included discussions of larger international issues, its focus remained primarily on how these global political forces affected Iran. In contrast, *Azadi-ye Sharq* was self-consciously
global, transnational, and Pan-Asian, combining a proto–Third Worldist
nationalism with leftist and Islamist vocabularies. One British intelligence assessment of *Azadi-ye Sharq* described its editorial policy as one
of combining Pan-Asian solidarity—what was described alternatively as
a policy of "Eastern solidarity" or one of "Asia for the Asiatics"—with
a pan-Islamist political program organized around the belief that "all
Muhammadan countries should be united under the Khalifa of Islam."[92]
According to another intelligence assessement, the tone of transregional
and transnational populism in the pages of *Azadi-ye Sharq* was especially
dangerous because it appealed "both to the intellectual class, but to the
masses as well."[93]

If the newspaper had a more localized concern, it was its interest in
the role of Afghanistan within the politics of a Pan-Asian solidarity. As
an intelligence agent wrote in one of the periodic reviews of Saif Azad's
work, "he regards Kabul as the place from which the main attack against
England is [to] be launched."[94] The special focus on Afghanistan's importance in the global struggle against empire grew in part out of Saif Azad's

own experience during World War I. Even after his participation in the Niedermayer-Hentig mission, Saif Azad maintained his commitment to Afghanistan's political independence and economic development, and its place in the politics of anti-imperialism. Perhaps an additional reason for the emphasis on Afghanistan in the pages of *Azadi-ye Sharq* was the financial support that the paper received from the Afghan government. This came primarily through the Afghan government's diplomatic missions in Berlin and Paris. Saif Azad's connection to the Afghan missions was noticed by the British intelligence services, and it was during the early 1920s that he fell under the scrutiny of security agencies. His declassified intelligence file reveals that his correspondence with key figures among the Afghan diplomatic corps in Europe was routinely intercepted. One British intelligence report, from October 1921, states that the Amir of Aghanistan "persuaded Abdulrahman Saif to accept the post of editor [of *Azadi-ye Sharq*] by paying him well and flattering his self-conceit, which is said to be one of his main characteristics."[95] Other intercepted correspondence includes exchanges with Mahmud Tarzi[96] and Muhammad Ali Khan,[97] both of whom served in the Afghan Foreign Ministry during the 1920s, as well as Ghulam Sadiq Khan, another Afghan nationalist and senior diplomat during the reign of Amanullah Khan.[98] Most of these exchanges passed through the Afghan government's Paris diplomatic mission, which was clearly under surveillance by British authorities. The details of this intercepted correspondence document Saif Azad's requests for and receipt of funds from Afghan government sources to publish the *Azadi-ye Sharq*.[99]

Other materials in his intelligence file are equally revealing. British authorities cast a rather wide net during the immediate post–World War I period. Intelligence officers from throughout South Asia, the Middle East, and Europe were particularly adept at identifying potential subversives and placing them under surveillance. Especially in Berlin—a city that had attracted large numbers of political refugees—British intelligence officers and their network of informants were diligent in gathering details relating to the activities and associations of figures such as Saif Azad. Another intelligence report from 1921 details Saif Azad's cooperation with Hossein Danesh, an Iranian leftist intellectual based in Istanbul, in their joint effort to ship arms, via a purported German front company, to the Turkish military during Turkey's war of independence. Danesh's trip to Berlin in 1921 to assist in arranging the arms shipment was monitored by British intelligence. The report notes that Danesh's address during his stay in Berlin was the same as Saif Azad's, 2 Savigny Platz, in the Charlottenburg district of central Berlin.[100] This neighborhood, which has been described as "Berlin's 'little Asia'"[101] during the 1920s, was the primary location for many of the politically engaged foreign nationals residing in the city. Taqizadeh and his associates had also lived and worked in this neighborhood, and the Kaviani press was located there as well. Saif Azad also resided in this neighborhood for much of his time in Berlin, and used it as his base of operations for the publication of *Azadi-ye Sharq* as well as his other political work.

By September of 1922 the success of the arms smuggling operation led the Berlin-based supporters of the Turkish nationalist movement to hold a clandestine victory celebration in Charlottenburg. British agents managed to infiltrate the meeting and document the identities of some of those in attendance, including Saif Azad. In a report describing the meeting of these "Orientals in Berlin," the informant provided a verbatim rendering of a speech given in Persian by Saif Azad during the meeting. The informant reported that in congratulating his Turkish comrades, Saif Azad stated:

> I speak on behalf of the Persians and my Afghan friends
> who are present tonight. We all congratulate Mustafa Kemal
> because it is a victory for all those who are fighting for
> freedom. . . . I should like to mention the names of all who
> fight in the same cause, and more especially Mr. Gandhi, who
> deserves all our praise and appreciation, the Amir [Amanul-
> lah Khan] of Afghanistan, and lastly Mustapha Kemal. May
> they all live long! Whether Persians, Afghans, or Indians, we
> should all unite to put an end to imperialism in our respec-
> tive countries. The English constitute the present menace. I
> hope this will soon be put an end to, so far as Turkey is con-
> cerned. Her example will, I think, soon be followed by other
> countries who will drive the English out of their respective
> countries.[102]

Saif Azad's invocation of Mahatma Gandhi, along with Amanullah Khan and Mustafa Kemal, during the celebration of the Turkish struggle for independence is suggestive of his larger global commitment to the anti-imperialist struggle. His speech in Persian, in which he spoke for both the Iranians and Afghans in the audience, is also an indication of how he saw his own position as part of a political movement that transcended the boundaries of Iran to forge solidarities across the Middle East and South Asia.

In addition to documenting Saif Azad's political commitments, the record of this speech is also suggestive of the extent to which his activities and associations were under surveillance. Saif Azad's intelligence file is replete with material documenting conversations that he had with individuals during his time in Berlin who, unbeknownst to him, were informants. Another report, based on information provided by an agent with the code name "T.C./19," documents a conversation in which Saif Azad explains his goal for *Azadi-ye Sharq*. According to the informant:

> During the course of the conversations Saif Azad stated that his newspaper was intended to represent all communities: Indians, Arabs, Persians, etc., and he hoped in time that it would develop and start branches in other European countries where there are Asiatics.[103]

Other reports from informants state that "he [Saif Azad] wants to join all the peoples of the East together to unite them in a fight against imperialism . . . and he regards Kabul as the place from which the main attack against England is to be launched."[104] His Pan-Asian politics were also documented by authorities through tracing his associations with other anti-imperialist nationalist groups, such as leaders of the Pan-Islamist and Egyptian nationalist movements in Berlin, including the key figure Abd al-Aziz Shawish (1872–1929), with whom the report states "he is in constant touch."[105] His meetings and associations with members of the Hindustan Ghadar Party were also monitored.[106] There was also speculation about his association with elements of the Communist Party in Berlin, including meetings he had with Wigdor Kopp, a known Soviet agent in Berlin during this period, as well as Leonid Krasin, a visiting Soviet diplomat.[107] According to the informant, Saif Azad "attached considerable importance" to the meeting with Krasin, "as there were several questions of propaganda to be discussed."[108] The speculation of his association with the Communist movement is not without some basis. Although he was always ideologically more committed to an anti-imperialism defined by Pan-Asian nationalism and an alliance with Germany, it is not inconceivable that he could have at least tactically associated himself with the political fortunes of revolutionary communism. Wipert von Blücher also commented on Saif Azad's optimistic analysis of the Russian Revolution, stating that he had described it as a potentially positive development for Iran and urged the Germans to make common cause with the Soviets against the British.[109]

IRAN-E BASTAN AND THE PARSI CONNECTION
Saif Azad's multiple associations and tactical alliances were very much in flux during his decade in Berlin. Bozorg Alavi's comment that he was a man of many "colors" is therefore perhaps the most accurate, as is Wipert von Blücher's comparison of Saif Azad's many self-reinventions to the legend of Shaharazad. Whatever his exact associations may have been during his time as an activist and journalist in Berlin—be they with Germans, Turks, Afghans, Egyptians, Iranians, Indians, or Bolsheviks—by 1931 he seemed to have once again felt the need to find new political allies and new financial patrons. During this period he ceased his journalistic activities in Berlin and left for Bombay and Tehran to begin the publication of *Iran-e Bastan*, the newspaper for which he is most remembered.

The circumstances that led to the closing of *Azadi-ye Sharq* in 1931 are not entirely clear. The newspaper had been published on an intermittent schedule since 1927. During this period Saif Azad was also publishing a number of other newspapers in Berlin, including the *Sana'-ye Alman va Sharq*. This journalistic enterprise was much less politically oriented in its content than *Azadi-ye Sharq*, focusing instead on the advances of German industrialization in the 1920s and advocating for stronger economic ties between German companies and countries in the Middle East and South Asia.[110] Like the *Azadi-ye Sharq*, the *Sana'-ye Alman va Sharq* was a multilingual paper that strove to reach a wide audience. Unlike the *Azadi-ye Sharq*, however, which published in Persian and German, the *Sana'-ye Alman va Sharq* also included articles in Ottoman and Urdu.[111] By 1931 both of these newspapers ceased publication; certainly the financial difficulties of sustaining a newspaper were a perennial challenge. The ten-year print run of *Azadi-ye Sharq* was itself remarkably long-lived compared to many other exile or expatriate newspapers of the same era. This longevity had likely been sustained in large part by the financial support that Saif Azad received from the Afghan government. When this funding ceased in 1929 following the fall of Amanullah Khan, it became much more difficult for him to sustain his journalistic efforts in Berlin. The newspapers now had to rely exclusively on paid subscriptions and advertising revenue from German industrial firms to sustain themselves. The global financial crisis following the crash of 1929 made advertising revenue increasingly difficult to come by. By 1931 it had become clear that neither *Azadi-ye Sharq* nor *Sana'-ye Alman va Sharq* would be able to survive.

Saif Azad's turn to the Parsi community of Bombay for financial support of his journalistic activities, beginning sometime in the second half of 1930, was therefore motivated by the decline of his fortunes in Berlin. As early as 1927 news of Parsi patronage for cultural, intellectual, and publishing initiatives had circulated widely among Iranians, both within Iran and in Europe. The efforts of the Iran League to sponsor the translation of the Zoroastrian texts into modern Persian were recognized as both a major scholarly achievement and a major investment of cultural philanthropy. The efforts of Dinshah Irani and Peshotanji Marker, in particular, to support Ebrahim Purdavud's translation of the *Gathas* suggested to many that a new era of Parsi engagement with Iran was beginning. Saif Azad was aware of these developments and concluded that traveling to Bombay to meet the leaders of the Parsi community could help to further his own interests.[112] In addition to the Parsi-sponsored translation initiative, rumors of Parsi philanthropy for Persian-language literary, cultural, and political journals had also circulated among intellectually engaged Iranians in Europe and Iran. Some of these rumors were levied to discredit those who were considered to be under the control of private donors. The Berlin-based Persian-language journal *Iranshahr*, edited by Hossein Kazemzadeh, had in particular been associated with Parsi benefactors. The journal's strong pre-Islamic and Zoroastrian themes lent an air of credence to these assertions. The Calcutta-based Islamic modernist newspaper *Habl al-Matin* publicly voiced these assertions, stating that *Iranshahr* was receiving funds from the Parsi community to advocate for a return to Zoroastrianism on the part of Iran's Muslim population.[113] The author of the column in *Habl al-Matin* wrote:

> [The writers of *Iranshahr*] try to write to please the Parsis of India in order to receive their £500 annual subsidy from them. . . . They are neglectful of the fact that the multitudes of people [in Iran] will never return to fire-worship and Zoroastrianism.[114]

Hossein Kazemzadeh's sharp retort to these accusations came in the July 23, 1926, issue of the journal. He wrote, "If the esteemed writer had carefully read the pages of *Iranshahr* . . . he would see that it is clear that promoting a specific religion is very far from our intention."[115] Instead, he went on to write, the main purpose of the newspaper was to "awaken the nation," to "fight moral decay," and to foster unity "without distinguishing on the basis of race or religion under a united flag representing Iranianness." Kazemzadeh also stated flatly that the journal "has not received a single dinar from the Parsis" and that it had fewer than thirty subscribers in all of India.[116]

Whatever the complete truth may have been regarding the relationship between Hossein Kazemzadeh and the Parsis—and there is no evidence in the Parsi sources to suggest that there was any relationship—this epistolary exchange in the pages of *Iranshahr* and *Habl al-Matin* does indicate that by the mid-1920s the growing involvement of Parsi philanthropy in shaping the nature of debates about contemporary Iran was gaining notice. For Saif Azad, the increased awareness of Parsi patronage toward Ebrahim Purdavud's translation efforts, and the rumors of Parsi support for journals such as *Iranshahr*, were the likely catalyst that encouraged him to reach out to the Parsis after the decline of his own fortunes in Berlin; by the early part of 1931 Saif Azad began making plans for a return to Iran by way of Bombay.

His efforts to reach out to the Parsis were made via correspondence with leaders of the Iran League. The League's activities included the publication of the long-running bilingual Persian and English quarterly journal *Iran League Quarterly*, which circulated within India and Iran as well as Europe, North America, East Asia, and East Africa. Saif Azad began a correspondence with the editors of the journal in late 1930, as well as with the leadership of the League and its sister organization, the Iranian Zoroastrian Anjoman of Bombay. Some of this correspondence was subsequently published in the pages of the *Quarterly*, as well as in the pages of what eventually became Saif Azad's Tehran-based newspaper, the *Iran-e Bastan*.

This correspondence indicates that sometime in the second half of 1930, Saif Azad began writing to the Parsi leadership from Berlin with an urgent appeal: "the Persians are ignorant of Parsi greatness,"[117] he wrote, and need to learn of Parsi industrial, commercial, and scientific achievements in order to foster Iran's own "regeneration." He went on to request support from the Parsis to establish a newspaper, in Persian, to be published in Tehran that would work to acquaint Iranians with the Parsi community: "I request that a private meeting of a few leaders interested in this question be called at an early date, and a bold, business-like decision taken to start the paper in its useful career."[118] He also requested the establishment of a community center in Tehran that would serve as both the editorial home of the newspaper and as an institution for cultural outreach to Iranians on behalf of the Parsis.

Saif Azad's correspondence with the Parsis also included a theme that was already prominent, both within the Parsi community and among some strands of the Iranian nationalist movement: the remigration of the Parsis to their ancestral homeland. The practicalities of land purchase in Khuzistan and other regions to establish a colony for future Parsi settlement, for example, was actively discussed both in the pages of the *Quarterly* and more broadly among the leaders of the Parsi community.[119] Saif Azad's correspondence with the Parsis broached this topic as well. In a long excerpt from one of his letters, published in the January 1932 issue of the *Iran League Quarterly*, he addressed the topic directly by making a striking comparison between the Parsis' connection to Iran and the then-active Zionist movement's project of promoting remigration to Palestine. He wrote:

> The right of the Jews in Palestine cannot at all be compared with those of Parsis in Persia, and yet the former have started intense propaganda all over the world and have several organs in Palestine itself. In [the] face of intense Arab animosity, and adverse opinion of a large sector of the world against their ways and methods, they are by dint of push and propaganda establishing their footing everywhere, and their right over Palestine, in face of bitter antagonism.[120]

Despite the thinly veiled tone of anti-Semitism in Saif Azad's assessment of "Jewish propaganda"—a tone that was also evident in the pages of *Iran-e Bastan*—he nevertheless seems to acknowledge a grudging respect for the success of the Zionist project of remigration. In the same letter, he also argued that the Zionist project should be seen as a model for the Parsis as they considered their own renewed connections with Iran. He continued:

On the other hand, Persia is the home of the Parsis and
there they do not possess a single newspaper of their own to
proclaim their very existence. You cannot imagine what an
immense appeal and impression such a paper would make on
the minds of your own brothers, sisters, and friends in Persia,
i.e., among your own nation.[121]

Saif Azad's appeal to the Parsis was met initially with a strong positive
response. By 1931 the Parsi community already had a long history of
supporting charity efforts to help alleviate the social and economic
conditions of the Zoroastrian communities in Kerman and Yazd. Their
sponsorship of Purdavud's translation efforts indicated that they were
also interested in supporting scholarly and intellectual exchanges. Saif
Azad's proposal for a Parsi-sponsored Persian-language newspaper, as
well as a Parsi-sponsored cultural center in Tehran, seemed to represent
the next stage of Parsi outreach and engagement with Iran. The leadership of the Iran League and the Iranian Zoroastrian Anjoman were
in fact eager to expand their engagement, and responded to Saif Azad's
proposal by extending an invitation for him to visit Bombay for several
weeks in June and July of 1931.

Not everyone, however, was eager to welcome Saif Azad to Bombay. British security forces, while granting him a visa, were well aware
of his activities in Berlin, as well as his earlier involvement with Afghan
politics, and therefore kept careful records of his movements and meetings while in the city. According to one anonymous informant whose
observations were documented in Saif Azad's intelligence file, "it is said
that the object of his visit is to rouse the Parsis in favor of Persia."[122] The
report also documented that Saif Azad was staying at the Taj Mahal Hotel
in the Colaba district of Bombay and was a guest of the Iran League and
the Iranian Zoroastrian Anjoman. It also documented meetings at the
hotel between Saif Azad and key Parsi civic and business leaders, including the prominent Parsi banker Phiroze Sethna, the former president
of the Iran League Hormusji Adenwalla, and the journalist and writer
Phiroze Jahangir Marzban. Two public events—one at the Willingdon
Sports Club and another at Sir Cowasji Jahangir Hall—were recorded
in the file.[123] The report also documented the skepticism of G. K. Nariman toward the intentions of Saif Azad. Nariman, a much-esteemed and
independent-minded scholar of Zoroastrianism and pre-Islamic Iranian

Iran-e Bastan *front page.* Iran-e Bastan, *Tehran, 1933.*

history, was among the few members of the community who was critical of Parsi initiatives toward Iran. He was quoted as describing Saif
Azad as a fraud who falsely presented himself as an emissary sent by
Reza Shah.[124] A news story from the *Bombay Chronicle* following Saif
Azad's speech and reception at the Willingdon Sports Club also states
that Saif Azad presented himself to the Parsi community as an emissary
of the Shah.[125] There is no indication to suggest that his visit to Bombay
was undertaken for any reason other than his own personal initiative.
Nariman's skeptical view of Saif Azad, in fact, seems to echo the views of
others who had crossed paths with him during his Berlin years, such as
Bozorg Alavi, Mortaza Moshfeq-Kazemi, and Wipert von Blücher, all of
whom emphasized his wily, mercurial, and capricious character.

Despite the skepticism of Nariman and other critical-minded members of the Parsi community, the civic, business, and financial leadership
of the Parsis nevertheless saw Saif Azad as a useful journalistic intermediary who could help to promote a new level of public engagement
with Iran. The result was a series of financial commitments to help him
establish both a newspaper and a cultural center in Tehran. By January
of 1933, *Iran-e Bastan* began publication with an initial print run of five
thousand biweekly issues; within the first year, the early success of the
newspaper led to an increase to eight thousand copies and a more ambitious publication schedule.[126] The cultural center, the "Kanun-e Iran-e
Bastan," was also inaugurated in the same year on Lalehzar Street, in the
heart of Tehran's new cultural and commercial district.[127] The cultural
center came to serve as both the editorial offices of the newspaper and a
location for meetings, lectures, and other community outreach activities.

PROMOTING PARSI REMIGRATION TO IRAN

The Parsi sponsorship of *Iran-e Bastan* was reflected in the subject matter and editorial content of the newspaper's first issues. While historians
of modern Iran have more conventionally regarded the newspaper as
principally an organ for the dissemination of Nazi propaganda,[128] the
early history of *Iran-e Bastan* should more accurately be tied to Saif
Azad's efforts to enlist Parsi support for the nation-building efforts of
Reza Shah. The shift toward an editorial policy of promoting Nazi cultural and political policies unfolded intermittently during the newspaper's inaugural year of publication, but in its inception and initial issues
Iran-e Bastan remained committed to carrying out the more limited mission that it proclaimed on its original masthead: "to encourage fraternal

Iran-e Bastan *with swastika masthead*. Iran-e Bastan, *Tehran, 1934.*

sentiments between the Parsees of India and Persians, to stimulate commercial relations, industrial enterprises, and to encourage Parsees to
visit Iran frequently."[129] This statement was included on the newspaper's
masthead from its inception in January of 1933 until the August 26 issue
of the same year.[130] In the fall of 1933 the newspaper's editorial position shifted more toward dissemination of pro-German and pro-Nazi
propaganda. This shift in editorial policy is best reflected in a graphic
change in the newspaper's front page; beginning with the September 2,
1933, issue, the initial reference to the Parsis was replaced with a series
of swastikas.[131]

For much of its first year, however, and only intermittently thereaf-
ter, *Iran-e Bastan* saw itself as committed to the goal of introducing the
Zoroastrian community of western India to an Iranian reading public,
and to fostering social, cultural, and economic ties between Parsis and
Iranians. Along with this broad goal, the newspaper sought to encourage
Zoroastrian remigration to Iran, and this also served as a prominent
editorial theme during its first eight months. These themes are reflected
through a number of different types of stories in the early issues of the
newspaper, including biographical portraits of prominent Parsis, the
publication of letters to the editor from members of the Parsi community, and editorials written by Saif Azad himself. In the case of the
biographical portraits, they were intended to present the great success
and prosperity of the Parsi community in Bombay to an Iranian audience, and to demonstrate to Iranian readers the Parsis' growing willingness to reach out to their Iranian compatriots. One such portrait, of
Sir Phiroze Sethna, appeared in the March 21, 1933, Nowruz issue of
Iran-e Bastan.[132] Sethna, a prominent banker in the Parsi community,
was one of the key civic leaders of the Bombay Parsi community and

had become an early supporter of Saif Azad's Parsi initiative. In *Iran-e Bastan*'s Nowruz issue of 1933, Saif Azad gave a detailed account of his own sojourn to Bombay in 1931, and of his visit with Sethna. He also included a description—along with photographs and an excerpt from the speech Sethna delivered—of the large gathering of Parsis who had attended the dinner banquet at the Willingdon Sports Club in Bombay held in Saif Azad's honor during the previous year.

The article began with the transcript of the speech, in which Sethna praised the achievements of Reza Shah: "Alahazrat Reza Shah Pahlavi has the same position and authority in Iran that Ghazi Mustafa Kemal has with respect to Turkey. . . . The progress of Turkey since the war has been stunning and tremendous. We hope that in the same way . . . Iran will follow this precedent."[133] Sethna also discussed Iran's progress in the ongoing construction of the trans-Iranian railroad, as well as the possibility of Parsi involvement in this and other infrastructure projects. He marveled at the progress of road construction inside Iran and the new ease of transport and travel: "what previously took several weeks now takes several days," he observed.[134] All of these achievements made the possibility of Parsi-Iranian economic and commercial ties much more viable than in the past. For Parsi civic, commercial, and financial leaders like Sethna, the possibilities of these new economic ties were very appealing not only for financial reasons, but also for reasons of philanthropy toward what the Parsis perceived as their ancestral homeland.

After describing these economic changes and investment possibilities, the article next described Sethna's comments regarding the newfound cultural appreciation of Iran's Zoroastrian heritage among contemporary Iranians:

Let me say something more about the Parsis of India and Iran. Until recently they [Iranians] did not interact with the Zoroastrians in the way that we would like, and they did not acknowledge the contributions of the ancient Zoroastrians to the majesty and greatness of ancient Iran. However, under the current leadership in Iran these sorts of ideas are no longer applicable. . . . Today in Iran, among all segments of society, there is a desire to become aware of the ancient literature and teachings which existed in Iran prior to the hijra. . . . This desire is so intense that they desire to know not only about their glorious past, but they are to the same degree eager to

learn how, and in what way, the Parsis in India . . . have made
such progress since our stay in India during the past twelve
centuries. . . . Iranians are of the opinion that if even a few of
us were to once more return to the country of our ancestors
and reside there we will also be successful there to the same
degree [as we have been in India]. . . . It is for this reason that
the present government of Iran is ready to provide assistance
to anyone who wants to migrate for purposes of trade and
commerce on a permanent basis.[135]

The social restrictions that had traditionally been in place on Zoroastrians and other religious minorities in Iran were a source of great concern for Parsis looking to reengage with their ancestral home. Lifting these restrictions had in fact become a prerequisite for effective Parsi economic and commercial engagement with Iran. Sethna's description of a newfound appreciation of Iran's Zoroastrian heritage by the Pahlavi government, and of efforts to lift traditionally imposed social restrictions on Zoroastrians inside Iran, was therefore important in making the case that a new era of social and economic possibilities had begun. To emphasize this point, Sethna described the recent visits to Iran by several key civic and commercial figures of the Parsi community, including the then-president of the Iran League, Hormusji Adenwalla. He also referenced the reports sent to Bombay from the Parsi community's permanent representative in Iran, Ardeshir Reporter. These firsthand accounts, Sethna argued, confirmed that the Pahlavi government had "awakened Iran, and placed her on the road of progress and modernization."[136] These changes, Sethna suggested, were necessary to enable Parsi remigration to Iran. As Saif Azad quotes him in the pages of *Iran-e Bastan*, "I know numerous eminent Parsi men and women who, if the opportunity was available, would be interested to personally go to Iran and assess the circumstances from up close and judge for themselves."[137] Social and economic progress under Reza Shah, along with a new cultural and ideological appreciation of Iran's Zoroastrian heritage, were themes that were emphasized throughout the early issues of *Iran-e Bastan*. As coverage of Sethna's speech in the pages of the newspaper suggested, segments of the Parsi community of Bombay were seriously considering a broader engagement with Iran, including economic investment, regular travel, and in some cases permanent remigration.

Sethna's speech concluded by emphasizing the growing anxiety felt by Parsis during the final decades of the British Raj. As the independence movement was gaining strength in the 1920s and 1930s, many Parsis began to question their social and political position in a post-independence India. This anxiety in fact permeated much of the subtext of Parsi engagement with Iran during the decades immediately preceding India's independence. While many Parsis were supporters of the independence movement, the history of the Parsi community's intimate relationship with the British colonial government opened many members of the Parsi community to considering alternative futures for the Parsis, including migration to the colonial metropole itself, emigration to more politically secure regions within the British Empire, or, finally, remigration to their ancestral homeland of Iran, now ruled by the welcoming Pahlavi monarch who was actively encouraging Parsi reengagement. As Sethna explained:

> I know that some Parsis are worried that if the movement
> for independence becomes successful their position in this
> country [India] will become uncertain. . . . For those who
> think this way . . . there is today an opportunity that they and
> their children can take advantage of. Even though it has been
> twelve hundred years since our immigration to India, I am
> confident that there remains a real love and loyalty within
> most Parsis towards the country of their ancestors . . . and if
> any Parsi friend of ours should be of the opinion to go there
> [Iran] I do not think that they will regret it in the future.[138]

With the advantage of hindsight, it is difficult to assign much credit to Sir Phiroze Sethna's predictions for Iran's political future. Nevertheless, from the vantage point of 1931, the political logic of Parsi anxiety within British India, coupled with the promise of a new era then unfolding inside Iran, seemed to suggest that remigration could serve as both a compelling possibility and a fortuitous future for the Parsi community.

While the biographical portrait of Phiroze Sethna and coverage of his speech at the Willingdon Sports Club was one of the most significant articles in the early issues of *Iran-e Bastan* that sought to highlight renewed Parsi-Iranian relations, there were many others during the newspaper's first eight months as well. Other biographical portraits of prominent Parsis also served as a convenient platform to introduce the Parsis to Iranian readers and to encourage further social, cultural, political, and economic connections. Biographies of Phiroze Jahangir Marzban, Sir Dinshaw Petit, Dinshah Fereydunji Molla, Nadirshah Noshirwan, Jamshid Mehta, Jehangir Vimadalal, and Sir Hormusji Adenwalla, were among others that Saif Azad included in the early issues of *Iran-e Bastan*. In all of these cases, their achievements were detailed, along with their endorsement of Reza Shah's modernization efforts, followed by a discussion of each individual's desire to assist in the development of their ancestral homeland.

In the case of Phiroze Jahangir Marzban, for example, Saif Azad describes the Marzban family as the owners of the *Jame-Jamshid*, one of the most successful and longest-running newspapers in India. In 1933 the *Jame-Jamshid* was celebrating its centennial, with public events held in Bombay to commemorate the newspaper's founding. The Marzban family, Saif Azad was quick to point out in his biographical portrait, was "among the wealthiest in India . . . and gives to charity for hospitals and to the poor."[139] He added that the *Jame-Jamshid* also regularly published articles about the achievements of Reza Shah. Saif Azad went on to describe how the *Jame-Jamshid*'s centennial was celebrated not only in Bombay, but also in Tehran. At the newly established Parsi community center in central Tehran—the so-called Kanun-e Iran-e Bastan on Lalehzar Street, established via Parsi financial support—prominent Iranian literati had gathered at Saif Azad's invitation to commemorate the centennial. Among those present were the poet Rashid Yasami, the historian Sa'id Nafisi, and the scholar of Perisan literature Sadeq Rezazadeh Shafaq. According to Saif Azad, each wrote an essay in honor of the centennial of the *Jame-Jamshid*, which was later to be published in book form as *Ghadrdani-ye Khedmat* (Appreciation for Support). The bilingual collection of essays was written, according to Saif Azad, to thank the Parsis for their support of Iran's modernization efforts and to encourage them to make a pilgrimage to Iran. As Saif Azad describes in the article describing the commemoration ceremony held in Tehran, upon receiving word of the gathering, "Phiruze Jahangir Marzban was very pleased."[140]

Like the biographical portrait of Marzban, Saif Azad's portraits of other prominent Parsis also emphasized their desire to reach out to Iran, and in particular to visit their ancestral homeland and participate in its social and economic development. In another article, Saif Azad quotes Sir Dinshaw Petit, the son of the founder of the Iranian Zoroastrian Amelioration Fund in the 1850s and among the Parsi families with the longest history of promoting charity work with respect to Iran: "nothing excites my heart more than the thought of paying pilgrimage to Iran . . . and to help it return to its past glory and splendor."[141] In another article about Sir Hormusji Adenwalla, one of the key civic leaders of the Iran League and a member of a prominent family of merchants and industrialists, Saif Azad quotes Adenwalla as saying, "Parsis are hopeful for the day when they can return and become part of the life of a new Iran in order to be a source of service . . . may God protect Iran and Iran's monarch."[142] Finally, in the portrait of Jamshid Mehta, another civic-minded Parsi from a prominent textile-industrialist and philanthropic family, and a key figure in the urban development of the city of Karachi, Saif Azad quotes him as saying, "If I can help the country of my forebears . . . I will devote myself to God in pursuit of this goal."[143]

The themes of Parsi support for Iran's development, as well as of return and remigration to Iran, were also discussed in other types of stories in the early issues of *Iran-e Bastan*. In the fourth issue of the newspaper, published on February 11, 1933, Saif Azad discusses economic development inside Iran and the possibility of establishing an infrastructure for Parsi tourism. He chronicles the efforts of two Parsi entrepreneurs, Visaji Tarapurvalla and Jehangir Katgara, who had recently traveled to Iran to prospect for suitable locations for visitor accommodations, as well as to assess the logistics of transportation between cities for the large number of Parsis whom they expected would be interested in visiting Iran. The two arrived in Iran via the port at Bushehr and traveled to Shiraz, Yazd, Kerman, Isfahan, and Tehran to build partnerships with locals for Parsi tourism. According to Saif Azad, who met with the two entrepreneurs during their visit to Shiraz, the people of that city were "eager to welcome and show hospitality to the visitors."[144] Saif Azad wrote that both Tarapurvalla and Katgara were very pleased with the progress underway in Iran through the efforts of Reza Shah "and will return to India and inform others."[145] In the years that followed, Parsi tourism in fact gained considerable momentum, and an economic infrastructure of Parsi travel to Iran had considerable success. Tour companies specializing in Parsi travel packages to Iran advertised in the pages of Bombay-based Parsi periodicals.[146] As early as 1935 the first Parsi-oriented guidebook for travel to Iran, *A Tourist Guide to Iran*, was published by Rustam Kharegat in Bombay.[147] The guidebook emphasized Iran's archaeological sites and Zoroastrian cultural monuments as destinations for travel, and was marketed specifically toward India's Parsi community.[148]

Another type of article that Saif Azad included in *Iran-e Bastan* to emphasize the theme of the Parsi return to Iran was the publication of his correspondence with Parsis in India. Via the supporters that he had cultivated in Bombay, Saif Azad had developed a cohort of contacts with whom he was in intermittent correspondence, especially during the early phase of the newspaper's publication. The occasional publication of these letters to the editor and his replies made it possible for his Iranian readers to gain a fuller appreciation of the emotional sentiments expressed by Parsis toward Iran. On the issue of tourism, for example, Saif Azad published a letter from Darabshah Jahangir and Hormozd Rustam-Pir, two young Parsis from Bombay who had undertaken a personal journey to see their ancestral homeland in 1933.[149] The two had traveled from Bombay prior to the formal establishment of a tourism infrastructure, but they were writing to Saif Azad to ask him to convey their deep appreciation to the Iranian people for the hospitality they received during their travels from Bushehr to Shiraz, Yazd, Isfahan, and Tehran. The letter, written originally in English and subsequently translated into Persian for publication in *Iran-e Bastan*, reflects the emotions of some Parsis upon returning to their ancestral homeland, an emotion that Saif Azad was eager to promote to help build bonds of connection and exchange between Parsis and Iranians. "I saw things that amazed me," the letter began, "such as Shiraz which I had heard was pleasant and beautiful . . . but now that I see it . . . my heart and soul and spirit have been reborn."[150] Upon traveling to the Achaemenid ruins at Takht-e Jamshid, Jahangir and Rustam-Pir described for Saif Azad, and for the readers of *Iran-e Bastan*, the "indescribable effect" that seeing the ruins had on them. One of them commented: "I stared as though in a trance (*zār-zār*), and I offered prayers and blessings to the spirit of my ancestors."[151] Their letter also describes a visit to the boys' and girls' schools in Yazd that had been established through the philanthropic efforts of Peshotanji Marker, one of the Parsi community's most generous benefactors toward the Zoroastrians of Iran. The authors describe "being very pleased to see all of the progress" and state their hope "that every day they [the Iranian Zoroastrians] will experience more and more progress."[152] They concluded their letter by thanking Saif Azad—"the esteemed editor of this newspaper"—for his help in arranging their travels through Iran. They also promised to "encourage more and more of our friends and acquaintances to make this pilgrimage. . . . We will invite our brothers and sisters who are in India and who are interested in making a pilgrimage to Iran to visit this land."[153]

The theme of encouraging Parsi return to Iran is also reflected in another notable epistolary exchange published in the pages of *Iran-e Bastan*. In one of the early issues of the newspaper, Saif Azad discusses a letter that he had received from one of his correspondents in Bombay. He does not give the name of the letter-writer, but in the letter, published under the headline of "Yadavari" (reminder), he describes the correspondent as "one of the wise elders of the Parsis."[154] The original letter, according to Saif Azad, posed the question of how Parsis and Iranians may overcome the obstacles standing in the way of closer contact between their two communities, as well as whether Parsis should consider permanent remigration to Iran. He reproduced his own reply in the form of an editorial open letter to the Parsi community, published in the February 4, 1933, issue. He began by suggesting that the question was central to his own concerns, and was the principal reason why he began publishing the newspaper, "as the esteemed gentleman knows the issue posed by the question is regularly addressed in these pages."[155] Saif Azad wrote:

> The Iran of today has changed dramatically from the Qajar era. Everything today is moving towards progress and is under the direction and leadership of the Pahlavi Shah. It is hoped that in the near future the country will be shoulder-to-shoulder with the civilized nations. Under these circumstances of inaugurating fundamental reforms to the ancient country of Iran, the goal of all true Iranians is to encourage the swift success of these reforms. . . . The Parsis of India, who are the revered offspring of Iran, if in previous eras had to flee their homeland because of terrible calamities, nevertheless have never lost their sense of Iranianness and love for Iran. Just as today, when all people of the Iranian race look with hope to a new auspicious day for the ancient land of Iran, so too the Parsis, who because of the particularities of their race, should also be hopeful and give Iran their greatest attention.[156]

Saif Azad's description of the reforms of the Reza Shah era were the foundation for promoting Parsi engagement with Iran. Throughout the early issues of *Iran-e Bastan*, discussions of Parsi remigration were always couched in terms of establishing the right conditions for further social and economic development. From the point of view of Saif Azad, and from the view of the Pahlavi state, these improved social and economic conditions were necessary to encourage the Parsis' return to Iran. As Saif Azad's letter to his Parsi correspondent expressed, he emphasized the economic opportunities in Iran for Parsi entrepreneurs, but also the cultural motivations for Parsi reengagement with Iran. The Parsis should be motivated to return to Iran "because returning to their dear homeland would not only result in innumerable material benefits, but will also be a source of pride and accomplishment . . . because this action would be motivated by a total devotion and a complete love for preserving their national identity."[157]

NAZIS, PARSIS, AND JEWS

In making his case for Parsi remigration, Saif Azad's open letter returned to the comparison between the Parsi project to Iran and the Zionist project of return to Palestine. Saif Azad made numerous references to Jewish history and the Zionist project of remigration in the pages of *Iran-e Bastan*. In his open letter to the Parsis, he once again argued that the Parsis should view the Zionist project as a model for reengaging with their own ancestral homeland. However, the broad cultural and historical comparison between the Jewish and Parsi experiences of diaspora and return quickly took an ideological turn:

> The scattered and weak Jewish nation, who from habit
> and custom think only of gaining money and wealth, have
> returned to Palestine through the unworkable promises of
> Balfour, and who once there are now only reproducing the
> insecurity and instability which has existed in their earlier
> history . . . and yet they do not complain, but instead strive to
> improve their homeland despite the hardships. Isn't it, there-
> fore, a cause of amazement that the pure Parsis, during a time
> of progress and security in their ancient Iranian homeland,
> are still wandering in a foreign land, even though they are
> allowed and encouraged to return to their dear home.[158]

Saif Azad's tone in making this comparison between Parsis and Jews works to illustrate one of the underlying tensions at the core of his efforts to encourage Parsi engagement with Iran. While the motivations of the Parsi community for reengagement with Iran were always rooted in a liberal ideal of cultural repatriation, for Saif Azad the arguments for

Parsi reengagement and remigration became increasingly shaped not by liberal ideas of charity, philanthropy, and social progress, but by a racialized and anti-Semitic language reflecting his increasing association with Nazi ideology.[159] As *Iran-e Bastan* continued to publish into the fall of 1933 and beyond, the editorial content of the newspaper took a decisive turn toward a Nazi ideological perspective. The characterization of Jews in the pages of *Iran-e Bastan* as disseminating pernicious propaganda, as seekers of wealth and money, and as embodiments of racial mongrelization all reflected vernacular stereotypes of early twentieth-century European anti-Semitism. In addition to the increasing presence of the swastika on the masthead of the newspaper, the shift toward Nazi ideology in the pages of *Iran-e Bastan* was also reflected in its lauditory coverage of Hitler's consolidation of power. The newspaper also began publishing a number of serialized translations into Persian from official Nazi Party magazines. An article by the notorious Nazi ideologue Alfred Rosenberg, for example, on the importance of studying ancient Iranian history to define the future of the German Reich, found its way into the pages of the April 14, 1934, issue of *Iran-e Bastan*.[160] Beginning with the August 25, 1934, issue, the newspaper published a serialized translation in six parts of Wolfgang Shultz Gurlitz's article "Iran and Zoroaster."[161] The article, first published in one of the official organs of the Nazi Party, hypothesized the racial evolution of Iranians and extolled the founder of Iran's ancient religion as "an Aryan prophet."[162]

Saif Azad and other contributors to the newspaper also began to publish their own original articles that now came to reflect Nazi ideology. One article, published in the October 7, 1934, issue, was titled "The Necessity of Knowing Races" and extolled Nazi innovations in the new "race science" (*'elm-e nezhād-shenāsi*).[163] The article states that "one of the accomplishments of the National Socialist party, for the benefit of the German nation, has been their effort to focus the attention of the nation on the issue of race."[164] The article continued by stating "a nation that does not give attention to this issue will be relegated to annihilation . . . in the same way that other nations in the past who have neglected this issue have likewise disappeared."[165] Another article proclaiming the virtues of nationhood and love of the homeland, written by a then young Davud Monshizadeh (1915–1989), the founder of what would become the SUMKA party—the Iranian equivalent of the Nazi Party—also appeared in the pages of *Iran-e Bastan*.[166] The paper's increasing affinity with racist ideology and fascist politics was also reflected in coverage of Nazi-affiliated political organizations outside of Germany, such as the Irish "Blueshirts,"[167] who fought alongside Franco in the Spanish civil war, and the radical wing of the Indian National Congress, as represented by coverage of the Indian nationalist Subhas Chandra Bose, whose "Azad Hind" movement would by the 1940s become an ally of the Nazi government.[168]

All of these examples of *Iran-e Bastan*'s shift toward a Nazi-affiliated editorial policy undermined what had been Saif Azad's original intention for the newspaper. His initial goal of using the newspaper as a platform for encouraging Parsi investment in Iran, remigration to Iran, and endorsement of the Pahlavi nation-building project was premised upon a shared understanding of Parsi-Iranian relations as part of a larger liberal and cosmopolitan project of national identity. While the language of race, religion, and cultural essentialism was always invoked by both Saif Azad and the Parsis in their mutual efforts to foster renewed ties, the political context of that language was—at least for the Parsis—never intended to promote an exclusionary, illiberal, or fascist style of politics. Nor, for that matter, were the Parsis generally interested in challenging the authority of the British Empire, within which they held the status of a privileged and protected minority community. For the Parsis, the increasingly unmistakable connection of Saif Azad's *Iran-e Bastan* with Nazi politics was therefore unsettling, and by the end of the first year of the newspaper's publication, in December of 1933, it seems clear that the Parsis had curtailed their ties with Saif Azad.

The Parsi sources are silent on the issue of curtailiing ties with Saif Azad. In none of the official sources is there a formal statement of why they chose to distance themselves from him by the fall of 1933. The decision was likely made after some internal deliberation following a more concerted examination of the newspaper's editorial content. We can infer this from an editorial by Saif Azad in the December 20, 1933, issue. In an annual assessment of the successes and challenges that the newspaper faced during its first year of publication, he made an elliptical comment in reference to the Parsis. After mentioning his initial visit to India and the hope that he had for help from the Parsi community there, he expresses disappointment:

> It is with the greatest regret and sadness . . . that because
> of bad intentions . . . our cooperation with some people,
> whose efforts were in harmony with our own before the

publication of the *Iran-e Bastan* journal, has now become
completely broken and I no longer have contact with them,
and the "kanun-e Iran-e bastan" is now nothing more than a
name and a sign. After the publication of *Iran-e Bastan* only
a handful of people . . . 10–15 who are members of the Iran
League of the Parsis and a few people, meaning 24 people,
who are members of the Iranian Zoroastrian Anjoman
are associated with this organization. . . . The details of the
founding of the "kanun-e Iran-e bastan" and its dismantling
is a story worth telling, and so it is better to leave that for a
time when there is more room to explain it in detail in order
to reveal much.[169]

Despite the suggestion that he would give a fuller explanation of this
"story worth telling" in a future issue of the newspaper, Saif Azad never
returned to the question of the break with the Parsis. As the newspaper continued into its second year and on to its final issue at the end of
1935, discussions of the Parsis, and Parsi-Iranian contact and cooperation, quickly disappeared. In the end, neither the Parsis nor Saif Azad
provided a full accounting of the details of their break. What Saif Azad
does suggest, however, in his December 1933 assessment of the journal's first year of publication, is in keeping with the trajectory of *Iran-e
Bastan*'s editorial content. His initiative to the Parsis in 1931 had been
made with the goal of reviving contact between the Parsi community of
India and their ancestral homeland to promote cultural ties, economic
investment, and political assistance for the nation-building project of
Reza Shah. The tension between these initial goals and the emerging
politics of national socialism, however, quickly produced a divergence
between the Parsis and the man they hoped would serve as their Iranian interlocutor. Saif Azad's background in the radical politics of early
twentieth-century anti-imperialism, including his ties to Berlin-based
revolutionary organizations and, ultimately, his Nazi associations, made
it clear to most members of the Parsi community by the fall of 1933 that
Saif Azad did not share their goals.

CONCLUSION

Despite the break with the Parsis and the eventual demise of *Iran-e
Bastan* in 1935, Saif Azad's commitment to the cause of India's independence continued. In 1937 he once again traveled to India with the

goal of establishing yet another newspaper, this time one extolling the social and economic progress achieved by semi-independent Rajas in the provinces.[170] The short-lived bilingual English-Persian newspaper, the *Salar-e Hend*, occupied his time during the final two years prior to his arrest and internment by British authorities in September of 1939. Like *Iran-e Bastan*, the *Salar-e Hend* clearly had associations with Nazi ideology, and according to British security officials it received funding from German government sources. While less overtly political than *Iran-e Bastan* and *Azadi-ye Sharq*, its emphasis on social and economic self-reliance and portrayal of ambitious local Indian Rajas as worthy leaders of India made it clear that the newspaper intended to promote the cause of Indian independence. Nazi symbols and references in the paper also made it clear that Saif Azad's latest newspaper—like his earlier journalistic ventures—had German connections. It was on the basis of these connections that British authorities arrested Saif Azad in Bombay on Septembrer 9, 1939.

Saif Azad's arrest at the outbreak of World War II and internment until the conclusion of the war represents a fitting final phase for Iranian nationalism's history during the interwar period. The many stages, changes, and transformations that he went through during this period— from his participation in the German-organized Afghan mission during World War I to his journalistic activism in Berlin during the 1920s, his attempt to enlist the Parsis to Iran's nation-building project, and finally his efforts in India on the eve of the war—all represent not only an unusually active period in Saif Azad's life, but also a period of remarkable dynamism for the history of Iranian nationalism. The course of Iranian nationalism during this period suggests that its political nature remained unresolved; that it was not monopolized by any single state, institution, or social class; and that it still retained the possibility of evolving along multiple, and often contradictory, political trajectories. From the point of view of someone like Saif Azad, Iranian nationalism's political nature was largely allied with the then-emerging politics of transnational anti-imperialism. For others—most notably, for the Parsis, as well as others who advocated for a more liberal, moderate, or conservative strand of Iranian nationalism—Saif Azad's version of Iranian nationalism represented a dangerous aberration that was not only ideologically unsound, but ultimately threatened to cost Iran its already precarious independence. The unsettled nature of Iranian nationalism during the interwar period ultimately enabled Iranian nationalism to simultaneously embrace these multiple ideological incarnations and political possibilities. These same incarnations and possibilities—and the inevitable tensions that went along with them—ultimately came to define the evolution of Saif Azad's life, and the same tensions came to define the interwar politics of Iranian nationalism.

CONCLUSION

Ebrahim Purdavud spent the final years of his life continuing to publish in the fields of ancient Iranian history and Zoroastrian studies. From the time of his retirement from the University of Tehran in 1964 until his death on November 17, 1968, he continued his work in collaboration with a small circle of friends, colleagues, and former students.[1] Those who regularly paid visits to the still much-esteemed scholar at his home on Aban Street in northern Tehran, such as Iraj Afshar, Mohammad Mo'in, Bahram Farahvashi, and Ehsan Yarshater,[2] were among those whom Purdavud considered to be his closest scholarly colleagues and intellectual heirs.

During this period Purdavud also began receiving anonymous death threats. According to one of his biographers, the immediate context of these threats, sent to him in the form of written notes, was Purdavud's advocacy for ending the mandatory instruction of Arabic in Iran's public school system.[3] Purdavud had given interviews and published newspaper articles suggesting that the methods and value of Arabic instruction in Iran's public schools were inefficient, unproductive, and ultimately did not serve the larger goal of Iran's modernization and nation-building goals. His arguments were principally grounded in criticisms of traditional pedagogical methods for Arabic instruction rather than on the basis of culture, politics, or nationalist ideology. Some readers of Purdavud's comments on these matters, however, saw in his criticism of Arabic instruction another example of what was perceived as Pahlavi nationalism's assault on the edifice of the Arab-Islamic culture within Iran. Purdavud made muted claims to the contrary, but as he was one of the chief intellectual architects of Pahlavi nationalism's mid-twentieth-century project of neoclassicism, the ideological subtext of his calls for a reconsideration of Arabic instruction was difficult for anyone to ignore. Purdavud, in fact, had a long history as an advocate for a linguistic policy that promoted Persian as Iran's national language.

Early in his career, as a member of the Farhangestan (the Iranian language academy), he had called on that body to seriously consider policies for both purifying Persian of Arabic loanwords and replacing the Arabic script with either the Latin system or a modernized and revived Middle Persian alternative.[4] While his stance on these issues evolved and became more realistic over the course of his career, given his history of promoting Iran's pre-Islamic cultural history, his advocacy for terminating Arabic instruction was seen by some as culturally and politically provocative.

What the threats against Purdavud also suggest was that Iran's political and cultural terrain had markedly shifted by the end of his life. When he died of natural causes while asleep in his private study in November of 1968,[5] the culture of Pahlavi nationalism had by that time achieved unprecedented political dominance inside Iran. Purdavud's role as one of the intellectual founders of this now-dominant culture was unmistakable. However, as the threats to his life suggest, the ideological dominance of Pahlavi nationalism had also engendered its own resentments, as well as a search for a new language of opposition. The anonymous, and ultimately unrealized, threats against Purdavud were likely part of this larger campaign of cultural and political contestation that was—by 1968—already underway, and which would reach its fullest stage of cultural and political mobilization a decade later.

The circumstances that had come to prevail inside Iran by the 1960s and 1970s were in stark contrast to the ones that had defined the origins of Iranian nationalism during the early decades of the twentieth century. While Iranian nationalism had started to take cultural shape during these early decades of the twentieth century—a period spanning the tumultuous years of the Constitutional Revolution of 1905 as well as the challenges and possibilities defining the years of World War I, the subsequent rise of Reza Shah, and the consolidation of the Pahlavi state during the 1920s and 1930s—Iranian nationalism had nevertheless not yet adopted a definitive political vocabulary of its own. Consequently, during these formative decades the entire range of political possibilities still remained available for Iran's nationalizing project. These possibilities extended from liberal, pluralistic, and democratic alternatives to more vigorously nationalist forms that advocated for policies of national authenticity and cultural purification.

As this book has detailed, the early twentieth-century Parsi-Iranian exchange was the cultural and intellectual context out of which

Iranian nationalism took shape during these formative decades. The Parsi-Iranian exchange had itself evolved out of a macrohistorical process involving the long-term decline of the Persianate system of knowledge and the simultaneous empowering of strands of culture that had long been subsumed within that system. The culture of Neo-Zoroastrianism was one of these strands of Persianate culture that found new opportunities to be redefined and reconfigured in the context of the new circulations of peoples and ideas enabled by the increasingly interconnected Indian Ocean world of the late nineteenth and early twentieth centuries. As the preceding chapters have argued, for both Parsis and Iranians, their mutual discoveries of the other inspired creative new formulations of the Zoroastrian heritage that, in turn, came to anticipate quite varied cultural and political projects of modernity. The nature of Parsi and Iranian appropriations of this common heritage differed depending on the respective historical and political contexts of Iran and India. For Parsis, their idealized future was imagined in terms of a "negation of exile" and a "return" to a mythic ancestral homeland. For Iranians, the discovery of the Parsis brought to life a blueprint for a reconstruction of a lost antiquity. These contrasting cultural imaginings were also coupled by contrasting political forms. For the Parsis, their long residence in the multiconfessional culture of the subcontinent and the prosperity that the community had achieved during the period of the liberal empire of the British Raj encouraged an understanding of Zoroastrianism that reflected cosmopolitan and ecumenical readings of the tradition. While strands of Parsi thought no doubt contained racialized and exclusivist understandings of the Zoroastrian heritage, it was the liberal ideals of a multiconfessional Bombay that characterized the mainstream of Parsi political thinking. Within the cultural and political terrain of the Iranian plateau, by contrast, the rethinking of the Zoroastrian tradition took form in the context of the Pahlavi state's project of a compensatory nation-building project that sought to revive Iran's pre-Islamic culture at the expense of its Arab-Islamicate heritage. While liberal ideals were not absent inside Iran, by the 1920s and 1930s Iran's political context produced a political appropriation of the Zoroastrian tradition that demonstrated affinities with increasingly conservative and quasi-fascist models of interwar nationalism.

As the chapters in this book have also illustrated, these contrasting appropriations of the Zoroastrian heritage meant that Parsis and Iranians were most often speaking through, past, and beyond each other, even as they were building new networks of contact, connection, and mutual exchange. The infinitely mutable cultural and political nature of nationalism enabled these starkly contrasting versions of the national idea to grow from the common heritage shared by Parsis and Iranians. The grounding of the cultural basis of nationalism in esoteric doctrines associated with faith traditions only further enabled the inherently ambiguous nature of the Zoroastrian tradition to be appropriated in multiple and varied political forms. By the end of Purdavud's life, the political trajectory of the Iranian pre-Islamic revival had changed from the possibilities of a utopian modernity that he had imagined as a young man traveling between Beirut, Berlin, and Bombay to become the conservative politics of official Pahlavi nationalism characterizing the late 1960s.

In the decade following his death, the intellectual project of Pahlavi nationalism was ultimately swept away by yet newer configurations of culture, politics, and ideology. While today the romanticized culture of Iranian neoclassicism that Purdavud had helped to construct retains important traces inside Iran, it is more fully represented in the exilic cultures of Iran's diaspora communities scattered across the many metropoles of our now-globalized ecumene. Like the doctrine of Nietzschean *eternal recurrence*, or perhaps like notions of time characteristic of Isma'ili cosmology, the legacy of twentieth-century Pahlavi nationalism therefore has not disappeared, but has followed—curiously and perhaps appropriately—the precedent of its medieval Parsi precursors to become a new iteration of a displaced Iranian culture, separated from its original "homeland" and, also like its Parsi precursors, a culture that has grown roots in new and more hospitable landscapes outside of its place of origin. These diasporic homelands, where the legacies of twentieth-century Pahlavi nationalism continue to thrive, can today be found in new global metropoles such as Los Angeles and London, or Toronto and Tel Aviv. While tracing the evolution of this analogous history lies outside the immediate framework of this discussion, the desires, anxieties, and potential historical trajectories of this more recent displacement—like the history investigated in this book—has its own cultural and political imagination that deserves consideration.

NOTES

INTRODUCTION

1. Ebrahim Purdavud, *Adabiyat-e Mazdayasna: Yashtha, Qesmati az Ketab-e Moqaddas-e Avesta, Jeld-e Dovvom*, P. D. Marker Avestan Series, vol. 3 (Bamba'i: Anjoman-e Zartoshtian-e Irani va Iran Lig, 1931), 11–13; Mohammad Mo'in, ed., *Yadnameh-ye Purdavud: Be Monasebat-e Shastomin Sal-e Tavallod-e Vay*, vol. 1 (Tehran: Asatir, 1946), 7; 'Ali Asghar Mostafavi, *Zaman va Zendegi-ye Ostad Purdavud* (Tehran: Mostafavi, 1991), 44.

2. Stephanie Jones, "British India Steamers and the Trade of the Persian Gulf, 1862–1914," *The Great Circle: Journal of the Australian Association for Maritime History* 7, no. 1 (April 1985): 23–44.

3. Monica Ringer, *Pious Citizens: Reforming Zoroastrianism in India and Iran* (Syracuse, NY: Syracuse University Press, 2011), 142.

4. Purdavud, *Adabiyat-e Mazdayasna: Jeld-e Dovvom*, 12.

5. Mohamad Tavakoli-Targhi, *Refashioning Iran: Orientalism, Occidentalism, and Historiography* (New York: Palgrave, 2001).

6. Raymond Schwab, *The Oriental Renaissance: Europe's Rediscovery of India and the East, 1680–1880* (New York: Columbia University Press, 1984), 8.

7. Nile Green, *Bombay Islam: The Religious Economy of the West Indian Ocean, 1840–1915* (Cambridge, UK: Cambridge University Press, 2011), 2, 8–12.

8. Tavakoli-Targhi, *Refashioning Iran*, 2.

9. Ibid., 3–4.

10. Nile Green, "The Waves of Heterotopia: Towards a Vernacular Intellectual History of the Indian Ocean," *American Historical Review* 123, no. 1 (June 2018): 846–874.

11. This conventional account is perhaps best represented in Dosabhoy Framjee, *Parsees: Their History, Manners, Customs, and Religion* (Bombay: Smith, Taylor and Co., 1858). For an assessment of Framjee's importance in establishing this conventional narrative, see Ringer, *Pious Citizens*, 154–158.

12. John Hinnells, "The Parsis," in *The Wiley Blackwell Companion to Zoroastrianism*, ed. Michael Stausberg and Yuhan Sohrab-Dinshaw Vevaina (West Sussex, UK: John Wiley and Sons, 2015), 157–159.

13. André Wink, *Al-Hind, the Making of the Indo-Islamic World*, vol. 1, *Early Medieval India and the Expansion of Islam, 7th–11th Centuries* (Leiden, Netherlands: Brill, 2002), 104–106.

14. Alan Williams, *The Zoroastrian Myth of Migration from Iran and Settlement in the Indian Diaspora: Text, Translation and Analysis of the 16th Century Qesse-ye Sanjan "The Story of Sanjan"* (Leiden, Netherlands: Brill, 2009), 218–220.

15. Mary Boyce, *Zoroastrians: Their Religious Beliefs and Practices* (London: Routledge, 1979), 156–160.

16. Ibid., 145–148.

17. Ibid., 161–162.

18. Jamsheed K. Choksy, "Despite Shāhs and Mollās: Minority Sociopolitics in Premodern and Modern Iran," *Journal of Asian History* 40, no. 2 (2006): 137–139. See also Jamsheed K. Choksy, *Conflict and Cooperation: Zoroastrian Subalterns and Muslim Elites in Medieval Iranian Society* (New York: Columbia University Press, 1997).

19. A. V. Williams Jackson, *Persia Past and Present: A Book of Travel and Research* (London: Macmillan and Co., 1906), 425.

20. Jesse S. Palsetia, *The Parsis of India: Preservation of Identity in Bombay City* (Leiden, Netherlands: Brill, 2001), 10.

21. Ibid., 48–50.

22. Ibid., 63.

23. Eckehard Kulke, *The Parsees in India: A Minority as Agent of Change* (Munich: Weltforum Verlag, 1974), 142–143.

24. There is a growing body of scholarship on Manekji Limji Hataria. The classic account is Mary Boyce, "Manekji Limji Hataria in Iran," in *K. R. Cama Oriental Institute Golden Jubilee Volume*, ed. N. D. Minochehr-Homji and M. F. Kanga (Bombay: K. R. Cama Oriental Institute, 1969), 19–31. See also Monica Ringer, "Reform Transplanted: Parsi Agents of Change amongst Zoroastrians in Nineteenth-Century Iran," *Iranian Studies* 42, no. 4 (2009): 549–560.

25. Reza Zia-Ebrahimi, "An Emissary of the Golden Age: Manekji Limji Hataria and the Charisma of the Archaic in Pre-Nationalist Iran," *Studies in Ethnicity and Nationalism* 10, no. 3 (2010): 377–390.

26. Mostafa Vaziri, *Iran as Imagined Nation: The Construction of National Identity* (New York: Paragon House, 1993). For a critique of Vaziri, see Mohamad Tavakoli-Targhi's book review in *International Journal of Middle East Studies* 26, no. 2 (May 1994): 316–318. For a larger discussion of the dialogic nature of nationalist thought outside of Europe, see Partha Chatterjee, *Nationalist Thought and the Colonial World: A Derivative Discourse?* (Minneapolis: University of Minnesota Press, 1993).

27. Talinn Grigor, "Parsi Patronage of the Urheimat," *Getty Research Journal* 2 (2010): 56. See also Talinn Grigor, "Persian Architectural Revivals in the British Raj and Qajar Iran," *Comparative Studies of South Asia, Africa, and the Middle East* 36, no. 3 (2016): 384–397.

28. Marshall Hodgson, *The Venture of Islam: Conscience and History in a World Civilization* (Chicago: University of Chicago Press, 1974), vol. 2, 293–314.

29. Richard Eaton and Phillip Wagoner, *Power, Memory, Architecture: Contested Sites on India's Deccan Plateau, 1300–1600* (New Delhi: Oxford University Press, 2014), 20–27. For the idea of the "cosmopolis," see Sheldon Pollock, *The Language of the Gods in the World of Men: Sanskrit, Culture, and Power in Premodern India* (Berkeley: University of California Press, 2006). For a broader discussion of the Persianate, see also Mana Kia and Afshin Marashi, "After the Persianate: Introduction," *Comparative Studies of South Asia, Africa, and the Middle East* 36, no. 2 (2016): 379–383; Nile Green, ed., *The Persianate World: The Frontiers of a Eurasian Lingua Franca* (Berkeley: University of California Press, 2019); Abbas Amanat and Assef Ashraf, eds., *The Persianate World: Rethinking a Shared Sphere* (Leiden, Netherlands: Brill, 2019).

30. Sanjay Subrahmanyam, "Connected Histories: Notes Towards a Reconfiguration of Early Modern Eurasia, 1400–1800," *Modern Asian Studies* 31, no. 3 (1997): 735–762.

31. Kathryn Babayan, *Mystics, Monarchs, and Messiahs: Cultural Landscapes of Early Modern Iran* (Cambridge, MA: Harvard University Press, 2002).

32. Mana Kia, "Indian Friends, Iranian Selves: Persianate Modern," *Comparative Studies of South Asia, Africa, and the Middle East* 36, no. 3 (2016): 398–417; Mana Kia, "Imagining Iran before Nationalism: Geocultural Meanings of Land in Azar's *Atashkadeh*," in *Rethinking Iranian Nationalism and Modernity*, ed. Kamran Aghaie

and Afshin Marashi (Austin: University of Texas Press, 2014), 89–112. See also Mana Kia, *Persianate Selves: Memories of Place and Origin before Nationalism* (Stanford, CA: Stanford University Press, 2020).

33. Daniel J. Sheffield, "Iran, the Mark of Paradise or the Land of Ruin? Approaches to Reading Two Parsi Zoroastrian Travelogues," in *On the Wonders of Land and Sea: Persianate Travel Writing*, ed. Sunil Sharma and Roberta Micallef (Boston: Ilex Foundation and Center for Hellenic Studies, 2013), 14–43.

34. In addition to his *Refashioning Iran*, cited previously, see also Mohamad Tavakoli-Targhi, "Early Persianate Modernity," in *Forms of Knowledge in Early Modern Asia: Explorations in the Intellectual History of India and Tibet, 1500–1800*, ed. Sheldon Pollock (Durham, NC: Duke University Press, 2011), 257–287.

35. In addition to his *Bombay Islam*, cited previously, see also Nile Green, *Terrains of Exchange: Religious Economies of Global Islam* (New York: Oxford University Press, 2015).

36. In addition to her *Pious Citizens*, cited previously, see also Monica Ringer, "The Discourse of Modernization and the Problem of Cultural Integrity in Nineteenth-Century Iran," in *Iran and Beyond: Essays in Middle Eastern History in Honor of Nikki R. Keddie*, ed. Rudi Matthee and Beth Baron (Costa Mesa, CA: Mazda, 2000), 56–69.

37. Wali Ahmadi, *Modern Persian Literature in Afghanistan: Anomalous Visions of History and Form* (London: Routledge, 2008). See also Farzin Vejdani, *Making History in Iran: Education, Nationalism, and Print Culture* (Stanford, CA: Stanford University Press, 2014), chapter 6; Alexander Jabbari, "The Making of Modernity in Persianate Literary History," *Comparative Studies of South Asia, Africa, and the Middle East* 36, no. 3 (2016): 418–434; Kevin L. Schwartz, "*Bâzgasht-i Adabî* (Literary Return) and Persianate Literary Culture in Eighteenth and Nineteenth Century Iran, India, and Afghanistan" (PhD diss., University of California, Berkeley, 2014).

38. Reza Zia-Ebrahimi, *The Emergence of Iranian Nationalism: Race and the Politics of Dislocation* (New York: Columbia University Press, 2016).

39. Ali M. Ansari, *The Politics of Nationalism in Modern Iran* (Cambridge, UK: Cambridge University Press, 2012), 110.

40. James L. Gelvin and Nile Green, eds., *Global Muslims in the Age of Steam and Print* (Berkeley: University of California Press, 2014).

41. In formal historiographic writing, Ghosh's reading of the Indian Ocean most resembles the work of Sugata Bose, *A Hundred Horizons: The Indian Ocean in the Age of Global Empire* (Cambridge, MA: Harvard University Press, 2006).

42. Green, "Waves of Heterotopia," 846. See also Meg Samuelson, "Crossing the Indian Ocean and Wading through the Littoral: Visions of Cosmopolitanism in Amitav Ghosh's 'Antique Land' and 'Tide Country,'" in *Cosmopolitan Asia: Littoral Epistemologies of the Global South*, ed. Sharmani Patricia Gabriel and Fernando Rosa (New York: Routledge, 2016), 105–122.

43. Alice Kaplan, *Looking for the Stranger: Albert Camus and the Life of a Literary Classic* (Chicago: University of Chicago Press, 2016); David Carroll, *Albert Camus the Algerian: Colonialism, Terrorism, Justice* (New York: Columbia University Press, 2007).

CHAPTER 1. TO BOMBAY AND BACK

1. "Marhum Kaykhosrow Shahrokh," *Ettela'at*, July 5, 1940 (Tir 14, 1319), 2.

2. There is some discrepancy regarding the exact date of his death. Most sources

indicate that he died on the night of July 2. See, for example, Rashid Shahmardan, *Farzanegan-e Zartoshti* (Tehran: Sazman-e Javanan-e Zartoshti-e Bamba'i, 1951), 569. "Ravanshad Kaykhosrow Shahrokh," *Andisheh-ye Ma* 2 (1945/1324): 20. Jahangir Oshidari, "Zendegani-ye Porarzesh va Kushesh," *Hukht* 23, no. 4 (1351/1972): 5–45.

3. "Shahrokh," *Ettela'at*, July 5, 1940, 2.

4. The details of Shahrokh's biography can be found in numerous sources, including his posthumously published memoir. See Kaykhosrow Shahrokh, *Yaddashtha-ye Kaykhosrow Shahrokh*, ed. Jahangir Oshidari (Tehran: Parcham, 2535/1977); Kaykhosrow Shahrokh, *Khaterat-e Arbab Kaykhosrow Shahrokh*, ed. Shahrokh Shahrokh and Rashna Rayter, trans. Gholamhosayn Mirza Saleh (Tehran: Mazyar, 2003); Kaykhosrow Shahrokh, *The Memoirs of Keikhosrow Shahrokh*, ed. and trans. Shahrokh Shahrokh and Rashna Writer (Lewiston, NY: Edwin Mellen Press, 1994). See also Ringer, *Pious Citizens*, 184–195.

5. Jamshid Oshidari, *Tarikh-e Pahlavi va Zartoshtian* (Tehran: Entesharat-e Hukht, 2535/1976), 383–397.

6. Shahmardan, *Farzanegan*, 563–569; Oshidari, *Tarikh-e Pahlavi va Zartoshtian*, 300–304.

7. Oshidari, *Tarikh-e Pahlavi va Zartoshtian*, 383–397; Grigor, "Parsi Patronage of the *Urheimat*," 59–60.

8. Sohrab Safrang, "Bazyadha'i az Zaman-e Riasat-e Ravanshad Arbab Kaykhosrow Shahrokh dar Anjoman-e Zartoshtian," *Hukht* 23, no. 4 (1351/1972): 26–29; Sarah Stewart, "The Politics of Zoroastrian Philanthropy and the Case of Qasr-e Firuzeh," *Iranian Studies* 45, no. 1 (2012): 69–71.

9. Shahrokh, *Memoirs*, 58; Oshidari, "Zendegani-ye Porarzesh," 24; Oshidari, *Tarikh-e Pahlavi va Zartoshtian*, 250; "Ravanshad Kaykhosrow Shahrokh," 5.

10. Shahmardan, *Farzanegan*, 565; Oshidari, *Tarikh-e Pahlavi va Zartoshtian*, 386–389.

11. Shahmardan, *Farzanegan*, 567; Oshidari, "Zendegani-ye Porarzesh," 6.

12. Oshidardi, *Pahlavi va Zartoshtian*, 388; Oshidari, "Zendegani-ye Porarzesh," 25.

13. Shamardan, *Farzanegan*, 567; "Ravanshad Kaykhosrow Shahrokh,"17; Oshidari, *Tarikh-e Pahlavi va Zartoshtian*, 131, 390–391; Oshidari, "Zendegani-ye Porarzesh," 29–35; Hosayn Mahbubi Ardakani, *Tarikh-e Mu'assesat-e Tamaddoni-ye Jadid dar Iran*, vol. 3 (Tehran: Anjoman-e Daneshjuyan-e Daneshgah-e Tehran, 1975), 5, 410, 426–428.

14. "Ravanshad Kaykhosrow Shahrokh," 17; Shahmardan, *Farzanegan*, 568; Oshidari, *Tarikh-e Pahlavi va Zartoshtian*, 387; Talinn Grigor, *Building Iran: Modernism, Architecture, and National Heritage under the Pahlavi Monarchs* (New York: Periscope, 2009), 52; Afshin Marashi, *Nationalizing Iran: Culture, Power, and the State, 1870–1940* (Seattle: University of Washington Press, 2008), 124–130.

15. The only extant copy appears to be of the second edition published in 1921, in Bombay. Kaykhosrow Shahrokh, *A'ineh-ye A'in-e Mazdayasna* (Bamba'i: Matba'-ye Mozaffari, 1921). This edition mentions that the first edition was published in Tehran in 1907. See Shahrokh, *A'ineh*, 2.

16. Ringer, *Pious Citizens*, 192.

17. Kaykhosrow Shahrokh, *Forugh-e Mazdayasna* (Tehran: Murteza al-Hosayni al-Baraghani, 1909).

18. Quoted in Mohammad Gholi Majd, *August 1941: The Anglo-Russian Occupa-*

tion of Iran and Change of Shahs (Lanham, MD: University Press of America, 2012), 124.

19. Ibid., 124–125. There has been a great deal of speculation regarding the possibility of foul play in Shahrokh's death. Much of it has found its way into the historiography of this period. See, for example, Ervand Abrahamian, *Iran between Two Revolutions* (Princeton, NJ: Princeton University Press, 1982), 163. Abrahamian writes that Shahrokh was "gunned down in the street." See also Arthur C. Millspaugh, *Americans in Persia* (Washington, DC: Brookings Institution, 1946), 37. Millspaugh writes that Shahrokh was "murdered by air injection." David Yaghoubian, *Ethnicity, Identity, and the Development of Nationalism in Iran* (Syracuse, NY: Syracuse University Press, 2014), 134. Yaghoubian states that Shahrokh was "killed by Iranian police." See also the memoir by Kaykhosrow Shahrokh's granddaughter, Nesta (Shahrokh) Ramazani, *The Dance of the Rose and the Nightingale* (Syracuse, NY: Syracuse University Press, 2002), 31–32. Ramazani recounts the family's version of Kaykhosrow's murder, including the speculation that "poison had been placed in Baba-joon's after-dinner coffee." Eliz Sanasarian and Hamid Naficy are more circumspect on this issue. See Sanasarian, *Religious Minorities in Iran* (Cambridge, UK: Cambridge University Press, 2000), 49, and Naficy, *A Social History of Iranian Cinema*, vol. 2 (Durham, NC: Duke University Press, 2011), 438n58. These speculations are also found in the Persian-language historiography. See, for example, Hosayn Makki, *Tarikh-e Bist Saleh-ye Iran*, vol. 7 (Tehran: 'Elmi, 2001), 269; Mehdi Bambad, *Sharh-e Hal-e Rejal-e Iran*, vol. 3 (Tehran: Zavar, 1978), 180.

20. Bahram Shahrokh recounts his wartime activities in a six-part serialized memoir titled "Khakestar-e Garm" (The Warm Ash) in the pages of the Tehran weekly, *Mard-e Emruz*. See "Khakestar-e Garm," December 27, 1947 (Dey 5, 1326), 1, 4–5; January 3, 1948 (Dey 12, 1326), 4–5; January 10, 1948 (Dey 19, 1326), 3, 6, 10; January 17, 1948 (Dey 26, 1326), 4, 9; January 24, 1948 (Bahman 3, 1326), 2, 6; January 31, 1948 (Bahman 10, 1326), 4.

21. Bahram Shahrokh's activities with "Radio Berlin" are detailed in Hamid Shokat, "Barnameh-ye Farsi-ye Radio Berlin dar Jang-e Jahani-ye Duvom," *Iran Nameh* 28, no. 1 (2013): 102–117.

22. US Army European Command, Intelligence Division, *Wartime Activities of the German Diplomatic and Military Services during World War II* (Ludwigsburg, Germany: US Army Intelligence, 1949), 61, 93. This report indicates that US intelligence officers interrogated Bahram Shahrokh after the war, before his return to Iran. The report also describes him as "about thirty-eight years of age, five feet two inches tall, has curly black hair, black eyes, wears glasses, and a mustache. He is a Zoroaster [*sic*] by religion. Subject came to Germany late in 1939 [Bahram's memoir indicates 1938] after he had become bankrupt as a merchant in Iran. He was engaged by the Ministry of Propaganda for Iranian broadcasts."

23. Mohammad-Reza Mo'in Samadani, "Havades-e Ayyam," in *Zendegi Nameh va Khadamat-e 'Elmi va Farhangi-e Shadravan Arbab Kaykhosrow Shahrokh*, ed. Omid Qanbari (Tehran: Anjoman-e Asar va Mafakher-e Farhangi, 2009), 112.

24. For a discussion of how fear and paranoia have shaped Iranian conceptions of the past, see H. E. Chehabi, "The Paranoid Style in Iranian Historiography," in *Iran in the 20th Century: Historiography and Political Culture*, ed. Touraj Atabaki (London: I. B. Tauris, 2009), 155–176.

25. Shahrokh, *Memoirs*, 1; Shahrokh, *Yaddashtha*, 28.

26. Shahrokh, *Memoirs*, 1–2; Shahrokh, *Yaddashtha*, 29; Shahmardan, *Farzanegan*, 561.

27. Boyce, *Zoroastrians*, 209; Choksy, "Despite Shāhs and Mollās," 141–144.

28. Oshidari, "Zendegani-ye Porarzesh," 20; Shahmardan, *Farzanegan*, 495, 563.

29. Janet Kestenberg Amighi, *The Zoroastrians of Iran: Conversion, Assimilation, or Persistence* (New York: AMS Press, 1990), 106.

30. Shahrokh, *Memoirs*, 1; Shahrokh, *Yaddashtha*, 28.

31. Shahmardan, *Farzanegan*, 563.

32. Shahrokh, *Memoirs*, 1; Shahrokh, *Yaddashtha*, 28.

33. Shahmardan, *Farzanegan*, 563.

34. Shahrokh, *Memoirs*, 2–3; Shahrokh, *Yaddashtha*, 31–32.

35. Shahrokh, *Yaddashtha*, 80.

36. Shahrokh, *Memoirs*, 17; Shahrokh, *Yaddashtha*, 80.

37. Shahmardan, *Farzanegan*, 641–642; Choksy, "Despite Shāhs and Mollās," 142; Firoze M. Kotwal, Jamsheed K. Choksy, Christopher J. Brunner, and Mahnaz Moazami, "Hatari, Manekji Limji," *Encyclopaedia Iranica*, http://www.iranicaonline.org/articles/hataria-manekji-limji, accessed September 24, 2018.

38. Shahrokh, *Memoirs*, 3–4; Shahrokh, *Yaddashtha*, 34–35.

39. Shahrokh, *Memoirs*, 17; Shahrokh, *Yaddashtha*, 81.

40. Shahmardan, *Farzanegan*, 360; Choksy, "Despite Shāhs and Mollās," 146.

41. Shahrokh, *Memoirs*, 2; Shahrokh, *Yaddashtha*, 31.

42. Shahrokh, *Memoirs*, 3; Shahrokh, *Yaddashtha*, 32.

43. A. Christian Van Gorder, *Christianity in Persia and the Status of Non-Muslims in Iran* (Lanham, MD: Lexington Books, 2010), 142.

44. Ibid.

45. Shahrokh, *Memoirs*, 3; Shahrokh, *Yaddashtha*, 32.

46. Ahmad Seyf, "Iran and Cholera in the Nineteenth Century," *Middle Eastern Studies* 38, no. 1 (2002): 172.

47. Shahrokh, *Memoirs*, 3–4; Shahrokh, *Yaddashtha*, 34–35.

48. Ibid.

49. Ibid.

50. Numerous sources have incorrectly reported that Kaykhosrow's journey to Bombay was arranged by Manakji Limji Hataria. For example, Mary Boyce writes that Shahrokh "had been sent by Manekji as a boy to study in Bombay"; see *Zoroastrians*, 219. Boyce is repeating an error also found in Shahmardan, *Farzanegan*, 563. As Shahrokh clearly states in his memoir (see footnote 35) that he never met Manekji, the source of Shahmardan and Boyce's claim is unclear. Shahrokh's father did, however, attend one of the schools established in Kerman by Manekji, before embarking on his own trip to India. Shahrokh may have received assistance from Manekji's successor, Kaykhosrow Tirandaz Khursand, who served in Iran as the Parsi community's official emissary from 1890 to 1893. Shahrokh's own account of his trip to India puts emphasis on his ability to correspond with his great-aunts then living in Bombay.

51. Jesse S. Palsetia, *Jamsetjee Jejeebhoy of Bombay: Partnership and Public Culture in Empire* (New Delhi: Oxford University Press, 2015), 121; Jivanji Jamshedji Modi, "A Short History of the Sir Jamsetjee Jejeebhoy Zarthoshti Madressa," in *Sir Jamsetjee Jejeebhoy Madressa Jubilee Volume*, ed. Jivanji Jamshedji Modi (Bombay: Fort Printing Press, 1914), 477–483; Boyce, *Zoroastrians*, 201–202.

52. Ringer, *Pious Citizens*, 38.

53. Shahrokh, *Memoirs*, 4; Shahrokh, *Yaddashtha*, 35.

54. Shahrokh, *Memoirs*, 4; Shahrokh, *Yaddashtha*, 57.

55. Kulke, *The Parsees in India*, 142–143.

56. Shahrokh, *Memoirs*, 18; Shahrokh, *Yaddashtha*, 37.

57. Shahrokh, *Memoirs*, 34; Shahrokh, *Yaddashtha*, 45.

58. Shahrokh, *Memoirs*, 19, Shahrokh, *Yaddashtha*, 40.

59. Shahrokh, *Memoirs*, 19; Shahrokh, *Yaddashtha*, 40–41.

60. Choksy, "Despite Shāhs and Mollās," 142.

61. Ibid.

62. Shahrokh, *Memoirs*, 33; Shahrokh, *Yaddashtha*, 45.

63. Mansoureh Ettehadieh, *The Lion of Persia: A Political Biography of Prince Farman-Farma* (Cambridge, MA: Tỹ Aur Press, 2012), 22–29.

64. Shahrokh, *Memoirs*, 19, 34; Shahrokh, *Yaddashtha*, 37–38, 45.

65. Shahrokh, *Memoirs*, 34; Shahrokh, *Yaddashtha*, 48.

66. Shahrokh, *Memoirs*, 35; Shahrokh, *Yaddashtha*, 49.

67. "Ravanshad Kaykhosrow Shahrokh," 5.

68. Shahrokh, *Memoirs*, 35; Shahrokh, *Yaddashtha*, 49.

69. Shahrokh, *Memoirs*, 37, 40; Shahrokh, *Yaddashtha*, 50–51, 68–69.

70. Shahrokh, *Memoirs*, 54–55; Shahrokh, *Yaddashtha*, 56.

71. Shahrokh, *Memoirs*, 55; Shahrokh, *Yaddashtha*, 55–56.

72. Shahrokh, *Memoirs*, 55; Shahrokh, *Yaddashtha*, 57, 63.

73. Shahrokh, *Memoirs*, 55; Shahrokh, *Yaddashtha*, 66.

74. Shahrokh, *Memoirs*, 55; Shahrokh, *Yaddashtha*, 66.

75. Shahrokh, *Memoirs*, 39; Shahrokh, *Yaddashtha*, 66.

76. Kestenberg Amighi, *The Zoroastrians of Iran*, 151–152; Shahmardan, *Farzanegan*, 432–445.

77. Shahrokh, *Memoirs*, 28; Shahrokh, *Yaddashtha*, 75.

78. Shahrokh, *Memoirs*, 58; Shahrokh, *Yaddashtha*, 127. There was considerable debate during the early constitutional era regarding the issue of representation of minority communities in the Majles. Conservatives initially intended to exclude Jews, Armenians, and Zoroastrians. With Arbab Jamshid Jamshidian's initial lobbying, Zoroastrians were granted a representation. It was only from the second Majles that Jews and Armenians also received representation on the Majles. See Janet Afary, *The Iranian Constitutional Revolution, 1906–1911: Grassroots Democracy, Social Democracy, and the Origins of Feminism* (New York: Columbia University Press, 1996), 70, 263.

79. Shahrokh, *Memoirs*, 58; Shahrokh, *Yaddashtha*, 127–128.

80. Shahrokh, *Memoirs*, 58; Shahrokh, *Yaddashtha*, 128. On Khorasani's correspondence with the constitutionalists in Tehran, see Mateo Mohammad Farzaneh, *The Iranian Constitutional Revolution and the Clerical Leadership of Khurasani* (Syracuse, NY: Syracuse University Press, 2015), 173–174.

81. Shahrokh, *Memoirs*, 58; Shahrokh, *Yaddashtha*, 129.

82. Shahrokh, *Memoirs*, 29; Shahrokh, *Yaddashtha*, 76.

83. Shahrokh, *A'ineh-ye A'in-e Mazdayasna*, preface, 2; Shahrokh, *Memoirs*, 26; Shahrokh; *Yaddashtha*, 82–83.

84. Shahrokh, *A'ineh-ye A'in-e Mazdayasna*, 131–145.

85. Ibid., preface, 2.

86. Both works had also been sponsored for publication for the purpose of gratis circulation to non-Zoroastrian communities. The Iranian historian Muhammad Ebrahim Bastani Parizi (1924–2014), for example, recalled being introduced to the *Forugh* text as a child via a copy in his father's library. The text had been given to his father by a Zoroastrian visitor to their hometown of Pariz sometime in 1924. The visiting Zoroastrian, Parizi recalled, was part of a crew of employees working for Kaykhosrow Shahrokh at that time to establish the telephone line connecting the cities of Sirjan and Rafsanjan. See Muhammad Ebrahim Bastani Parizi, "Yaddashti bar Yaddashtha-ye Shadravan Arbab Kaykhosrow Shahrokh," in *Yaddashtha-ye Kaykhosrow Shahrokh*, ed. Jahangir Oshidari (Tehran: Parcham, 2535/1977), preface, n.p., "zhe." Shahrokh himself tells the story of his books helping to promote a new positive understanding of Zoroastrianism among an audience of 'ulama who also encountered the books. See Shahrokh, *Memoirs*, 27–28; Shahrokh, *Yaddashtha*, 83–84; Pheroza J. Godrej and Firoza Punthakey Mistree, eds., *A Zoroastrian Tapestry: Art, Religion and Culture* (Middletown, NJ: Mapin Publishing, 2002), 290.

87. See, for example, "Chidag Andarz i Poryotkeshan: A Zoroastrian Catechism," in *The Teachings of the Magi: A Compendium of Zoroastrian Beliefs*, ed. and trans. R. C. Zaehner (Oxford: Oxford University Press, 1976), 20–28. See also Jenny Rose, *Zoroastrianism: An Introduction* (London: I. B. Tauris, 2010), 117–118. There were also numerous Zoroastrian catechisms published in India by Parsi reformists in the nineteenth and early twentieth century. See Philip G. Kreyenbroek, "Catechisms," *Encyclopaedia Iranica*, http://www.iranicaonline.org/articles/catechisms-treatises-for-instruction-in-the-fundamental-tenets-of-a-religious-faith-cast-in-the-form-of-questions-and-answe, accessed September 26, 2018.

88. Ringer, *Pious Citizens*, 187.

89. Shahrokh, *A'ineh-ye A'in-e Mazdayasna*, 1–3.

90. Ibid., 40–44.

91. Ibid., 20–33.

92. Ibid., 58–59.

93. Ibid., 59–60.

94. Ibid., 65–67.

95. Ibid., 1.

96. Ibid., 2.

97. Ibid.

98. Ibid.

99. Ibid., 22.

100. Ibid., 21.

101. Ibid., 24.

102. Ibid.

103. Ibid.

104. Ibid., 32.

105. Irach Taraporewala's free English translation of *Yasna* 30.2 is: "Hear with your ears the Highest Truths I preach / And with illumined minds weigh them with care / Before you choose which of the two Paths to tread / Deciding man by man, each one for each / Before the New Age is ushered in / Wake up, alert to spread Ahura's word." On the debates relating to proselytism and conversion within the Parsi community, see Ringer, *Pious Citizens*, 139–141. See also Pargol Saati, "Conversion

vii. To the Zoroastrian Faith in the Modern Period," *Encyclopaedia Iranica*, http://www.iranicaonline.org/articles/conversion-vii, accessed October 3, 2018.

106. Shahrokh, *A'ineh-ye A'in-e Mazdayasna*, 64.

107. Shahrokh, *Yaddashtha*, 101; Shahrokh, *Memoirs*, 11–12.

108. Ringer, *Pious Citizens*, 190.

109. Ibid., 136–137.

110. Shahrokh, *A'ineh-ye A'in-e Mazdayasna*, 65.

111. Shahrokh, *Forugh-e Mazdayasna*, 103.

112. Ibid.

113. Samuel Laing, *A Modern Zoroastrian* (London: Watts and Co., 1903), 4. Shahrokh translated the term "law of polarity" as "*qānūn-e qovā'-ye motazād.*" See Shahrokh, *Forugh-e Mazdayasna*, 276.

114. Laing, *A Modern Zoroastrian*, 2–4; Shahrokh, *Forugh-e Mazdayasna*, 276.

115. Laing, *A Modern Zoroastrian*, 197–198; Shahrokh, *Forugh-e Mazdayasna*, 280–281.

116. Edward Said, *Orientalism* (New York: Vintage Books, 1978), 115. See also Schwab, *The Oriental Renaissance*.

117. Laing, *A Modern Zoroastrian*, 203; Shahrokh, *Forugh-e Mazdayasna*, 287.

118. Laing, *A Modern Zoroastrian*, 203; Shahrokh, *Forugh-e Mazdayasna*, 287.

119. Laing, *A Modern Zoroastrian*, 205; Shahrokh, *Forugh-e Mazdayasna*, 289.

120. Shahrokh, *Forugh-e Mazdayasna*, 7.

121. Ibid.

122. The Mazdaznan movement has yet to receive serious attention from historians of religion. There are brief treatments in Richard Noll, *The Jung Cult: Origins of a Charismatic Movement* (Princeton, NJ: Princeton University Press, 1994), 105–106, and James Webb, *The Occult Establishment* (La Salle, IL: Open Court Publishing, 1976), 32–33. See also discussion in Michael Stausberg, "Para-Zoroastrianism: Memetic Transmissions and Appropriations," in *Parsis in India and the Diaspora*, ed. John Hinnells and Alan Williams (London: Routledge, 2007), 236–254.

123. His background and origins remain obscure. Some sources describe him as having been born in the American Midwest to Polish immigrant parents. See Pádraic E. Moore, "One Could Almost Call It Holiness," in Otoman Zar-Adusht Hanish, *The Egyptian Postures*, edited by Ian Whittlesea (London: Everyday Press, 2017).

124. The magazine was published in Chicago and Los Angeles intermittently between 1902 and 1953 as *The Sun-Worshiper*, *Mazdaznan*, and *The Messenger*. Among the cult's most notable publications was a cookbook, Otoman Zar-Adusht Hanish, *Mazdaznan Encyclopedia of Dietics and Home Cook Book* (Chicago: Mazdaznan Press, 1901), as well as Otoman Zar-Adusht Hanish, *Inner Studies: A Course of Twelve Studies* (Chicago: Sun-Worshiper Publishing Co., 1902).

125. Some members of India's Parsi community remained skeptical of the Hanish cult. See, for example, Maneckji Musserwanji Dhalla, *Dastur Dhalla, The Saga of a Soul: An Autobiography*, trans. Gool and Behram Sohrab H. J. Rustomji (Karachi: Dhalla Memorial Institute, 1975), 716–721.

126. Shahrokh, *Forugh-e Mazdayasna*, 8.

127. Ibid.

128. Shahrokh, *A'ineh-ye A'in-e Mazdayasna*, 2.

129. Shahrokh, *A'ineh-ye A'in-e Mazdayasna*, 16; Ali-Akbar Dehkhoda, "*farjūd,*" *Loghatnameh* 37: 128.

130. Shahrokh, *A'ineh-ye A'in-e Mazdayasna*, 22; Ali-Akbar Dehkhoda, "*varshīm*," *Loghatnameh* 49: 164.

131. Shahrokh, *A'ineh-ye A'in-e Mazdayasna*, 22; Ali-Akbar Dehkhoda, "farāzmān," *Loghatnameh* 37: 100.

132. Shahrokh, *A'ineh-ye A'in-e Mazdayasna*, 108–130.

133. Shahrokh, *Forugh-e Mazdayasna*, 9.

134. Ibid.

135. Shahrokh, *A'ineh-ye A'in-e Mazdayasna*, 7.

136. Ibid., 67.

137. Ibid. On the complexity of Ferdowsi's use of the myth of Zahhāk, see Babayan, *Mystics, Monarchs, and Messiahs*, 27; and Zia-Ebrahimi, *The Emergence of Iranian Nationalism*, 104.

138. Shahrokh, *A'ineh-ye A'in-e Mazdayasna*, 67.

139. Ibid., 68.

140. Ibid.

141. Ibid., 69.

142. Ibid.

143. Ibid.

144. Shahrokh, *Forugh-e Mazdayasna*, 12.

145. Ibid.

146. Ibid.

147. Shahrokh, *A'ineh-ye A'in-e Mazdayasna*, 71.

148. Ibid.

149. Ibid., 72.

150. Ibid.

151. The dates for the six-part memoire are as follows: Bahram Shahrokh, "Khakestar-e Garm," *Mard-e Emruz*, December 27, 1947 (issue #131); January 3, 1948 (issue #132); January 10, 1948 (issue #133); January 17, 1948 (issue #134); January 24, 1948 (issue #135); January 31, 1948 (issue #136).

152. L. P. Elwell-Sutton, "The Iranian Press, 1941–1947," *Iran* 6 (1968): 97. See also Hasan Mirabedini, "Mard-e Emruz," *Encyclopaedia Iranica*, http://www.iranicaonline.org/articles/mard-e-emruz, accessed October 7, 2018. The newspaper ultimately ceased publication in February of 1948, following Masud's assassination, as Ervand Abrahamian argues, because of his "gadfly articles." See Abrahamian, *Iran Between Two Revolutions*, 202.

153. Mohammad Masud, "Khakestar-e Garm," *Mard-e Emruz*, December 27, 1947, 1, 4.

154. Shahmardan, *Farzanegan*, 569; "Ravanshad Kaykhosrow Shahrokh," 5, 17, 20; Oshidari, *Tarikh-e Pahlavi va Zartoshtian*, 62, 389; "Shahrokh," *Ettela'at*, July 5, 1940, 2; Bambad, *Sharh-e Hal-e Rejal-e Iran*, vol. 3, 179–180. Bahram Shahrokh claims that the wedding reception was at the home of Hassan Esfandiary (Mohtashem al-Saltaneh). This would have made the distance from the reception to Shahrokh's home approximately one mile. See Bahram Shahrokh, "Khakestar-e Garm," *Mard-e Emruz*, January 17, 1948, 4. The location of Shahrokh's home is also detailed in Monica Ringer, "Din-e 'Aqlani va Asl-e Shahrvandi dar Iran," *Iran Nameh* 26, no. 1–2 (2011), photo caption, 72.

155. Bahram Shahrokh, "Khakestar-e Garm," *Mard-e Emruz*, January 17, 1948, 4.

156. Ramazani, *Dance of the Rose and the Nightingale*, 31.

157. Mohammad Reza Nasiri, "Yek Zendegi," in *Zendegi Nameh va Khadamat-e 'Elmi va Farhangi-e Shadravan Arbab Kaykhosrow Shahrokh*, ed. Omid Qanbari (Tehran: Anjoman-e Asar va Mafakher-e Farhangi, 2009), 30–31.

158. Accoding to this theory, Kaykhosrow Shahrokh was another victim of the infamous prison doctor, Ahmad Ahmadi (1885–1944). Ahmadi, known colloquially as "pezeshk Ahmadi," was reportedly responsible for numerous state-sanctioned murders via air injection during the Reza Shah years, including the murders of Abdolhossein Teymurtash (1883–1933), Taqi Arani (1903–1940), Mohammad Farrokhi Yazdi (1889–1939), Shemuel Hayim (1891–1931), and Jafar Quli Khan Sardar As'ad Bakhtari (1879–1934). For a summary of this wave of police executions in the Reza Shah period, see Stephanie Cronin, "Riza Shah, the Fall of Sardar Asad, and the 'Bakhtiari Plot,'" *Iranian Studies* 38, no. 2 (2005): 244.

159. Bahram Shahrokh, "Khakestar-e Garm," *Mard-e Emruz*, January 17, 1948, 4.

160. Annabelle Sreberny and Massoumeh Torfeh, *Persian Service: The BBC and the British Interests in Iran* (London: I. B. Tauris, 2014), 34.

161. Abbas Milani, *The Shah* (New York: Palgrave, 2011), 81, 194. Shahrokh also provided voice-over narration for German newsreel coverage of the war. See Naficy, *A Social History of Iranian Cinema*, vol. 2, 438.

162. Jaleh Pirnazar, "Jang-e Bainolmelal-e Dovvum va Jam'eh-ye Yahud dar Iran," in *Teru'a: Yahudian-e Irani dar Tarikh-e Mo'aser*, ed. Homa Sarshar (Beverly Hills, CA: Entesharat-e Tarikh-e Shafahi-ye Yahudian-e Irani, 1996), 103.

163. Shokat, "Barnameh-ye Farsi-ye Radio Berlin," 105.

164. Ibid. There is some discrepancy as to when the Persian service of Radio Berlin began its broadcasts. Bahram Shahrokh gives the date of November 22, 1939. Shokat gives a date of August of 1939. See Bahram Shahrokh, "Khakestar-e Garm," *Mard-e Emruz*, January 3, 1948, 5.

165. Shokat, "Barnameh-ye Farsi-ye Radio Berlin," 108.

166. Pirnazar, "Jang-e Bainolmelal-e Dovvum," 103.

167. Fakhreddin Azimi, *The Quest for Democracy in Iran: A Century of Struggle against Authoritarian Rule* (Cambridge, MA: Harvard University Press, 2008), 112; Milani, *The Shah*, 81. The rumors of an impending pro-Nazi coup are also detailed in Bahram Shahrokh, "Khakestar-e Garm," *Mard-e Emruz*, January 3, 1948, 5, and January 31, 1948, 1.

168. Bahram Shahrokh, "Khakestar-e Garm," *Mard-e Emruz*, January 24, 1948, 2.

169. Bahram Shahrokh, "Khakestar-e Garm," *Mard-e Emruz*, January 3, 1948, 5. Shahrokh's primary contact was with the Foreign Ministry's "Eastern Office" and its experienced Iran expert, Werner Otto von Hentig (1886–1984). Hentig was a veteran of the Jihad mission to Afghanistan in World War I, as discussed in chapter 5. The German Reich Ministry of Propaganda was, by contrast, under the direction of Josef Goebbels. Shahrokh describes writing a report that was read by Goebbels, but otherwise does not seem to have worked directly with him. See also Shokat, "Barnameh-ye Farsi-ye Radio Berlin," 114.

170. Bahram Shahrokh, "Khakestar-e Garm," *Mard-e Emruz*, January 24, 1948, 2.

171. Bahram Shahrokh, "Khakestar-e Garm," *Mard-e Emruz*, January 17, 1948, 4.

172. Ibid., 4, 9.

173. Ibid., 4.

174. Ibid.

175. Ibid.

176. Ibid.

177. For a related discussion, see Monica Ringer, "Iranian Nationalism and Zoroastrian Identity: Between Cyrus and Zoroaster," in *Iran Facing Others: Iranian Identity Boundaries and Modern Political Culture*, ed. Abbas Amanat and Farzin Vejdani (New York: Palgrave Macmillan, 2012), 267–277.

CHAPTER 2. PATRON AND PATRIOT

This chapter is a revised and expanded version of a previously published article, Afshin Marashi, "Patron and Patriot: Dinshah J. Irani and the Revival of Indo-Iranian Culture," *Iranian Studies* 46, no. 2 (2013): 186–206. Copyright © The International Society for Iranian Studies. Reprinted by permission of Taylor & Francis Ltd, www.tandfonline.com on behalf of The International Society for Iranian Studies.

1. Biographical information for Dinshah Irani can be found in the following sources: Sir Jehangir C. Coyajee, "A Brief Life-Sketch of the Late Mr. Dinshah Irani," *Dinshah Irani Memorial Volume: Papers on Zoroastrianism and Iranian Subjects*, ed. Jahangir Coyajee et al. (Bombay, 1943), i–xiii; Shahmardan, *Farzanegan*, 490–499; "Shadravan Dinshah Irani," *Andisheh-ye Ma* 1, no. 5 (1946): 4–6; Ebrahim Purdavud, "Goftar-e Agha-ye Purdavud," *Iran League Quarterly* 9, no. 1 (October 1938), Persian section: 1–6; Kaikhosrov D. Irani, "Dinshah J. Irani, 1881–1938," http://www.zarathushtra.com/z/gatha/dji/dinshah.htm, accessed May 2, 2018; Kaikhusroo M. JamaspAsa, "Dinshah Jijibhoy Irani," *Encyclopaedia Iranica*, http://www.iranicaonline.org/articles/irani-dinshah-jijibhoy, accessed May 2, 2018.

2. Coyajee, "A Brief Life-Sketch," xiii.

3. For the Zoroastrian charitable foundations in Bombay, see Christine Dobbin, "The Parsi Panchayat in Bombay City in the Nineteenth Century," *Modern Asian Studies* 4, no. 2 (1970): 149–164; John R. Hinnells, "The Flowering of Zoroastrian Benevolence: Parsi Charities in the 19th and 20th Centuries," in *Papers in Honour of Professor Mary Boyce*, vol. 1, ed. Jacques Duchesne-Guillemin and Mary Boyce (Leiden, Netherlands: Brill, in association with Centre International d'Études Indo-iraniennes, 1985), 282–286. On the history of the Iran League I am grateful to Dinyar Patel for sharing with me his unpublished master's thesis, "The Iran League of Bombay: Parsis, Iran, and the Appeal of Iranian Nationalism" (Harvard University, 2008).

4. Purdavud, "Goftar-e Agha-ye Purdavud," *Iran League Quarterly* 9, no. 1 (October 1938): 1–2.

5. Coyajee, "A Brief Life-Sketch," xiii. For Jalal al-Din Kayhan, see also *Iran League Quarterly* 2, no. 2–3 (January-April, 1932): 119.

6. Irani's collaborations with his Iranian colleagues led him to support the Iranian nationalist movement of "literary return" (*bāzgasht-e adabī*) to classical Persian poetic forms, and he became a South Asian critic of the Persian literary tradition in India (the so-called *sabk-e hendī* style). Irani's literary collaborations and positions are well documented in, among other sources, his annotated anthology of contemporary Persian poetry, Dinshah J. Irani, ed., *Poets of the Pahlavi Regime* (Bombay: Fort Printing Press, 1933). On these and related issues, see Farzin Vejdani, "Indo-Iranian Linguistic, Literary, and Religious Entanglements: Between Nationalism and Cosmopolitanism, ca. 1900–1940," *Comparative Studies of South Asia, Africa, and the Middle*

East 36, no. 3 (2016): 443–446. On the politics and poetics of the "literary return" movement, see Kevin Schwartz, "*Bazgasht-i Adabi* and Persianate Literary Culture in Eighteenth and Nineteenth Century Iran, India, and Afghanistan" (PhD diss., University of California, Berkeley, 2014).

7. The Firuz Bahram School was itself built with funds donated by Parsi benefactors. See Shahrokh, *Memoirs*, 23. See also "Firoze Behram Middle School," *Iran League Quarterly* 3, no. 2 (January 1933): 109–111.

8. "Late Mr. Dinshah J. Irani: Great Grief Felt in Iran at His Loss," *Iran League Quarterly* 9, no. 2 (January 1939): 97–98.

9. A definitive critical history of the Parsi intellectual renaissance of the nineteenth century has yet to be completed. The following works may serve as preludes to that history: Ringer, *Pious Citizens*; Sheffield, "Iran, the Mark of Paradise or the Land of Ruin?" 15–43; Palsetia, *The Parsis of India*; Kulke, *The Parsees in India*; Susan Maneck, *The Death of Ahriman: Culture, Identity, and Theological Change among the Parsis of India* (Bombay: K. R. Cama Oriental Institute, 1997).

10. For the broader history of this phenomenon, see Hamid Dabashi, *Persophilia: Persian Culture on the Global Scene* (Cambridge, MA: Harvard University Press, 2015). See also Schwab, *The Oriental Renaissance*.

11. For the rise and fall of the Persianate, see Hodgson, *The Venture of Islam*, especially vol. 2, 293–314. See also Kia and Marashi, "After the Persianate: Introduction," 379–383; Tavakoli-Targhi, *Refashioning Iran*.

12. Coyajee, "A Brief Life-Sketch," iii; Shahmardan, *Farzanegan*, 492. For the condition of Iran's Zoroastrian community during the nineteenth century, see Kestenberg Amighi, *The Zoroastrians of Iran* and Michael Stausberg, "Zoroastrians in Modern Iran," in *The Wiley Blackwell Companion to Zoroastrianism*, ed. Michael Stausberg and Yuhan Sohrab-Dinshaw Vevaina (West Sussex, UK: John Wiley and Sons, 2015), 173–176.

13. For the most detailed account of P. D. Marker's philanthropy, see Mirza Sarosh Lohrasb, ed., *Peshotanji Marker Memorial Volume/Yadnameh-ye Peshotan Dusabai Marker* (Bombay: Iranian Zoroastrian Anjoman, 1966), English section, 17–20, and Persian section, 5–55.

14. Dinshah Jijibhoy Irani, *Peyk-e Mazdayasnan* (Bamba'i: Anjoman-e Zartoshtian-e Irani-ye Bamba'i, 1927).

15. Dinshah Jijibhoy Irani, *Akhlaq-e Iran-e Bastan* (Bamba'i: Anjoman-e Zarthostian-e Irani-ye Bamba'i, 1930). The book has been republished in numerous editions in both Tehran and Bombay, in 1933, 1955, 1974, and 1982.

16. Dinshah J. Irani, *Falsafeh-ye Iran-e Bastan* (Bamba'i: Anjoman-e Zarthostian-e Irani-ye Bamba'i, 1933).

17. Irani completed his legal education in 1904, received multiple awards and scholarships to further his study of the law, and passed the solicitor's examination in 1908. He then joined the prominent Bombay law firm of Mulla and Mulla. Specializing in tax law, he rose to become a senior partner in the firm. See Coyajee, "A Brief Life-Sketch," ii. For the importance of the Parsi community in the legal history of colonial India, see Mitra Sharafi, *Law and Identity in Colonial South Asia: Parsi Legal Culture, 1772–1947* (Cambridge, UK: Cambridge University Press, 2014).

18. For the relationship between modernity, liberalism, and religious reform in the Middle East and South Asia, see, for example, Juan Cole, *Modernity and the*

Millennium: The Genesis of the Baha'i Faith in the Nineteenth-Century Middle East (New York: Columbia University Press, 1998), 13–14. For the history of Zoroastrian reformism, see Ringer, *Pious Citizens*, 71–90.

19. For the most comprehensive critique of this conservative and proto-fascist reading of Iranian nationalism, see Zia-Ebrahimi, *The Emergence of Iranian Nationalism*.

20. Vejdani, "Indo-Iranian Linguistic, Literary, and Religious Entanglements," 437.

21. Shahmardan, *Farzanegan*, 498.

22. The total population of Parsis in Bombay, according to the 1872 census, was 44,091, or 6.8 percent of the urban population. See Dobbin, "The Parsi Panchayat," 157. The exact number of "Iranis" is difficult to estimate but likely numbered a few thousand. On Iranian migration to India more generally in the nineteenth century, see John R. Hinnells, *The Zoroastrian Diaspora: Religion and Migration* (Oxford, UK: Oxford University Press, 2005), 79–81; Kestenberg Amighi, *The Zoroastrians of Iran*, 129–131; Palsetia, *The Parsis of India*, 169. For a firsthand account of Iranians in nineteenth-century Bombay, see Haji Ali Mohammad Pirzadeh, *Safarnameh-ye Haji Mohammad Ali Pirzadeh*, vol. 1, ed. Hafez Farmanfarmaian (Tehran: Entesharat-e Daneshgah-e Tehran, 1963), 130–133.

23. For the role of the Parsis in the commercial history of Bombay, see Christine Dobbin, *Asian Entrepreneurial Minorities: Conjoint Communities in the Making of the World-Economy, 1570–1940* (London: Routledge 1996), 77–104; Palsetia, *The Parsis of India*, 35–64. For the Parsi role in the opium economy, see Jesse S. Palsetia, "The Parsis of India and the Opium Trade in China," *Contemporary Drug Problems* 35, no. 4 (Winter 2008): 647–678.

24. Delphine Menant, *Les Parsis: Histoire des Communautés Zoroastriennes de l'Inde* (Paris: Leroux, 1898), 427–428; S. M. Edwardes, *Memoir of Sir Dinshaw Manockjee Petit, First Baronet* (Oxford, UK: Oxford University Press, 1923), 5–11. Lady Sakarbai was reportedly the daughter of one of the earliest "Irani" migrants to India, who married the prominent Parsi textile merchant Framji Panday. See "Obituary for Lady Sakarbai," *Indian Magazine* 233 (May 1890): 278–279; Choksy, "Despite Shāhs and Mollās," 152–153. Lady Sakarbai's brother Merwanji Framji Banday (1812–1876), another successful "Irani" businessman in mid-nineteenth-century Bombay, also played a central role in establishing the Persian Zoroastiran Amelioration Fund. See also M. M. Murzban, *The Parsis in India: Being an Enlarged and Copiously Annotated, Up to Date English Edition of Delphine Menant's Les Parsis*, vol. 1 (Bombay: Murzan, 1917), 132.

25. Palsetia, *The Parsis of India*, 169–170; Kulke, *The Parsees in India*, 142–143; Menant, *Les Parsis*, 44–45.

26. The "Irani" community of Bombay even developed its own *migration narrative* reminiscent of the *Qesseh-ye Sanjan*, in which a Kermani Zoroastrian, Kaikhosrow Yazdyar, fled to India with his daughter "Golestan Banu" in the late eighteenth century, who in turn became the founder of the "Irani" community in Bombay. This narrative of "Irani" origins in Bombay came to circulate increasingly from the mid-nineteenth century onward and may have first found its way into written form in Manekji Limji Hataria's account of his first decade in Iran, written in 1863. See Boyce, *Zoroastrians*, 209–212; Boyce, "Manekji Limji Hataria in Iran," 20. On the travels of Manekji Limji, see also Zia-Ebrahimi, "An Emissary of the Golden Age,"

377–390. For the "Irani" migration narrative, see also Shahmardan, *Farzanegan*, 495–498; Coyajee, "A Brief Life-Sketch," vii-viii.

27. Irani, "Dinshah J. Irani, 1881–1938"; JamaspAsa, "Dinshah Jijibhoy Irani." For the importance of Elphinstone College in nineteenth-century Bombay, see Boyce, *Zoroastrians*, 196; Palsetia, *The Parsis of India*, 140; Ringer, *Pious Citizens*, 37–46.

28. The gradual decline of Persian as both a vernacular and administrative language began after the 1835 English Education Act, which made English the administrative language of India and the language of instruction in Indian schools. Persian gradually became a literary language studied by "academic specialists" like Dinshah Irani; see Muzaffar Alam, "The Culture and Politics of Persian in Precolonial Hindustan," in *Literary Cultures in History: Reconstructions from South Asia*, ed. Sheldon Pollock (Berkeley: University of California Press, 2003), 188–189.

29. The texts include: *Saadi's Odes 1–60: With Persian Text, Full Translation, Exhaustive Introduction and Complete Notes*, ed. and trans. K. B. Irani and D. J. Irani (Bombay, 1913); *Saadi's Qasayed-i Farsiye: With Persian Text, Full Translation, Exhaustive Introduction and Complete Notes*, trans. K. B. Irani and D. J. Irani (Bombay, 1914); *Translation of Nizam-ul-Mulk's Siasat-nameh*, ed. and trans. K. B. Irani and D. J. Irani (Bombay, 1916); *Hafez Odes 1–75*, ed. and trans. K. B. Irani and D. J. Irani (Bombay, 1917 [revised 2nd ed., 1925]); *Full Translation and Explanation of Anwar-e-Sohaili, Chapters II and III*, ed. and trans. K. B. Irani and D. J. Irani (Bombay, 1917).

30. Purdavud, "Goftar-e Agha-ye Purdavud," 3; K. A. Fitter, "League's Efforts to Popularize Persian among the Parsis," *Iran League Quarterly* 7, no. 3 (April 1937): 192.

31. For the history of this important Parsi institution, see Modi, "A Short History," 477–483.

32. Kharshedji Rustomji Cama, *The Collected Works of K. R. Cama* (Bombay: K. R. Cama Institute, 1968), vol. 1, i-x; James Russell, "Kharshedji Rustamh Cama," *Encyclopaedia Iranica*, http://www.iranicaonline.org/articles/cama-kharshedji-rustamh-b, accessed May 7, 2018.

33. For the role of K. R. Cama at the J. J. Zartoshti Madressa, see Modi, "A Short History," 480–481; Dinshah Kapadia, "Renaissance of Zoroastrian Studies among the Parsis," in *Sir J. J. Zarthoshti Madressa Centenary Volume*, ed. Dinshah D. Kapadia (Bombay: Dorabji and Co., 1967), vii-xvi.

34. D. J. Irani, *Gems from the Divine Songs of Zoroaster* (Bombay: E. G. Pearson, 1922), i.

35. Coyajee, "A Brief Life-Sketch," iii. For these reform groups, see Boyce, *Zoroastrians*, 200; Ringer, *Pious Citizens*, 72–74, 112–114.

36. Palsatia, *The Parsis of India*, 65–104; Dobbin, "The Parsi Panchayet," 149–164; Hinnells, "The Flowering of Zoroastrian Benevolence," 261–326.

37. Ringer, *Pious Citizens*, 161–162; Coyajee, "A Brief Life-Sketch," iii.

38. See, for example, "The Iran League: Aims and Objectives," *Iran League Quarterly* 1, no. 1, n.p. The "aims and objectives" of the Iran League, along with the names and positions of key stakeholders, were published in multiple issues of the journal during its print run. See also K. A. Fitter, "Summary of Work Done by Iran League between September 1931, and September 1934," part I, *Iran League Quarterly* 7, no. 3 (April 1937): 187–196; K. A. Fitter, "Summary of Work Done by Iran League between

September, 1931, and September, 1934," part II, *Iran League Quarterly* 7, no. 4 (July 1937): 259–263.

39. Mary Boyce, "Maneckji Limji Hataria in Iran," 19–31; Murzban, *The Parsis in India*, vol.1, 132–136; Shahmardan, *Farzanegan*, 617–643; Ardeshir Reporter, "The Education Movement among the Zoroastrians of Iran," *Iran League Quarterly* 1, no. 1–2 (April–July 1930): 75–81.

40. Murzban, *The Parsis in India*, vol. 1, 132; Shahmardan, *Farzanegan*, 639–642. For a complete list of the schools built through local and Parsi philanthropy during this period, see Jamshid Pishdadi, *Yadnameh-ye Sorush Lohrasb* (Los Angeles, 1998), 80–82.

41. Irach J. S. Taraporewala, "Mrs. Ratanbanu E. Bamji," *Iran League Quarterly* 1, no. 1–2 (April–July 1930): 112; Sohrab J. Bulsara, "The Late Mrs. Ratanbanu E. Bamji," *Iran League Quarterly* 1, no. 3–4 (October 1930–January 1931): 249.

42. Sohrab J. Bulsara, "Anosheravan Dadgar High School for Girls in Tehran," *Iran League Quarterly* 7, no. 3 (April 1937): 199–202. The article includes statistical data on students at the school. Approximately two-thirds of the students were from Muslim families, with the remaining third from the local Zoroastrian community as well as six students from Armenian Christian backgrounds. The Tata endowment also subsidized tuition at the school, with approximately 25 percent of those enrolled paying little or no fees.

43. Sohrab J. Bulsara, "Parsi Charitable Organizations in Persia," *Iran League Quarterly* 1, no. 3–4 (October 1931–July 1932): 236; Arbab Kaykhosrow Shahrokh, "Anowshirwan Dadgar High School in Tehran," *Iran League Quarterly* 10, no. 2 (January 1940): 88–89.

44. The school opened in December of 1932. "Feroze Behram Middle School," *Iran League Quarterly* 3, no. 2 (January 1933): 108–111.

45. Lohrasb, *Marker Memorial Volume*, Persian section, 8; Sohrab J. Bulsara, "Editor's Notes," *Iran League Quarterly* 3, no. 3 (April 1933): 137.

46. The details of Reporter's life and work in Iran remain controversial and undocumented. For the most reliable biographical details, see Shahmardan, *Farzanegan*, 360–368. See also Sohrab J. Bulsara, "The Late Mr. Ardeshirji Reporter," *Iran League Quarterly* 3, no. 2 (January 1933): 61. On the first anniversary of his death an expanded obituary of Reporter was published in the *ILQ*. There is a reference in the obituary to the existence of his diaries: "luckily he has left his precious diaries behind." See also Sohrab J. Bulsara, "Ardeshirji Reporter," *Iran League Quarterly* 4, no. 2–3 (January–April 1934): 119–121. An unauthenticated fragment from these diaries was published in Iran in Abdollah Shahbazi, ed., *Zohur va Soqut-e Saltanat-e Pahlavi*, vol. 2 (Tehran: Entesharat-e Etella'at, 1991), 146–159. This source should be approached with caution. Also to be approached with caution is Abdollah Shahbazi, "Ser Ardeshir Ripurter: Servis-e Ettela'ati-ye Britania va Iran," http://www.shahbazi.org/Articles/Reporter_Ardeshirji.pdf, 1–29.

47. Irach J. S. Taraporewala, "Active Propaganda in Bombay by the Iran League," *Iran League Quarterly* 1, no. 1–2 (April–July 1930): 111–112.

48. Ibid.

49. Reporter, "The Education Movement among the Zoroastrians of Iran," 76.

50. Ibid.

51. Ibid.

52. Ibid., 77–78.

53. Sohrab J. Bulsara, "Parsees and Iran: The Late Editor's Services," *Iran League Quarterly* 2, no. 1 (October 1931): 1.

54. Ibid., 2.

55. Nariman's criticisms of the Iran League's policies toward Iran were prescient. See chapter 4, note 167, and chapter 5 discussion of Saif Azad's 1931 visit to India. Nariman was a consistent critic of many of the pious orthodoxies of more conservative members of the Parsi community. He wrote, for example, "there is hardly any of the alleged meretricious usages of modern Islam which had no parallel, sometimes in an aggravated from, in the later Zoroastiran period. Let us be loyal to Truth and just to our [Muslim] confreres in Persia." See G. K. Nariman, *Persia and Parsis: Part I* (Bombay: Iran League, 1925), iv.

56. Bulsara, "Parsees and Iran," 2–3.

57. Ardeshirji Edulji Reporter, "Iran Revived," *Iran League Quarterly* 2, no. 2–3 (January–April 1932): 157.

58. Ibid., 156.

59. Ibid.

60. M. A. Mazandi, "Acquisition of Land in Khuzeestan," *Iran League Quarterly* 2, no. 2–3 (January–April 1932): 175–178; Sohrab J. Bulsara, "Personal Labour Essential for Working Agricultural Colony," *Iran League Quarterly* 5, no. 2 (January 1935): 80.

61. Sohrab J. Bulsara, "Acquisition of Land in Iran for the Unemployed Zoroastrians There," *Iran League Quarterly* 7, no. 1 (January 1937): 93–95.

62. K. A. Fitter, "Summary of the Work Done by the Iran League between September 1931 and September 1934," *Iran League Quarterly* 7, no. 4 (July 1937): 259.

63. R. P. Masani, "With Dinshah Irani in New Iran," in *Dinshah Irani Memorial Volume: Papers on Zoroastrianism and Iranian Subjects*, ed. Jehangir Coyajee et al. (Bombay: Dinshah Irani Memorial Committee, 1948), xxiv; Lohrasb, *Marker Memorial Volume*, 5–6.

64. Sohrab J. Bulsara, "Parsis and Persia," *Iran League Quarterly* 3, no. 1 (October 1932): 1.

65. Sohrab J. Bulsara, "Persia's Long Foreshores," *Iran League Quarterly* 4, no. 2–3 (January–April 1934): 117. The new port had been rebuilt in 1932 and also came to serve as the southern terminus of the trans-Iranian railroad. It was renamed Bandar-e Khomeini following the 1979 revolution. See also X. De Planhol, "Bandar-e Šāhpūr," *Encyclopaedia Iranica*, http://www.iranicaonline.org/articles/bandar-e-sahpur, accessed May 10, 2018.

66. Bulsara, "Acquisition of Land in Iran," 93–95. I am using the term "Parsi settler colony" casually. These Parsi-Iranian proposals for remigration and resettlement require additional consideration within the typologies and theoretical debates relating to settler colonialism. See Patrick Wolfe, *Settler Colonialism and the Transformation of Anthropology: The Politics and Poetics of an Ethnographic Event* (London: Cassell, 1999); Edward Cavanagh and Lorenzo Veracini, eds., *The Routledge Handbook of the History of Settler Colonialism* (London: Routledge, 2017).

67. Bulsara, "Personal Labour Essential for Working Agricultural Colony," 80.

68. Sohrab J. Bulsara, "Textile Mill in Mashhad," *Iran League Quarterly* 4, no. 4 (July 1934): 108; K. A. Fitter, "Scheme to Start Spinning/Weaving Factory in Iran," *Iran League Quarterly* 7, no. 3 (April 1937): 189, 195; Sohrab J. Bulsara, "Khosrovi Mill in Mashhad," *Iran League Quarterly* 8, no. 2–3 (January–April 1938): 159. The mill project was not a success and closed within a short time. R. P. Masani, one of

the participants in the project, described it as a "sordid business." See Masani, "With Dinshah Irani in New Iran," xvi.

69. Bulsara, "Personal Labour Essential for Working Agricultural Colony," 80.

70. The *Iran League Quarterly* serialized portions of what became Phiroz Sakatvala's *Rich Fields in Persia* (Bombay: Iran League Quarterly, 1933). See Phiroz Sakatvala, "Rich Fields in Persia," *Iran League Quarterly* 3, no. 1 (October 1932): 17–20; Phiroz D. Sakatvala, "Rich Fields in Persia," *Iran League Quarterly* 3, no. 2 (January 1933): 75–80; Phiroz Sakatvala, "Rich Fields in Persia," *Iran League Quarterly* 3, no. 3 (April 1933): 143–150.

71. Dinshah J. Irani, "Regenerated Iran," *Iran League Quarterly* 2, no. 4 (July 1932): 206.

72. Tanya H. Luhrmann, *The Good Parsi: The Fate of a Colonial Elite in a Postcolonial Society* (Cambridge, MA: Harvard University Press, 1996).

73. William Safran, "Diasporas in Modern Societies: Myths of Homeland and Return," *Diaspora: A Journal of Transnational Studies* 1, no. 1 (Spring 1991): 83–99.

74. Biographical details for P. D. Marker and his family can be found in the following sources: Lohrasb, *Marker Memorial Volume*, English section, 1–23, and Persian section, 5–55; K. A. Fitter, "Peshotanji D. Marker: An Appreciation, Part I," *Iran League Quarterly* 5, no. 1 (October 1934): 33–35; K. A. Fitter, "Peshotanji D. Marker: An Appreciation, Part II," *Iran League Quarterly* 5, no. 4 (July 1935): 235–240; Kekobad Ardeshir Marker, *A Petal from the Rose*, 2 vols. (Karachi: Rosette, 1985); John Hinnells, *The Zoroastrian Diaspora: Religion and Migration* (Oxford, UK: Oxford University Press, 2005), 224–226.

75. Hinnells, *Zoroastrian Diaspora*, 224.

76. Fitter, "Peshotanji D. Marker: An Appreciation, Part I," 34.

77. Hinnells, *Zoroastrian Diaspora*, 202.

78. Fitter, "Peshotanji D. Marker: An Appreciation, Part II," 236.

79. Fitter, "Peshotanji D. Marker: An Appreciation, Part I," 33. Marker had also read the reports about the social conditions in Yazd and Kerman produced by Manakji Limji Hataria, Ardeshir Reporter, and others associated with charity and relief efforts in Iran. See J. D. Daruwala, "P. D. Marker, Founder of Educational Institutions for Boys and Girls in Yazd," in *Marker Memorial Volume*, ed. Mirza Sarosh Lohrasb (Bombay: Iranian Zoroastrian Anjoman, 1966), 2.

80. Ibid., 7–14.

81. Fitter, "Peshotanji D. Marker: An Appreciation, Part II," 240.

82. Lohrasb, *Marker Memorial Volume*, 19. In 1934, corresponding with the Ferdowsi Millennium Celebrations of that year, Marker also provided funds for the erection of the "Ferdowsi Memorial Clock Tower" not far from the Marker School, in what became known as Marker Square. See Lohrasb, *Marker Memorial Volume*, 15–16, 24–26; K. A. Fitter, "Ferdawsi Memorial Clock Tower in Yezd," *Iran League Quarterly* 5, no. 2 (January 1935): 93–97.

83. Lohrasb, *Marker Memorial Volume*, 12, 56–57; Pishdadi, *Yadnameh-ye Sorush Lohrasb*, 95–96. Sorush Lohrasb also compiled statistical data on Zoroastrian literacy in Yazd and the surrounding areas. He estimated that the total Zoroastrian population in this region was 7,610, with aggregate literacy rates at about 44 percent. He observed, "this shows the average percentage literacy to be above 44, which should be regarded as fair in the circumstances, but not satisfactory." See Sorush Lohrasb, "Literacy among the Zoroastrians of Yazd and Surrounding Villages," *Iran League*

Quarterly 6, no. 2–3 (January–April 1936): 153–155. Similar surveys, with lower literacy rates, were also collected for Kerman and its hinterlands. See P. P. Barucha, "Literacy Census of the Zoroastrians of Kerman," *Iran League Quarterly* 7, no. 3 (April 1937): 197.

84. Irach J. S. Taraporewala, "Some Statistics of Zoroastrian Educational Institutions in Persia," *Iran League Quarterly* 1, no. 5 (April 1931): 30–31. There is a large literature on the history of education policy in modern Iran. See, for example, David Menashri, *Education and the Making of Modern Iran* (Ithaca, NY: Cornell University Press, 1992); Jasamin Rostam-Kolayi, "From Evangelizing to Modernizing Iranians: The American Presbyterian Mission and Its Iranian Students," *Iranian Studies* 41, no. 2 (March 2008): 213–240.

85. Lohrasb, *Marker Memorial Volume*, 13.

86. Ibid., 14. Marker and Irani had reached out to the leaders of the Bombay Parsi community to invest and possibly remigrate to Iran. Marker spent considerable effort to reach out to the Tata family to encourage their investment in the trans-Iranian railroad project. Despite their initial inquiries, the Tata firm ultimately did not participate in the construction of the railroad. See Marker, *Petal from the Rose*, vol. 1, 177–178.

87. Marker made three trips to Iran, in 1924, 1934, and 1949.

88. Marker, *Petal from the Rose*, vol. 1, 163.

89. Ibid., 164.

90. Ibid., 169; Lohrasb, *Marker Memorial Volume*, 3–5.

91. Lohrasb, *Marker Memorial Volume*, 7–9; Pishdadi, *Yadnameh-ye Sorush Lohrasb*, 91. In the following years, local Iranian Zoroastrian doctors trained in Bombay assumed the responsibilities for overseeing the medical facilities.

92. Lohrasb, *Marker Memorial Volume*, 5–29. Lohrasb would continue his role as headmaster of the Marker schools until the late 1960s.

93. Ibid.

94. Marker, *Petal from the Rose*, vol. 1, 174.

95. Ibid.

96. Ibid., 173.

97. Ibid.

98. Ibid., 172.

99. Fitter, "Peshotanji D. Marker: An Appreciation, Part II," 236; "List of Publications on Iran," *Iran League Quarterly* 7, no. 3 (April 1937): 198.

100. Fitter, "Summary of Work Done by Iran League between September, 1931, and September, 1934," Part II, 196. On page 189 of the same article, Fitter describes the Iran League's effort to raise funds for a "Parsi Preacher" who would travel to Iran to facilitate "the spread of religious knowledge among [the] coreligionists."

101. See chapter 4, footnotes 674–677.

102. The most important of these was the Persian translation of S. M. Taher Rezwi, *Parsis: A People of the Book, Being a Survey of the Zoroastrian Religion in Light of Biblical and Quranic Teachings* (Calcutta: N. C. Roy, 1928). The book was translated by Mirza Ali Mazandi as *Parsian Ahl-e Ketaband* (Bamba'i: Anjoman-e Iran Lig, 1936). Mazandi's translation was also serialized in the Persian section of the *Iran League Quarterly*. The other key English-language text on Zoroastrianism and ancient Iran that was translated into Persian was Pestanji Phirozshah Balsara's *Ancient Iran: Its Contribution to Human Progress* (Bombay: Iran League, 1936).

The Persian translation was made by Abdolhossein Sepanta as *Iran va Ahmiat-e an dar Taraqqi va Tamaddon-e Bashar* (Bamba'i: Anjoman-e Iran Lig, 1936). Sepanta worked closely with Dinshah Irani during this period. He also became a pioneering Iranian filmmaker.

103. Muzaffar Alam and Sanjay Subrahmanyam, *Indo-Persian Travels in the Age of Discoveries, 1400–1800* (Cambridge, UK: Cambridge University Press, 2010).

104. On the history of modern printing in Iran and India and its effects on the production and circulation of Persian-language books, see Nile Green, "Stones from Bavaria: Iranian Lithography in Its Global Contexts," *Iranian Studies* 43, no. 3 (June 2010): 305–331; Green, *Bombay Islam*, chapter 4; Shahla Babazadeh, *Tarikh-e Chap dar Iran* (Tehran: Tahuri, 1991); Ulrich Marzolph, *Narrative Illustration in Persian Lithographed Books* (Leiden, Netherlands: Brill, 2001); Willem Floor, "ČĀP," *Encyclopaedia Iranica*, http://www.iranicaonline.org/articles/cap, accessed May 15, 2018; Iraj Afshar, "Ketabha-ye Chap-e Qadim dar Iran va Chap-e Ketabha-ye Farsi dar Jahan," *Hunar va Mardom* 5 (1966): 26–33.

105. Afshin Marashi, "Print Culture and Its Publics: A Social History of Bookstores in Tehran, 1900–1950," *International Journal of Middle East Studies* 47, no. 1 (2015): 89–108.

106. Green, "Stones from Bavaria," 321; Marzolph, *Narrative Illustration*, 14.

107. The centrality of profit has been a key theme in most discussions of the early social history of print technology. See Benedict Anderson, *Imagined Communities: Reflections on the Origins and Spread of Nationalism*, rev. ed. (New York: Verso Books, 2006), 38; Lucien Febvre and Henri-Jean Martin, *The Coming of the Book: The Impact of Printing, 1450–1800* (New York: Verso, 1991), 248–250.

108. Leslie Howsman, *Cheap Bibles: Nineteenth Century Publishing and the British and Foreign Bible Society* (Cambridge, UK: Cambridge University Press, 1991).

109. Irani, *Peyk-e Mazdayasnan*.

110. Ibid., preface. Irani also states that some of the essays were previously published in English in the *British Mazdaznan Magazine: The Official Organ of the Mazdaznan Association of Great Britain*. The Mazdaznan Association of Great Britain followed the spiritualist cult of Otto Hanish (1854–1936). See Noll, *The Jung Cult*, 104–106; Webb, *The Occult Establishment*, 32–33. The cult of Otto Hanish also attracted interest among the Parsis of Bombay, including Dinshah Irani, who discusses the movement's magazine in the *Peyk-e Mazdayasnan*, 20–23. The movement was also discussed with some reverence in the pages of the *Iran League Quarterly*; see Nanabhai F. Mama, "The Rev. Dr. Otoman Zar'adusht Hanish, a Short Sketch of His Life," *Iran League Quarterly* 8, no. 1 (October 1937): 45–49; Behram H. Santook, "The Great Teacher—Rev. Dr. Otoman Zar-Adusht Hanish," *Iran League Quarterly* 8, no. 2–3 (January–April 1938): 145–156.

111. Dinshaw J. Irani, *Understanding the Gathas: Hymns of Zarathustra*, ed. Kaikhosrov D. Irani (Womelsdorf, PA: Ahura Publishers, 1994), i.

112. Irani, *Peyk-e Mazdayasnan*, n.p., preface.

113. Ibid., 8.

114. Ibid., 8–9.

115. Dan Sheffield, "Primary Sources: New Persian (Persian Revāyats)," in *The Wiley Blackwell Companion to Zoroastrianism*, ed. Michael Stausberg and Yuhan Sohrab-Dinshaw Vevaina (West Sussex, UK: John Wiley and Sons, 2015), 533–534.

116. Boyce, *Zoroastrians*, 190–191. Shifts in the balance of religious authority

between Iranian Zoroastrians and Paris began as early as the eighteenth century. On this issue see also Ringer, *Pious Citizens*, 143–147.

117. Irani, *Peyk-e Mazdayasnan*, 8–9.

118. Ibid., 11.

119. Ibid., 93.

120. Ibid., 94.

121. Ansari, *The Politics of Nationalism in Modern Iran*, 65–67.

122. Irani, *Peyk-e Mazdayasnan*, 97–98.

123. Choksy, "Despite Shāhs and Mollās," 141–144.

124. Irani, *Peyk-e Mazdayasnan*, 98.

125. Ibid., 99.

126. Ibid.

127. Irani, *Akhlaq-e Iran-e Bastan*.

128. Irani, *Falsafeh-ye Iran-e Bastan*.

129. The second edition was published in Tehran at the Majles Press, and a third edition was produced again in Bombay.

130. Irani, *Akhlaq-e Iran-e Bastan*, 13. An English rendering of the diagram was produced in his posthumously published *Path to Happiness, or Ethical Teachings of Zoroaster* (Bombay: Jehangir B. Karant's Sons, 1939), 6. It was also reproduced in the inaugural issue of the *Iran League Quarterly* 1, no. 1–2 (October 1930): 72–73. The diagram reproduced in the *Iran League Quarterly* was accompanied by commentary from Irach Taraporewalla, who wrote, "D. J. Irani…to whom we owe this wonderful 'circle of perfection' has clearly caught the underlying principles of the Amesha-Spentas."

131. Boyce, *Zoroastrians*, 21–24.

132. Irani, *Akhlaq-e Iran-e Bastan*, 13.

133. Ibid., 16.

134. Ibid., 18.

135. Ibid., 20.

136. Ibid., 21.

137. Ibid., 22.

138. Ibid., 12.

139. Ibid.

140. Ibid., 23.

141. Ibid.

142. For the most complete discussion of Azar Kayvan and the Kayvani sect, see Daniel J. Sheffield, "The Language of Heaven in Safavid Iran: Speech and Cosmology in the Thought of Azar Kayvan and His Followers," in *No Tapping Around Philology: A Festschrift in Honor of Wheeler McIntosh Thackston Jr.'s 70th Birthday*, ed. Alireza Korangy and Daniel J. Sheffield (Wiesbaden: Harrassowitz Verlag, 2014), 161–183. See also Daniel J. Sheffield, "In the Path of the Prophet: Medieval and Early Modern Narratives of the Life of Zarathustra in Islamic Iran and Western India," PhD diss., Harvard University, 2012, 88–95; Tavakoli-Targhi, *Refashioning Iran*, 86–89; Maneck, *The Death of Ahriman*, 49–70; Henry Corbin, "Āzar Kayvān," *Encyclopaedia Iranica*, http://www.iranicaonline.org/articles/azar-kayvan-priest, accessed May 17, 2018.

143. Babayan, *Mystics, Monarchs, and Messiahs*, 484.

144. On the Theosophical Society, see Gauri Viswanathan, *Outside the Fold: Conversion, Modernity, and Belief* (Princeton, NJ: Princeton University Press, 1998),

179–184; Gauri Viswanathan, "In Search of Madame Blavatsky: Reading the Exoteric, Retrieving the Esoteric," *Representations* 141, no. 1 (Winter 2018): 67–94. See also Bruce F. Campbell, *Ancient Wisdom Revived: A History of the Theosophical Movement* (Berkeley: University of California Press, 1980); Charles J. Ryan, *H. P. Blavatsky and the Theosophical Movement: A Brief Historical Sketch* (Point Loma, CA: Theosophical University Press, 1937). On the theme of heterodoxy in the religious history of colonial India, see Mitchell Numark, "Translating Religion: British Missionaries and the Politics of Knowledge in Colonial India and Bombay," PhD diss., UCLA, 2006; Mitchell Numark, "Translating Dharma: Scottish Missionary-Orientalists and the Politics of Religious Understanding in Nineteenth-Century Bombay," *Journal of Asian Studies* 70, no. 2 (May 2011): 471–500.

145. Irani, *Fasafeh-ye Iran-e Bastan*, n.p., preface.

146. On the complexities of this issue, see Farzin Vejdani, "The Place of Islam in Interwar Iranian Nationalist Historiography," in *Rethinking Iranian Nationalism and Modernity*, ed. Kamran Aghaie and Afshin Marashi (Austin, TX: University of Texas Press, 2014), 205–218.

147. Ibid., 61.

148. On the concept of stages, the path, or *tariqa* in Persianate mystical and poetic traditions, see Annemarie Schimmel, *Mystical Dimensions of Islam*, 2nd ed. (Chapel Hill: University of North Carolina Press, 2011), 98–129.

149. Irani, *Falsafeh-ye Iran-e Bastan*, 61.

150. Ibid., 66.

151. Ibid., 72.

152. Ibid., 83.

153. Ibid., 96.

154. Ibid., 102.

155. Ibid., 113.

156. Ibid., 114

157. Ibid.

158. On the history and usage of this term in referring to Hafez, see Hossein Ziai, "Hāfez, *Lisān al-Ghayb* of Persian Poetic Wisdom," in *Gott ist schön und er liebt die schönheit—God is beautiful and he loves beauty: Festschrift für Annemarie Schimmel zum 7. April 1992 dargebracht von schulern, freunden und kollegen*, ed. Alma Giese and Christoph Bürgel (Bern: Peter Lang, 1994), 449–469. For a broader discussion of the place of Hafez in the modern Iranian national imaginary, see Ali Ferdowsi, "The 'Emblem of the Manifestation of the Iranian Spirit': Hafiz and the Rise of the National Cult of Persian Poetry," *Iranian Studies* 41, no. 5 (December 2008): 667–691.

159. Irani, *Falsafeh-ye Iran-e Bastan*, 117.

160. Ibid., 120.

161. On this concept see William W. Malandra, "*Garōdmān*," *Encyclopaedia Iranica*, http://www.iranicaonline.org/articles/garodman, accessed May 18, 2018; G. W. Bowersock, Peter Brown, and Oleg Grabar, eds., *Late Antiquity: A Guide to the Postclassical World* (Cambridge, MA: Harvard University Press, 1999), 485.

162. Irani, *Falsafeh-ye Iran-e Bastan*, 116.

163. Ibid., 119.

164. Ibid., 36.

165. Irani does not go into great detail in highlighting the connection, but references to the *'eshraqi* tradition of Shehab al-din Yahya Sohrewardi (1154–1191) are

quite vivid. On the connection between Zoroastrianism and *'eshraqi* Sufism, see John Walbridge and Hossein Ziai, *Suhrawardi: The Philosophy of Illumination* (Provo, UT: Brigham Young Universtiy, 1999); Henry Corbin, *Spiritual Body and Celestial Earth: From Mazdean Iran to Shi'ite Iran*, trans. Nancy Pearson (Princeton, NJ: Princeton University Press, 1977); Henry Corbin, *The Man of Light in Iranian Sufism*, trans. Nancy Pearson (New Lebanon, NY: Omega Books, 1994). See also Maneck, *The Death of Ahriman*, 56–58.

166. Irani, *Falsafeh-ye Iran-e Bastan*, 119.

167. Ibid., 120.

CHAPTER 3. IMAGINING HAFEZ

This chapter is a revised and expanded version of a previously published article, Afshin Marashi, "Imagining Hafez: Rabindranath Tagore in Iran, 1932," *Journal of Persianate Studies* 3, no. 1 (2010): 46–77. Republished with permission of Brill Academic Publishers. Permission conveyed through Copyright Clearance Center, Inc.

1. Rabindranath Tagore, *Journey to Persia and Iraq: 1932*, trans. Surendranath Tagore and Sukhendu Ray (Kolkata: Visva-Bharata, 2003), 22, 121–129. Excerpts of Tagore's travelogue of this trip, originally published in Bengali as *Parasya-Yatri*, were partially translated into English by Surendranath Tagore in the *Modern Review* (October 1932) and the *Visva-Bharati Quarterly* (April and August 1937). Sri Sukhendu Ray translated the remainder of the travelogue for the 2003 edition. All references in this article are to the full translation published in 2003. Other sources detailing the itinerary of Tagore's trip to Iran can be found in *Indo-Iranica* 9, no. 2 (1961) and *Bokhara* 45 (2005).

2. Mohammad Golbon, "Tagur va Iran," *Bokhara* 45 (2005): 130.

3. Ibid., 131; Tagore, *Journey to Persia*, 113.

4. Irani, "Regenerated Iran," 192.

5. Tagore, *Journey to Persia*, 31. Tagore had also become eager to visit Iran after visiting the 1931 International Exhibition of Persian Art in London; see Irani, "Regenerated Iran," 191. The London exhibition was organized by the British Royal Academy with the curatorial assistance of Arthur Upham Pope. For a discussion of this exhibition, see Barry D. Wood, "'A Great Symphony of Pure Form': The 1931 International Exhibition of Persian Art and Its Influence," *Ars Orientalis* 30 (2000): 113–130.

6. Tagore had only one previous experience with air travel, from London to Paris in 1921. See Krishna Dutta and Andrew Robinson, *Rabindranath Tagore: The Myriad-Minded Man* (New York, St. Martin's, 1995), 315–316; Bose, *A Hundred Horizons*, 261. The most complete itinerary of his many travels can be found in Dutta and Robinson, Appendix 2, and in *Rabindranath Tagore: A Centenary Volume, 1861–1961* (New Delhi: Sahitya Akademi, 1961).

7. Tagore, *Journey to Persia*, 18. The Calcutta to Bushehr journey was part of Royal Dutch Airlines' regular air service linking Amsterdam and Batavia. The route ran regularly during the 1920s and 1930s, pioneering long-distance commercial aviation.

8. Ibid., 18–19.

9. Ibid., 25.

10. Ibid.

11. Bose, *A Hundred Horizons*, chapter 7; Ashis Nandy, *The Illegitimacy of*

Nationalism: Rabindranath Tagore and the Politics of Self (New Delhi: Oxford University Press, 1994), 2–8; Michael Adas, "Contested Hegemony: The Great War and the Afro-Asian Assault on the Civilizing Mission Ideology," *Journal of World History* 15, no. 1 (2004): 50–52.

12. On the idea of "strategic essentialism," see Gayatri Chakravorty Spivak, "Subaltern Studies: Deconstructing Historiography," in *Selected Subaltern Studies*, ed. Ranajit Guha and Gayatri Chakravorty Spivak (New York: Oxford University Press, 1988), 13.

13. Rabindranath Tagore, *Nationalism* (New Delhi: Rupa and Co., 2005), 70.

14. Stephen N. Hay, *Asian Ideas of East and West: Tagore and His Critics in Japan, China, and India* (Cambridge, MA: Harvard University Press, 1970), 14–26.

15. Nandy, *The Illegitimacy of Nationalism*, 5. Less sympathetic commentators, such as E. M. Forster, famously described his writing as riddled with "Babu sentences." Part of the problem was the difficulty of accurate translation. On this issue, see also Nabaneeta Sen, "The 'Foreign Reincarnation' of Rabindranath Tagore," *Journal of Asian Studies* 25, no. 2 (1966): 275–286.

16. There is considerable primary and secondary writing on Tagore's travels to Europe: see Dutta and Robinson, *Rabindranath Tagore*, 266–305; Alex Aronson, *Rabindranath through Western Eyes* (Calcutta: Rdhhi-India, 1978); Martin Kampchen, *Rabindranath Tagore in Germany: Four Responses to a Cultural Icon* (Shimla: Indian Institute for Advanced Study, 1999); Martin Kampchen, ed., *Rabindranath Tagore and Germany: A Documentation* (Calcutta: Mueller Bhavan, 1991); Dietmar Rothermund, ed. and trans., *Rabindranath Tagore in Germany: A Cross-Section of Contemporary Reports* (New Delhi: Mueller Bhavan, 1961).

17. For Western culture's moment of crisis following World War I, see Michael Adas, *Machines as the Measure of Men: Science, Technology, and Ideologies of Western Dominance* (Ithaca, NY: Cornell University Press, 1989), 365–380.

18. Prasenjit Duara, "The Discourse of Civilization and Pan-Asianism," *Journal of World History* 12, no. 1 (2001): 99–130; Prasenjit Duara, "The Discourse of Civilization and Decolonization," *Journal of World History* 15, no. 1 (2004): 1–5.

19. Duara, "The Discourse of Civilization," 99.

20. For the pre-Islamic revival in modern Iranian thought, see Tavakoli-Targhi, *Refashioning Iran*; Marashi, *Nationalizing Iran*; Ringer, *Pious Citizens*; Zia-Ebrahimi, *The Emergence of Iranian Nationalism*.

21. Tagore, *Journey to Persia*, introduction.

22. Hay, *Asian Ideas of East and West*, has the most detailed analysis of Tagore's visits to China and Japan. For Tagore's travels to Indonesia, see Arun Das Gupta, "Rabindranath Tagore in Indonesia: An Experiment in Bridge-Building," *Koninklijk Instituut Voor Taal-, Land- En Volkendunde (Royal Institute of Linguistics and Anthropology)* 158, no. 2 (2002): 451–477.

23. Okakura Tenshin (Kakuzo) was in many ways the Japanese version of Tagore, a public intellectual and advocate for Japanese modernity who simultaneously emphasized the cultural rootedness of Japan within "Pan-Asian" culture; see his *The Ideals of the East, with Special Reference to the Art of Japan* (Rutland, VT: C. E. Tuttle Co., 1970 [1903]); *The Book of Tea* (Rutland, VT: C. E. Tuttle Co., 1956 [1906]); *The Awakening of Japan* (New York: Century Co., 1904). See also Victoria Weston, *Japanese Painting and National Identity: Okakura Tenshin and His Circle* (Ann Arbor: Center for Japanese Studies, University of Michigan, 2003); Stefan Tanaka, "Imaging

History: Inscribing Belief in the Nation," *Journal of Asian Studies* 53, no. 1 (1994): 24–44; F. G. Notehelfer, "On Idealism and Realism in the Thought of Okakura Tenshin," *Journal of Japanese Studies* 16, no. 2 (1990): 309–355. For the friendship between Tagore and Tenshin, see Rustom Bharucha, *Another Asia: Rabindranath Tagore and Okakura Tenshin* (New Delhi: Oxford University Press, 2006).

24. Tagore, like many early twentieth-century Asian nationalists, was an avid consumer of the scientific orientalism of his day. During his tours of Europe he made great effort to meet with scholars of Indian culture. Tagore's Visva Bharati academy also became a research institute that hosted many orientalist scholars during the interwar period, including such key figures in Indic and Indo-Iranian studies as Sylvain Levi, Moriz Winternitz, Vincenc Lesny, Carlo Formici, and Giuseppe Tucci. Interestingly, Tagore's orientalist interlocutors were primarily non-Anglophone. Ebrahim Purdavud makes this point in his "Rabindranat Tagur," *Majalleh-ye Daneshkadeh-ye Adabiyat* 9, no. 2 (1962): 22.

25. For Tagore and the "Greater India Society," see Susan Bayly, "Imagining 'Greater India': French and Indian Visions of Colonialism in the Indic Mode," *Modern Asian Studies* 38, no. 3 (2004): 710. Among Tagore's closest intellectual associates within the Greater India Society was the comparative philologist of Indo-Iranian studies Suniti Kumar Chatterji (1890–1977). Among Chatterji's key works was his *Iranianism: Iranian Culture and Its Impact on the World from Achamenian Times* (Calcutta: Asiatic Society, 1972). Chatterji also accompanied Tagore on his Southeast Asian tour of 1927. See Das Gupta, "Rabindranath Tagore in Indonesia," 451.

26. Coyajee, "A Brief Life-Sketch," i–xiii. Irani was instrumental in publishing Ebrahim Purdavud's first modern Persian translations of the Avestan literature, as discussed in chapter 4. Irani also composed a number of his own works in Persian, most importantly his *Akhlaq-e Iran-e Bastan* and *Falsafeh-ye Iran-e Bastan*. In addition to his native Gujarati and his proficiency in English, Irani had also studied Avestan at the University of Bombay. His Persian-language writings indicate that he also acquired proficiency in modern Persian, although he indicates that he was assisted by his friend (and pioneer Iranian filmmaker) Abdolhossein Sepanta; see Irani, *Akhlaq-e Iran-e Bastan*, preface/dibacheh.

27. The Zoroastrian Society endowed the Visva-Bharati academy for the study and teaching of Persian and Avestsan. The endowment also allowed for the acquisition of a library of original texts for the study of Iranian and Zoroastrian topics.

28. Dinshah J. Irani, *The Divine Songs of Zarathustra* (New York: Allen and Unwin, 1924).

29. The introductory essay was originally published, in a slightly longer form, in the Visva Bharati academy's own quarterly journal as Rabindranath Tagore, "The Indo-Iranians," *Visva-Bharati Quarterly* 1, no. 3 (1923): 191–207.

30. Ibid., 191.

31. Ibid., 192.

32. Ibid.

33. Ibid., 201.

34. Ibid., 206.

35. Tagore, *Journey to Persia*, 37.

36. Golbon, "Tagur va Iran," 134; A. Hafez Azhar, "Gurudev Tagore's Visit to Persia and the Persian Translations of His Works," in *Profile of Rabindranath Tagore in World Literature*, ed. Rita D. Sil (New Delhi: Khama Publishers, 2000), 177. Bozorg

Alavi's Tagore translations were made from the German editions of Tagore's poetry, which Alavi acquired during his time in Germany in the 1920s, a period during which Tagore was at the height of European popularity.

37. Stephanie Cronin, "An Experiment in Revolutionary Nationalism: The Rebellion of Colonel Mohammad Taqi Khan Pasyan in Mashhad, April-October 1921," *Middle Eastern Studies* 33, no. 4 (1997): 699.

38. Mohammad Mohit Tabataba'i, *Rabindranat Tagur: Sha'er va Filsuf-e Bozorg-e Hend* (Tehran, 1932); see also the "Tagur" entry in Ali-Akbar Dehkhoda's *Loghat-nameh* for bibliographic information on translations of Tagore into Persian and other languages.

39. Rabindranat Tagur, *Sad Band-e Tagur: Mushtamel bar Yek Sad Tarajim az Manzumat-e Bengali-ye Rabindranat Tagur*, trans. M. Zia al-Din (Calcutta, 1935); Purdavud, "Rabindranat Tagur," 23; Ebrahim Purdavud, "Sad Band-e Tagur," *Bokhara* 45 (2005): 187–193. For the most complete discussion of translations of Tagore's work into Persian, see M. Firoze, "Recent Studies of Rabindranath Tagore in Iran," *Indo-Iranica* 51, no. 1–4 (1998): 118–131. Translations of Tagore's work increased dramatically from the 1950s.

40. *Ettela'at*, April 20, 1932.

41. Ibid.

42. *Ettela'at*, April 28, 1932.

43. Ibid.

44. Ibid.

45. Ibid.

46. Ibid.

47. Ibid.

48. Tagore, *Journey to Persia*, 37.

49. Ibid.

50. Ibid.

51. Ibid.

52. There is a large literature on the cultural and political history of the "Aryan theory." The most comprehensive and useful treatments are Leon Poliakov, *The Aryan Myth: A History of Racist and Nationalistic Ideas in Europe* (New York: Barnes and Noble Books, 1996); Thomas R. Trautmann, *Aryans and British India* (Berkeley: University of California Press, 1997); Tzvetan Todorov, *On Human Diversity: Nationalism, Racism, and Exoticism in French Thought* (Cambridge, UK: Cambridge University Press, 1993). See also Zia-Ebrahimi, *The Emergence of Iranian Nationalism*.

53. K. N. Chatterji, "Itinerary of the Persian Tour," *Modern Review* 53 (March 1933): 330.

54. His most famous and controversial work is *Bist-u-Sih Sal* (Beirut, n.d.); *Twenty-Three Years: A Study of the Prophetic Career of Mohammad*, trans. F. R. C. Bagley (Costa Mesa, CA: Mazda Publishers, 1994); J. E. Knörzer, *Ali Dashti's Prison Days: Life under Reza Shah* (Costa Mesa, CA: Mazda Publishers in Association with Bibliotheca Persica, 1994).

55. K. N. Chatterji, "Itinerary of the Persian Tour," 329; Tagore, *Journey to Persia*, 126.

56. Tagore, *Journey to Persia*, 35.

57. Ibid., 154.

58. Ibid.

59. Ibid., 156.

60. Ibid.

61. Hay, *Asian Ideas of East and West*, 63–64. The same theme runs through chapter 1 ("Nationalism in Japan") of Tagore's 1917 book, *Nationalism*.

62. Ibid., 157.

63. Ibid., 155.

64. Dutta and Robinson, *Rabindranath Tagore*, 17–18.

65. Tagore, *Journey to Persia*, 64.

66. Ibid., 49.

67. Ibid., 38.

68. Golbon, "Tagur va Iran," 131; Tagore, *Journey to Persia*, 122.

69. Tagore, *Journey to Persia*, 47; S. B. Ray, "Tagore's Visit to Shiraz," *Indo-Iranica* 39, no. 1–4 (1986): 85–87.

70. Tagore, *Journey to Persia*, 47.

71. Legend has it that Sultan Mahmud Bahmani (r. 1378–1397), king of Deccan, also invited Hafez to India. Hafez went as far as Hurmuz before becoming homesick for Shiraz, ultimately declining the offers to visit India. This legend is reproduced and analyzed in many sources. See E. G. Browne, *A Literary History of Persia*, vol. 3 (London: Cambridge University Press, 1959 [1920]), 285–287; M. Kalim, "Hafiz Shirazi and Bengal," *Indo-Iranica* 38, no. 1–2 (1985): 42–51; S. M. Mohit Tabatabai, "Hafiz and India," *Indo-Iranica* 4, no. 2–3 (1951): 45–47; S. A. Hafez Abdi, "Hafiz and India," *Indo-Iranica* 31, no. 3–4 (1978): 5–7; Firoze Cowasji Davar, *Iran and India through the Ages* (New York: Asia Publishing House, 1962), 160–161; A. J. Arberry, *Shiraz: Persian City of Saints and Poets* (Norman: University of Oklahoma Press, 1960), 150–151. Both the Bahmani Kingdom of the Deccan and the Ilyas Shahi dynasty of Bengal invoked Iranian and Persianate imagery as the basis of their legitimacy. For the Ilyas Shahi court at Pandua, see Richard Eaton, *The Rise of Islam and the Bengal Frontier, 1204–1760* (Berkeley: University of California Press, 1993), 42–50.

72. For the influence of Hafez on Tagore, see Saleem Ahmed, "Hafiz and Tagore: A Study in Influence," in *Essays on Rabindranath Tagore in Honor of D. M. Gupta*, ed. T. R. Sharma (Ghaziabad, 1987), 231–282.

73. Maharishi Devendranath Tagore, *The Autobiography*, trans. Satyendranath Tagore and Indira Devi (London: Macmillan, 1961), 250.

74. Dutta and Robinson, *Rabindranath Tagore*, 315; Tagore, *Journey to Persia*, 133–134, 140–141.

75. Alam and Subrahmanyam, *Indo-Persian Travels in the Age of Discoveries*, 359–360. See also Sanjay Subrahmanyam, "Iranians Abroad: Intra-Asian Elite Migration and Early Modern State Formation," *Journal of Asian Studies* 51, no. 2 (1992): 340–363.

76. For the idea of Tagore and the "spectral" I am grateful to Alexander Jabbari. See also Jacques Derrida, *Specters of Marx: The State of the Debt, the Work of Mourning, and the New International* (New York: Routledge, 1994).

77. The building of cultural sites and national monuments was carried out by the Society for National Monuments. See Hosayn Bahr al-'Olumi, *Karnameh-ye Anjoman-e Asar-e Melli: Az Aghaz to 2535 Shahanshahi, 1301–1355 Hejri Shamsi* (Tehran, 1977); Talinn Grigor, "Recultivating 'Good Taste': The Early Pahlavi Modernists

and Their Society for National Heritage," *Iranian Studies* 37, no. 1 (2004): 17–45; Grigor, *Building Iran*; Mina Marefat, "Building to Power: Architecture of Tehran 1921–1941," PhD diss., Massachusetts Institute of Technology, 1988.

78. *Ettela'at*, April 30, 1932; Tagore, *Journey to Persia*, 122.

79. Kuros Kamali Sarvestani, "Hafez xiii–xiv. Hafez's Tomb (Hafeziya)," *Encyclopaedia Iranica*, http://www.iranicaonline.org/articles/hafez-xiii, accessed October 3, 2018.

80. Tagore, *Journey to Persia*, 49.

81. Ibid., 50.

82. Bose, *A Hundred Horizons*, 260.

83. This idea would eventually find its most developed expression in the work of the generation of scholars following World War II. See Abdolhosayn Zarinkub, *Du Qarn-e Sokut* (Tehran: Amir Kabir, 1951), and Corbin, *Spiritual Body and Celestial Earth*, among many others. For the place of Hafez within the literary and cultural history of Iranian nationalism, see also Ferdowsi, "The 'Emblem of the Manifestation of the Iranian Spirit,'" 667–691. Ferdowsi identifies the 1928 publication of the book *Hafez-tashrih* as the foundational text in the "national sacrilization of Hafez."

84. Suniti Kumar Chatterji, "Tagore, the Full Man and Iran," *Indo-Iranica* 14, no. 2 (1961): 7.

85. Sadeq Rezazadeh-Shafaq, "Zartosht Az Nazar-e Tagur," *Majalleh-ye Daneshkadeh-ye Adabiyat* 9, no. 2 (1962): 34–35.

86. Ibid., 34–35.

87. For a more detailed discussion of Tagore's ideas with respect to the Persian literary tradition, see Leonard Lewisohn, "Rabindranath Tagore's Syncretistic Philosophy and the Persian Sufi Tradition," *International Journal of Persian Literature* 2, no. 1 (2017): 2–41.

88. Tagore, *Journey to Persia*, 53.

89. For Herzeld's archaeological work in Iran, see Jennifer Jenkins, "Excavating Zarathustra: Ernst Herzfeld's *Archaeological History of Iran*," *Iranian Studies* 45, no. 1 (2012): 1–27; Elspeth R. M. Dusinberre, "Herzfeld in Persepolis," in *Ernst Herzfeld and the Development of Near Eastern Studies, 1900–1950*, ed. Ann Clyburn Gunter and Stefan R. Hauser (Leiden, Netherlands, 2005), 137–180; Kamyar Abdi, "Nationalism, Politics, and the Development of Archaeology in Iran," *American Journal of Archaeology* 105, no. 1 (2001): 51–76.

90. The public symbolism of Tagore's meeting with Herzfeld was later recounted in *Ettela'at* along with a transcript of a telegraph sent by Tagore to Herzfeld thanking the professor for the tour of Persepolis. *Ettela'at*, May 7, 1932.

91. Tagore, *Journey to Persia*, 55.

92. Ibid., 55.

93. Ibid., 54.

94. Ibid., 54–55.

95. For the Mohenjodaro and the history of archaeology, see Bruce G. Trigger, *A History of Archaeological Thought* (Cambridge, UK: Cambridge University Press, 1989), 181–182.

96. For the life and work of Aurel Stein, see Jeannette Mirsky, *Sir Aurel Stein: Archaeological Explorer* (Chicago: University of Chicago Press, 1977).

97. Tagore, *Journey to Persia*, 56.

98. Ibid., 59.

99. *Salnameh-ye Pars*, 1933, 68–70.

100. Isa Sadiq, *Yadegar-e 'Omr*, vol. 2 (Tehran: Amir Kabir, 1966), 156.

101. Ibid., 156–157.

102. "Qiyafeh-yi Tagur," *Ettela'at*, May 5, 1932.

103. Frontispiece, *Iran League Quarterly* 2, no. 4 (July 1932): 177. For more on M. F. Pithawala, see Anil Relia, *The Indian Portrait: An Artistic Journey from Miniature to Modern* (Ahmedabad: Archer House, 2010), 52.

104. For Tagore and the visual arts, see Andrew Robinson, *The Art of Rabindranath Tagore* (London: Deutsch, 1989).

105. *Ettela'at*, May 4, 1932; Sadiq, *Yadegar-e 'Omr*, 158.

106. The poem itself read: "I carry in my heart a golden lamp of remembrance of an illumination that is past / I keep it bright against the tarnishing touch of time / Thine is a fire of a new magnanimous life / Allow it, my brother, to kiss my lamp with its flame." *Ettela'at*, May 4, 1932; Tagore, *Journey to Persia*, 124.

107. Sadiq, *Yadegar-e 'Omr*, 157; *Ettela'at*, May 10, 1932.

108. Sadiq, *Yadegar-e 'Omr*, 158; *Ettela'at*, May 4, 7, 1932.

109. Sadiq, *Yadegar-e 'Omr*, 158; *Ettela'at*, May 4, 7, 1932.

110. Sadiq, *Yadegar-e 'Omr*, 158; *Ettela'at*, May 4, 7, 1932.

111. Masani, "With Dinshah Irani in New Iran," xxiv. Dinshah Irani recounts this meeting in similar terms. See Irani, "Regenerated Iran," 205–206.

112. The endowment was established in 1933 at Visva-Bharati University. See Ahmed, "Hafiz and Tagore," 240; and 'Ali Asghar Mostafavi, *Zaman va Zendegi-ye Ostad Purdavud* (Tehran: Mostafavi, 1991), 67.

113. *Ettela'at*, May 7, 8, 9, and 10, 1932; K. N. Chatterji, "Itinerary of the Persian Tour," 328–329.

114. *Ettela'at*, May 7, 8, 9, and 10, 1932; K. N. Chatterji, "Itinerary of the Persian Tour," 328–329.

115. Tagore, *Journey to Persia*, 89; *Ettela'at*, May 7, 8, and 12, 1932; K. N. Chatterji, "Itinerary of the Persian Tour," 328–329; *Salnameh-ye Pars*, 1932, 68–73.

116. *Ettela'at*, May 5, 7, 1932; K. N. Chatterji, "Itinerary of the Persian Tour," 328–329.

117. *Ettela'at*, May 7, 1932; "Victory to Iran!" *Indo-Iranica* 14, no. 2 (1961): 1. The poem read in part: "Iran, thy brave sons have brought their priceless gifts of friendship on this birthday of the poet of a faraway shore / for they have known him in their hearts as their own. Iran, crowned with a new glory by the honor from thy hand this birthday of the poet of a faraway shore finds its fulfillment / and in return I put this wreath of a verse on thy forehead and cry: 'victory to Iran.'"

118. *Ettela'at*, May 21, 1932. Tagore spent an additional twelve days in Iraq before beginning the return journey to India on May 31.

119. Vejdani, "Indo-Iranian Linguistic, Literary, and Religious Entanglements," 449–450.

120. Ibid.

121. Hosayn-Ali Nowzari, "Makatebat-e Allameh Mohammad Eqbal Lahuri va Abbas Aram," *Tarikh-e Mo'aser-e Iran* 1, no. 1 (1997): 169, cited in Vejdani, "Indo-Iranian Linguistic, Literary, and Religious Entanglements."

122. Ibid.

123. Ibid.

124. Ibid., 176.

125. Abolqasem Lahuti, "Maktub-e Sargoshadeh beh Rabindranat Tagur," *Paykar* 1, no. 10 (August 1, 1931/ Mordad 9, 1310), in *Paykar dar Berlin*, ed. Reza Azari

Shaherza'i (Tehran: Shirazeh Ketab, 2016), 76. According to an editorial note at the end of the open letter, Lahuti also forwarded it to numerous Indian newspapers. I am grateful to Houchang Chehabi for providing me with this source. There seems to be some discrepancy as to the authorship of this letter. There is a notation in a subsequent issue of the newspaper stating that there had been a misprint in the typesetting of the original letter, and that an Indian Communist named "Lahuri," and not Abolqasem Lahuti, was the author. See "Tashih va Tazakkur," *Paykar* 1, no. 13 (September 19, 1931/ Shahrivar 27, 1310), in *Paykar dar Berlin*, 90. I am grateful to Samuel Hodgkin for providing me with this source. On Lahuti, see also Samuel Gold Hodgkin, "Lahuti: Persian Poetry in the Making of the Literary International, 1906–1957" (PhD diss., University of Chicago, 2018).

126. Lahuti, "Maktub-e Sargoshadeh beh Rabindranat Tagur," 76.

127. For Soviet cultural policies in Iran, see James Pickett, "Soviet Civilization through a Persian Lens: Iranian Intellectuals, Cultural Diplomacy and Socialist Modernity, 1941–55," *Iranian Studies* 48, no. 5 (September 2015): 805–826. See also Christine Philliou, "Postcolonial Worlds in the Soviet Imaginary," *Comparative Studies in South Asia, Africa, and the Middle East* 33, no. 2 (2013): 197–200.

128. Ringer, *Pious Citizens*, 163–183.

CHAPTER 4. EBRAHIM PURDAVUD AND HIS INTERLOCUTORS

1. Nawaz B. Mody, "Madame Bhikhaiji Rustom Cama—Sentinel of Liberty," in *The Parsis of Western India: 1818–1920*, ed. Nawaz B. Mody (Bombay: Allied Publishers Ltd.), 62, 66–69; Iran League, "Address and Souvenir Presented to Prof. Pour-e Davoud," *Iran League Quarterly* 4, no. 4 (July 1934): 229; Rustam Masani, "Foreword," in *Professor Poure Davoud Memorial Volume II: Papers on Zoroastrian and Iranian Subjects*, ed. Rustam Masani et al. (Bombay: Iran League, 1951), viii; Mansour Bonakdarian, "Iranian Nationalism and Global Solidarity Networks 1906–1918: Internationalism, Transnationalism, Globalization, and Nationalist Cosmopolitanism," in *Iran in the Middle East: Transnational Encounters and Social History*, ed. H. E. Chehabi, Peyman Jafari, and Maral Jefroudi (London: I. B. Tauris, 2015), 80–81; Panchanan Saha, *Madam Cama: Mother of Indian Revolution* (Calcutta: Manisha, 1975), 36–38.

2. Mo'in, "Purdavud," in *Yadnameh-ye Purdavud*, 1–5; Mostafavi, *Zaman va Zendegi*, 13–36; Hushang Ettehad, *Pezhuheshgaran-e Mu'aser-e Iran* (Tehran: Farhang-e Mu'aser, 2001), 27–30; Mahmud Nikuyeh, *Purdavud: Pezhuhandeh-ye Ruzegar-e Nokhost* (Rasht: Gilan, 1999), 1–12.

3. Mo'in, *Yadnameh-ye Purdavud*, 56–57; Mostafavi, *Zaman va Zendegi*, 355–356; Isa Sadiq, "Sokhanrani-ye Profesor Isa Sadiq," *Hukht* 25, no. 10 (1353/2524): 5.

4. W. Scott Haine, *The World of the Paris Café: Sociability among the French Working Class, 1789–1914* (Baltimore: Johns Hopkins University Press, 1996), 229; Gary P. Steenson, *After Marx, Before Lenin: Marxism and Socialist Working-Class Parties in Europe, 1884–1914* (Pittsburgh: University of Pittsburgh Press, 1991), 115–116; Auguste Lepage, *Les Cafés Artistiques et Littéraires de Paris* (Paris: M. Bousin, 1882), 81; Maxim Rude, *Toute Paris au Café* (Paris: M. Dreyfous, 1877), 101–110; Noel Riley Fitch, *The Grand Literary Cafes of Europe* (London: New Holland, 2006), 33–38.

5. Mody, *The Parsis of Western India*, 66.

6. Ibid., 46.

7. Ibid., 48–49.

8. Ibid., 61; Saha, *Madam Cama*, 28–29, 32; Bonakdarian, "Iranian Nationalism and Global Solidarity Networks," 80; Mansour Bonakdarian, *Britain and the Iranian Constitutional Revolution of 1906–1911: Foreign Policy, Imperialism, and Dissent* (Syracuse, NY: Syracuse University Press, 2006), xx.

9. Mody, *The Parsis of Western India*, 58–62, 66–67.

10. *Iran League Quarterly* 4, no. 4 (July 1934): 229.

11. Mostafavi, *Zaman va Zendegi*, 113–114; Ebrahim Purdavud, "Yadi Digar az Qazvini," in *Yadnameh-ye Allameh Mohammad Qazvini*, ed. Ali Dehbashi (Tehran: Ketab va Farhang, 1999), 157; Hossein Kazemzadeh-Iranshahr, *Asar va Ahval-e Kazemzadeh-Iranshahr* (Tehran: Eqbal, 1971), 108.

12. Moʻin, *Yadnameh-ye Purdavud*, 56–57.

13. *Iran League Quarterly* 4, no. 4 (July 1934): 229.

14. Anklesaria was primarily a scholar of the Pahlavi tradition of Zoroastrian literature. He also served as the principal of the Sir J. J. Zartoshti and Mulla Firoza Maddressas. See K. M. JamaspAsa and Mary Boyce, "Bahramgore Tahmuras Anklesaria," *Encyclopaedia Iranica*, http://www.iranicaonline.org/articles/anklesaria-bahramgore-tahmuras, accessed July 6, 2019. See also Moʻin, *Yadnameh-ye Purdavud*, 25.

15. Nariman's scholarly interests were wide-ranging across the fields of Sanskrit literature, Zoroastrian and Buddhist studies, as well as classical and medieval history. He was also a translator of multiple scholarly works in these fields from German, French, and Russian into English. Moʻin, *Yadnameh-ye Purdavud*, 23.

16. Modi received both a traditional initiation into the Zoroastrian priesthood as well as a modern education in Zoroastrian studies. He was closely associated with K. R. Cama and later served as director of the Cama Institute. Modi was also among the most prolific scholars of the modern Parsi scholarly tradition, and contributed an English-language forward to Purdavud's translation of the *Gatha*. See Michael Stausberg and Ramiyar P. Karanjia, "Modi, Jivanji Jamshedji." See also Moʻin, *Yadnameh-ye Purdavud*, 22.

17. Sanjana was another major figure in the modern Parsi intellectual tradition. Born into a priestly family, he went on to study at the J. J. Zartoshti Madressa and the University of Bombay. Proficient in German and French in addition to Sanskrit, Avestan, and Pahlavi, he published numerous translations in English. See Michael Stausberg, "Sanjana, Darab Dastur Peshotan," *Encyclopaedia Iranica*, http://www.iranicaonline.org/articles/sanjana-darab, accessed October 12, 2017. See also Ringer, *Pious Citizens*, 119–128; Moʻin, *Yadnameh-ye Purdavud*, 28.

18. Taraporewalla was another major figure in the modern Zoroastrian scholarly tradition. His primary education in the field of Zoroastrian studies took place at the German University of Würzburg. Taraporewalla is perhaps most noted for his major free English translation of the *Gathas*, with accompanying notes and commentary. He worked closely with Purdavud during the latter's time in India and contributed an English-language introduction to his first volume of Persian translations of the *Yashtha*. See Moʻin, *Yadnameh-ye Purdavud*, 27–28.

19. Ebrahim Purdavud, *Gatha: Sorudha-ye Moqaddas-e Payghambar-e Iran*, with introductory notes in English by Dinshah J. Irani, Jivanji Jamshedji Modi, and G. K. Nariman, P. D. Marker Avestan Series, vol. 1 (Bambaʾi: Anjoman-e Zartoshtian-e Irani va Iran Lig, 1927); Ebrahim Purdavud, *Gatha: Sorudha-ye Minovi-ye Payghambar-e Iran* (Bambaʾi: Anjoman-e Zartoshtian-e Irani, 1952); Ebrahim Purdavud and Bahram Farahvashi, *Yaddashtha-ye Gatha* (Tehran: Chapkhaneh-ye Atashkadeh, 1957).

20. Purdavud, *Adabiyat-e Mazdayasna: Jeld-e Aval*; Purdavud, *Adabiyat-e Maz-dayasna: Jeld-e Dovvom*.

21. Ebrahim Purdavud, *Yasna (Jeld-e Aval): Jozvi az Nameh-ye Minovi-ye Avesta*, P. D. Marker Avestan Series, vol. 1 (Bamba'i: Anjoman-e Zartoshtian-e Irani va Iran Lig, 1938); Ebrahim Purdavud and Bahram Farahvashi, *Yasna (Jeld-e Dovvom): Jozvi az Nameh-ye Minovi-ye Avesta* (Tehran: Entesharat-e Anjoman-e Iran Shenasi, 1958).

22. Ebrahim Purdavud, *Khordeh Avesta: Jozvi az Nameh-ye Minovi-ye Avesta* (Bamba'i: Anjoman-e Zartoshtian-e Irani va Iran Lig, 1931).

23. Ebrahim Purdavud and Bahram Farahvashi, *Vesperad* (Tehran: Mu'asseseh-ye Entesharat va Chap-e Danishgah-e Tehran, 1961).

24. Among the most important of these volumes are: Ebrahim Purdavud, *Iran-shah: Tarikhcheh-ye Mohajerat-e Zartoshtian be Hendustan* (Bamba'i: Anjoman-e Zartoshtian-e Irani, 1925); Ebrahim Purdavud, *Khorramshah: Konferansha-ye Purdavud dar Hend* (Bamba'i: Anjoman-e Zartoshtian-e Irani, 1926); Ebrahim Purdavud, *Sushians: Ma'ud-e Mazdayasna* (Bamba'i: Chapkhaneh-ye Hur, 1927); Ebrahim Purdavud, *Purandokht-Nameh: Divan-e Purdavud* (Bamba'i: Anjoman-e Zartoshtian-e Irani, 1928).

25. Ringer, "Reform Transplanted," 549–560. See also her *Pious Citizens*.

26. Daniel Sheffield, *Cosmopolitan Zarathustras: Religion, Translation, and Prophethood in Iran and South Asia*, forthcoming.

27. Peter van der Veer, *Imperial Encounters: Religion and Modernity in India and Britain* (Princeton, NJ: Princeton University Press, 2001); Talal Asad, *Genealogies of Religion: Discipline and Reasons of Power in Christianity and Islam* (Baltimore: Johns Hopkins University Press, 1993).

28. Zia-Ebrahimi, *The Emergence of Iranian Nationalism*.

29. Mo'in, *Yadnameh-ye Purdavud*, 2; Mostafavi, *Zaman va Zendegi*, 13; Etehad, *Pezhuheshgaran*, 27; Nikuyeh, *Purdavud*, 1.

30. Mostafavi, *Zaman va Zendegi*, 13–16.

31. Ibid.

32. Ibid.

33. Purdavud, *Purandokht-Nameh*, 10.

34. Ibid.; Mostafavi, *Zaman va Zendegi*, 14.

35. Mo'in, *Yadnameh-ye Purdavud*, 11–12; Mostafavi, *Zaman va Zendegi*, 17; Nikuyeh, *Purdavud*, 2; Purdavud, *Purandokht-Nameh*, 10.

36. Ibid.

37. *Iran League Quarterly* 4, no. 4 (July 1934): 228–229.

38. Ibid.

39. Purdavud, *Purandokht-Nameh*, 10–11.

40. Ibid.

41. Mostafavi, *Zaman va Zendegi*, 20; Mo'in, *Yadnameh-ye Purdavud*, 12; Ni-kuyeh, *Purdavud*, 3–5; Purdavud, *Purandokht-Nameh*, 11.

42. Purdavud, *Purandokht-Nameh*, 11.

43. For discussion of Iranians in Beirut during this period, see Richard Hollinger, "An Iranian Enclave in Beirut: Baha'i Students at the American University of Beirut, 1906–1948," in *Distant Relations: Iran and Lebanon in the Last 500 Years*, ed. H. E. Chehabi (New York: I. B. Tauris/Centre for Lebanese Studies, 2006), 96–119; H. E. Chehabi, "An Iranian in First World War Beirut: Qasem Ghani's Reminiscences," in *Distant Relations*, 120–136. See also Betty S. Anderson, *The American University of*

Beirut: Arab Nationalism and Liberal Education (Austin: University of Texas Press, 2011), 159.

44. Mostafavi, *Zaman va Zendegi*, 20–21.

45. Ibid.

46. Ibid.

47. Ibid., 101.

48. Tavakoli-Targhi, *Refashioning Iran*, 86–89; Boyce, *Zoroastrians*, 197–198; Sheffield, "Primary Sources: New Persian," 538–540; Sheffield, "The Language of Heaven in Safavid Iran," 161–183.

49. Ebrahim Purdavud, *Farhang-e Iran-e Bastan* (Tehran: Mu'asseseh-ye Entesharat va Chap-e Danishgah-e Tehran, 1976), 17.

50. Ibid., 19. Purdavud had also written an earlier essay, in 1927, documenting the *Dasatir* as a forged text, "or, as the Europeans say, a *satire.*" See Purdavud, *Sushians*, 50. Purdavud's sober and scientific assessment of the *Dasatir* finally became the official understanding of the text with Ali-Akbar Dehkhoda's entry in the *Loghatnameh*; see "Dasatir," *Loghatnameh*, vol. 6, pt. 1 (Tehran: University of Tehran, 1958), 611.

51. Rose, *Zoroastrianism: An Introduction*, 203; William Jones, "The Sixth Anniversary Discourse, on the Persians, Delivered 19th February, 1789," in *The Works of Sir William Jones*, ed. John Shore Teignmouth, vol. 3 (London: Stockdale and Walker, 1807), 110–111; Mulla Firuz Bin Kaus, *The Desatir: Or Sacred Writings of the Ancient Persian Prophets* (Bombay: Courier Press, 1818 [repr., Wizard Bookshelf, 1975]), 12; Fath-Allah Mojtaba'i, "Dasatir," in *Encyclopaedia Iranica*, http://www.iranicaonline.org/articles/dasatir, accessed October 17, 2017.

52. See for example, Sheriarji Dadabhai Bharucha, *The Dasatir: Being a Paper Prepared for the Tenth International Congress of Orientalists Held at Geneva in 1894 A.C.* (Bombay: Fort Printing Press, 1907 [repr., K. R. Cama Oriental Institute, 2006]).

53. Mostafavi, *Zaman va Zendegi*, 12; Nikuyeh, *Purdavud*, 5; Mo'in, *Yadnameh-ye Purdavud*, 12–13; Etehad, *Pezhuheshgaran*, 29.

54. Iraj Afshar, ed., *Namehha-ye Paris az Qazvini be Taqizadeh* (Tehran: Qatreh, 2005), 354.

55. Purdavud, "Yadi Digar az Qazvini," 157–162; Purdavud, *Purandokht-Nameh*, 14–15; Mo'in, *Yadnameh-ye Purdavud*, 18; Mostafavi, *Zaman va Zendegi*, 112.

56. Qazvini and Purdavud had an ongoing debate regarding the influence of Arabic on Persian. Purdavud had been one of the earliest proponents of replacing the Arabic script for the writing of Persian, before changing his mind in later years. Their disagreements on this issue were mostly amicable. See, for example, Qazvini's comments regarding Purdavud's harsh criticism of the Arabic language: "although I am not in agreement with him in regards to his bias against the Arabic language . . . I respect his intellect and passion"; Mohammad Qazvini, "Sharh-e Zendegani," in *Bist Maqaleh-ye Qazvini*, ed. Ebrahim Purdavud (Bamba'i: Intesharat-e Anjoman-e Zartoshtian-e Irani, 1928), 16. Qazvini also praised Purdavud's Persian translation of the *Gathas* and the first volume of the *Yashts*, but cautioned against the avoidance of Arabic vocabulary in producing the translation; see Mohammad Qazvini, *Bist Maqaleh-ye Qazvini: Dowreh-ye Kamel* (Tehran: Ibn Sina, 1953), 337. Despite the criticism, Purdavud included Qazvini's written review as a preface to the second volume of his translation of the *Yashts*; see Purdavud, *Adabiyat-e Mazdayasna: Jeld-e Dovvom*, vol. 2, preface, n.p., "maktub."

57. Mahmoud Omidsalar, "Qazvini, Mohammad," in *Encyclopaedia Iranica*,

http://www.iranicaonline.org/articles/qazvini-mohammad, accessed October 18, 2017; Qazvini, *Bist Maqaleh*, 3–10; Shahpar Ansari, "The Life, Works, and Times of Muhammad Qazvini (1875–1949)" (master's thesis, University of Utah, 1990).

58. Qazvini, *Bist Maqaleh*, 10–23. For Qazvini's relationship to E. G. Browne, see also Vejdani, *Making History in Iran*, 155–156.

59. Purdavud, *Farhang-e Iran-e Bastan*, 18. Purdavud was not the only person to adopt the Dasatir's neologisms in modern Persian literature; see discussion in Ali-Akbar Dehkhoda, ed., "Dasatir," *Loghatnameh*, 611.

60. Mostafavi, *Zaman va Zendegi*, 101.

61. Purdavud, *Farhang-e Iran-e Bastan*, 18.

62. Ibid.

63. Ibid.

64. Ibid., 19.

65. Mo'in, *Yadnameh-ye Purdavud*, 57; Mostafavi, *Zaman va Zendegi*, 29.

66. Afshar, *Namehha-ye Paris*, 354–355; Kazemzadeh-Iranshahr, *Asar va Ahval*, 108–109.

67. Mo'in, *Yadnameh-ye Purdavud*, 57. The practice of renting rooms at these cafés for "private meetings" was common in this era; see Haine, *The World of the Paris Café*, 229.

68. Sadiq, "Sokhanrani-ye Profesor Isa Sadiq," 4–5.

69. Ibid., 5.

70. Ibid., 5–6, E. G. Browne translation. See also Edward G. Browne, *The Press and Poetry of Modern Persia* (Cambridge, UK: Cambridge University Press, 1914), 290–292. Browne became aware of Purdavud's poetry through their mutual friend and colleague, Hossein Kazemzadeh-Iranshahr. Kazemzadeh spent several years working closely with Browne at Cambridge University. See Mostafavi, *Zaman va Zendegi*, 105–107.

71. Sadiq, "Sokhanrani-ye Profesor Isa Sadiq," 6. See also Mostafavi, *Zaman va Zendegi*, 355–357.

72. Kazemzadeh-Iranshahr, *Asar va Ahval*, 109.

73. Ibid. In addition to his work as a dramatist, Poirier went on to become a pioneering filmmaker of the silent era, with a well-developed interest in the visual culture of exoticism. See Andrew Dudley, "Praying Mantis: Enchantment and Violence in French Cinema of the Exotic," in *Visions of the East: Orientalism in Film*, ed. Matthew Bernstein and Gaylyn Studlar (New Brunswich, NJ: Rutgers University Press, 1997), 232–252.

74. Kazemzadeh-Iranshahr, *Asar va Ahval*, 109. For more on Armen Ohanian, see her autobiography, Armen Ohanian, *The Dancer of Shamahka*, trans. Rose Wilder Lane (New York: E. P. Dutton and Co., 1923). See also Diana Souhami, *Wild Girls: Paris, Sappho, and Art: The Lives and Loves of Natalie Barney and Romaine Brooks* (New York: St. Martin's, 2004), 67. In addition to her notoriety as a dancer, actress, and libertine, Ohanian also circulated in the same Parisian political circles as Madame Cama and Ebrahim Purdavud; see Bonakdarian, "Iranian Nationalism and Global Solidarity Networks," 80–81.

75. Kazemzadeh-Iranshahr, *Asar va Ahval*, 109.

76. Ibid.

77. Mohammad Sadr-Hashemi, *Tarikh-e Jara'ed va Majallat-e Iran*, vol. 1 (Esfahan: Kamal, 1948), 337–340.

78. Nasredin Parvin, "Tarikhcheh-ye Yek Ruznameh: Iranshahr-e Paris," *Dabireh* 4 (1988): 103–106.

79. Kazemzadeh-Iranshahr, *Asar va Ahval*, 109; Mostafavi, *Zaman va Zendegi*, 105–106.

80. Moʻin, *Yadnameh-ye Purdavud*, 29; Mostafavi, *Zaman va Zendegi*, 30–31, 93; Nikuyeh, *Purdavud*, 5–6.

81. Parvin, "Tarikhcheh," 104.

82. Afshar, *Namehha-ye Paris*, 357.

83. Ibid.

84. Ibid., 355; Bonakdarian, "Iranian Nationalism and Global Solidarity Networks," 81.

85. Afshar, *Namehha-ye Paris*, 355–356.

86. Ibid.

87. Ibid., 357.

88. Rüdiger Schmitt, "Markwart, Josef," *Encyclopaedia Iranica*, http://www.iranicaonline.org/articles/markwart-josef, accessed October 23, 2017.

89. Moʻin, *Yadnameh-ye Purdavud*, 16; Purdavud, *Adabiyat-e Mazdayasna: Jeld-e Dovvom*, 4–5.

90. In the first issue of the newspaper, the front-page editorial also makes reference to the term "Iranshahr" as mentioned in the Avestan sources and in the geographic and astronomical writings of Abu Rayhan Biruni. The editorial reads, "this name should be considered sacred and prodigious by all who have been born in the land of Iran." See Parvin, "Tarikhcheh," 106. For more on Biruni and the idea of "Iranshahr," see Roy Parviz Mottahadeh, "The Idea of Iran in the Buyid Dominions," in *Early Islamic Iran: The Idea of Iran*, vol. 5, ed. Edmund Herzig and Sarah Stewart (London: I. B. Tauris, 2012), 156–157.

91. Parvin, "Tarikhcheh," 105.

92. Ibid., 107.

93. Ibid.

94. Ibid.

95. Hasan Taqizadeh, *Zendegi-ye Tufani: Khaterat-e Sayyid Hasan Taqizadeh*, ed. Iraj Afshar (Tehran: ʻElmi, 1993), 481–482; Purdavud, *Purandokht-Nameh*, 11–12.

96. Taqizadeh, *Zendegi-ye Tufani*, 181–185.

97. Ibid., 185. For the work of the "Information Bureau of the East/Nachrichtenstelle für den Orient," see Kris Manjapra, *Age of Entanglement: German and Indian Intellectuals across Empire* (Cambridge, MA: Harvard University Press, 2014), 88–89.

98. Taqizadeh, *Zendegi-ye Tufani*, 185.

99. Ibid., 481.

100. Purdavud, *Purandokht-Nameh*, 11; Mohammad-Ali Jamalzadeh, "Yek Dusti-ye Shast Saleh," *Vahid* 6, no. 2–3 (1969): 198–199.

101. Jamalzadeh, "Yek Dusti-ye Shast Saleh," 199.

102. Moʻin, *Yadnameh-ye Purdavud*, 30–32; Mostafavi, *Zaman va Zendegi*, 31–33, 94–100; Nikuyeh, *Purdavud*, 7–10. For *Rastakhiz*, see also Nasereddin Parvin, "Rastkiz," *Encyclopaedia Iranica*, http://www.iranicaonline.org/articles/rastakhiz, accessed October 24, 2017.

103. Purdavud, *Purandokht-Nameh*, 44–45, Dinshah Irani translation.

104. Moʻin, *Yadnameh-ye Purdavud*, 30; Mostafavi, *Zaman va Zendegi*, 94.

105. Jamalzadeh, "Yek Dusti-ye Shast Saleh," 199.

106. Ibid., 199–200.

107. Purdavud, *Purandokht-Nameh*, 11–12.

108. Ibid. See also Nikolas Gardner, *The Siege of Kut-al-Amara: At War in Mesopotamia, 1915–1916* (Bloomington: Indiana University Press, 2014).

109. Erik-Jan Zürcher, *Jihad and Islam in World War I: Studies on the Ottoman Jihad on the Centenary of Snouck Hurgronje's "Holy War Made in Germany"* (Leiden, Netherlands: Leiden University Press, 2016). See also David Motadel, *Islam and Nazi Germany's War* (Cambridge, MA: Harvard University Press, 2014).

110. Purdavud, *Purandokht-Nameh*, 12.

111. Ibid.

112. For the history of *Kaveh*, see Iraj Afshar, "Kāva Newspaper," *Encyclopaedia Iranica*, http://www.iranicaonline.org/articles/kava, accessed October 25, 2017; Gholamreza Vatandoust, "Sayyid Hasan Taqizadeh and Kaveh: Modernism in Post-Constitutional Iran (1916–1921)" (PhD diss., University of Washington, 1977); Afshin Matin-Asgari, "The Berlin Circle: Iranian Nationalism Meets German Countermodernity," in *Rethinking Iranian Nationalism*, ed. Kamran Aghaie and Afshin Marashi (Austin: University of Texas Press, 2014), 49–66; Afshin Matin-Asgari, *Both Eastern and Western: An Intellectual History of Iranian Modernity* (New York: Cambridge University Press, 2018).

113. Mo'in, *Yadnameh-ye Purdavud*, 31.

114. Mostafavi, *Zaman va Zendegi*, 39; Jamalzadeh, "Yek Dusti-ye Shast Saleh," 201; Qazvini, *Bist Maqaleh*, 15.

115. Mo'in, *Yadnameh-ye Purdavud*, 6–7.

116. Schmitt, "Markwart, Josef."

117. Qazvini and Markwart also developed a friendship during this period. See Qazvini, *Bist Maqaleh*, 16. Qazvini was very discerning in his assessment of orientalist scholars, and the list of European scholars whom he deemed worthy of his respect was very short. Markwart was on this list, alongside Browne and Theodor Nöldeke. For a discussion of Qazvini and orientalism, see Hamid Dabashi, *Post-Orientalism: Knowledge and Power in a Time of Terror* (New York: Routledge, 2017), 73–81.

118. Purdavud, *Adabiyat-e Mazdayasna: Jeld-e Dovvom*, 4–5.

119. Ibid.

120. Ibid.

121. Ibid.

122. Ibid.

123. For Purdavud's evolving ideas with respect to language policy, see Ebrahim Purdavud, "Taghir-e Khat?" in *Anahita: Panjah Goftar-e Purdavud*, ed. Morteza Gorji (Tehran: Amir Kabir, 1963), 36–40.

124. Mo'in, *Yadnameh-ye Purdavud*, 17; Mostafavi, *Zaman va Zendegi*, 111; Joseph Hell, *Die Kulter der Araber* (Leipzig, Germany: Quelle and Meyer, 1909); Joesph Hell, *The Arab Civilization*, trans. S. Khuda Buksh (Cambridge, UK: W. Heffer and Sons, 1926).

125. Mo'in, *Yadnameh-ye Purdavud*, 17; Mostafavi, *Zaman va Zendegi*, 110–111; Isaac Landman, ed., *Universal Jewish Encyclopedia* (New York: Universal Jewish Encyclopedia, Inc., 1942), vol. 7, 591; Hilmar Kaiser, *Imperialism, Racism, and Development Theories: The Construction of a Dominant Paradigm on Ottoman Armenians* (Ann Arbor, MI: Gomidas Institute Books, 2009), 26–29.

126. Moʻin, *Yadnameh-ye Purdavud*, 17; Fritz Wolff, *Avesta: Die Heiligen Bücher der Parsen, Übersetzt auf der Grundlage von Christian Batholomae's Altiranischem Wörterburch* (Berlin: W. de Guyter, 1924). Wolff is also famous for his important glossary of the *Shahnameh*; see his *Glossar zu Firdosis Schahname* (Berlin: Gerdruckt in der Reichsdruckerei, 1935).

127. Moʻin, *Yadnameh-ye Purdavud*, 16–17; Mostafavi, *Zaman va Zendegi*, 107–112.

128. For Oskar Mann's interaction with the Berlin Iranians, see Matin-Asgari, *Both Eastern and Western*, 52; Vejdani, *Making History*, 184n50.

129. Moʻin, *Yadnameh-ye Purdavud*, 4; Mostafavi, *Zaman va Zendegi*, 40–42; Etehad, *Pezhuheshgaran*, 31; Nikuyeh, *Purdavud*, 10–11.

130. Mostafavi, *Zaman va Zendegi*, 40–42.

131. Ibid.

132. Kazemzadeh-Iranshahr, *Asar va Ahval*, 174–177.

133. Ibid.

134. Ebrahim Purdavud, "Nameh-ye Yazdegerd-e Dovvom be Isayuan-e Armanestan," *Iranshahr* 1, no. 5 (October 25, 1922): 107–116.

135. Ibid., 110–111. Purdavud did not provide complete citations in these references, but he was likely drawing from available German and English translations such as Theodoretus, *Kirchengeschichte*, trans. Leon Parmentier (Leipzig: J. C. Hinrichs, 1911); Elisaeus, *The History of Vartan and of the Battle of the Armenians: Containing an Account of the Religious Wars between the Persians and Armenians*, trans. Karl Friedrich Neumann (London: Murray, Parbury, Allen and Co., 1830); and Gazar P'arpec'I, *Geschichte Armenians* (Venedig, 1873). Purdavud may have also cultivated an interest in Armenian sources through his intellectual mentorship with Josef Markwart, who made extensive use of Armenian sources in his *Untersuchungen zur Geschichte von Eran* (Göttingen, Germany: Dieterich, 1896).

136. Purdauvd, "Nameh-ye Yazdegerd," 112.

137. Hossein Kazemzadeh-Iranshahr, "Be Qalam-e Aqa-ye Purdavud," *Iranshahr* 1, no. 5 (October 25, 1922): 107.

138. Ibid.

139. Ebrahim Purdavud, "Negahi be Ruzegaran-e Gozashteh-ye Iran va Pishgu'i-ye *Bahman Yasht* az Fetneh-ye Moghul," *Iranshahr* 1, no. 12 (June 15, 1923): 342–352.

140. The first translation into a European language appeared in 1880 in F. Max Müller, ed., *Sacred Books of the East, Pahlavi Tests*, vol. 5, pt. 1, trans. E. W. West (Oxford, UK: Oxford University Press, 1880), 189–235. A New Persian translation had also appeared in Bombay in the year just prior to Purdavud's essay in *Iranshahr*; see Ervad Manockji Rustamji Unvala, ed., *Darab Hormazyar's Rivayat, with an Introduction by Shams-ul-Ulma Jivanji Jamshedji Modi*, vol. 2 (Bombay: British India Press, 1922), 86–101. See also W. Sundermann, "Bahman Yast," *Encyclopaedia Iranica*, http://www.iranicaonline.org/articles/bahman-yast-middle-persian-apocalyptical-text, accessed October 31, 2017.

141. Purdavud, "Negahi be Ruzegaran-e Gozashteh-ye Iran," 350.

142. Ibid.

143. Ibid.

144. Ibid.

145. Ibid., 351.

146. Ibid., 342.

147. Ibid., 343.

148. Ibid.

149. Ibid., 344.

150. Sheffield, "Primary Sources: New Persian," 541.

151. Boyce, *Zoroastrians*, 220. As discussed in chapter 1, Kaykhosrow Shahrokh wrote two works in this form, his *A'ineh-ye A'in-e Mazdayasna* and *Forugh-e Mazdayasna*.

152. Shahrokh, *Yaddashtha-ye Kaykhosrow Shahrokh*, 83.

153. Shahmardan, *Farzanegan*, 363.

154. Shahrokh, *Yaddashtha*, 112.

155. D. J. Irani, *Gems from the Divine Songs of Zoroaster* (Bombay: E. G. Pearson, 1922); Irani, *Divine Songs of Zarathustra*.

156. For the life and work of Peshotanji Marker, see Lohrasb, *Marker Memorial Volume*. See also Hinnells, *The Zoroastrian Diaspora*, 79–80. Shahmardan states that the endowment to fund the translations was in the amount of 200,000 rupees; see Shahmardan, *Farzanegan*, 495.

157. Mo'in, *Yadnameh-ye Purdavud*, 7; Mostafavi, *Zaman va Zendegi*, 44; Nikuyeh, *Purdavud*, 12–13.

158. There are references to Dinshah Irani in some of Qazvini's letters. See, for example, Dehbashi, *Yadnameh-ye Allameh Mohammad Qazvini*, 348. Irani also mentions Qazvini's approval for Purdavud's translation work in his introductory note to the 1927 Gatha translation; see Purdavud, *Gatha*, translator's note, ix. In this introductory note, Irani also states that "hence for several years we strove hard but in vain to get a translation made by a person worthy of the task. At the very last we were fortunate enough to come into touch with Aga Poure Davoud." For Qazvini's correspondence, see also Afshar, *Namehha-ye Paris*. For the suggestion that Qazvini was the person to recommend Purdavud for the translation project to Dinshah Irani, see also Jamshed C. Tarapore, "Professor Poure Davoud, a Life Sketch," in Masani et al., *Professor Poure Davoud Memorial Volume II*, 14.

159. Ardeshir Reporter spent the years from 1893 to 1933 in Iran. As the successor of Manekji Limji Hataria, he was the official representative of Bombay's Parsi community in Iran during these years. Kaykhosrow Shahrokh was the Zoroastrian representative to the Iranian Majles, and was active during the 1920s in many aspects of Reza Shah's cultural policy of nationalization. In his memoir he makes multiple references to his associations with Purdavud, Reporter, and Irani.

160. Tarapore, "Professor Poure Davoud," 14.

161. Ibid.; Abdol-Hosayn Sepanta, the Iranian filmmaker and translator who worked with Dinshah Irani in Bombay during the 1920s, also recalled that it was Dinshah Irani who issued the formal invitation to Purdavud. See Abdol-Hosayn Sepanta, "Sokhanrani-ye Agha-ye Abdol-Hossayn Sepanta," *Hukht* 19, no. 10 (January 1969): 93.

162. Mo'in, *Yadnameh-ye Purdavud*, 7; Mostafavi, *Zaman va Zendegi*, 44.

163. Mo'in, *Yadnameh-ye Purdavud*, 21–22; Purdavud, *Adabiyat-e Mazdayasna: Jeld-e Dovvom*, vol. 3, 12.

164. Purdavud, *Adabiyat-e Mazdayasna: Jeld-e Dovvom*, vol. 3, 12.

165. Sepanta gives an account of his time in Bombay with Irani and Purdavud. See Sepanta, "Sokhanrani-ye Agha-ye Abdol-Hossayn Sepanta," 92–95.

166. Mo'in, *Yadnameh-ye Purdavud*, 23; Purdavud, *Adabiyat-e Mazdayasna: Jeld-e Aval*, 56.

167. Nariman, for example, was critical of the thesis that the Arab-Muslim conquest of Iran was the precipitating factor for the Zoroastrian exodus to the subcontinent. See Nariman, "Was It Religious Persecution Which Compelled the Parsis to Migrate from Persia into India?" *Islamic Culture* 7 (1933): 277–280.

168. Mo'in, *Yadnameh-ye Purdavud*, 23; Purdavud, *Adabiyat-e Mazdayasna: Jeld-e Aval*, 56.

169. Ibid.

170. JamaspAsa and Boyce, "Bahramgore Tahmuras Anklesaria."

171. Ebrahim Purdavud, "Bahramgur Anklesaria," *Sokhan* 2, no. 6 (1944): 418.

172. Most of the first editions of Purdavud's books published in Bombay bear the Fort Printing Press imprint. The Iran League and the Iranian Zoroastrian Anjoman collaborated closely with this printing house, which specialized in producing difficult multilingual texts containing Sanskrit, Avestan, Pahlavi, and New Persian typescripts. Fort was also the printer of many other Zoroastrian books and periodicals, including the *Iran League Quarterly*.

173. For the life and work of Sadeq Hedayat, including his time in Bombay, see Homa Katouzian, *Sadeq Hedayat: The Life and Literature of an Iranian Writer* (London: I. B. Tauris, 2000). For Hedayat's association with Anklesaria, see also Mohamad Tavakoli-Targhi, "Narrative Identity in the Works of Hedayat and His Contemporaries," in *Sadeq Hedayat: His Work and His Wondrous World*, ed. Homa Katouzian (New York: Routledge, 2008), 113. See also Nadeem Akhtar, "Hedayat, Sadeq v. Hedayat in India," *Encyclopaedia Iranica*, http://www.iranicaonline.org/articles/hedayat-sadeq-v, accessed November 6, 2017.

174. Katouzian, *Sadeq Hedayat*, 60.

175. Purdavud, "Bahramgur Anklesaria," 418.

176. For a discussion and description of the ceremony, see Dastur Firoze M. Kotwal and James W. Boyd, *A Persian Offering: The Yasna, A Zoroastrian High Liturgy* (Paris: Association Pour l'Avancement des Études Iranieness, 1991).

177. Boyce, *Zoroastrians*, 23.

178. Kotwal and Boyd, *A Persian Offering*, 3.

179. Mo'in, *Yadnameh-ye Purdavud*, 76–78; Purdavud, *Khorramshah*, 15.

180. Purdavud, *Khorramshah*, 15. Purdavud gives the names of the priests as Dastur Firuz and Dastur Kaywoji.

181. Ibid., 16.

182. Ibid.

183. Ibid.

184. Ibid.

185. Purdavud, *Iranshah*.

186. Purdavud, *Iranshah*, dedication.

187. Ibid., 26.

188. Ibid., 1.

189. Ibid.

190. Ibid., 2.

191. Ibid.

192. For a critical analysis of this text, see Williams, *The Zoroastrian Myth of Migration from Iran and Settlement in the Indian Diaspora*.

193. Purdavud, *Iranshah*, 22.

194. Ibid., 4–5.

195. Purdavud, *Iranshah*, appendix, photos 5–57. For the architectural and aesthetic exchange between Iran and the Parsis, see Talinn Grigor, "Parsi Patronage of the Urheimat," 53–68.

196. Mostafavi, *Zaman va Zendegi*, 400–406; Purdavud, *Farhang-e Iran-e Bastan*, 24–25. A complete two-volume edition of the *Yasna* was published in 1958 by Ibn Sina Press, in collaboration with the Institute for Iranain Studies established by Purdavud at the University of Tehran. See Purdavud and Farahvashi, *Yasna (Jeld-e Dovvom)*.

197. Coyajee, "A Brief Life-Sketch," i–ii. Coyajee states that Irani personally contributed 10,000 rupees of his own money toward the Peshotanji Marker endowment to support the publishing costs of Purdavud's translations.

198. Purdavud, *Yashtha*, vol. 2, 24.

199. Ibid.

200. Purdavud, *Gatha: Sorudha-ye Moqaddas-e Payghambar-e Iran*, translator's note, n.p.

201. Ibid., 9–10.

CHAPTER 5. SWORD OF FREEDOM

1. Saif Azad, *Demokrasi va Azadi dar Hend* (Tehran: Majles, 1950), "Yadegari az ruzha-ye zendan," n.p.; National Archives of the UK (TNA): KV 2/3857, September 18, 1939. For more details regarding Saif Azad's internment, see Government of India, Home Department archives, File No. 59/10-A/39-Political. I am grateful to Dinyar Patel for this reference.

2. J. Chinn Durai, "Indian Prisons," *Journal of Comparative Legislation and International Law* 11, no. 4 (1929): 245–249; Amarendra Mohanty and Narayan Hazary, *Indian Prison Systems* (New Delhi: Ashish Publishing House, 1989), 23–28.

3. Azad, *Demokrasi va Azadi*, "Yadegari," n.p.

4. Ibid.

5. His exact birthdate is not recorded. Information listed on his visa applications indicates his date of birth as February 18, 1891. Other sources suggest that he was born in 1884. TNA: KV 2/3857, February 20, 1937.

6. Yasmin Khan, *India at War: The Subcontinent and the Second World War* (Oxford, UK: Oxford University Press, 2015), 11–16. For the larger engagement between Germany and India during this period, see Manjapra, *Age of Entanglement*.

7. TNA: KV 2/3857, August 31, 1939. British surveillance of Saif Azad noted his contacts with the main Nazi Party agent in Bombay, Georg Leszczynski, observing that he was "a regular visitor to Leszczynski at the Indo-German institute . . . calls himself a national socialist Aryan . . . and refers to Germans as possible saviors of India from slavery." For more on Leszczynski's role in promoting the Nazi Party in India, see Manjapra, *Age of Entanglement*, 207–208.

8. TNA: KV 2/3857, February 19, 1921.

9. TNA: KV 2/3857, August 31, 1921; Ludwig W. Adamec, *Afghanistan, 1900–1923: A Diplomatic History* (Berkeley: University of California Press, 1967), 123–135.

10. TNA: KV 2/3857, February 19, 1921.

11. TNA: KV 2/3857, November 25, 1921.

12. TNA: KV 2/3857, October 10, 1935.

13. Bonakdarian, "Iranian Nationalism and Global Solidarity Networks," 77–79.

14. TNA: KV 2/3857, February 20, 1937. Other sources indicate that he was born as early as 1884.

15. Ibid.

16. TNA: KV 2/3857, January 13, 1922. In this early record documenting his Afghan connections, for example, British authorities note that Saif Azad is known by multiple aliases. He is initially referred to in the file as "Saif Effendi," but a note within the document indicates that this person is the same as "Sheikh Abdul Rahman Seif, the publisher of the 'Azadi-i-Sharq' who has been mentioned in many previous notes."

17. The issue of Saif Azad's multiple names is mentioned by Wipert von Blücher, the former German ambassador in Tehran and one of Saif Azad's closest German associates. See Wipert von Blücher, *Safarnameh-ye Blusher: neveshteh-ye Vipert Blusher*, trans. Kaykavus Jahandari (Tehran: Khwarazmi, 1985), 137. Saif Azad is initially referred to as "the messenger" (a reference to his work for the German embassy in Tehran), and is later referred to as "Abdurahman," and later as "Saif Islam." For different iterations of his name, see also Bozorg Alavi, *Khaterat-e Bozorg Alavi*, ed. Hamid Ahmadi (Spanga, Sweden: Baran Press, 1998), 105.

18. TNA: KV 2/3857, November 3, 1921.

19. TNA: KV 2/3857, July 21, 1931.

20. Yitzhak Nakash, *The Shi'is of Iraq* (Princeton, NJ: Princeton University Press, 1995), 49.

21. Priya Satia, *Spies in Arabia: The Great War and the Cultural Foundations of Britain's Covert Empire in the Middle East* (Oxford, UK: Oxford University Press, 2009), 214.

22. Ibid.

23. Ibid., 215.

24. Ibid.

25. Nakash, *The Shi'is of Iraq*, 51–53.

26. Ibid.; Farzaneh, *The Iranian Constitutional Revolution and the Clerical Leadership of Khurasani*, 131–133.

27. Motadel, *Islam and Nazi Germany's War*, 18–19, 337–338; Nakash, *The Shi'is of Iraq*, 60.

28. Ulrich Gehrke, *Pish beh su-ye Sharq*, vol. 1, trans. Parviz Sadri (Tehran: Ketab-e Siamak, 1998), 111–112.

29. Motadel, *Islam and Nazi Germany's War*, 24; Nakash, *The Shi'is of Iraq*, 57–58.

30. Motadel, *Islam and Nazi Germany's War*, 25–27; Adamec, *Afghanistan, 1900–1923: A Diplomatic History*, 83–95; Jules Stewart, *The Kaiser's Mission to Kabul: A Secret Expedition to Afghanistan in World War I* (London: I. B. Tauris, 2014); Peter Hopkirk, *Like Hidden Fire: The Plot to Bring Down the British Empire* (New York: Kodansha International, 1994); Thomas Hughes, "The German Mission to Afghanistan, 1915–1916," *German Studies Review* 25 (2002): 447–476. Niedermayer and Hentig both wrote memoirs of their experiences during the war. See Werner-Otto von Hentig, *Ins Verscholossene Land: Ein Kampf mit Mensch und Meile* (Berlin: Ullstein, 1918), and Oskar von Niedermayer, *Unter der Glutsonne Irans: Krigserlebnisse der dentschen Expedition nach Persien und Afganistan* (Munich: Einhornverlag, 1925). The Niedermayer memoir has also been translated into Persian as *Zir-e Aftab-e Suzan-e Iran*, trans. Kaykavus Jahandari (Tehran: Tarikh-e Iran, 1984).

31. The Indian nationalists who accompanied the German-Turkish mission were Maulana Barakatullah (1854–1927), the Indian revolutionary who helped found

the Ghadar Party, and Mahendra Pratap (1886–1979), the former Raja who would later become a leading Indian Bolshevik. In addition to Niedermayer and Hentig's accounts, Pratap also wrote a detailed account of the mission, "My German Mission to High Asia: How I Joined Forces with the Kaiser to Enlist Afghanistan against Great Britain," *Asia: The Journal of the American Asiatic Association* 25 (May 1925): 382–455.

32. Adamec, *Afghanistan, 1900–1923: A Diplomatic History*, 83–84. The important German orientalist and political strategist Max von Oppenheim was also critical in devising this plan; see Motadel, *Islam and Nazi Germany's War*, 20–21; Hopkirk, *Like Hidden Fire*, 53–54; Stewart, *The Kaiser's Mission to Kabul*, 30–33. See also Jennifer Jenkins, "Germany's Eurasian Strategy in 1918," in *The World During the First World War*, ed. Helmut Bey and Anorthe Kremers (Essen: Klartext, 2014), 291-302.

33. Hughes, "The German Mission to Afghanistan, 1915–1916," 453.

34. For the most vivid account of the journey's travails, see Niedermayer, *Zir-e Aftab-e Suzan-e Iran*, 100–139; Hopkirk, *Like Sudden Fire*, 123–127.

35. Hughes, "The German Mission to Afghanistan, 1915–1916," 460.

36. Ibid., 461. For the German presence in Iran during World War I, see also Oliver Bast, "Germany ix. Germans in Persia: Agents and Soldiers," *Encyclopaedia Iranica*, http://www.iranicaonline.org/articles/germany-ix, accessed June 22, 2016; Oliver Bast, *Les Allemands en Perse pendant la Première Guerre mondiale* (Paris: Peeters, 1997); George Lenczowski, *Russia and the West in Iran, 1918–1948* (Ithaca, NY: Cornell University Press, 1949), 145–150.

37. Pratap, "My German Mission to High Asia," 386–388.

38. Ibid., 450–453.

39. Ibid., 383; Stewart, *The Kaiser's Mission to Kabul*, 59–62; Hopkirk, *Like Hidden Fire*, 137–142.

40. Hughes, "The German Mission to Afghanistan, 1915–1916," 462.

41. Blücher, *Safarnameh-ye Blusher: neveshteh-ye Vilpert Blusher*, 90–93.

42. Ibid.

43. Adamec, *Afghanistan, 1900–1923: A Diplomatic History*, 93–94, 178–179; Hughes, "The German Mission to Afghanistan, 1915–1916," 468.

44. Stewart, *The Kaiser's Mission to Kabul*, 115.

45. Stephanie Cronin, "Gendarmerie. The Swedish Period," *Encyclopaedia Iranica*, http://www.iranicaonline.org/articles/gendarmerie, accessed June 22, 2016; Stephanie Cronin, *The Army and the Creation of the Pahlavi State in Iran, 1910–1926* (London: I. B. Tauris, 1997), 29–34; Lenczowski, *Russia and the West in Iran*, 151.

46. Niedermayer, *Zir-e Aftab-e Suzan-e Iran*, 208; Bast, *Les Allemands en Perse*, 101–113.

47. Mirza Abulqasem Khan Kahhalzadeh, *Didehha va Shenidehha: Khaterat-e Mirza Abulqasem Khan Kahhalzadeh, Monshi-ye Sefarat-e Emperatori-ye Alman dar Iran, 1914–1918*, ed. Mortezah Kamran (Tehran: Nashr-e Farhang, 1984), 224–225.

48. Niedermayer, *Zir-e Aftab-e Suzan-e Iran*, 211.

49. Ibid., 265–268.

50. Kahhalzadeh, *Didehha va Shenidehha*, 220.

51. Ibid., 224; Bast, *Les Allemands en Perse*, 111.

52. Kahhalzadeh, *Didehha va Shenidehha*, 224.

53. Ibid., 226.

54. Ibid., 237; Niedermayer, *Zir-e Aftab-e Suzan-e Iran*, 267–268.

55. Niedermayer, *Zir-e Aftab-e Suzan-e Iran*, 268.

56. Kahhalzadeh, *Didehha va Shenidehha*, 238–240.

57. Ibid.

58. Stephanie Cronin, "Iranian Nationalism and the Government Gendarmerie," in *Iran and the First World War: Battleground of the Great Powers*, ed. Touraj Atabaki (London: I. B. Tauris, 2006), 52.

59. Kahalzadeh, *Didehha va Shenidehha*, 239.

60. Niedermayer, *Zir-e Aftab-e Suzan-e Iran*, 269–270.

61. Kahhalzadeh, *Didehha va Shenidehha*, 240.

62. Niedermayer, *Zir-e Aftab-e Suzan-e Iran*, 282.

63. Kahhalzadeh, *Didehha va Shenidehha*, 241.

64. Jamshid Behnam, *Berlaniha: Andishmandan-e Irani dar Berlan* (Tehran: Farzan, 2000), 38–57; Matin-Asgari, "The Berlin Circle," 49–66; Matin-Asgari, *Both Eastern and Western*, 49–63; Ansari, *The Politics of Nationalism in Modern Iran*, 68–69.

65. Behnam, *Berlaniha: Andishmandan-e Irani dar Berlan*, 17–21; Morteza Moshfeq-Kazemi, *Ruzegar va Andishehha*, vol. 1 (Tehran: Ibn Sina, 1971), 167–170; Asghar Schirazi, "Germany X. The Persian Community in Germany," *Encyclopaedia Iranica*, http://www.iranicaonline.org/articles/germany-x, accessed June 22, 2016.

66. Blücher, *Safarnameh-ye Blusher: neveshteh-ye Vilpert Blusher*, 137.

67. Ibid.

68. TNA: KV 2/3857, February 19, 1921. He is referred to as "Sheikh Abdul Rahman Saif"; the first use of the name "Saif Azad" appears in the British surveillance source TNA: KV 2/3857, February 23, 1926.

69. Blücher, *Safarnameh-ye Blusher: neveshteh-ye Vilpert Blusher*, 138–139.

70. Ibid.

71. Ibid. British surveillance also took notice of Saif Azad's tobacco kiosk and café in Berlin; see TNA: KV 2/3857, April 16, 1921; TNA: KV 2/3857, February 19, 1921; TNA: KV 2/3857, August 31, 1921.

72. Blücher, *Safarnameh-ye Blusher: neveshteh-ye Vilpert Blusher*, 139.

73. Alavi, *Khaterat-e Bozorg Alavi*, 105–106.

74. Ibid.

75. Moshfeq-Kazemi, *Ruzegar va Andishehha*, 183–184.

76. Ibid., 184.

77. The shift toward a more pan-Asianist and internationalist direction also involved the growing influence of Bolshevism among the expatriate communities in Berlin. For this shift among some Iranian students, see Behnam, *Berlaniha: Andishmandan-e Irani dar Berlan*, 70–71; Hamid Ahmadi, *Tarikhcheh-ye Ferqeh-ye Jumhuri-ye Inqilabi-ye Iran va Goruh-e Arani* (Tehran: Atiyeh, 2000), 9–14; Younes Jalali, *Taghi Erani, a Polymath in Interwar Berlin: Fundamental Science, Psychology, Orientalism, and Political Philosophy* (London: Palgrave, 2019). See also Manjapra, *Age of Entanglement*, 91–95.

78. TNA: KV 2/3857, April 11, 1921; TNA: KV 2/3857, August 31, 1921. For the League of Oppressed Peoples, see also Bonakdarian, "Iranian Nationalism and Global Solidarity Networks," 113n53. In addition to Berlin, the League had offices and solidarity groups in other cities as well, such as in New York, where the secretary was the noted Iranian art and antiquities expert Arthur Upham Pope; see his letter on behalf of the League to W. E. B Du Bois, http://credo.library.umass.edu/view/pageturn/mums312-b014-i260/#page/1/mode/1up, accessed June 24, 2016.

79. TNA: KV 2/3857, April 23, 1921.

80. TNA: KV 2/3857, October 24, 1921.

81. Barry Rubin and Wolfgang G. Schwanitz, *Nazis, Islamists, and the Making of the Modern Middle East* (New Haven, CT: Yale University Press, 2014), 75; David Motadel, "The Making of Muslim Communities in Western Europe, 1914–1939," in *Transnational Islam in Interwar Europe*, ed. Götz Nordbruch and Umar Ryad (New York: Palgrave, 2014), 27.

82. Rubin and Schwanitz, *Nazis, Islamists, and the Making of the Modern Middle East*, 73.

83. Manjapra, *Age of Entanglement*, 89.

84. Ibid.

85. Iraj Afshar, "Kāva Newspaper," *Encyclopaedia Iranica*, http://www.iranicaonline.org/articles/kava, accessed June 27, 2016.

86. In addition to Taqizadeh, the other owners were Ezzatollah Hedayat and Mirza Abdul Shakur Tabrizi.

87. Mirza Abdul Shakur Tabrizi was a longtime Iranian resident of Berlin and merchant in the carpet trade; TNA: KV 2/3857, October 4, 1921.

88. Ibid.; E. G. Browne, "Some Recent Persian Books: Publications of the 'Kaviani' Press, Berlin," *Journal of the Royal Asiatic Society* 56 (April 1924): 279–280.

89. Sadr-Hashemi, *Tarikh-e Jaraed va Majallat-e Iran*, vol. 1, 148. In addition to the *Azadi-ye Sharq*, Saif Azad also published a number of other shorter-lived newspapers during his years in Berlin, including *Rahnama-ye Banuan, Iran-e Nou*, and *Sana'-ye Alman va Sharq*. See Sadr-Hashemi, *Tarikh-e Jaraed va Majallat-e Iran*, vol. 2, 337–338, and vol. 3, 127–129. According to British surveillance records, Saif Azad terminated his association with the Kaviani press after its owners abruptly increased their printing fees. He subsequently acquired a new press and began printing the newspaper on his own. TNA: KV 2/3857, November 18, 1921.

90. *Azadi-ye Sharq*, April 1930, 1.

91. Ibid. The first line reads: "The Children of Adam are like limbs of each other, since in their creation they are of one essence."

92. TNA: KV 2/3857, October 24, 1921, and November 25, 1921.

93. TNA: KV 2/3857, November 25, 1921.

94. Ibid.

95. TNA: KV 2/3857, October 24, 1921.

96. TNA: KV 2/3857, January 31, 1923.

97. TNA: KV 2/3857, November 11, 1921.

98. TNA: KV 2/3857, March 15, 1935.

99. TNA: KV 2/3857, January 31, 1923.

100. TNA: KV 2/3857, April 16, 1921, April 11, 1921, April 23, 1921, and August 31, 1921.

101. Manjapra, *Age of Entanglement*, 89.

102. TNA: KV 2/3857, September 21, 1922.

103. TNA: KV 2/3857, October 4, 1921.

104. TNA: KV 2/3857, November 25, 1921.

105. Ibid.

106. TNA: KV 2/3857, April 23, 1921.

107. TNA: KV 2/3857, November 3, 1921.

108. Ibid.

109. Blücher, *Safarnameh-ye Blusher: neveshteh-ye Vilpert Blusher*, 120–121.

110. Sadr-Hashemi, *Tarikh-e Jara'ed va Majallat-e Iran*, vol. 3, 127–129.

111. Ibid., 127.

112. TNA: KV 2/3857, July 21, 1931. British intelligence authorities speculated about the connection between Ebrahim Purdavud's translation work and Saif Azad's outreach to the Parsis: "Four years ago [1927] the Bombay Parsis had invited one Puray Dawood [*sic*] . . . to translate their religious books. The Parsis had paid him [Purdavud] about Rs. 20,000 for that work. Seeing this Saif Azad wrote some articles in praise of Parsis and came down to Bombay hoping to get some money from them . . ."

113. Mohammed Alsulami, "Iranian Journals in Berlin during the Interwar Period," in *Transnational Islam in Interwar Europe*, ed. Götz Nordbruch and Umar Ryad (New York: Palgrave, 2014), 157–171.

114. "Jang ba Fesad-e Akhlaq," *Iranshahr* 4, no. 5 (July 23, 1926): 319.

115. Ibid., 320.

116. Ibid.

117. *Iran League Quarterly* 2, no. 2–3 (1932): 160.

118. Ibid.

119. Ibid.; *Iran League Quarterly* 7, no. 2 (1937): 93–95.

120. *Iran League Quarterly* 2, no. 2–3 (1932): 160.

121. Ibid.

122. TNA: KV 2/3857, May 30, 1931.

123. TNA: KV 2/3857, July 1, 1931.

124. Ibid.

125. TNA: KV 2/3857, July 6, 1931.

126. Sadr-Hashemi, *Tarikh-e Jara'ed va Majallat-e Iran*, vol. 1, 330–331.

127. Ibid.

128. Miron Rezun, *The Soviet Union and Iran: Soviet Policy in Iran from the Beginning of the Pahlavi Dynasty until the Soviet Invasion of 1941* (Genève: Institut Universitaire de Hautes Etudes Internationales, 1981), 319; Zia-Ebrahimi, *The Emergence of Iranian Nationalism*, 121; Reza Zia-Ebrahimi, "Self-Orientalization and Dislocation: The Uses and Abuses of the 'Aryan' Discourse in Iran," *Iranian Studies* 44 (2011): 458; Oliver Bast, "Germany: German-Persian Diplomatic Relations," *Encyclopaedia Iranica*, http://www.iranicaonline.org/articles/germany-i, accessed June 22, 2016. For German cultural and political policy toward Iran in the interwar period, see also Lenczowski, *Russia and the West in Iran*, 158–166.

129. *Iran-e Bastan*, January 14, 1933, 1; Sadr-Hashemi, *Tarikh-e Jara'ed va Majallat-e Iran*, vol. 1, 330.

130. *Iran-e Bastan*, August 26, 1933, 1.

131. *Iran-e Bastan*, September 2, 1933, 1.

132. *Iran-e Bastan*, March 21, 1933, 11.

133. Ibid.

134. Ibid.

135. Ibid.

136. Ibid.

137. Ibid.

138. *Iran-e Bastan*, April 1, 1933, 9.

139. *Iran-e Bastan*, January 14, 1933, 4.

140. Ibid.

141. *Iran-e Bastan*, January 14, 1933, 5.

142. Ibid.

143. Ibid.

144. *Iran-e Bastan*, February 11, 1933, 5.

145. Ibid.

146. *Iran League Quarterly* 7, no. 4 (July 1937): frontispiece.

147. Rustam Kharegat, *A Tourist Guide to Iran* (Bombay: G. Clarige Publishers, 1935).

148. The book was regularly advertised in the pages of the *Iran League Quarterly*. See, for example, *Iran League Quarterly* 7, no. 4 (July 1937): 240.

149. *Iran-e Bastan*, June 29, 1933, 10.

150. Ibid.

151. Ibid.

152. Ibid.

153. Ibid.

154. *Iran-e Bastan*, February 4, 1933, 3.

155. Ibid.

156. Ibid.

157. Ibid.

158. Ibid.

159. Tavakoli-Targhi, "Narrative Identity in the Works of Hedayat and His Contemporaries," 118–119.

160. *Iran-e Bastan*, April 14, 1934, 5.

161. *Iran-e Bastan*, August 25, 1934, 3; September 1, 1934, 3; September 15, 1934, 3; September 22, 1934, 3; September 30, 1934, 3; October 17, 1934, 3.

162. Tavakoli-Targhi, "Narrative Identity in the Works of Hedayat and His Contemporaries," 118.

163. *Iran-e Bastan*, October 7, 1934, 8.

164. Ibid.

165. Ibid.

166. *Iran-e Bastan*, March 15, 1933, 9.

167. *Iran-e Bastan*, December 20, 1933, 22.

168. *Iran-e Bastan*, November 25, 1933, 2. On Subhas Chandra Bose's work with the Germans during World War II, see Bose, *A Hundred Horizons*, 172–192.

169. *Iran-e Bastan*, December 20, 1933, 2.

170. Said Azad had not severed all contact with the Parsis, and during his 1937 trip to India he met with some of his remaining allies within the Iran League, including its former president, Hormusji Cowasji. See Government of India, Home Department archives, File No. 59/10-A/39-Political, 116. I am grateful to Dinyar Patel for this reference.

CONCLUSION

1. Nikuyeh, *Purdavud*, 18.

2. Mostafavi, *Zaman va Zendegi*, 323–335; Ehsan Yarshater, "Be Yad-e Purdavud," *Farhang-e Iran Zamin* 21, no. 1–4 (2535/1976): 15.

3. Mostafavi, *Zaman va Zendegi*, 52–53.

4. Purdavud, *Anahita: Panjah Goftar-e Purdavud*, 36–40, 51–54.

5. Mostafavi, *Zaman va Zendegi*, 52.

BIBLIOGRAPHY

Abdi, Kamyar. "Nationalism, Politics, and the Development of Archaeology in Iran." *American Journal of Archaeology* 105, no. 1 (2001): 51–76.

Abdi, S. A. Hafez. "Hafiz and India." *Indo-Iranica* 31, no. 3–4 (1978): 1–36.

Abrahamian, Ervand. *Iran between Two Revolutions*. Princeton, NJ: Princeton University Press, 1982.

Adamec, Ludwig W. *Afghanistan, 1900–1923: A Diplomatic History*. Berkeley: University of California Press, 1967.

Adas, Michael. "Contested Hegemony: The Great War and the Afro-Asian Assault on the Civilizing Mission Ideology." *Journal of World History* 15, no. 1 (2004): 31–63.

———. *Machines as the Measure of Men: Science, Technology, and Ideologies of Western Dominance*. Ithaca, NY: Cornell University Press, 1989.

Afary, Janet. *The Iranian Constitutional Revolution, 1906–1911: Grassroots Democracy, Social Democracy, and the Origins of Feminism*. New York: Columbia University Press, 1996.

Afshar, Iraj. "Kāva Newspaper." *Encyclopaedia Iranica*, vol. 16.2, 132–135. Available online at http://www.iranicaonline.org/articles/kava. Accessed October 25, 2017.

———. "Ketabha-ye Chap-e Qadim dar Iran va Chap-e Ketabha-ye Farsi dar Jahan." *Hunar va Mardom* 5 (1966): 26–33.

Afshar, Iraj, ed. *Namehha-ye Paris az Qazvini be Taqizadeh*. Tehran: Qatreh, 2005.

Ahmadi, Hamid. *Tarikhcheh-ye Ferqeh-ye Jumhuri-ye Inqilabi-ye Iran va Goruh-e Arani*. Tehran: Atiyeh, 2000.

Ahmadi, Wali. *Modern Persian Literature in Afghanistan: Anomalous Visions of History and Form*. London: Routledge, 2008.

Ahmed, Saleem. "Hafiz and Tagore: A Study in Influence." In *Essays on Rabindranath Tagore in Honor of D. M. Gupta*, edited by T. R. Sharma, 231–282. Ghaziabad: Vimal Prakashan, 1987.

Akhtar, Nadeem. "Hedayat, Sadeq v. Hedayat in India." *Encyclopaedia Iranica*. Available online at http://www.iranicaonline.org/articles/hedayat-sadeq-v. Accessed November 6, 2017.

Alam, Muzaffar. "The Culture and Politics of Persian in Precolonial Hindustan." In *Literary Cultures in History: Reconstructions from South Asia*, edited by Sheldon Pollock, 131–198. Berkeley: University of California Press, 2003.

Alam, Muzaffar, and Sanjay Subrahmanyam. *Indo-Persian Travels in the Age of Discoveries, 1400–1800*. Cambridge, UK: Cambridge University Press, 2010.

Alavi, Bozorg. *Khaterat-e Bozorg Alavi*. Edited by Hamid Ahmadi. Spanga, Sweden: Baran Press, 1998.

Alsulami, Mohammad. "Iranian Journals in Berlin during the Interwar Period." In *Transnational Islam in Interwar Europe*, edited by Götz Nordbruch and Umar Ryad, 151–171. New York: Palgrave, 2014.

Amanat, Abbas, and Assef Ashraf, eds. *The Persianate World: Rethinking a Shared Sphere*. Leiden, Netherlands: Brill, 2019.

Anderson, Benedict. *Imagined Communities: Reflections on the Origins and Spread of Nationalism*. Rev. ed. New York: Verso Books, 2006.

Anderson, Betty S. *The American University of Beirut: Arab Nationalism and Liberal Education*. Austin: University of Texas Press, 2011.

Ansari, Ali M. *The Politics of Nationalism in Modern Iran*. Cambridge, UK: Cambridge University Press, 2012.

Ansari, Shahpar. "The Life, Works, and Times of Muhammad Qazvini (1875–1949)." Master's thesis, University of Utah, 1990.

Arberry, A. J. *Shiraz: Persian City of Saints and Poets*. Norman: University of Oklahoma Press, 1960.

Aronson, Alex. *Rabindranath through Western Eyes*. Calcutta: Rdhhi-India, 1978.

Asad, Talal. *Genealogies of Religion: Discipline and Reasons of Power in Christianity and Islam*. Baltimore: Johns Hopkins University Press, 1993.

Azad, Saif. *Demokrasi va Azadi dar Hend*. Tehran: Majles, 1950.

Azadi-ye Sharq. Berlin, 1921–1930.

Azari Shahrzai, Reza, ed. *Paykar dar Berlin*. Tehran: Shirazeh Ketab, 2016.

Azhar, A. W. "Gurudev Tagore's Visit to Persia and the Persian Translations of His Works." In *Profile of Rabindranath Tagore in World Literature*, edited by Rita D. Sil, 171–184. New Delhi: Khama Publishers, 2000.

Azimi, Fakhreddin. *The Quest for Democracy in Iran: A Century of Struggle against Authoritarian Rule*. Cambridge, MA: Harvard University Press, 2008.

Babayan, Kathryn. *Mystics, Monarchs, and Messiahs: Cultural Landscapes of Early Modern Iran*. Cambridge, MA: Harvard University Press, 2002.

Babazadeh, Shahla. *Tarikh-e Chap dar Iran*. Tehran: Tahuri, 1991.

Bahr al-'Olumi, Hosayn. *Karnameh-ye Anjoman-e Asar-e Melli: Az Aghaz to 2535 Shahanshahi, 1301–1355 Hejri Shamsi*. Tehran, 1977.

Balsara, Pestanji Phirozshah. *Ancient Iran: Its Contribution to Human Progress*. Bombay: Iran League, 1936.

———. *Iran va Ahmiat-e an dar Taraqqi va Tamaddon-e Bashar*. Translated by Abdolhossein Sepanta. Bamba'i: Anjoman-e Iran Lig, 1936.

Bambad, Mehdi. *Sharh-e Hal-e Rejal-e Iran*. 3 vols. Tehran: Zavar, 1978.

Bast, Oliver. "Germany i: German-Persian Diplomatic Relations." *Encyclopaedia Iranica*, vol. 10.5, 506–519. Available online at http://www.iranicaonline.org/articles/germany-i. Accessed June 22, 2016.

———. "Germany ix. Germans in Persia: Agents and Soldiers." *Encyclopaedia Iranica*, vol. 10.6, 567–572. Available online at http://www.iranicaonline.org/articles/germany-ix. Accessed June 22, 2016.

———. *Les Allemands en Perse pendant la Première Guerre mondiale*. Paris: Peeters, 1997.

Bastani-Parizi, Mohammad Ebrahim. "Yaddashti bar Yaddashtha-ye Shadravan Arbab Kaykhosrow Shahrokh." In *Yaddashtha-ye Kaykhosrow Shahrokh*, edited by Jahangir Oshidari, n.p. Tehran: Parcham, 2535/1977.

Bayly, Susan. "Imagining 'Greater India': French and Indian Visions of Colonialism in the Indic Mode." *Modern Asian Studies* 38, no. 3 (2004): 703–744.

Behnam, Jamshid. *Berlaniha: Andishmandan-e Irani dar Berlan*. Tehran: Farzan, 2000.

Bharucha, Rustom. *Another Asia: Rabindranath Tagore and Okakura Tenshin*. New Delhi: Oxford University Press, 2006.

Bharucha, Sheriarji Dadabhai. *The Dasatir: Being a Paper Prepared for the Tenth International Congress of Orientalists Held at Geneva in 1894 A.C.* Bombay: Fort Printing Press, 1907. Repr., K. R. Cama Oriental Institute, 2006.

Blücher, Wipert von. *Safarnameh-ye Blusher: neveshteh-ye Vilpert Blusher.* Translated by Kaykavus Jahandari. Tehran: Khwarazmi, 1985.

Bonakdarian, Mansour. *Britain and the Iranian Constitutional Revolution of 1906–1911: Foreign Policy, Imperialism, and Dissent.* Syracuse, NY: Syracuse University Press, 2006.

———. "Iranian Nationalism and Global Solidarity Networks 1906–1918: Internationalism, Transnationalism, Globalization, and Nationalist Cosmopolitanism." In *Iran in the Middle East: Transnational Encounters and Social History,* edited by H. E. Chehabi, Peyman Jafari, and Maral Jefroudi, 77–119. London: I. B. Tauris, 2015.

Bose, Sugata. *A Hundred Horizons: The Indian Ocean in the Age of Global Empire.* Cambridge, MA: Harvard University Press, 2006.

Bowersock, G. W., Peter Brown, and Oleg Grabar, eds. *Late Antiquity: A Guide to the Postclassical World.* Cambridge, MA: Harvard University Press, 1999.

Boyce, Mary. "Manekji Limji Hataria in Iran." In *K. R. Cama Oriental Institute Golden Jubilee Volume,* edited by N. D. Minochehr-Homji and M. F. Kanga, 19–31. Bombay: K. R. Cama Oriental Institute, 1969.

———. *Zoroastrians: Their Religious Beliefs and Practices.* London: Routledge, 1979.

British Mazdaznan Magazine: The Official Organ of the Mazdaznan Association of Great Britain.

Browne, Edward G. *A Literary History of Persia.* 4 vols. London: Cambridge University Press, 1959.

———. *The Press and Poetry of Modern Persia.* Cambridge, UK: Cambridge University Press, 1914.

———. "Some Recent Persian Books: Publications of the 'Kaviani' Press, Berlin." *Journal of the Royal Asiatic Society* 56 (April 1924): 279–280.

Cama, Kharshedji Rustomji. *The Collected Works of K. R. Cama.* Bombay: K. R. Cama Institute, 1968.

Campbell, Bruce F. *Ancient Wisdom Revived: A History of the Theosophical Movement.* Berkeley: University of California Press, 1980.

Carroll, David. *Albert Camus the Algerian: Colonialism, Terrorism, Justice.* New York: Columbia University Press, 2007.

Cavanagh, Edward, and Lorenzo Veracini, eds. *The Routledge Handbook of the History of Settler Colonialism.* London: Routledge, 2017.

Chatterjee, Partha. *Nationalist Thought and the Colonial World: A Derivative Discourse?* Minneapolis: University of Minnesota Press, 1993.

Chatterji, K. N. "Itinerary of the Persian Tour." *Modern Review* 53 (March 1933): 327–332.

Chatterji, Suniti Kumar. *Iranianism: Iranian Culture and Its Impact on the World from Achamenian Times.* Calcutta: Asiatic Society, 1972.

———. "Tagore, the Full Man and Iran." *Indo-Iranica* 14, no. 2 (1961): 7.

Chehabi, H. E. "An Iranian in First World War Beirut: Qasem Ghani's Reminiscences." In *Distant Relations: Iran and Lebanon in the Last 500 Years,* edited by H. E. Chehabi, 120–136. New York: I. B. Tauris/Centre for Lebanese Studies, 2006.

———. "The Paranoid Style in Iranian Historiography." In *Iran in the 20th Century: Historiography and Political Culture,* edited by Touraj Atabaki, 155–176. London: I. B. Tauris, 2009.

Choksy, Jamsheed K. *Conflict and Cooperation: Zoroastrian Subalterns and Muslim Elites in Medieval Iranian Society.* New York: Columbia University Press, 1997.

————. "Despite Shāhs and Mollās: Minority Sociopolitics in Premodern and Modern Iran." *Journal of Asian History* 40, no. 2 (2006): 129–184.

Cole, Juan R. I. *Modernity and the Millennium: The Genesis of the Baha'i Faith in the Nineteenth-Century Middle East.* New York: Columbia University Press, 1998.

Corbin, Henry. "Āzar Kayvān." *Encyclopaedia Iranica*, vol. 3.2, 183–187. Available online at http://www.iranicaonline.org/articles/azar-kayvan-priest. Accessed May 17, 2018.

————. *The Man of Light in Iranian Sufism.* Translated by Nancy Pearson. New Lebanon, NY: Omega Books, 1994.

————. *Spiritual Body and Celestial Earth: From Mazdean Iran to Shi'ite Iran.* Translated by Nancy Pearson. Princeton, NJ: Princeton University Press, 1977.

Coyajee, Jehangir C. "A Brief Life-Sketch of the Late Mr. Dinshah Irani." In *Dinshah Irani Memorial Volume: Papers on Zoroastrianism and Iranian Subjects*, edited by Jehangir Coyajee et al., i–xiii. Bombay: Dinshah Irani Memorial Committee, 1948.

Cronin, Stephanie. *The Army and the Creation of the Pahlavi State in Iran, 1910–1926.* London: I. B. Tauris, 1997.

————. "An Experiment in Revolutionary Nationalism: The Rebellion of Colonel Mohammad Taqi Khan Pasyan in Mashhad, April-October 1921." *Middle Eastern Studies* 33, no. 4 (1997): 693–750.

————. "Gendarmerie. The Swedish Period." *Encyclopaedia Iranica*, vol. 10.4, 398–405. Available online at http://www.iranicaonline.org/articles/gendarmerie. Accessed June 22, 2016.

————. "Iranian Nationalism and the Government Gendarmerie." In *Iran and the First World War: Battleground of the Great Powers*, edited by Touraj Atabaki, 43–68. London: I. B. Tauris, 2006.

————. "Riza Shah, the Fall of Sardar Asad, and the 'Bakhtiari Plot.'" *Iranian Studies* 38, no. 2 (2005): 211–245.

Dabashi, Hamid. *Persophilia: Persian Culture on the Global Scene.* Cambridge, MA: Harvard University Press, 2015.

————. *Post-Orientalism: Knowledge and Power in a Time of Terror.* New York: Routledge, 2017.

Daruwala, J. D. "P. D. Marker, Founder of Educational Institutions for Boys and Girls in Yazd." In *Peshotanji Marker Memorial Volume/Yadnameh-ye Peshotan Dusabai Marker*, edited by Mirza Sarosh Lohrasb, 1–3. Bombay: Iranian Zoroastrian Anjoman, 1966.

Das Gupta, Arun. "Rabindranath Tagore in Indonesia: An Experiment in Bridge-Building." *Koninklijk Instituut Voor Taal-, Land- En Volkendunde (Royal Institute of Linguistics and Anthropology)* 158, no. 2 (2002): 451–477.

Dashti, Ali. *Twenty-Three Years: A Study of the Prophetic Career of Mohammad.* Translated by F. R. C. Bagley. Costa Mesa, Calif.: Mazda Publishers, 1994.

Davar, Firoze Cowasji. *Iran and India through the Ages.* New York: Asia Publishing House, 1962.

De Planhol, X. "Bandar-e Šāhpūr." *Encyclopaedia Iranica*, vol. 3.7, 689. Available online at http://www.iranicaonline.org/articles/bandar-e-sahpur. Accessed May 10, 2018.

Derrida, Jacques. *Specters of Marx: The State of the Debt, the Work of Mourning, and the New International.* New York: Routledge, 2006.

Dhalla, Maneckji Musserwanji. *Dastur Dhalla, The Saga of a Soul: An Autobiography.* Translated by Gool and Behram Sohrab H. J. Rustomji. Karachi: Dhalla Memorial Institute, 1975.

Dobbin, Christine. *Asian Entrepreneurial Minorities: Conjoint Communities in the Making of the World-Economy, 1570–1940.* London: Routledge, 1996.

———. "The Parsi Panchayat in Bombay City in the Nineteenth Century." *Modern Asian Studies* 4, no. 2 (1970): 149–164.

Duara, Prasenji. "The Discourse of Civilization and Decolonization." *Journal of World History* 15, no. 1 (2004): 1–5.

———. "The Discourse of Civilization and Pan-Asianism." *Journal of World History* 12, no. 1 (2001): 99–130.

Dudley, Andrew. "Praying Mantis: Enchantment and Violence in French Cinema of the Exotic." In *Visions of the East: Orientalism in Film,* edited by Matthew Bernstein and Gaylyn Studlar, 232–252. New Brunswick, NJ: Rutgers University Press, 1997.

Durai, J. Chinn. "Indian Prisons." *Journal of Comparative Legislation and International Law* 11, no. 4 (1929): 245–249.

Dusinberre, Elspeth R. M. "Herzfeld in Persepolis." In *Ernst Herzfeld and the Development of Near Eastern Studies, 1900–1950,* edited by Ann Clyburn Gunter and Stefan R. Hauser, 137–180. Leiden, Netherlands: E. J. Brill, 2005.

Dutta, Krishna, and Andrew Robinson. *Rabindranath Tagore: The Myriad-Minded Man.* New York: St. Martin's, 1995.

Eaton, Richard. *The Rise of Islam and the Bengal Frontier, 1204–1760.* Berkeley: University of California Press, 1993.

Eaton, Richard, and Phillip Wagoner, eds. *Power, Memory, Architecture: Contested Sites on India's Deccan Plateau, 1300–1600.* New Delhi: Oxford University Press, 2014.

Edwardes, S. M. *Memoir of Sir Dinshaw Manockjee Petit, First Baronet.* Oxford, UK: Oxford University Press, 1923.

Elisaeus. *The History of Vartan and of the Battle of the Armenians: Containing an Account of the Religious Wars between the Persians and Armenians.* Translated by Karl Friedrich Neumann. London: Murray, Parbury, Allen and Co., 1830.

Elwell-Sutton, L. P. "The Iranian Press, 1941–1947." *Iran* 6 (1968): 65–104.

Ettehad, Hushang. *Pezhuheshgaran-e Muʿaser-e Iran.* Tehran: Farhang-e Muʿaser, 2001.

Ettehadieh, Manoureh. *The Lion of Persia: A Political Biography of Prince Farman-Farma.* Cambridge, MA: Tŷ Aur Press, 2012.

Ettelaʿat. Tehran, 1925.

Farzaneh, Mateo Mohammad. *The Iranian Constitutional Revolution and the Clerical Leadership of Khurasani.* Syracuse, NY: Syracuse University Press, 2015.

Febvre, Lucien, and Henri-Jean Martin. *The Coming of the Book: The Impact of Printing, 1450–1800.* Translated by David Gerard. New York: Verso, 1991.

Ferdowsi, Ali. "The 'Emblem of the Manifestation of the Iranian Spirit': Hafiz and the Rise of the National Cult of Persian Poetry." *Iranian Studies* 41, no. 5 (December 2008): 667–691.

Firoze, M. "Recent Studies of Rabindranath Tagore in Iran." *Indo-Iranica* 51, no. 1–4 (1998): 118–131.

Fish, Laura. "The Bombay Interlude: Parsi Transnational Aspirations in the First Persian Sound Film." *Transnational Cinemas* 9, no. 2 (2018): 197–211.

Fitch, Noel Riley. *The Grand Literary Cafes of Europe*. London: New Holland, 2006.
Floor, Willem. "ČĀP." *Encyclopaedia Iranica*, vol. 4.7, 760–764. Available online at http://www.iranicaonline.org/articles/cap-print-printing-a-persian-word-prob-ably-derived-from-hindi-chapna-to-print-see-turner-no. Accessed June 23, 2019.
Framjee, Dosabhoy. *Parsees: Their History, Manners, Customs, and Religion*. Bombay: Smith, Taylor and Co., 1858.
Gardner, Nikolas. *The Siege of Kut-al-Amara: At War in Mesopotamia, 1915–1916*. Bloomington: Indiana University Press, 2014.
Gehrke, Ulrich. *Pish beh su-ye Sharq*. Translated by Parviz Sadri. 2 vols. Tehran: Ketab-e Siamak, 1998.
Gelvin, James, and Nile Green, eds. *Global Muslims in the Age of Steam and Print*. Berkeley: University of California Press, 2014.
Godrej, Pheroza J., and Firoza Punthakey Mistree, eds. *A Zoroastrian Tapestry: Art, Religion and Culture*. Middletown, NJ: Mapin Publishing, 2002.
Golbon, Mohammad. "Tagur va Iran." *Bokhara* 45 (Fall 2005): 130–140.
Green, Nile. *Bombay Islam: The Religious Economy of the West Indian Ocean, 1840–1915*. Cambridge, UK: Cambridge University Press, 2011.
———. "Stones from Bavaria: Iranian Lithography in Its Global Contexts." *Iranian Studies* 43, no. 3 (June 2010): 305–331.
———. "The Waves of Heterotopia: Towards a Vernacular Intellectual History of the Indian Ocean." *American Historical Review* 123, no. 1 (June 2018): 846–874.
Green, Nile, ed. *The Persianate World: The Frontiers of a Eurasian Lingua Franca*. Berkeley: University of California Press, 2019.
———. *Terrains of Exchange: Religious Economies of Global Islam*. New York: Oxford University Press, 2015.
Grigor, Talinn. *Building Iran: Modernism, Architecture, and National Heritage under the Pahlavi Monarchs*. New York: Periscope Books, 2009.
———. "Parsi Patronage of the *Urheimat*." *Getty Research Journal* 2 (2010): 53–68.
———. "Persian Architectural Revivals in the British Raj and Qajar Iran." *Comparative Studies in South Asia, Africa, and the Middle East* 36, no. 3 (2016): 384–397.
———. "Recultivating 'Good Taste': The Early Pahlavi Modernists and Their Society for National Heritage." *Iranian Studies* 37, no. 1 (2004): 17–45.
Haine, W. Scott. *The World of the Paris Café: Sociability among the French Working Class, 1789–1914*. Baltimore: Johns Hopkins University Press, 1996.
Hanish, Otoman Zar-Adusht. *The Egyptian Postures*. Edited by Ian Whittlesea. London: Everyday Press, 2017.
———. *Inner Studies: A Course of Twelve Studies*. Chicago: Sun-Worshiper, 1902.
———. *Mazdaznan Encyclopedia of Dietics and Cookery Book*. Chicago: Mazdaznan Press, 1901.
Hay, Stephen N. *Asian Ideas of East and West: Tagore and His Critics in Japan, China, and India*. Cambridge, MA: Harvard University Press, 1970.
Hell, Joseph. *The Arab Civilization*. Translated by S. Khuda Buksh. Cambridge, UK: W. Heffer and Sons, 1926.
———. *Die Kulter der Araber*. Leipzig, Germany: Quelle and Meyer, 1909.
Hentig, Werner-Otto von. *Ins Verscholossene Land: Ein Kampf mit Mensch und Meile*. Berlin: Ullstein, 1918.
Hinnells, John R. "The Flowering of Zoroastrian Benevolence: Parsi Charities in the

19th and 20th Centuries." In *Papers in Honour of Professor Mary Boyce*, vol. 1, edited by Jacques Duchesne-Guillemin and Mary Boyce, 261–327. Leiden, Netherlands: E. J. Brill, in association with Centre International d'Études Indo-iraniennes, 1985.

———. "The Parsis." In *The Wiley Blackwell Companion to Zoroastrianism*, edited by Michael Stausberg and Yuhan Sohrab-Dinshaw Vevaina, 157–172. West Sussex, UK: John Wiley and Sons, 2015.

———. *The Zoroastrian Diaspora: Religion and Migration*. Oxford, UK: Oxford University Press, 2005.

Hodgkin, Samuel. "Lahuti: Persian Poetry in the Making of the Literary International, 1906–1957." PhD diss., University of Chicago, 2018.

Hodgson, Marshall G. S. *The Venture of Islam: Conscience and History in a World Civilization*. 3 vols. Chicago: University of Chicago Press, 1974.

Hollinger, Richard. "An Iranian Enclave in Beirut: Baha'i Students at the American University of Beirut, 1906–1948." In *Distant Relations: Iran and Lebanon in the Last 500 Years*, edited by H. E. Chehabi, 96–119. New York: I. B. Tauris/Centre for Lebanese Studies, 2006.

Hopkirk, Peter. *Like Hidden Fire: The Plot to Bring Down the British Empire*. New York: Kodansha International, 1994.

Howsam, Leslie. *Cheap Bibles: Nineteenth Century Publishing and the British and Foreign Bible Society*. Cambridge, UK: Cambridge University Press, 1991.

Hughes, Thomas. "The German Mission to Afghanistan, 1915–1916." *German Studies Review* 25 (2002): 447–476.

Hukht. Tehran, 1950–1984.

Iran-e Bastan. Tehran, 1933–1935.

Iran League Quarterly: Official Organ of the Iran League, Bombay. Bombay, 1930–1953.

Irani, Dinshah J. *Akhlaq-e Iran-e Bastan*. Bamba'i: Anjoman-e Zartoshtian-e Irani-ye Bamba'i, 1930.

———. *The Divine Songs of Zarathustra*. With an introduction by Rabindranath Tagore. New York: Allen and Unwin, 1924.

———. *Falsafeh-ye Iran-e Bastan*. Bamba'i: Anjoman-e Zartoshtian-e Irani-ye Bamba'i, 1933.

———. *Gems from the Divine Songs of Zoroaster*. Bombay: E. G. Pearson, 1922.

———. *The Path to Happiness, or Ethical Teachings of Zoroaster*. Bombay: Jehangir B. Karant's Sons, 1939.

———. *Peyk-e Mazdayasnan*. Bamba'i: Anjoman-e Zartoshtian-e Irani-ye Bamba'i, 1927.

———. *Understanding the Gathas: Hymns of Zarathustra*. Edited by Kaikhosrov D. Irani. Womelsdorf, PA: Ahura Publishers, 1994.

Irani, Dinshah J., ed. *Full Translation and Explanation of Anwar-e-Sohaili, Chapters II and III*. Edited and translated by K. B. Irani and D. J. Irani. Bombay, 1917.

———. *Hafez Odes 1–75*. Edited and translated by K. B. Irani and D. J. Irani. Bombay, 1917.

———. *Poets of the Pahlavi Regime*. Bombay: Fort Printing Press, 1933.

———. *Saadi's Odes 1–60: With Persian Text, Full Translation, Exhaustive Introduction and Complete Notes*. Bombay, 1913.

———. *Saadi's Qasayed-i Farsiye: With Persian Text, Full Translation, Exhaustive*

Introduction and Complete Notes. Translated by K. B. Irani and D. J. Irani. Bombay, 1914.

———. *Translation of Nizam-ul-Mulk's Siasat-nameh.* Edited and translated by K. B. Irani and D. J. Irani. Bombay, 1916.

Irani, Kaikhosrov D. "Dinshah J. Irani, 1881–1938." http://www.zarathushtra.com/z/ gatha/dji/dinshah.htm. Accessed May 2, 2018.

Iranshahr: Majalleh-ye Mosavvar, 'Elmi, va Adabi. Berlin, 1922–1927.

Jabbari, Alexander. "The Making of Modernity in Persianate Literary History." *Comparative Studies of South Asia, Africa, and the Middle East* 36, no. 3 (2016): 418–434.

Jackson, A. V. Williams. *Persia Past and Present: A Book of Travel and Research.* London: Macmillan and Co., 1906.

Jalali, Younes. *Taghi Erani, a Polymath in Interwar Berlin: Fundamental Science, Psychology, Orientalism, and Political Philosophy.* London: Palgrave, 2019.

Jamalzadeh, Mohammad-Ali. "Yek Dusti-ye Shast Saleh." *Vahid* 6, no. 2–3 (1969): 194–204.

JamaspAsa, Kaikhusroo M. "Dinshah Jijibhoy Irani." *Encyclopaedia Iranica,* vol. 13.5, 500–501. Available online at http://www.iranicaonline.org/articles/irani-dinshah-jijibhoy. Accessed May 2, 2018.

JamaspAsa, Kaikhusroo M., and Mary Boyce. "Bahramgore Tahmuras Anklesaria." *Encyclopaedia Iranica,* vol. 2.1, 96. Available online at http://www.iranicaonline. org/articles/anklesaria-bahramgore-tahmuras. Accessed June 24, 2019.

Jenkins, Jennifer. "Excavating Zarathustra: Ernst Herzfeld's *Archaeological History of Iran.*" *Iranian Studies* 45, no. 1 (2012): 1–27.

———. "Germany's Eurasian Strategy in 1918." In *The World during the First World War,* edited by Helmut Bley and Anorthe Kremers, 291-302. Essen: Klartext, 2014.

Jones, Stephanie. "British India Steamers and the Trade of the Persian Gulf, 1862–1914." *The Great Circle: Journal of the Australian Association for Maritime History* 7, no. 1 (April 1985): 23–44.

Jones, William. "The Sixth Anniversary Discourse, on the Persians, Delivered 19th February, 1789." In *The Works of Sir William Jones,* edited by John Shore Teignmouth, vol. 3, 110–111. London: Stockdale and Walker, 1807.

Kahhalzadeh, Mirza Abulqasem Khan. *Didehha va Shenidehha: Khaterat-e Mirza Abulqasem Khan Kahhalzadeh, Monshi-ye Sefarat-e Emperatori-ye Alman dar Iran, 1914–1918.* Edited by Mortezah Kamran. Tehran: Nashr-e Farhang, 1984.

Kaiser, Hilmar. *Imperialism, Racism, and Development Theories: The Construction of a Dominant Paradigm on Ottoman Armenians.* Ann Arbor, MI: Gomidas Institute Books, 2009.

Kalim, M. "Hafiz Shirazi and Bengal." *Indo-Iranica* 38, no. 1–2 (1985): 42–51.

Kampchen, Martin. *Rabindranath Tagore in Germany: Four Responses to a Cultural Icon.* Shimla: Indian Institute for Advanced Study, 1999.

Kampchen, Martin, ed. *Rabindranath Tagore and Germany: A Documentation.* Calcutta: Mueller Bhavan, 1991.

Kapadia, Dinshah D. "Renaissance of Zoroastrian Studies among the Parsis." In *Sir J. J. Zarthoshti Madressa Centenary Volume,* edited by Dinshah D. Kapadia, viii–xvi. Bombay: Dorabji and Co., 1967.

Kaplan, Alice. *Looking for the Stranger: Albert Camus and the Life of a Literary Classic*. Chicago: University of Chicago Press, 2016.

Katouzian, Homa. *Sadeq Hedayat: The Life and Literature of an Iranian Writer*. London: I. B. Tauris, 2000.

Kaus, Mulla Firuz Bin. *The Desatir: Or Sacred Writings of the Ancient Persian Prophets*. Bombay: Courier Press, 1818.

Kaveh. Berlin, 1916–1922.

Kazemzadeh-Iranshahr, Hossein. *Asar va Ahval-e Kazemzadeh-Iranshahr*. Tehran: Eqbal, 1971.

———. "Be Qalam-e Aqa-ye Purdavud." *Iranshahr* 1, no. 5 (October, 25, 1922): 107.

Kestenberg Amighi, Janet. *The Zoroastrians of Iran: Conversion, Assimilation, or Persistence*. New York: AMS Press, 1990.

Khan, Yasmin. *India at War: The Subcontinent and the Second World War*. Oxford, UK: Oxford University Press, 2015.

Kharegat, Rustam. *A Tourist Guide to Iran*. Bombay: G. Clarige, 1935.

Kia, Mana. "Imagining Iran before Nationalism: Geocultural Meanings of Land in Azar's *Atashkadeh*." In *Rethinking Iranian Nationalism and Modernity*, edited by Kamran Aghaie and Afshin Marashi, 89–112. Austin: University of Texas Press, 2014.

———. "Indian Friends, Iranian Selves: Persianate Modern." *Comparative Studies of South Asia, Africa, and the Middle East* 36, no. 3 (2016): 398–417.

———. *Persianate Selves: Memories of Place and Origin before Nationalism*. Stanford, CA: Stanford University Press, 2020.

Kia, Mana, and Afshin Marashi. "After the Persianate: Introduction." *Comparative Studies of South Asia, Africa, and the Middle East* 36, no. 3 (2016): 379–383.

Knörzer, J. E. *Ali Dashti's Prison Days: Life under Reza Shah*. Costa Mesa, CA: Mazda Publishers in Association with Bibliotheca Persica, 1994.

Kotwal, Dastur Firoze M., and James W. Boyd. *A Persian Offering: The Yasna, a Zoroastrian High Liturgy*. Paris: Association Pour l'Avancement des Études Iranieness, 1991.

Kotwal, Dastur Firoze M., Jamsheed K. Choksy, Christopher J. Brunner, and Mahnaz Moazami. "Hatari, Manekji Limji." *Encyclopaedia Iranica*. http://www.iranica-online.org/articles/hataria-manekji-limji. Accessed September 24, 2018.

Kreyenbroek, Philip G. "Catechisms." *Encyclopaedia Iranica*. http://www.iranicaon-line.org/articles/catechisms-treatises-for-instruction-in-the-fundamental-te-nets-of-a-religious-faith-cast-in-the-form-of-questions-and-answe. Accessed June 24, 2019.

Kulke, Eckehard. *The Parsees in India: A Minority as Agent of Social Change*. Munich: Weltforum Verlag, 1974.

Lahuti, Abolqasem. "Maktub-e Sargoshadeh beh Rabindranat Tagur." *Paykar* 1, no. 10 (August 1, 1931): 76.

Laing, Samuel. *A Modern Zoroastrian*. London: Watts and Co., 1903.

Landman, Isaac, ed. *Universal Jewish Encyclopedia*. New York: Universal Jewish Encyclopedia, Inc., 1942.

Lenczowski, George. *Russia and the West in Iran, 1918–1948*. Ithaca, NY: Cornell University Press, 1949.

Lepage, Auguste. *Les Cafés Artistiques et Littéraires de Paris*. Paris: M. Bousin, 1882.

Lewisohn, Leonard. "Rabindranath Tagore's Syncretistic Philosophy and the Persian Sufi Tradition." *International Journal of Persian Literature* 2, no. 1 (2017): 2–41.

Lohrasb, Mirza Sarosh, ed. *Peshotanji Marker Memorial Volume/Yadnameh-ye Peshotan Dusabai Marker*. Bombay: Iranian Zoroastrian Anjoman, 1966.

Luhrmann, Tanya H. *The Good Parsi: The Fate of a Colonial Elite in a Postcolonial Society*. Cambridge, MA: Harvard University Press, 1996.

Mahbubi Ardakani, Hosayn. *Tarikh-e Mu'assesat-e Tamaddoni-ye Jadid dar Iran*. 3 vols. Tehran: Anjoman-e Daneshjuyan-e Daneshgah-e Tehran, 1975.

Majd, Mohammad Gholi. *August 1941: The Anglo-Russian Occupation of Iran and Change of Shahs*. Lanham, MD: University Press of America, 2012.

Makki, Hosayn. *Tarikh-e Bist Saleh-ye Iran*. 7 vols. Tehran: 'Elmi, 2001.

Malandra, William W. "*Garōdmān*." *Encyclopaedia Iranica*, vol. 10.3, 317–318. Available online at http://www.iranicaonline.org/articles/garodman-. Accessed May 18, 2018.

Maneck, Susan. *The Death of Ahriman: Culture, Identity, and Theological Change among the Parsis of India*. Bombay: K. R. Cama Oriental Institute, 1997.

Manjapra, Kris. *Age of Entanglement: German and Indian Intellectuals across Empire*. Cambridge, MA: Harvard University Press, 2014.

Marashi, Afshin. *Nationalizing Iran: Culture, Power, and the State, 1870–1940*. Seattle: University of Washington Press, 2008.

———. "Print Culture and Its Publics: A Social History of Bookstores in Tehran, 1900–1950." *International Journal of Middle East Studies* 47, no. 1 (2015): 89–108.

Mard-e Emruz. Tehran, 1942–1948.

Marefat, Mina. "Building to Power: Architecture of Tehran 1921–1941." PhD diss., Massachusetts Institute of Technology, 1988.

Marker, Kekobad Ardeshir. *A Petal from the Rose*. 2 vols. Karachi: Rosette, 1985.

Markwart, Josef. *Untersuchungen zur Geschichte von Eran*. Göttingen, Germany: Dieterich, 1896.

Marzolph, Ulrich. *Narrative Illustration in Persian Lithographed Books*. Leiden, Netherlands: Brill, 2001.

Masani, R. P. "With Dinshah Irani in New Iran." In *Dinshah Irani Memorial Volume: Papers on Zoroastrianism and Iranian Subjects*, edited by Jehangir Coyajee et al., xv-xxiv. Bombay: Dinshah Irani Memorial Committee, 1948.

———. "Foreword." In *Professor Poure Davoud Memorial Volume II: Papers on Zoroastrian and Iranian Subjects*, edited by Rustam Masani et. al., i-x. Bombay: Iran League, 1951.

Matin-Asgari, Afshin. "The Berlin Circle: Iranian Nationalism Meets German Countermodernity." In *Rethinking Iranian Nationalism and Modernity*, edited by Kamran Aghaie and Afshin Marashi, 49–66. Austin: University of Texas Press, 2014.

———. *Both Eastern and Western: An Intellectual History of Iranian Modernity*. New York: Cambridge University Press, 2018.

Menant, Delphine. *Les Parsis: Histoire des Communautés Zoroastriennes de l'Inde*. Paris: Leroux, 1898.

Menashri, David. *Education and the Making of Modern Iran*. Ithaca, NY: Cornell University Press, 1992.

Milani, Abbas. *The Shah*. New York: Palgrave, 2011.

Millspaugh, Arthur C. *Americans in Persia*. Washington, DC: Brookings Institution, 1946.

Mirabedini, Hasan. "Mard-e Emruz." *Encyclopaedia Iranica*. http://www.iranicaonline.org/articles/mard-e-emruz. Accessed October 7, 2018.

Mirsky, Jeannette. *Sir Aurel Stein: Archaeological Explorer*. Chicago: University of Chicago Press, 1977.

Modi, Jivanji Jamshedji. "A Short History of the Sir Jamsetjee Jejeebhoy Zarthoshti Madressa." In *Sir Jamsetjee Jejeebhoy Madressa Jubilee Volume*, edited by Jivanji Jamshedji Modi, 477–483. Bombay: Fort Printing Press, 1914.

Mody, Nawaz B. "Madame Bhikhaiji Rustom Cama—Sentinel of Liberty." In *The Parsis of Western India: 1818–1920*, edited by Nawaz B. Mody, 46–106. Bombay: Allied Publishers Ltd., 1998.

Mohanty, Amarendra, and Narayan Hazary. *Indian Prison Systems*. New Delhi: Ashish Publishing House, 1989.

Mohit Tabataba'i, Mohammad. "Hafiz and India." *Indo-Iranica* 4, no. 2–3 (1951): 45–49.

———. *Rabindranat Tagur: Sha'er va Filsuf-e Bozorg-e Hend*. Tehran, 1932.

Mo'in, Mohammad, ed. *Yadnameh-ye Purdavud: Be Monasebat-e Shashtomin Sal-e Tavallod-e Vay*. Vol. 1. Tehran: Asatir, 1946.

Mojtaba'i, Fath-Allah. "Dasatir." *Encyclopaedia Iranica*, vol. 7.1, 84. Available online at http://www.iranicaonline.org/articles/dasatir. Accessed October 17, 2017.

Moshfeq-Kazemi, Morteza. *Ruzegar va Andishehha*. 2 vols. Tehran: Ibn Sina, 1971.

Mostafavi, 'Ali Asghar. *Zaman va Zendegi-ye Ostad Purdavud*. Tehran: Mostafavi, 1991.

Motadel, David. *Islam and Nazi Germany's War*. Cambridge, MA: Harvard University Press, 2014.

———. "The Making of Muslim Communities in Western Europe, 1914–1939." In *Transnational Islam in Interwar Europe*, edited by Götz Nordbruch and Umar Ryad, 13–43. New York: Palgrave, 2014.

Mottahedeh, Roy Parviz. "The Idea of Iran in the Buyid Dominions." In *Early Islamic Iran: The Idea of Iran*. The Idea of Iran Series, vol. 5, edited by Edmund Herzig and Sarah Stewart, 153–160. London: I. B. Tauris, 2012.

Müller, F. Max, ed. *Sacred Books of the East: Pahlavi Texts*. Vol. 5, pt. 1. Translated by E. W. West. Oxford, UK: Oxford University Press, 1880.

Murzban, M. M. *The Parsis in India: Being an Enlarged and Copiously Annotated, Up to Date English Edition of Delphine Menant's Les Parsis*. Bombay: Murzban, 1917.

Naficy, Hamid. *A Social History of Iranian Cinema*. 4 vols. Durham, NC: Duke University Press, 2012.

Nakash, Yitzhak. *The Shi'is of Iraq*. Princeton, NJ: Princeton University Press, 1995.

Nandy, Ashis. *The Illegitimacy of Nationalism: Rabindranath Tagore and the Politics of Self*. New Delhi: Oxford University Press, 1994.

Nariman, G. K. *Persia and Parsis: Part I*. Bombay: Iran League, 1925.

———. "Was It Religious Persecution Which Compelled the Parsis to Migrate from Persia into India?" *Islamic Culture* 7 (1933): 277–280.

Nasiri, Mohmmad Reza. "Yek Zendegi." In *Zendegi Nameh va Khadamat-e 'Elmi va Farhangi-e Shadravan Arbab Kaykhosrow Shahrokh*, edited by Omid Qanbari, 13–42. Tehran: Anjoman-e Asar va Mafakher-e Farhangi, 2009.

Niedermayer, Oskar von. *Unter der Glutsonne Irans: Krigserlebnisse der dentschen Expedition nach Persien und Afganistan*. Munich: Einhornverlag, 1925.

———. *Zir-e Aftab-e Suzan-e Iran*. Translated by Kaykavus Jahandari. Tehran: Tarikh-e Iran, 1984.

Nikuyeh, Mahmud. *Purdavud: Pezhuhandeh-ye Ruzegar-e Nokhost*. Rasht: Gilan, 1999.

Noll, Richard. *The Jung Cult: Origins of a Charismatic Movement*. Princeton, NJ: Princeton University Press, 1994.

Notehelfer, F. G. "On Idealism and Realism in the Thought of Okakura Tenshin." *Journal of Japanese Studies* 16, no. 2 (1990): 309–355.

Nowzari, Hosayn-Ali. "Makatebat-e Allameh Mohammad Eqbal Lahuri va Abbas Aram." *Tarikh-e Mo'aser-e Iran* 1, no. 1 (1997): 161–177.

Numark, Mitchell. "Translating Dharma: Scottish Missionary-Orientalists and the Politics of Religious Understanding in Nineteenth-Century Bombay." *Journal of Asian Studies* 70, no. 2 (May 2011): 471–500.

———. "Translating Religion: British Missionaries and the Politics of Knowledge in Colonial India and Bombay." PhD diss., UCLA, 2006.

"Obituary for Lady Sakarbai." *Indian Magazine* 233 (May 1890): 278–279.

Ohanian, Armen. *The Dancer of Shamahka*. Translated from French by Rose Wilder Lane. New York: E. P. Dutton and Co., 1923.

Okakura, Kakuzo. *The Awakening of Japan*. New York: Century Co., 1904.

———. *The Book of Tea*. Rutland, VT: C. E. Tuttle Co., 1956 [1906].

———. *The Ideals of the East, with Special Reference to the Art of Japan*. Rutland, VT: C. E. Tuttle Co., 1970 [1903].

Omidsalar, Mahmud. "Qazvini, Mohammad." *Encyclopaedia Iranica*. http://www.iranicaonline.org/articles/qazvini-mohammad. Accessed October 18, 2017.

Oshidari, Jamshid. *Tarikh-e Pahlavi va Zartoshtian*. Tehran: Entesharat-e Hukht, 2535/1976.

———. "Zendegani-ye Porarzesh va Kushesh," *Hukht* 23, no. 4 (1351/1972): 5–45.

Palsetia, Jesse S. *Jamsetjee Jejeebhoy of Bombay: Partnership and Public Culture in Empire*. New Delhi: Oxford University Press, 2015.

———. *The Parsis of India: Preservation of Identity in Bombay City*. Leiden, Netherlands: Brill, 2001.

———. "The Parsis of India and the Opium Trade in China." *Contemporary Drug Problems* 35, no. 4 (Winter 2008): 647–678.

P'arpec'i, Gazar. *Geschichte Armenians*. Venedig: n.p., 1873.

Parvin, Nassereddin. "Rastkiz." *Encyclopaedia Iranica*. http://www.iranicaonline.org/articles/rastakhiz. Accessed October 24, 2017.

———. "Tarikhcheh-ye Yek Ruznameh: Iranshahr-e Paris." *Dabireh* 4 (1988): 103–116.

Patel, Dinyar. "Between Two Nationalisms: The Iran League of Bombay." Unpublished manuscript, 2018.

———. "The Iran League of Bombay: Parsis, Iran, and the Appeal of Iranian Nationalism." Master's thesis, Harvard University, 2008.

———. *Naoroji: Pioneer of Indian Nationalism*. Harvard University Press, in press.

Philliou, Christine. "Postcolonial Worlds in the Soviet Imaginary." *Comparative Studies of South Asia, Africa, and the Middle East* 33, no. 2 (2013): 197–200.

Pickett, James. "Soviet Civilization through a Persian Lens: Iranian Intellectuals,

Cultural Diplomacy and Socialist Modernity, 1941–55." *Iranian Studies* 48, no. 5 (September 2015): 805–826.

Pirnazar, Jaleh. "Jang-e Bainolmelal-e Dovvum va Jam'eh-ye Yahud dar Iran." In *Teru'a: Yahudian-e Irani dar Tarikh-e Mo'aser*, edited by Homa Sarshar, 93–105. Beverly Hills, CA: Entesharat-e Tarikh-e Shafahi-ye Yahudian-e Irani, 1996.

Pirzadeh, Haji Ali Mohammad. *Safarnameh-ye Haji Mohammad Ali Pirzadeh*. Vol. 1. Edited by Hafez Farmanfarma'ian. Tehran: Entesharat-e Daneshgah-e Tehran, 1963.

Pishdadi, Jamshid. *Yadnameh-ye Sorush Lohrasb*. Los Angeles: n.p., 1998.

Poliakov, Leon. *The Aryan Myth: A History of Racist and Nationalistic Ideas in Europe*. New York: Barnes and Noble Books, 1996.

Pollock, Sheldon. *The Language of the Gods in the World of Men: Sanskrit, Culture, and Power in Premodern India*. Berkeley: University of California Press, 2006.

Pratap, Mahendra. "My German Mission to High Asia: How I Joined Forces with the Kaiser to Enlist Afghanistan against Great Britain." *Asia: The Journal of the American Asiatic Association* 25 (May 1925): 382–455.

Purdavud, Ebrahim. *Adabiyat-e Mazdayasna: Yashtha, Qesmati az Ketab-e Moqaddas-e Avesta, Jeld-e Aval*. P. D. Marker Avestan Series, vol. 2. Bamba'i: Anjoman-e Zartoshtian-e Irani va Iran Lig, 1928.

———. *Adabiyat-e Mazdayasna: Yashtha, Qesmati az Ketab-e Moqaddas-e Avesta, Jeld-e Dovvom*. P. D. Marker Avestan Series, vol. 3. Bamba'i: Anjoman-e Zartoshtian-e Irani va Iran Lig, 1931.

———. *Anahita: Panjah Goftar-e Purdavud*. Edited by Morteza Gorji. Tehran: Amir Kabir, 1963.

———. "Bahramgur Anklesaria." *Sokhan* 2, no. 6 (1944): 417–419.

———. *Farhang-e Iran-e Bastan*. Tehran: Mu'asseseh-ye Entesharat va Chap-e Danishgah-e Tehran, 1976.

———. *Gatha: Sorudha-ye Minovi-ye Payghambar-e Iran*. Bamba'i: Anjoman-e Zartoshtian-e Irani, 1952.

———. *Gatha: Sorudha-ye Moqaddas-e Payghambar-e Iran*. With introductory notes in English by Dinshah J. Irani, Jivanji Jamshedji Modi, and G. K. Nariman. P. D. Marker Avestan Series, vol. 1. Bamba'i: Anjoman-e Zartoshtian-e Irani va Iran Lig, 1927.

———. "Goftar-e Agha-ye Purdavud." *Iran League Quarterly* 9, no. 1 (October 1938), Persian section: 1–6.

———. *Iranshah: Tarikhcheh-ye Mohajerat-e Zartoshtian be Hendustan*. Bamba'i: Anjoman-e Zartoshtian-e Irani, 1925.

———. *Khordeh Avesta: Jozvi az Nameh-ye Minovi-ye Avesta*. Bamba'i: Anjoman-e Zartoshtian-e Iran va Iran Lig, 1931.

———. *Khorramshah: Konferansha-ye Purdavud dar Hend*. Bamba'i: Anjoman-e Zartoshtian-e Irani, 1926.

———. "Nameh-ye Yazdegerd-e Dovvom be Isayuan-e Armanestan." *Iranshahr* 1, no. 5 (October 25, 1922): 107–116.

———. "Negahi be Ruzegaran-e Gozashteh-ye Iran va Pishgu'i-ye *Bahman Yasht* az Fetneh-ye Moghul." *Iranshahr* 1, no. 12 (June 15, 1923): 342–352.

———. *Purandokht-Nameh: Divan-e Purdavud*. Bamba'i: Anjoman-e Zartoshtian-e Irani, 1928.

——. "Rabindranat Tagur." *Majalleh-ye Daneshkadeh-ye Adabiyat* 9, no. 2 (1962): 13–30.

——. "Sad Band-e Tagur." *Bokhara* 45 (2005): 187–193.

——. *Sushians: Ma'ud-e Mazdayasna.* Bamba'i: Chapkhaneh-ye Hur, 1927.

——. "Yadi Digar az Qazvini." In *Yadnameh-ye Allameh Mohammad Qazvini*, edited by Ali Dehbashi, 157–162. Tehran: Ketab va Farhang, 1999.

——. *Yasna (Jeld-e Aval): Jozvi az Nameh-ye Minovi-ye Avesta.* P. D. Marker Avestan Series, vol. 5. Bamba'i: Anjoman-e Zartoshtian-e Irani va Iran Lig, 1938.

Purdavud, Ebrahim, and Bahram Farahvashi. *Vesperad.* Tehran: Mu'asseseh-ye Entesharat va Chap-e Danishgah-e Tehran, 1961.

——. *Yaddashtha-ye Gatha.* Tehran: Chapkhaneh-ye Atashkadeh, 1957.

——. *Yasna (Jeld-e Dovvom): Jozvi az Nameh-ye Minovi-ye Avesta.* Tehran: Entesharat-e Anjoman-e Iran Shenasi, 1958.

Qazvini, Mohammad. *Bist Maqaleh-ye Qazvini.* Edited by Ebrahim Purdavud. Bamba'i: Intesharat-e Anjoman-e Zartoshtian-e Irani, 1928.

——. *Bist Maqaleh-ye Qazvini: Dowreh-ye Kamel.* Edited by Ebrahim Purdavud. Tehran: Ibn Sina, 1953.

Ramazani, Nesta. *The Dance of the Rose and the Nightingale.* Syracuse, NY: Syracuse University Press, 2002.

Ray, S. B. "Tagore's Visit to Shiraz." *Indo-Iranica* 39, no. 1–4 (1986): 85–95.

Relia, Anil. *The Indian Portrait: An Artistic Journey from Miniature to Modern.* Ahmedabad: Archer House, 2010.

Rezazadeh-Shafaq, Sadeq. "Zartosht Az Nazar-e Tagur." *Majalleh-ye Daneshkadeh-ye Adabiyat* 9, no. 2 (1962): 31–36.

Rezun, Miron. *The Soviet Union and Iran: Soviet Policy in Iran from the Beginning of the Pahlavi Dynasty until the Soviet Invasion of 1941.* Genève: Institut Universitaire de Hautes Etudes Internationales, 1981.

Rezwi, S. M. Taher. *Parsian Ahl-e Ketaband.* Translated by Mirza Ali Mazandi. Bamba'i: Anjoman-e Iran Lig, 1936.

——. *Parsis: A People of the Book, Being a Survey of the Zoroastrian Religion in Light of Biblical and Quranic Teachings.* Calcutta: N. C. Roy, 1928.

Ringer, Monica M. "Din-e 'Aqlani va Asl-e Shahrvandi dar Iran." *Iran Nameh* 26, no. 1–2 (2011): 71–86.

——. "The Discourse of Modernization and the Problem of Cultural Integrity in Nineteenth-Century Iran." In *Iran and Beyond: Essays in Middle Eastern History in Honor of Nikki R. Keddie*, edited by Rudi Matthee and Beth Baron, 56–69. Costa Mesa, CA: Mazda, 2000.

——. "Iranian Nationalism and Zoroastrian Identity: Between Cyrus and Zoroaster." In *Iran Facing Others: Iranian Identity Boundaries and Modern Political Culture*, edited by Abbas Amanat and Farzin Vejdani, 267–277. New York: Palgrave Macmillan, 2012.

——. *Pious Citizens: Reforming Zoroastrianism in India and Iran.* Syracuse, NY: Syracuse University Press, 2011.

——. "Reform Transplanted: Parsi Agents of Change amongst Zoroastrians in Nineteenth-Century Iran." *Iranian Studies* 42, no. 4 (September 2009): 549–560.

Robinson, Andrew. *The Art of Rabindranath Tagore.* London: Deutsch, 1989.

Rose, Jenny. *Zoroastrianism: An Introduction.* London: I. B. Tauris, 2010.

Rostam-Kolayi, Jasamin. "From Evangelizing to Modernizing Iranians: The American Presbyterian Mission and Its Iranian Students." *Iranian Studies* 41, no. 2 (March 2008): 213–240.

Rothermund, Dietmar, ed. and trans. *Rabindranath Tagore in Germany: A Cross-Section of Contemporary Reports*. New Delhi: Mueller Bhavan, 1961.

Rubin, Barry, and Wolfgang G. Schwanitz. *Nazis, Islamists, and the Making of the Modern Middle East*. New Haven, CT: Yale University Press, 2014.

Rude, Maxim. *Toute Paris au Café*. Paris: M. Dreyfous, 1877.

Russell, James. "Kharshedji Rustamh Cama." *Encyclopaedia Iranica*, vol. 4.7, 722. Available online at http://www.iranicaonline.org/articles/cama-kharshedji-rustamh-b. Accessed September 10, 2018.

Ryan, Charles J. *H. P. Blavatsky and the Theosophical Movement: A Brief Historical Sketch*. Point Loma, CA: Theosophical University Press, 1937.

Rybitschka, Emil. *Im gottgegebenen Afghanistan als gäste des emirs*. Leigzig: F. A. Brockhaus, 1927.

Saati, Pargol. "Conversion vii. To the Zoroastrian Faith in the Modern Period." *Encyclopaedia Iranica*, vol. 6.3, 242–243. Available online at http://www.iranicaonline.org/articles/conversion-vii. Accessed October 3, 2018.

Sadiq, Isa. "Sokhanrani-ye Profesor Isa Sadiq." *Hukht* 25, no. 10 (1353/2524): 4–6.

———. *Yadegar-e 'Omr*. Tehran: Amir Kabir, 1966.

Sadr-Hashemi, Mohammad. *Tarikh-e Jara'ed va Majallat-e Iran*. 4 vols. Esfahan: Kamal, 1984.

Safran, William. "Diasporas in Modern Societies: Myths of Homeland and Return." *Diaspora: A Journal of Transnational Studies* 1, no. 1 (Spring 1991): 83–99.

Safrang, Sohrab. "Bazyadha'i az Zaman-e Riasat-e Ravanshad Arbab Kaykhosrow Shahrokh dar Anjoman-e Zartoshtian," *Hukht* 23, no. 4 (1351/1972): 26–29.

Saha, Panchanan. *Madam Cama: Mother of Indian Revolution*. Calcutta: Manisha, 1975.

Said, Edward. *Orientalism*. New York: Vintage Books, 1978.

Sakatvala, Phiroz. *Rich Fields in Persia*. Bombay: Iran League Quarterly, 1933.

Samadani, Mohammad-Reza Mo'in. "Havades-e Ayyam." In *Zendegi Nameh va Khadamat-e 'Elmi va Farhangi-e Shadravan Arbab Kaykhosrow Shahrokh*, edited by Omid Qanbari, 105–120. Tehran: Anjoman-e Asar va Mafakher-e Farhangi, 2009.

Samuelson, Meg. "Crossing the Indian Ocean and Wading through the Littoral: Visions of Cosmopolitanism in Amitav Ghosh's 'Antique Land' and 'Tide Country.'" In *Cosmopolitan Asia: Littoral Epistemologies of the Global South*, edited by Sharmani Patricia Gabriel and Fernando Rosa, 105–122. New York: Routledge, 2016.

Sanasarian, Eliz. *Religious Minorities in Iran*. Cambridge, UK: Cambridge University Press, 2000.

Sarvestani, Kuros Kamali. "Hafez xiii–xiv. Hafez's Tomb (Hafeziya)." *Encyclopaedia Iranica*, vol. 11.5, 505–507. Available online at http://www.iranicaonline.org/articles/hafez-xiii. Accessed October 3, 2018.

Satia, Priya. *Spies in Arabia: The Great War and the Cultural Foundations of Britain's Covert Empire in the Middle East*. Oxford, UK: Oxford University Press, 2009.

Schimmel, Annemarie. *Mystical Dimensions of Islam*. 2nd ed. Chapel Hill: University of North Carolina Press, 2011.

Schirazi, Asghar. "Germany x. The Persian Community in Germany." *Encyclopaedia*

Iranica, vol. 10.6, 572–574. Available online at http://www.iranicaonline.org/articles/germany-x. Accessed June 22, 2016.

Schmitt, Rüdiger. "Markwart, Josef." *Encyclopaedia Iranica*. http://www.iranicaonline.org/articles/markwart-josef. Accessed October 23, 2017.

Schwab, Raymond. *Oriental Renaissance: Europe's Rediscovery of India and the East, 1680–1880*. New York: Columbia University Press, 1984.

Schwartz, Kevin L. "*Bâzgasht-i Adabî* (Literary Return) and Persianate Literary Culture in Eighteenth and Nineteenth Century Iran, India, and Afghanistan." PhD diss., University of California, Berkeley, 2014.

Sen, Nabaneeta. "The 'Foreign Reincarnation' of Rabindranath Tagore." *Journal of Asian Studies* 25, no. 2 (1966): 275–286.

Sepanta, Abdol-Hosayn. "Sokhanrani-ye Agha-ye Abdol-Hossayn Sepanta." *Hukht* 19, no. 10 (January 1969): 92–95.

Seyf, Ahmad. "Iran and Cholera in the Nineteenth Century." *Middle Eastern Studies* 38, no. 1 (2002): 169–178.

"Shadravan Dinshah Irani." *Andisheh-ye Ma* 1, no. 5 (1946): 4–6.

Shahbazi, Abdollah. "Ser Ardeshir Ripurter: Servis-e Ettela'ati-ye Britania va Iran." http://www.shahbazi.org/Articles/Reporter_Ardeshirji.pdf. Accessed September 10, 2018.

Shahbazi, Abdollah, ed. *Zohur va Soqut-e Saltanat-e Pahlavi*. 2 vols. Tehran: Entesharat-e Etella'at, 1991.

Shahmardan, Rashid. *Farzanegan-e Zartoshti*. Tehran: Sazman-e Javanan-e Zartoshti-e Bamba'i, 1951.

Shahrokh, Kaykhosrow. *A'ineh-ye A'in-e Mazdayasna*. Bamba'i: Matba'-ye Mozaffari, 1921.

———. *Forugh-e Mazdayasna*. Tehran: Murteza al-Hosayni al-Baraghani, 1909.

———. *Khaterat-e Arbab Kaykhosrow Shahrokh*. Edited by Shahrokh Shahrokh and Rashna Rayter. Translated by Gholamhosayn Mirza Saleh. Tehran: Mazyar, 2003.

———. *The Memoirs of Keikhosrow Shahrokh*. Edited and translated by Shahrokh Shahrokh and Rashna Writer. Lewiston, NY: Edwin Mellen Press, 1994.

———. *Yaddashtha-ye Kaykhosrow Shahrokh*. Edited by Jahangir Oshidari. Tehran: Parcham, 2535/1977.

Sharafi, Mitra. *Law and Identity in Colonial South Asia: Parsi Legal Culture, 1772–1947*. Cambridge, UK: Cambridge University Press, 2014.

Sheffield, Daniel J. "In the Path of the Prophet: Medieval and Early Modern Narratives of the Life of Zarathustra in Islamic Iran and Western India." PhD diss., Harvard, 2012.

———. "Iran, the Mark of Paradise or the Land of Ruin? Historical Approaches to Reading Two Parsi Zoroastrian Travelogues." In *On the Wonders of Land and Sea: Persianate Travel Writing*, edited by Sunil Sharma and Roberta Micallef, 15–43. Boston: Ilex Foundation and Center for Hellenic Studies, 2013.

———. "The Language of Heaven in Safavid Iran: Speech and Cosmology in the Thought of Azar Kayvan and His Followers." In *No Tapping Around Philology: A Festschrift in Honor of Wheeler McIntosh Thackston Jr.'s 70th Birthday*, edited by Alireza Korangy and Daniel J. Sheffield, 161–183. Wiesbaden: Harrassowitz Verlag, 2014.

———. "Primary Sources: New Persian." In *The Wiley Blackwell Companion to Zoro-*

astrianism, edited by Michael Stausberg and Yuhan Sohrab-Dinshaw Vevaina, 529–542. West Sussex, UK: John Wiley and Sons, 2015.

Shokat, Hamid. "Barnameh-ye Farsi-ye Radio Berlin dar Jang-e Jahani-ye Duvom." *Iran Nameh* 28, no. 1 (2013): 102–117.

Souhami, Diana. *Wild Girls: Paris, Sappho, and Art—The Lives and Loves of Natalie Barney and Romaine Brooks*. New York: St. Martin's, 2004.

Spivak, Gayatri Chakravorty. "Subaltern Studies: Deconstructing Historiography." In *Selected Subaltern Studies*, edited by Ranajit Guha and Gayatri Chakravorty Spivak, 3–32. New York: Oxford University Press, 1988.

Sreberny, Annabell, and Massoumeh Torfeh. *Persian Service: The BBC and the British Interests in Iran*. London: I. B. Tauris, 2014.

Stausberg, Michael. "Para-Zoroastrianism: Memetic Transmissions and Appropriations." In *Parsis in India and the Diaspora*, edited by John Hinnells and Alan Williams, 236–254. London: Routledge, 2007.

———. "Sanjana, Darab Dastur Peshotan." *Encyclopaedia Iranica*. http://www.iranicaonline.org/articles/sanjana-darab. Accessed October 12, 2017.

———. "Zoroastrians in Modern Iran." In *The Wiley Blackwell Companion to Zoroastrianism*, edited by Michael Stausberg and Yuhan Sohrab-Dinshaw Vevaina, 173–190. West Sussex, UK: John Wiley and Sons, 2015.

Stausberg, Michael, and Ramiyar P. Karanjia. "Modi, Jivanji Jamshedji." *Encyclopaedia Iranica*. http://www.iranicaonline.org/articles/modi-jivanji-jamshedji. Accessed October 12, 2017.

Steenson, Gary P. *After Marx, Before Lenin: Marxism and Socialist Working-Class Parties in Europe, 1884–1914*. Pittsburgh: University of Pittsburgh Press, 1991.

Stewart, Jules. *The Kaiser's Mission to Kabul: A Secret Expedition to Afghanistan in World War I*. London: I. B. Tauris, 2014.

Stewart, Sarah. "The Politics of Zoroastrian Philanthropy and the Case of Qasr-e Firuzeh." *Iranian Studies* 45, no. 1 (2012): 59–80.

Subrahmanyam, Sanjay. "Connected Histories: Notes Towards a Reconfiguration of Early Modern Eurasia, 1400–1800." *Modern Asian Studies* 31, no. 3 (1997): 735–762.

———. "Iranians Abroad: Intra-Asian Elite Migration and Early Modern State Formation." *Journal of Asian Studies* 51, no. 2 (1992): 340–363.

Sundermann, W. "Bahman Yašt." *Encyclopaedia Iranica*, vol. 3.5, 492–493. Available online at http://www.iranicaonline.org/articles/bahman-yast-middle-persian-apocalyptical-text. Accessed October 31, 2017.

Tagore, Maharishi Devendranath. *The Autobiography*. Translated by Satyendranath Tagore and Indira Devi. London: Macmillan, 1961.

Tagore, Rabindranath. "The Indo-Iranians." *Visva-Bharati Quarterly* 1, no. 3 (1923): 191–207.

———. *Journey to Persia and Iraq: 1932*. Translated by Surendranath Tagore and Sukhendu Ray. Kolkata: Visva-Bharata, 2003.

———. *Nationalism*. New Delhi: Rupa and Co., 2005.

———. *Rabindranath Tagore: A Centenary Volume, 1861–1961*. New Delhi: Sahitya Akademi, 1961.

Tagur, Rabindranat. *Sad Band-e Tagur: Mushtamel bar Yek Sad Tarajim az Manzumat-e Bengali-ye Rabindranat Tagur*. Translated by M. Zia al-Din. Calcutta, 1935.

Tanaka, Stefan. "Imaging History: Inscribing Belief in the Nation." *Journal of Asian Studies* 53, no. 1 (1994): 24–44.

Taqizadeh, Hasan. *Zendegi-ye Tufani: Khaterat-e Sayyid Hasan Taqizadeh.* Edited by Iraj Afshar. Tehran: 'Elmi, 1993.

Tarapore, Jamshed C. "Professor Poure Davoud, a Life Sketch." In *Professor Poure Davoud Memorial Volume II: Papers on Zoroastrian and Iranian Subjects,* edited by Rustam Masani et. al., 1–49. Bombay: Iran League, 1951.

Taraporewala, Irach. *The Divine Songs of Zarathushtra: A Philological Study of the Gathas.* Bombay: Hukhta Foundation, 1993.

Tavakoli-Targhi, Mohamad. "Early Persianate Modernity." In *Forms of Knowledge in Early Modern Asia: Explorations in the Intellectual History of India and Tibet, 1500–1800,* edited by Sheldon Pollock, 257-287. Durham, NC: Duke University Press, 2011.

———. "Narrative Identity in the Works of Hedayat and his Contemporaries." In *Sadeq Hedayat: His Work and His Wondrous World,* edited by Homa Katouzian, 107–128. New York: Routledge, 2008.

———. *Refashioning Iran: Orientalism, Occidentalism, and Historiography.* New York: Palgrave, 2001.

Theodoretus. *Kirchengeschichte.* Translated by Leon Parmentier. Leipzig: J. C. Hinrichs, 1911.

Todorov, Tzvetan. *On Human Diversity: Nationalism, Racism, and Exoticism in French Thought.* Cambridge, MA: Harvard University Press, 1993.

Trautmann, Thomas R. *Aryans and British India.* Berkeley: University of California Press, 1997.

Trigger, Bruce G. *A History of Archaeological Thought.* Cambridge, UK: Cambridge University Press, 1989.

Unvala, Ervad Manockji Rustamji, ed. *Darab Hormazyar's Rivayat, with an Introduction by Shams-ul-Ulma Jivanji Jamshedji Modi.* Vol. 2. Bombay: British India Press, 1922.

US Army European Command, Intelligence Division. *Wartime Activities of the German Diplomatic and Military Services During World War II.* Ludwigsburg, Germany: US Army Intelligence, 1949.

van der Veer, Peter. *Imperial Encounters: Religion and Modernity in India and Britain.* Princeton, NJ: Princeton University Press, 2001.

Van Gorder, A. Christian. *Christianity in Persia and the Status of Non-Muslims in Iran.* Lanham, MD: Lexington Books, 2010.

Vatandoust, Gholamreza. "Sayyid Hasan Taqizadeh and Kaveh: Modernism in Post-Constitutional Iran (1916–1921)." PhD diss., University of Washington, 1977.

Vaziri, Mostafa. *Iran as Imagined Nation: The Construction of National Identity.* New York: Paragon House, 1993.

Vejdani, Farzin. "Indo-Iranian Linguistic, Literary, and Religious Entanglements: Between Nationalism and Cosmopolitanism, ca. 1900–1940." *Comparative Studies of South Asia, Africa, and the Middle East* 36, no. 3 (2016): 435–454.

———. *Making History in Iran: Education, Nationalism, and Print Culture.* Stanford, CA: Stanford University Press, 2014.

———. "The Place of Islam in Interwar Iranian Nationalist Historiography." In *Rethinking Iranian Nationalism and Modernity,* edited by Kamran Aghaie and Afshin Marashi, 205–218. Austin: University of Texas Press, 2014.

Viswanathan, Gauri. "In Search of Madame Blavatsky: Reading the Exoteric, Retrieving the Esoteric." *Representations* 141, no. 1 (Winter 2018): 67–94.

———. *Outside the Fold: Conversion, Modernity, and Belief*. Princeton, NJ: Princeton University Press, 1998.

Webb, James. *The Occult Establishment*. La Salle, IL: Open Court Publishing, 1976.

Weston, Victoria. *Japanese Painting and National Identity: Okakura Tenshin and His Circle*. Ann Arbor: Center for Japanese Studies, University of Michigan, 2003.

Williams, Alan. *The Zoroastrian Myth of Migration from Iran and Settlement in the Indian Diaspora: Text, Translation and Analysis of the 16th Century Qesse-ye Sanjan "The Story of Sanjan."* Leiden, Netherlands: Brill, 2009.

Wink, André. *Al-Hind, the Making of the Indo-Islamic World*. Vol. 1, *Early Medieval India and the Expansion of Islam, 7th–11th Centuries*. Leiden, Netherlands: Brill, 2002.

Wolfe, Patrick. *Settler Colonialism and the Transformation of Anthropology: The Politics and Poetics of an Ethnographic Event*. London: Cassell, 1999.

Wolff, Fritz. *Avesta: Die Heiligen Bücher der Parsen, Übersetzt auf der Grundlage von Christian Batholomae's Altiranischem Wörterburch*. Berlin: W. de Guyter, 1924.

———. *Glossar zu Firdosis Schahname*. Berlin: Gerdruckt in der Reichsdruckerei, 1935.

Wood, Barry D. "'A Great Symphony of Pure Form': The 1931 International Exhibition of Persian Art and Its Influence." *Ars Orientalis* 30 (2000): 113–130.

Yaghoubian, David. *Ethnicity, Identity, and the Development of Nationalism in Iran*. Syracuse, NY: Syracuse University Press, 2014.

Zaehner, R. C., ed. "Chidag Andarz i Poryotkeshan: A Zoroastrian Catechism." In *The Teachings of the Magi: A Compendium of Zoroastrian Beliefs*, edited and translated by R. C. Zaehner, 20–28. Oxford, UK: Oxford University Press, 1976.

Zarinkub, Abdolhosayn. *Du Qarn-e Sokut*. Tehran: Amir Kabir, 1957.

Zia-Ebrahimi, Reza. *The Emergence of Iranian Nationalism: Race and the Politics of Dislocation*. New York: Columbia University Press, 2016.

———. "An Emissary of the Golden Age: Manekji Limji Hataria and the Charisma of the Archaic in Pre-Nationalist Iran." *Studies in Ethnicity and Nationalism* 10, no. 3 (2010): 377–390.

———. "Self-Orientalization and Dislocation: The Uses and Abuses of the 'Aryan' Discourse in Iran." *Iranian Studies* 44 (2011): 445–472.

Ziai, Hossein. "Hāfez, Lisān al-Ghayb of Persian Poetic Wisdom." In *Gott ist schön und er liebt die schönheit—God is beautiful and he loves beauty: Festschrift für Annemarie Schimmel zum 7. April 1992 dargebracht von schulern, freunden und kollegen*, edited by Alma Giese and Christoph Bürgel, 449–469. Bern: Peter Lang, 1994.

———. *Suhrawardi: The Philosophy of Illumination*. Provo, UT: Brigham Young University, 1999.

Zürcher, Erik-Jan. *Jihad and Islam in World War I: Studies on the Ottoman Jihad on the Centenary of Snouck Hurgronje's "Holy War Made in Germany."* Leiden, Netherlands: Leiden University Press, 2016.

INDEX

306 | Index